797,885 Books
are available to read at

Forgotten Books

www.ForgottenBooks.com

Forgotten Books' App
Available for mobile, tablet & eReader

ISBN 978-1-332-16559-9
PIBN 10180525

This book is a reproduction of an important historical work. Forgotten Books uses state-of-the-art technology to digitally reconstruct the work, preserving the original format whilst repairing imperfections present in the aged copy. In rare cases, an imperfection in the original, such as a blemish or missing page, may be replicated in our edition. We do, however, repair the vast majority of imperfections successfully; any imperfections that remain are intentionally left to preserve the state of such historical works.

Forgotten Books is a registered trademark of FB &c Ltd.
Copyright © 2015 FB &c Ltd.
FB &c Ltd, Dalton House, 60 Windsor Avenue, London, SW19 2RR.
Company number 08720141. Registered in England and Wales.

For support please visit www.forgottenbooks.com

1 MONTH OF FREE READING

at

www.ForgottenBooks.com

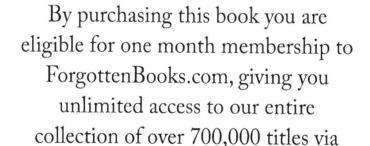

By purchasing this book you are eligible for one month membership to ForgottenBooks.com, giving you unlimited access to our entire collection of over 700,000 titles via our web site and mobile apps.

To claim your free month visit:
www.forgottenbooks.com/free180525

* Offer is valid for 45 days from date of purchase. Terms and conditions apply.

English
Français
Deutsche
Italiano
Español
Português

www.forgottenbooks.com

Mythology Photography **Fiction** Fishing Christianity **Art** Cooking Essays Buddhism Freemasonry Medicine **Biology** Music **Ancient Egypt** Evolution Carpentry Physics Dance Geology **Mathematics** Fitness Shakespeare **Folklore** Yoga Marketing **Confidence** Immortality Biographies Poetry **Psychology** Witchcraft Electronics Chemistry History **Law** Accounting **Philosophy** Anthropology Alchemy Drama Quantum Mechanics Atheism Sexual Health **Ancient History Entrepreneurship** Languages Sport Paleontology Needlework Islam **Metaphysics** Investment Archaeology Parenting Statistics Criminology **Motivational**

LIFE AND TIMES

OF

JOSEPH WARREN.

BY

RICHARD FROTHINGHAM.

BOSTON:
LITTLE, BROWN, & COMPANY.
1865.

THE NEW YORK
PUBLIC LIBRARY

170193

ASTOR, LENOX AND
TILDEN FOUNDATIONS.
1900.

Entered, according to Act of Congress, in the year 1865, by
RICHARD FROTHINGHAM,
In the Clerk's Office of the District Court of the District of Massachusetts.

Cambridge · Stereotyped and Printed by John Wilson and Sons

TO

THOMAS AUSTIN GODDARD,

This Volume is Inscribed,

WITH RESPECT AND AFFECTION,

BY THE AUTHOR.

PREFACE.

WHEN preparing, in 1849, an introduction to a narrative of the military transactions in 1775 and 1776, contained in a volume entitled "History of the Siege of Boston," &c., I found but meagre accounts of the revolutionary movement in the town from 1767 to 1775. The space allotted to it in Dr. Snow's History is about thirty pages. It was not a part of the plan of William Tudor, in his "Life of James Otis," or of Josiah Quincy, in his "Memoir of the Life of Josiah Quincy, jun.," to describe it in these valuable works; nor could the subject be treated with the fulness it requires in a history of Massachusetts or of the United States.

I found, moreover, that Joseph Warren was identified with the whole of this movement as an efficient political leader. The only accounts of his great service, however, were a brief memoir by Rev. Dr. John Eliot, in the "Boston Magazine" of 1784, which, in 1809, was enlarged into the five pages of his "Biographical Dictionary;" an interesting sketch of his life, in 1816, in "Rees's Cyclopædia," supplied by Dr. John C. Warren; the "Memoir of Joseph Warren," of ten pages, by Samuel L. Knapp, in the "Boston Monthly Magazine" of April, 1826, which was enlarged from his "Biographical Sketches," printed in 1821; a little volume, entitled "Stories of General

Warren in relation to the Fifth-of-March Massacre and the Battle of Bunker Hill, by a Lady of Boston," printed in 1835; and the "Life of Joseph Warren by Alexander H. Everett," printed in 1845, incorporated into Sparks's "American Biography," the most of which will be found in an oration delivered in 1836. This "Life" contains ninety pages, fifty-five being devoted to a description of the Battle of Bunker Hill. These publications do not contain one of Warren's letters.

In 1849, I began to frame a narrative of Warren's career, and my collections soon became large. In 1852, fresh material was supplied in the valuable historical contribution of "The Hundred Boston Orators," by James S. Loring, who devotes to Warren twenty-six pages. In 1854, additional matter relative to him was printed in Mr. Bancroft's fourth volume of the "History of the United States," in which Warren is assigned a just position in our revolutionary story. That year, Dr. John C. Warren issued the elegant volume of the genealogy of the family, which contains several of the letters of Warren, and Dr. John Warren's Journal. In 1855, Samuel G. Drake printed his elaborate "History of Boston," which, however, does not come down later than 1770. In 1857, there appeared a pamphlet entitled "Biography of General Joseph Warren by a Bostonian," which consists of eighty-five pages, forty of them being taken up with three orations.

None of these publications contain a description of the proceedings of the patriots of Boston from 1767 to 1775. I have attempted in this volume to supply a deficiency in American history, by describing those scenes which had a direct bearing on momentous political events. From the date of 1774, the material for biography is abundant; and I have given Warren's letters in full, and have dwelt on his personal action.

I am indebted to JARED SPARKS for the free use of the collection, in folio volumes, of the "Letters and Papers" of Francis Bernard; to GEORGE BANCROFT for the use of a manuscript life of Samuel Adams by Samuel Adams Wells, the Journals of the Boston Committee of Correspondence, and the papers of Samuel Adams, in which were preserved the letters addressed by Warren to Samuel Adams, now carefully bound in a separate volume, none of which have been printed; to the librarians of the Boston Athenæum, Harvard College, the American Academy of Arts and Sciences, the American Antiquarian Society, and the New-York Historical Society, for every facility in making researches; to the courteous City Clerk of Boston, SAMUEL F. M'CLEARY, for access to the files of papers and records in his office; to the successive Secretaries of State for facilities in consulting the Massachusetts archives; and to Dr. J. MASON WARREN for the use of the plate from which is printed the portrait of the General. I am indebted for favors to Dr. NATHANIEL B. SHURTLEFF. I am under special obligations to Dr. JOHN APPLETON, Assistant Librarian of the Massachusetts Historical Society, for the drawing of the *fac-simile* of Warren's last letter, and for critical service in revising the proof-sheets.

In all cases where it was possible, I have resorted to original authorities. I have spent much time in examining the letter books and papers of Thomas Hutchinson, which are among the rich collection of Massachusetts archives at the State House; and I have copied much from them. This material and the papers of Francis Bernard contain authentic revelations of the principles and objects of two confidential agents of the British Administration, who exerted an important influence in bringing about the events that were the proximate cause of the Revolution.

PREFACE.

I will only add, that I have aimed to be precise and accurate, not only in the construction of the narrative, but in the statement of opinion. The history contained in this volume has a general bearing. There will be found in it much to show the beginnings of that Union which the Fathers of the Republic recognized to be a manifestation of the Providence of God; and much to illustrate the way in which the thirteen English colonies passed from the sovereignty of Great Britain to become an American nationality.

CHARLESTOWN, MASS., October 2, 1865.

CONTENTS.

CHAPTER I.

EARLY DAYS.—1741 TO 1763.

	PAGE.		PAGE.
Introductory	1	Mary Warren	7
Warren's Position	1	Her Domestic Life	8
His Public Life	1	Her Character	8
His Civic Career	2	Obituary Notice of her	9
His Utterances	3	Warren enters College	9
His Fields of Labor	3	His Life-long Friends	10
The Warren Family	4	His College Reputation	11
The Warren Surname	4	Anecdote	11
Warren's Ancestry	4	Poem ascribed to him	11
His Birthplace	4	Master of a Grammar-school	12
His Father	5	Warren to the School Committee	12
Warren in Boyhood	6	Member of St. Andrew's Lodge	13
Joseph Warren's Death	7	Studies Medicine	13
His Sons	7	Takes his College Degree	13

CHAPTER II.

PRINCIPLES AND PARTY.—1763 TO 1767.

	PAGE.		PAGE.
Warren's Marriage	14	His Ruling Passion	18
Elizabeth Warren	14	Key to his Political Life	19
Warren's Domestic Virtues	14	Warren to Edmund Dana	20
His Settlement in Boston	15	On Self-taxation	20
Character of the Town	15	On Equality of Property	21
The Small Pox	15	On Freedom and Equality	21
Warren's Prospects as a Physician	16	On the Genius of the People	21
The Political World	16	On the Value of Union	21
Parties in Boston	17	On French Interference	22
Leading Objects of the Whigs	17	Character of this Letter	23
Leading Objects of the Tories	17	The Popular Leaders	24
Sympathies of Physicians	17	Samuel Adams	25
Warren's Study of Politics	18	His Influence on Young Men	26
He joins the Whigs	18	Friendship of Warren and Adams	26

CHAPTER III.

CONNECTION WITH THE PRESS. — 1767 TO MARCH, 1768.

	PAGE.		PAGE.
The Townshend Revenue Acts	28	Meeting October Twenty-eighth	37
Francis Bernard	29	Hand-bill on Liberty Tree	37
His Sketch of Boston Politics	29	Speech of Otis on Mobs	38
Divisions in the Popular Party	30	Bernard's Misrepresentations	39
Hutchinson on their Origin	31	Lord Shelburne on the Press	40
Warren's Theory of Taxation	31	"A True Patriot," by Warren	40
American Theory of Local Rights	31	Bernard's Message	41
Constitutional Action enjoined	32	Answer of the Council	42
Warren's Aims at Twenty-six	33	Answer of the House	43
Gordon on his Motives	34	Bernard asks a Prosecution	44
His Connection with the Press	34	Hutchinson's Charge	44
Journalism in Boston	34	Warren's Review of the Case	45
The "Boston Gazette"	35	The Chagrin of the Tories	45
Warren as a Writer	35	The Exultation of the Whigs	46
Bernard's Statement of the Press	36	The Liberty of the Press	47
His Charge of Insurrection	37	The Service of the Newspapers	47

CHAPTER IV.

CONNECTION WITH PUBLIC MEETINGS. — 1768. MARCH TO JUNE.

Public Meetings	49	Commissioners order her Seizure	57
Political Clubs	49	The Tenth-of-June Riot	57
Warren's Connection with them	49	Commissioners call it Rebellion	59
Their Number	50	Warren as a Pacificator	59
Anecdote of Warren and J. Adams	51	Commissioners go to the Castle	61
Warren and the Farmer's Letters	51	Meeting at Liberty Tree	61
The Commissioners of the Customs	52	Town-meeting at Faneuil Hall	62
They misrepresent the Patriots	52	Adjourned to the Old South	62
Bernard on asking for Troops	53	Petition to the Governor	63
The Commissioners odious	53	His Fear of Insurrection	64
Eighteenth-of-March Holiday	54	His Reception of a Committee	64
Misrepresented as a Riot	55	His Answer to the Petition	65
Naval Force ordered to Boston	55	The Officials demand Troops	66
A Press-gang	55	Meeting of June Seventeenth	67
The People sullen	56	Vote on Introducing Troops	68
Hutchinson on the Politicians	56	Service of Warren	68
Bernard predicts Insurrection	57	Officials on the Petition	68
The Sloop "Liberty"	57	Opinions on the Meeting	69

CONTENTS.

CHAPTER V.

PROTEST AGAINST A STANDING ARMY. — 1768. JULY TO OCTOBER.

	PAGE.		PAGE.
Influence of Town-meetings	71	Ask Bernard his Reasons	83
Massachusetts Circular Letter	71	Answer of Bernard	83
Refusal to rescind it	72	Report and Debate	83
The Union Spirit	72	A Convention resolved on	86
Troops to be posted in Boston	73	Character of this Meeting	87
Hillsborough's Instructions	73	Stirring News from England	88
Commissioners desire Troops	73	Memorial in behalf of Boston	88
Gage on asking for Troops	73	The Selectmen's Circular	89
Excitement of the People	74	The Spirit of the Country	90
Hutchinson on Constitutional Mobs	74	Meeting of the Convention	90
Council vote Troops not needed	75	Declared a High Offence	91
Bernard's Comment on this Vote	76	Bernard's Proclamation	91
His Perversion of a Celebration	76	Tone of the Press	92
Knox on the State of Boston	77	Parties in the Convention	93
Bernard advised of the Troops	77	Bancroft on this Measure	94
"Reader, Attend"	78	Effect of Popular Action	94
Bernard's Views of it	79	Termed the Source of Rebellion	94
States that Troops were coming	79	Termed the Origin of a Republic	94
Petition for Town-meeting	79	Elicits Lord North's Declaration	95
Officials afraid of Insurrection	80	Proposal to arrest Americans	96
The Tar-barrel Affair	81	Position of the Popular Leaders	97
The Popular Leaders at Warren's	81	The Status of Civil Freedom	97
Town-meeting September Twelfth	82	The Glory of their Pioneer Stand	97

CHAPTER VI.

THE BOSTON MASSACRE AND A CIVIC TRIUMPH. — OCTOBER, 1768, TO MARCH, 1770.

The Landing of the Troops	99	Bernard's View of his Successor	106
Contest about their Quarters	100	Thomas Hutchinson	107
Disposition of the Troops	101	His Political Career	107
The Question of their Removal	102	His Estimate of his Times	109
Warren's Identification with it	102	His View of Local Government	110
Town's Petition to the King	102	His Policy on American Union	111
Hillsborough's Letter on Treason	103	Warren and Hutchinson	112
Instructions to Representatives	103	Hutchinson in favor of Troops	113
Gage orders off Two Regiments	104	Declines to suppress Meetings	113
Surprise of Bernard	104	Boston's Appeal to the World	114
Joy of the Patriots	104	Hutchinson on Public Meetings	114
Town asks the Removal of all	104	Warren Grand Master	115
Supersedure of Bernard	105	Lieutenant-Colonel Dalrymple	116

CONTENTS.

	PAGE.		PAGE.
Inadequacy of his Force	116	Troops go to their Quarters	131
Hutchinson on the Public Peace	117	Proceedings in the Night	132
Troops occasion Quarrels	117	Morning of March Sixth	133
Question of Firing on the People	118	Question of Removal	133
Franklin fears a Collision	119	Hutchinson's Denial of Power	134
Hutchinson dreads a Tragic Scene	119	Meeting in Faneuil Hall	134
General Interest in the Question	119	Ask a Removal of the Troops	137
Inflamed State of the People	120	Decision to Remove a Part	138
The Localities of the Troops	121	Town-meeting in the Afternoon	139
Fight at Gray's Ropewalk	121	Report of the Committee	141
Laid before the Council	122	The Cry, "Both Regiments or none"	142
Members for a Removal	122		
The Press and a Hand-bill	123	The Second Committee	142
Evening of March Fifth	124	The Council Chamber	143
Affray at Murray's Barracks	124	Demand by Samuel Adams	144
A Sentinel assaults a Boy	124	Agitation of Hutchinson	145
Twenty Minutes of Interval	125	Vacillation of Dalrymple	146
A Party threatens the Sentinel	126	Unanimity of the Council	147
Preston protects the Sentinel	126	Decision to remove the Troops	148
The People and the Soldiers	127	Report of the Committee	149
The Soldiers fire on the People	127	Formation of the Watch	149
Carr parades his Men	128	Warren on the Removal	150
The Night Alarm	128	John Adams on the Bloodshed	150
Summons of Hutchinson	129	The Surprise in England	151
His Meeting with Preston	130	Eulogy on Boston	152
His Speech to the People	130	Medford to Boston	152
Arrest of Preston	131	Boston for a Common Cause	154

CHAPTER VII.

ORATION ON THE MASSACRE. — MARCH, 1770, TO MARCH, 1772.

	PAGE.		PAGE.
Warren's next Service	155	Anecdote of his Firmness	161
Urges Trials of the Soldiers	156	Differences among the Patriots	162
Appointed on Committees	156	Eliot on their Causes	162
Union the Desire of Americans	156	Hancock and Samuel Adams	163
Warren at a Merchants' Meeting	157	Declining Health of Otis	163
Repeal of the Townshend Act	157	J. Adams removes to Braintree	164
Retention of the Tea Duty	157	Anecdote of Cushing	165
Non-importation Plan a Failure	158	Warren at Thirty	166
The General Apathy	158	His Household	166
Hutchinson and Samuel Adams	159	His Bargain for a Slave	166
Hutchinson on Local Government	159	His Professional Life	167
		His Irritability	168
Hutchinson on Union	159	His Reputation	168
Samuel Adams on Union	159	His Social Walks	169

CONTENTS.

	PAGE		PAGE
His Connection with the Clubs	170	Oration on the American Principle	174
The Fifth-of-March Orator	171	On Violations of it	175
Tory View of Local Government	171	On Love of Liberty	176
The Whig View	172	Hutchinson on the Oration	178
The Town-meeting	172	Comment of the Press	178
Oration on Civil Government	173	Vote of Thanks by the Town	178
On Consent as its Basis	174	Main Purpose of the Oration	178

CHAPTER VIII.

COMMITTEES OF CORRESPONDENCE. — MARCH, 1772, TO JANUARY, 1773.

Object of the Tory Party	180	Answer to the Petition	199
Designs of the Patriots	180	Resolve on the Right of Petition	200
Question of the Judges' Salaries	181	Committee of Correspondence	201
Differences among the Whigs	182	Otis, S. Adams, and Warren	201
Samuel Adams on Parties	182	Organization of the Committee	202
The Press urges Action	183	Sub-committee to frame a Report	202
The Public continue Apathetic	183	Hutchinson on the Movement	202
Alarms and Petitions for Action	184	Samuel Adams's Faith	204
The Need of an Issue	185	Cheering Letter from Gerry	205
Resignation of Hillsborough	185	Meeting November Twentieth	206
Appointment of Dartmouth	185	Report on Colonial Rights	207
His Instructions on Salaries	186	On Expatriation	207
The Popular Leaders not agreed	186	On Equality	207
Their Relations to Politics	187	On Government	207
Samuel Adams urges Union	187	On Personal Freedom	207
Hutchinson on a Broken Union	187	On Taxation	208
His View of Local Rights	189	On Local Rights	208
Salaries freed from Local Law	189	On Jury Trials	209
Committees of Correspondence	189	On Commercial Freedom	210
Hutchinson on the Popular Clamor	190	On Americanism	211
Union a Plan of Providence	191	Doubts of James Warren	212
Petitions for a Town-meeting	191	Faith of Samuel Adams	212
The Press urges Attendance	192	The Report its own Orator	213
Hutchinson on Political Causes	192	Read by the Selectmen	214
Meeting October Twenty-eighth	193	Reception by the People	214
Letter read from Gerry	194	Their Response to Boston	214
Message to the Governor	194	The Answer of Cambridge	214
Samuel Adams on Politics	196	All the Towns urged to act	215
Answer of the Governor	197	Blindness of the Tories	216
Petition for a General Court	198	The Judgment of Hutchinson	217
Town-meeting November Second	198	Influence of the Report on Public Opinion	217
An Independent Commonwealth	198		

CONTENTS.

CHAPTER IX.

THE DESTRUCTION OF THE TEA. — 1773. JANUARY TO DECEMBER.

	PAGE		PAGE
Sequence of destroying the Tea	218	Conference of Committees	252
Warren on New Year's Day	219	Consignees and Selectmen	253
Faith in Divine Providence	219	Arrival of a Tea Ship	254
Union the Paramount Object	220	Proceedings of the Selectmen	255
Committee of Correspondence	220	Committee of Correspondence	255
Hutchinson on the Signs	221	Their Circular to the Towns	255
His Speech to the Legislature	222	The Pledge of Cambridge	556
The Answer of the House	223	Meeting November Twenty-ninth	257
On its Authorship	223	The Debates in the Old South	258
Hutchinson on Popular Action	224	The Proceedings of the Council	259
Fifth-of-March Oration	225	Obstinacy of Hutchinson	262
Town defends its Action	225	Firmness of the Consignees	263
A National Party organized	226	Vote to risk Life and Fortune	264
Adams on the Virginia Action	227	Comment on this Meeting	265
Death of Elizabeth Warren	228	The Watch over the Teas	265
Society for the Bill of Rights	229	Joy at the Action of Boston	266
The Town responds to Virginia	230	Urged to save the Country	267
Progress of the Union	231	Arrival of Two more Tea Ships	267
Demand for a Congress	231	Vigilance of the Patriots	267
Hutchinson on the Whig Party	232	Temper of the People	268
Passage of the Tea Act	233	Abigail Adams on the Temper	268
East-India Company's Plans	234	The Legal Status of the Teas	269
The Determination to defeat them	234	The Press on Public Meetings	269
Action of Philadelphia	235	Meeting December Fourteenth	271
Spirit of Massachusetts	236	Hutchinson December Fifteenth	271
The Boston Consignees	238	Boston on December Sixteenth	272
Action of North-end Caucus	238	A Revolutionary Deed required	273
The Summons to Liberty Tree	239	Meeting at the Old South	274
Vote of the North-end Caucus	240	Rotch told to get a Pass	275
Meeting at Liberty Tree	240	Speech of Josiah Quincy, jun.	276
The People and the Consignees	241	Hutchinson at Milton	277
They decline to resign	241	Rotch applies for a Pass	277
Town-meeting November Fifth	243	Hutchinson's Denial	278
Adopts the Philadelphia Resolves	243	The Old South at Sunset	278
Consignees evade the Demand	244	Dissolution of the Meeting	279
The Tone of the Press	245	A Party in Indian Costume	279
Hutchinson on the Exigency	246	The People at Griffin's Wharf	280
Firmness of Samuel Adams	247	The Destruction of the Tea	281
The Tea Issue and the Union	248	The General Joy	281
A Compromise impossible	248	Response from the Colonies	282
News from the Tea Ships	250	Comment on the Destruction of the Tea	283
Meeting November Eighteenth	251	Contemporary Vindication	284
Declination of the Consignees	251	Warren's Service	285
Their Application to the Council	252		

CONTENTS. xv

CHAPTER X.

BOSTON PORT ACT AND THE AMERICAN UNION. — DECEMBER, 1773, TO JUNE, 1774.

	PAGE		PAGE
Letters of Warren	287	Arrival of General Gage	307
Warren to Arthur Lee	288	His Character and Reception	307
His Service in Committees	290	Hutchinson's last Official Acts	308
The Reply to Newport	290	On paying for the Tea	310
The Union and a Congress	291	Bearing of the People	310
Tea Issue promotes Union	292	Port Act under the Colonies	311
Isaac Royall on Loyalty	294	Solemn League and Covenant	313
Samuel Adams on his Party	294	Appeal for Union	314
Anxiety to hear from England	295	Interesting Week	315
Hancock on the Fifth of March	295	Franklin on paying for the Tea	315
Warren on a new Post-Office	296	Meeting of Tradesmen	316
Reports from England	298	Warren to Samuel Adams	317
Views of Samuel Adams	299	Letter from Baltimore	318
England's Nationality roused	299	Warren to Baltimore	318
The Boston Port Bill	299	Seventeenth of June	319
Reception by the Committee	300	Town-meeting in Faneuil Hall	320
Circular drafted by Warren	300	John Adams as Moderator	320
State of the American Mind	301	His Political Career	320
Committees meet May Twelfth	301	Success of the Meeting	322
Samuel Adams the Chairman	302	Samuel Adams at Salem	322
His Fame at Fifty-two	302	Gage dissolves the General Court	324
His Invective on the Port Act	303	Delegates chosen to Congress	325
Circular of the Conference	304	Close of British Authority in Massachusetts	325
Town-meeting May Twelfth	305		
The Donation Committee	306	Rejoicing at Warren's House	325

CHAPTER XI.

THE REGULATING ACT AND THE SUFFOLK RESOLVES. — 1774. JUNE TO SEPTEMBER.

Two additional Penal Acts	327	Pledges to Massachusetts	336
Hutchinson and George III.	327	Words of Prescott and Gardner	337
The King and the Colonies	331	S. Adams leaves for Congress	338
Effect of the New Acts	331	Supply of his Necessities	338
Samuel Adams on the Crisis	332	Warren as a Popular Leader	338
Meeting June Twenty-eighth	333	Warren to Samuel Adams	339
Donation Committee organized	334	Putnam the Guest of Warren	341
Gage receives the Two Acts	334	Suffolk Convention at Stoughton	341
His Instructions	334	Dunbar's Liberty Prayer	342
Greatness of the Issue	335	William Eustis	342

xvi   CONTENTS.

	PAGE.		PAGE.
Warren to Samuel Adams	343	Paul Revere on Boston	359
Warren to Stonington	345	British Force in Boston	360
Warren to Preston	346	Suffolk Convention re-assembles	360
Gage forbids a Town-meeting	348	Warren reports the Suffolk Resolves	361
Conference August Twenty-sixth	349	Address to Gage	362
Provincial Congress resolved on	349	His Reply	363
Warren to Norwich	350	Second Address	363
Warren to Samuel Adams	351	Warren's Meeting with Plucker	364
The Powder Alarm	352	Boldness of the Suffolk Resolves	365
Warren at Cambridge	353	Warren sends them to Congress	366
Warren to East Haddam	354	Their Reception	367
Warren on Government	355	Their Indorsement	367
Warren to Samuel Adams	355	Joy of the Patriots	367
One Colony of Freemen a Bulwark for the Rights of America	358	Surprise of Gage	367
Expression of Popular Feeling	358	Violence of the Tories	368
Gage fortifies Boston Neck	359	Union of the Colonies	369

CHAPTER XII.

MASSACHUSETTS AND THE GENERAL CONGRESS. — SEPTEMBER, 1774, TO JANUARY, 1775.

Description of Massachusetts	370	Decline to Form a Government	390
The First Charter	371	Middletown on the Penal Acts	391
Charter of William and Mary	372	Warren to Middletown	391
Local Government dissolved	373	Citation from Josiah Quincy, jun.	393
Condition of the People	374	Warren to Josiah Quincy, jun.	393
On forming Government	375	Gage on the Union	396
Extremists among the Whigs	375	The Provincial Congress	397
Class who aimed at Union	375	Its Address to the People	397
Warren to Samuel Adams	375	Warren to Newport	398
Samuel Adams to Warren	377	His General Activity	398
Warren chosen a Delegate	378	Spirit of the Tory Party	399
Instructions of Boston	379	Firmness of the Whigs	400
Card by Warren	380	Non-importation Policy	400
Committee of Correspondence	380	American Union fully reached	401
Warren to Samuel Adams	381	Voices from South Carolina	401
A Provincial Congress	383	Prediction for 1874	402
Prominent Members	384	Meaning of Union	403
On Forming a Government	385	Washington's Interpretation	404
Letter of John Adams	386	Motto on the American Flag, "Liberty and Union"	403
Action in the Union Spirit	387	Pledge from Durham	403
Reliance on the General Congress	388	Military Preparation	404
Its Pledge to Massachusetts	388	Warren's "Song on Liberty"	405
The Provincial Congress	389		

CHAPTER XIII.

WARREN'S SECOND ORATION. — 1775. JANUARY TO MARCH.

	PAGE.		PAGE.
Warren in favor of Bold Action .	406	Leslie at Salem .	422
His Service on Committees	406	Firmness of the Patriots	422
Inspection Committees . .	407	The Pledge of Falmouth	423
Greatness of the Question .	407	Reply of Boston . .	423
Objects of the Patriots . .	408	Inspiring Signs of Union	424
Ministry give up Taxation	409	Contemporary Interpretation .	424
Retain the Right to alter Charters	409	William H. Drayton's Charge	424
		John Adams's "Novanglus" . .	424
Franklin on this Claim	409	Abraham Cowley's Prophecy .	425
Army sent to enforce it . . .	410	The American Ensign	426
Spirit of Resistance to it . . .	410	Fifth-of-March Anniversary .	426
Dartmouth on Hostilities . . .	411	Warren selected as the Orator	426
Samuel Adams on Hostilities .	411	Town-meeting	427
Second Provincial Congress . .	412	Appearance of the Old South	427
Re-elect the Committee of Safety	412	The Audience	428
Enlarge their Powers . .	412	Description of the Orator .	429
Tory Action and Hand-bill	413	Oration, exordium .	430
The Troops create Alarm .	413	On Personal Freedom	430
Warren to Samuel Adams	414	On Colonial Freedom .	431
Warren on Committees .	415	On Aggressions .	432
Appeal of Congress . . .	416	On their Consequences	432
Gage on the Congress . .	417	On the Massacre	433
Warren to Arthur Lee . .	418	On Hostilities .	433
The Committee of Safety .	419	On the Duty of the Hour	435
Hawley against Hostilities . .	420	Behavior of the Officers	437
Josiah Quincy, jun., on Hostilities	421	Samuel Adams on the Scene .	438
Gage on disarming the People .	422	Samuel L. Knapp on the Scene .	439

CHAPTER XIV.

THE NINETEENTH OF APRIL. — 1775. FROM THE 5TH OF MARCH TO THE 19TH OF APRIL.

Action of the Committee of Safety	441	Summons of Absent Members .	445
The Army watched	441	Irritations of the Army	445
George III. confident	442	Mock Oration by the Officers .	446
Patriots hold Union their Anchor	442	Marches of the Army . . .	457
Warren to Montreal . . .	442	Warren to Arthur Lee . . .	457
Spirit of the National Life .	444	Francis Dana on the Colony . .	448
The Provincial Congress meet .	444	Samuel Cooper on Union	448
Its Conciliatory Spirit	444	Warren to Franklin . .	448
Alarming News from England .	445	Caution of Congress . . .	449

CONTENTS.

	PAGE.
Numbers of the Army	450
Its Officers expect Submission	450
Warren on Cowardice	451
Apprehensions of Arrests	451
Anecdotes of Warren	452
Warren decides on a Military Life	452
Movements of Gage	453
Warren informs Hancock and Adams	454
Troops on the March	454
Warren sends Word to Lexington	455
Smith's Expedition to Concord	455
Anecdote of Lord Percy	455
The Alarm of the Country	456
Day of Lexington and Concord	456
Express to Warren	456
His Departure from Boston	456
Meets Charlestown Men	457
Meets Officers in Cambridge	457
Meets the Committee of Safety	458
Question of beginning War	458
Hancock and Adams	459
Anecdote of Samuel Adams	459
Warren joins Heath	460
Percy rescues Smith	460
Warren and West Cambridge	461
British reach Bunker Hill	462
Comment on Warren's Service	462

CHAPTER XV.

SIXTY DAYS OF SERVICE. — 1775. FROM THE 19TH OF APRIL TO THE 17TH OF JUNE.

	PAGE.
Day of Lexington and Concord	464
Boards of Selectmen	464
Circular penned by Warren	466
Warren to General Gage	467
Eliot on Warren's Influence	468
The Provincial Congress	468
Warren President *pro tem.*	469
His Autographs	470
Warren to Arthur Lee	470
Report made by Warren	471
Warren to the Selectmen	472
Warren to Alexander M'Dougal	473
Warren to Connecticut	475
Warren on Committees	476
Warren drafts Papers	477
Warren on the Situation of Boston	478
Character of William Cooper	480
Warren on a Government	481
Warren to Committee of Safety	482
Warren to Moses Gill	482
Warren to Samuel Adams	483
On taking up Government	485
Warren to Joseph Reed	486
Warren to Continental Congress	487
Its Admirable Statesmanship	487
Warren to Arther Lee	488
Warren on Ticonderoga	490
Re-chosen on Committee of Safety	490
Warren on giving Commissions	491
Warren at Grape Island	493
His Connection with the Press	493
Benjamin Edes and John Gill	493
Warren on Arnold's Success	494
Warren to Samuel Adams	495
Warren to Continental Congress	496
Warren to New Hampshire	497
Third Provincial Congress	498
Warren elected President	498
Dr. Langdon's Sermon	498
Testimony to Social Order	499
Warren on the Appointment of Washington	500
Warren on Exchange of Prisoners	501
Report on the Army	502
Warren on Committees	503
Warren chosen Major-General	503
Decision to occupy Bunker Hill	504
Relations of Warren's Views	504
Warren's last Letter	506
Occupation of Breed's Hill	507

CHAPTER XVI.

THE CLOSING SCENE. — 1775. THE SEVENTEENTH OF JUNE.

	PAGE		PAGE
The Seventeenth of June .	508	His Death	517
Warren in the Morning .	509	His Burial on the Field .	518
He goes to Cambridge	510	Relations of his Fall . .	519
Meets the Committee of Safety .	510	The General Mourning .	520
Letters from Congress . . .	511	Individual Expressions	520
Alarm in Cambridge . . .	512	John Warren on the Battle-field .	522
Warren goes to Charlestown .	513	Discovery of the Body .	522
His View from Bunker Hill	513	The Public Funeral	523
His Interview with Putnam	514	Perez Morton's Eulogy .	524
His Meeting with Prescott	515	The Remains	524
His Service as a Volunteer	515	Warren's Friends .	525
Capture of the Redoubt . . .	516	Conclusion	525

APPENDIX.

I. THE SUFFOLK RESOLVES 529
II. EULOGIES ON WARREN 535
III. WARREN'S CHILDREN 542
IV. RELICS OF WARREN 546
V. MONUMENTS TO WARREN 547

LIFE AND TIMES

OF

JOSEPH WARREN.

CHAPTER I.

EARLY DAYS.

INTRODUCTORY. — FAMILY OF WARREN. — HIS BOYHOOD. — DEATH OF HIS FATHER. — HIS COLLEGE DAYS. — POLITICAL EVENTS. — ANECDOTE. — A SCHOOL-TEACHER. — A MASON. — HIS PROFESSION.

1741 TO 1763.

JOSEPH WARREN was one of the popular leaders of Boston during the early stage of the American Revolution. He grasped its basis idea of civil freedom, and aimed to impress on the public mind its dignity and glory. By ten years of devotion to the patriot cause, he rose to be the head of public affairs in Massachusetts, and became one of the most prominent characters of New England.[1]

Warren, through life, was a man of action, whose words were deeds. To repel the aggressions of arbitrary power, and to maintain the principles of liberty, he wrote in the political journals, was zealous in the private clubs, and was a leader in the public meetings.

---

[1] Both in civil and military affairs, the most prominent man in New England. — *Life of Warren*, by Alexander H. Everett, 107.

When his townsmen desired an exponent of their sentiment, he became their orator; when the time arrived for American union, he was active in organizing committees of correspondence; and, when revolutionary action was required, he appeared in the front of responsibility in destroying the tea, and in resisting the acts altering the Massachusetts Charter. As the virtual executive of a free State, he acted with the comprehensiveness of the patriot, and the administrative ability of the statesman. On the field of war, he impressed his associates with his coolness, judgment, and resources. He volunteered to share with a band of militia, the perils of an extreme post; and, when he fell in the Bunker-hill battle, co-laborers in the cause, who felt the magnetism of his influence, and knew the value of his service, declared that his memory would be endeared to the worthy, in every part and age of the world, as long as virtue and valor should be esteemed among mankind.[1]

The tributes paid to Warren, when he was crowned an immortal, indicate a career of no ordinary character; and the future seemed burdened with his honors.[2] But so scanty is the material relative to him, of a strictly personal cast, that the greater part of his civic service has been overlooked.[3] The Boston records place him in the front rank of great political action, but are barren of details. Contemporary eulogy, however abundant, is not copious in facts; and his letters are but few in number, until the last fifteen months of his life. Then, utterances,

---

[1] Massachusetts Committee of Safety, July 25, 1775.   [2] Bancroft, vii. 433.

[3] The first public appearance of Dr. Warren, in connection with the political affairs of the day, was on the occasion of the delivery of the Anniversary Address of 1772. — *Everett's Life of Warren*, 114.

elicited by his public labors, often in a prophet's tone, and always aglow with patriotic fire, reveal the inner springs of a noble life, and justify the judgment, that Warren lived an ornament to his country.[1]

His words, interpreted in action, show his grasp of issues, his motive, and his aim; but, to see him as a social power, it is necessary to follow him through scenes when the public passion was roused, and high resolve ruled the hour, and when he was a leader in company with kindred spirits. These scenes must ever be of interest from their connection with the events that led to national independence. In weaving descriptions of them into a biography which demands traits of personal character, there is a liability of encroaching on the province of history on the one hand, and, on the other, of being incomplete; and, while a view will be given of the great popular demonstrations in which he was an actor, only so much general history will be related as may be necessary to show the working of political influences on the community among whom he passed his life.

The career of many of the revolutionary men extends over a longer period than that of Warren; but few have connected their names more enduringly with vital principles or salient events, and seldom is there seen a life of nobler devotion to country, and hence better calculated, by its lesson, to strengthen patriotic influences. The contemplation of such a character as the self-devoted martyr of Bunker Hill is the noblest spectacle which the moral world affords.[2]

---

[1] As he lived an ornament to his country, his death reflected a lustre upon himself, and the cause he so warmly espoused. — *Eliot's Biographical Dictionary.*

[2] Everett's Warren, 182.

In a genealogy of the Warren Family, the name is traced back to William, Earl Warren, a Norman baron of Danish extraction. He accompanied William the Conqueror on his expedition to England; fought at the battle of Hastings; was rewarded with riches that were shorn from the intrepid Saxons; and won the confidence of the Court to such an extent, that, when the king left England on a visit to his native land, Earl Warren was appointed one of the two guardians of the kingdom. From this ancestry, the Warrens are followed down through earls, knights, and commoners, to the period of the colonization of our country.[1] Then emigrants of this name settled in Plymouth, Watertown, and Boston; but no proof has been discovered of a connection between these families.[2] A careful examination of the records of the parish in England, whence the Watertown family came, fails to connect it with the Boston family.[3] Joseph Warren's ancestry have not been authen-

---

[1] I am indebted to the late Dr. J. C. Warren for a copy of his beautiful "Genealogy of Warren, with some Historical Sketches," printed in 1854. In "Patronymica Britannica" is an account of the Warren surname, dated Oct. 1, 1860: "Warren. — William de Warene, or Warrena, who married Gundrada, a daughter of William the Conqueror, received great possessions in Sussex, Surry, Norfolk, Suffolk, &c., and became progenitor of the Earls of Warenne and Surry. His chief seat, anterior to the Conquest, was at Bellencombre, a small town in the arrondissement of Dieppe, in Normandy, on the little river Varenne. By this name, the town itself was anciently known, until, upon the erection of a fortress upon an artificial mound, or *bellus cumulus*, it received, from that circumstance, the appellation of Bellencombre. — *Arch. Journal*, iii. 6. The Norman de Warrennes were doubtless progenitors of many existing families of Warren; but it must not be forgotten that the surname may have a totally different source, — namely, warren, which Baily defines as "a franchise, or place privileged by the king, for keeping conies, hares, partridges, pheasants," &c.; though the phrase is now more commonly applied to a colony of rabbits. Thirdly, Warran, or Warinus, is an old baptismal name, whence Fitz Warine."

[2] Savage's Genealogical Dictionary.   [3] H. G. Somerby, MS. letter.

EARLY DAYS.

tically traced beyond Peter Warren, whose name appears first on the Boston records, in 1659, where he is called Mariner. His second son, Joseph, a housewright, built a house, in 1720, in Roxbury, and died in 1729. His son Joseph, born in 1696, married, May 29, 1740, Mary, the daughter of Dr. Samuel Stevens, of Roxbury; and here their son Joseph, the subject of this biography, was born, on the 11th of June, 1741. The family mansion, which was substantial and commodious, stood in what is now Warren Street, and was then near the centre of the principal village. On the site of it there is now a modern house, built of stone, which has two inscriptions on the front of the second story. One is: "On this spot stood the house erected, in 1720, by Joseph Warren, of Boston, remarkable for being the birthplace of General Joseph Warren, his grandson, who was killed at the Battle of Bunker Hill, June 17, 1775." The other is: "John Warren, a distinguished physician and anatomist, was also born here. The original mansion being in ruins, this house was built by John C. Warren, M.D., in 1846, son of the last named, as a permanent memorial of the spot."[1]

Roxbury, which borders on Boston, is characterized, by an early writer, as having been settled by a laborious people, who turned its swamps into fruitful fields, and planted flocks and herds on its rocky hills.[2] The father of Warren was a farmer, who was highly esteemed and respected, led an exemplary life, and held several municipal offices to the acceptance of his townsmen. He paid much attention to fruit-raising, and introduced into the neigborhood of Boston the

---
[1] Loring's Hundred Boston Orators, 47.   [2] Hubbard.

apple denominated from him the "Warren Russet."[1] Warren's mother had a fine mind and a lovely disposition; and her long and useful life was imbued with fervent piety.

Warren, happy in a parentage of independence and virtue, passed his childhood under careful eyes and healthy influences. He was instructed in the rudiments of knowledge in the public school of Roxbury; but nothing is related specially of his studies. He is described in boyhood as manly, generous, fearless, and independent.[2] He raised himself, a Tory writer said, from ambition only, from a bare-legged milk-boy to be a major-general.[3] The history of the time could hardly have failed to arrest his attention and excite his ambition. The journals then seen in most families contained accounts of the encroachments of the French in the Valley of the Ohio; and Washington's daring feats and dawning fame would naturally be the household talk[4] There was in Boston the uncommon spectacle of the gathering of an army, and

---

[1] Everett's Warren, 95. [2] Stories of Gen. Warren, 18.
[3] News Letter, Jan. 11, 1776.
[4] The following, from the newspapers of this period, shows the manner in which Washington was named when Warren was a boy:—

A brief chronology of remarkable events relating chiefly to the present war.

Since first the Sparks of this dire War begun, } 1749.
In this new World, which into Europe run.
Since the perfidious *French* in hostile Ranks } 1751.
The *English* drove from smooth Ohio's Banks
Since *Washington* entered the List of Fame, } October, 1753.
And by a Journey to Lake *Erie* came.
Since he defeats a *French* detached Band, } May 24, 1754.
Under the brave *Jumonville's* command.
Since *Contrecoeur* took hold of English Claim, } June 13, 1754.
His Fortress builds and calls it Fort *Du Quesne*.
Since *Beau Se Jour* yielded to British Fame, } June 20, 1754.
And *Cumberland* adorns its present name
Since Fortune turned to *Washington* adverse, } July 3, 1754.
Who makes good Terms with a superior Force

its embarkation for Nova Scotia, in order to act against the enemy.

When Warren was fourteen, his father, while in his orchard, gathering fruit from a tree, fell from the ladder on which he was mounted, and was instantly killed. His son John, subsequently a celebrated surgeon, who was sent by his mother to call his father to dinner, met the body as two laborers were bearing it towards the house. A letter in the "Boston News Letter" (Roxbury, Oct. 25, 1755) thus relates this calamity· "On Wednesday last, a sorrowful accident happened here. As Mr. Joseph Warren, of this town, was gathering apples from a tree, standing upon a ladder considerable distance from the ground, he fell from thence, broke his neck, and expired in a few minutes. He was esteemed a man of good understanding; industrious, upright, honest, and faithful; a serious, exemplary Christian; a useful member of society. He was generally respected among us, and his death is universally lamented." His widow was left with the charge of four sons, — Joseph, the patriot; Samuel, who continued to live with his mother, and cultivate the paternal estate; Ebenezer, who settled in Foxboro', and was a member of the Convention which ratified the Federal Constitution, and of the General Court, and a judge of the Court of Common Pleas in Norfolk County; and John, who was educated at Harvard College, studied medicine with his brother, was a surgeon in the army of the Revolution, rose to eminence in his profession, was a distinguished literary and political writer, and an eloquent lecturer. The fidelity with which the mother executed her arduous trust is attested by the virtues of her children.

She lived to see her sons attain fame and honor, was an object of general interest in Roxbury, reached an advanced age, and continued until her death to live in the family mansion. She was hospitable, kind to her neighbors, benevolent to the poor, and reaped, in the affectionate attention of the younger members of the family, the best reward for the exemplary care with which she had discharged her maternal duties. This excellent woman appears to have much resembled the mother of Washington, in the skill and care with which she infused generous sentiments and virtuous principles into the bosoms of her children; and she reaped, almost as richly as Mrs. Washington, the fruits of her labors.[1] It has been said[2] that it is not easy to imagine a lovelier scene than the following paragraph, from the "Stories of General Warren," presents, of the evening of a well-spent life, still warmed and brightened by the benign spirit which had been the sun of this life's long day: "In her old age, when her own children had left their fireside to take their part in the active scenes of life, it was one of her dearest pleasures to gather a group of their children and the children of others around her. She did all in her power to promote their enjoyment, and her benevolent smile was always ready to enliven and encourage them. On Thanksgiving Day, she depended on having all her children and grandchildren with her; and, until she was eighty years of age, she herself made the pies with which her table was loaded."[3]

Mary Warren died in 1803. Several of the Boston journals of Jan. 20 have this obituary notice: "At

---

[1] Southern Literary Messenger, i. 750.   [2] Ib.   [3] Stories of Gen. Warren, 17.

Roxbury, on Friday last, Mrs. Mary Warren, aged ninety. Few among the sons and daughters of Adam have attained so advanced an age, fewer still with faculties so unimpaired, very few with a character so unspotted. An unshaken confidence in the rectitude of the Divine government rendered her firm and serene through every stage of life. Of the cup of adversity she had sometimes drank deeply; but the religion of Jesus was her never-failing support. It was this that prompted to the exercise of universal beneficence; it was this which heightened her relish for social intercourse and enjoyment; and the cheerfulness it inspired, together with an uncommon strength of mind, made her, at a period of life which is usually but labor and sorrow, the welcome companion of the young and the aged. And it was this which at last enabled her to meet the approach of death, for which she, at that interesting hour, expressed herself she had been all her life preparing, without a terror and without a groan."

In 1755, Warren, at fourteen, entered Harvard College, which was presided over by the prudent Holyoke, a man of a just and noble spirit. Great political events occurred during the four years of his college course. The struggle between England and France, for empire in this western world, filled every locality with politics. The humiliation to which unworthy counsels brought British arms was typified in the defeat of Braddock; and the victory of Wolfe was an earnest of the fresh life which Pitt infused into his countrymen. Harvard graduates, with whom Warren was afterwards intimately associated, were, during this period, beginning their career. Samuel

Adams was of the class of 1740; and, three years later, he maintained, in a thesis before the faculty, the doctrine, that it was lawful to resist by force the supreme magistrate, if the commonwealth otherwise could not be preserved; and was recognized already as a champion of the popular cause in Boston. James Otis, of the class of 1743, had acquired such fame for genius, learning, and eloquence at the bar, that lawyers spoke of him to John Adams, then at Worcester, as the greatest, the most learned and honest young man of his age.[1] Samuel Cooper, of the same class, the patriot divine, who became Warren's pastor, was settled at Brattle-street Church, and appeared, like the rising light, shining more and more unto his meridian splendor.[2] James Bowdoin, of the class of 1745, was an eminent merchant, and a member of the General Court. John Hancock, of the class of 1754, was in the counting-room of his uncle, the largest merchant of Boston. John Adams, of the class of 1755, was master of a grammar school at Worcester, and was speculating on the removal, from the West, of the turbulent Gallies, an American Union, and on the progress of his country in power, until the united force of Europe would be unable to subdue it;[3] and, the year Warren was graduated, his life-long and dear friend, Josiah Quincy, jun., entered as a student.

Warren sustained in college the character of a youth of talents, fine manners, and a generous, independent deportment, united to great personal courage and perseverance.[4] He exhibited, in union with manliness, spirit, and resolution, that gentleness of nature

---

[1] John Adams, in a letter, says he had not met Otis in 1758.   [2] Dr. Eliot
[3] Letter, 1755.   [4] Knapp's Biographical Sketches, 107.

which characterized his career.¹ An anecdote is related showing his fearlessness. Several of his class, in the course of a college frolic, to exclude him, shut themselves in a chamber, and barred the door so effectually that he could not force it. Warren, bent on joining them, saw that their chamber-window was open, and that a spout was near it which reached from the roof to the ground; and he went to the top of the house, walked to the spout, slid by it down to the window, and threw himself into the room. At this instant, the spout fell; when he quietly remarked, that it had served his purpose. He then entered into the sport of his classmates. "A spectator of this feat and narrow escape," Knapp says, "related this fact to me in the college-yard, nearly half a century afterwards; and the impression it made on his mind was so strong that he seemed to feel the same emotion as though it happened but an hour before." ²

During Warren's collegiate course, Washington and other Virginians visited Cambridge, and were received with marked attention; but no memorials connect Warren thus early with public men or affairs. It is said that he distinguished himself highly as a student, and had a part assigned to him on the day he was graduated.³ It is related, that, soon after he left college, he gained a premium which was offered by gentlemen of the province for the best poem on the death of George the Second and the accession of George the Third.⁴ A volume was published, in Boston, in 1761, under the title of *Pietas et Gratulatio*, containing thirty-one poems, on these themes,

---

¹ Everett's Warren, 96. ² Knapp's Sketches, 108. ³ Rees' Cyclopædia. ⁴ *Ib.*

which were written by the alumni of Harvard; but he is not named among their authors.

In April succeeding his graduation, at nineteen, he was appointed master of the grammar school in Roxbury, which was one of the best endowed, oldest, and most successful schools in Massachusetts. His immediate predecessor was Mr. Fairfield; and the feoffees' or trustees' records say: "1760. April ye 11. Then the Feoffees agreed with Mr. Joseph Warren to take the school for one quarter of a year at ye rate of fortey three pounds nine shillings & fourpence a year, he to board himself and his time to commence until about the second of May (as he was to keep a week or ten days for Mr. Fairfield)." Warren taught this school about a year, as appears from the following letter, addressed " To the gentlemen intrusted with the care of the school in Roxbury: " —

BOSTON, December, 1761.

GENTLEMEN, — You may remember that you agreed with me to teach the school in Roxbury for forty-four pounds sixteen shillings a year; of which I have received from Deacon Gridley twenty-five pounds twelve shillings, of the Rev. Mr. Adams about five pounds, of the school-boys, to pay for the carting of wood, two pounds and eight pence, of which by your direction I expended eleven shillings and two pence in buying a lock, hooks, staples, and nails for the repairing of the school-house. So that there remains due to me about thirteen pounds, by payment of which to my mother or order, you will greatly oblige, Gentlemen, your
H. Servant, JOSEPH WARREN.

P. S. — I am not certain of the particular sums received of the Rev. Mr. Adams; but his receipts will determine.[1]

[1] I copy from the original, in the files in possession of the Secretary of the Trustees, Mr. C. K. Dillaway, the author of the interesting history of this school, who obligingly submitted the papers to me.

On the back of the original of this letter is the autograph of Mary Warren, acknowledging the receipt of thirteen pounds six shillings and eight pence, in full for her son's keeping this grammar school.

About the time Warren left this school, he was initiated (Sept. 10, 1761) a member of the St. Andrew's Lodge of Masons, which had been formed but a few years. He was regular at its meetings, and made earnest effort to establish the character and widen the influence of this association. "It was his *Alma Mater*," it has been said; "and, as such, he was ever zealous to defend its honor and promote its welfare." He continued through life a member of this institution, and rose, as will be seen, to its highest honors; and the craft have affectionately and gratefully cherished his memory.[1]

Warren chose the profession of medicine for his calling. Dr. James Lloyd, who had recently returned from London with a high reputation for learning and skill, was now an eminent physician in Boston. He kept a genteel equipage, entertained company with great liberality, commanded a more respectable circle of practice than any other physician of his day, and was considered highly accomplished in all branches of the profession.[2] Warren went through the usual preparatory course of study under his direction; but I have no memorials of this portion of his life. He took his degree as master of arts in course at Harvard, in 1762.

---

[1] Memoir of Warren, by Charles W. Moore.
[2] Thacher's Medical Biography, 24.

CHAPTER II.

PRINCIPLES AND PARTY.

Marriage. — Settlement in Boston. — As a Physician. — As a Politician. — His Ruling Passion. — Letter. — The Popular Leaders. Samuel Adams. — Warren and Adams.

1763 to 1767.

WARREN was united in marriage, on the 6th of September, 1764, with Miss Elizabeth Hooton, of Boston. The event was announced in the following way: "Last Thursday evening was married Dr. Joseph Warren, one of the physicians of this town, to Miss Elizabeth Hooton, only daughter of the late Mr. Richard Hooton, merchant, deceased, an accomplished young lady with a handsome fortune." A gentle, sensitive nature, good sense, and accomplishments of a high order, formed a character worthy to share his fortunes. A tribute on her decease says she had —

> "Good sense and modesty with virtue crowned;
> A sober mind, when fortune smiled or frowned;
> So keen a feeling for a friend distressed,
> She could not bear to see a worm oppressed." [1]

The eulogies on Warren specialize the social qualities and domestic virtues "which endeared him to the honest among the great, and the good among the humble;" and made him, "in the private walks of life, a pattern for mankind."[2] The love which he bore his

---

[1] Boston Gazette, May 3, 1773.   [2] Perez Morton's Oration.

mother attests his filial piety; and his care for his children, his parental affection: and the devoted patriot was the faithful head of a happy home. He lived in Hanover Street, on the estate on which the American House stands, being but a short distance from Faneuil Hall and the old Town House; and attended the Congregational Church in Brattle Street, of which Samuel Adams was a member, and Dr. Cooper the pastor.

Thus, at twenty-three, Warren established himself permanently as a physician. Boston was the metropolis of New England, and was noted as the largest town, and best situated for trade, in British North America. Its population, almost wholly of English extraction, was estimated at sixteen or eighteen thousand; and the number who could take part in politics, at thirty-five hundred. It presented an attractive field for professional life. It was emphatically republican in politics; and this element, in a century and a quarter of its history, had become so interwoven with the feelings, habits, and customs of its inhabitants, that, along with whatever it contained of the provincial and transient, it had the heirloom of principles that were national and enduring.

It happened that the small-pox, which was then dreaded as a scourge, prevailed in the town this year to such an extent that business was mostly suspended; and many of the inhabitants retreated into the country. A great number were inoculated. One of Warren's patients was John Adams, when the two patriots formed an acquaintance which ripened into friendship; and, until near the day on which Warren fell, the Adams Family continued to enjoy the benefit of his skill in his profession.[1] He was especially attentive to the poor,—a service which drew the public eye upon him. He had a graceful figure, was scrupulously neat in his person, of thorough culture, and had an elegant address; and these traits rendered him a welcome visitor in polite circles, while a frank and genial manner made him a general favorite. He had a great love for his fellow-men; and being a stranger to the passion of avarice, and even neglectful to a fault in pecuniary matters, he had an ear ever open to the claims of want, and a hand ever extended to afford relief. Thus imbued with the qualities that characterize the good physician, the path before him to success was easy and wide. "In person, mind, and manners, he was equally well accomplished," Dr. Eliot, a Whig, says;[2] and a Tory, Dr. Perkins, used to remark, "If Warren were not a Whig, he might soon be independent, and ride in his chariot."[3] Thus the quiet walks of private life allured him, not only with the promise of a fortune, but with the crowning honors of his profession.

Great events, however, growing out of the spirit of the age, and exciting powerfully the liberty-loving people of the colonies, attracted Warren to a wider stage of action, and gave direction to the current of his life. The progress of his countrymen in numbers and wealth, and their large and successful exercise of popular power, roused the jealousy of England; and, with the end ever in view of checking the democratic principle and of increasing a dependence on the Crown, its ministry entered on the policy of subject-

[1] John Adams's Works, i. 64.   [2] Eliot's Biographical Dictionary.
[3] Rees's Cyclopædia.

ing the colonies to taxes which they had no voice in imposing, and to plans of internal government which they had no hand in framing. The Stamp Act provoked discussions on profound questions connected with natural rights and constitutional law, which divided the community of Boston into two political parties, — the supporters of the Administration, who were called Loyalists, Tories, and Friends of Government, and the opponents of the Administration, who held the new policy to be unconstitutional, who were styled Whigs, Patriots, and Sons of Liberty. The Tories claimed to be friends of freedom, because they upheld the supremacy of law; and the Whigs said they were loyal to the mother country, because they recognized the executive functions of the Crown and the sovereignty of Great Britain. As it was not the original purpose of the Tories to invoke for their country the curse of arbitrary power, so it was not the early programme of the Whigs to sever political relations with the British Crown. Men are but instruments in the hands of Providence. Both parties drifted into measures which neither party originally proposed, or even desired; and thus the Tory, to uphold the sovereignty of parliament, grew into the defender of arbitrary power; and the Whig, to preserve his constitutional rights, became the assertor of national independence.

Warren's natural bent would not permit him to be a cold looker-on in this struggle of parties, in which he saw involved the issue of freedom. It is worthy of remark, that Dr. Lloyd, who was an ornament of his profession, with whom Warren studied medicine, did not join in the movements of the patriots; and

Dr. Rand, one of Lloyd's students at this time, sympathized with the Tory side. Other physicians of the town took the same view, and with these Warren would naturally be thrown frequently in contact. But his professional associations did not govern his political course. It is related, that, " after the passing of the Stamp Act, he undertook a serious examination of the right of parliament to tax the colonies; and, as his time was not at his command during the day, his nights were spent in this investigation. He devoted himself to the common cause with a zeal extremely prejudicial to his private interests. While he was engaged in disseminating the great truths he had learned, his pecuniary affairs were neglected, and became greatly deranged."[1] His love of country and of liberty was ardent and absorbing; and, when he reached settled convictions as to the aggressive nature of the new policy of the Administration on popular rights, he desired to influence the public mind. In aiming at this, instead of wasting effort in individual and unsystematic action, he put himself in a situation to wield power, by joining the political party that was opposing these aggressions. He gave his heart and hand to the Whigs, and it was the ruling passion of his life to promote their cause. But though he became a warm party man, was high-spirited, had sensibilities uncommonly strong, " and a zeal which blazed in the cause of liberty, he was candid, generous, and ready to do kind offices to those who had different sentiments about the cause in which he was engaged."[2] This warrants the remark, that he mingled among his fellow-citizens as though

[1] Rees's Cyclopædia.   [2] Boston Magazine, April, 1784.

it were his endeavor to rear into vigor and maturity the generous and honest feelings that belong to our nature; to bring the dispositions that are lovely in private life into the service and conduct of the commonwealth; and so to be the patriot as not to forget to be the gentleman.[1] " He gained the love of those who lived with him in habits of intimacy, while the public voice celebrated his virtues."[2]

Warren left a precious early memorial, showing the feelings and ideas with which he engaged in public life. One of his college classmates (Edmund Dana) had emigrated to England, married there happily, and was settled as the rector of Wroxeter in Salop. Warren addressed to this friend the following letter, which reveals much of his genius and his aims. It shows his sympathy with the free spirit of his age, his broad union and national ideas, contains a sagacious view of the temper of his countrymen, and may be said to be the key to his political life. Boston, when this letter was written, was alive with politics. Its daring spirit had been evinced in the memorable uprising of the Fourteenth of August, 1765, against the Stamp Act; it was welcoming John Adams's high-toned dissertation on the canon and feudal law; and Warren was taking part with his townsmen in their bold action. The letter is dated the day after the repeal of the Stamp Act, which, of course, was unknown in the colonies: —

---

[1] Edmund Burke.

[2] Eliot's Biographical Dictionary. Dr. Eliot repeated, in 1809, on this trait of Warren, the sentiments which he expressed in the "Boston Magazine," in 1784, and adds: "There are persons now living who recollect his polite attentions, when they were slighted and wounded by others whose minds were less liberal, or more corroded with party spirit."

Joseph Warren to Edmund Dana.

BOSTON, NEW ENGLAND, March 19, 1766.[1]

DEAR SIR, — I have not had the pleasure of a line from you since you left this country. I wrote to you soon after I heard of your arrival in England; and I have not at any time been negligent in inquiring concerning you, whenever an opportunity presented. I have with great satisfaction heard of that agreeable life which you lead amidst all the gayeties and diversions of that jovial city, London; but I received a peculiar pleasure from the intelligence which I have lately had of your happy marriage with a lady of noble birth and every accomplishment, both natural and acquired. Accept the sincerest wishes of your long-absent (but I hope not forgotten) friend, that you may long enjoy, with your charming consort, that unequalled happiness which must arise from a union of persons so amiable.

Perhaps it may not be disagreeable at this time to hear something of the present state of your native country. Never has there been a time, since the first settlement of America, in which the people had so much reason to be alarmed as the present. The whole continent is inflamed to the highest degree. I believe this country may be esteemed as truly loyal in their principles as any in the universe; but the strange project of levying a stamp duty, and of depriving the people of the privilege of trial by jury, has roused their jealousy and resentment. They can conceive of no liberty when they have lost the power of taxing themselves, and when all controversies between the Crown and the people are to be determined by the opinion of one dependent man; and they think that slavery is not only the greatest misfortune, but that it is also the greatest crime, if there be a possibility of escaping it. You are sensible that the inhabitants of this country have ever been zealous lovers of their civil and religious liberties. For the enjoyment of these, the first settlers fought battles, left a pleasant and populous country, and exposed themselves to all the dangers and hardships in this new world; and their laudable attachment to freedom has hitherto been transmitted to their posterity. Moreover, in all new countries (and especially in this, which was settled by private adventurers), there is a more equal division of property amongst the people; in conse-

---

[1] This letter is printed in Loring's "Hundred Orators," also in the "Warren Genealogy;" but I have followed the copy in the archives of the Massachusetts Historical Society, which differs from both in a few words.

quence of which, their influence and authority must be nearly equal, and every man will think himself deeply interested in the support of public liberty. Freedom and equality is the state of nature; but slavery is the most unnatural and violent state that can be conceived of, and its approach must be gradual and imperceptible in many old countries, where, in a long course of years, some particular families have been able to acquire a very large share of property, from which must arise a kind of aristocracy: that is, the power and authority of some persons or families is exercised in proportion to the decrease of the independence and property of the people in general. Had America been prepared in this manner for the Stamp Act, it might perhaps have met with a more favorable reception; but it is absurd to attempt to impose so cruel a yoke on a people who are so near to the state of original equality, and who look upon their liberties, not merely as arbitrary grants, but as their unalienable, eternal rights, purchased by the blood and treasure of their ancestors, — which liberties, though granted and received as acts of favor, could not, without manifest injustice, have been refused, and cannot now, or at any time hereafter, be revoked. Certainly, if the connection was rightly understood, Great Britain would be convinced, that, without laying arbitrary taxes upon her colonies, she may and does reap such advantages as ought to satisfy her. Indeed, it amazes the more judicious people on this side the water, that the late minister was so unacquainted with the state of America, and the manners and circumstances of the people; or, if he was acquainted, it still surprises them to find a man in his high station so ignorant of nature and of the operations of the human mind, as madly to provoke the resentment of millions of men, who would esteem death, with all its tortures, preferable to slavery. Most certainly, in whatever light the Stamp Act is viewed, an uncommon want of policy is discoverable. If the real and only motive of the minister was to raise money from the colonies, that method should undoubtedly have been adopted which was least grievous to the people. Instead of this, the most unpopular that could be imagined is chosen. If there was any jealousy of the colonies, and the minister designed by this act more effectually to secure their dependence on Great Britain, the jealousy was first groundless. But, if it had been founded on good reasons, could any thing have been worse calculated to answer this purpose? Could not the minister have found out, either from history or from his own observation, that the strength of any country depended on its being united within itself? Has he not by this act brought about what the most zealous colonist never could have expected? The colonies, until now, were ever at variance, and foolishly jealous of each other. They are now, by the refined policy of Mr. George Grenville, united for their common defence against what they believe to be oppression; nor will they soon forget the weight which this close union gives them. The impossibility of accounting in any other way for the imposition of the stamp duty has induced some to imagine that the minister designed by this act to force the colonies into a rebellion, and from thence to take occasion to treat them with severity, and, by military power, to reduce them to servitude. But this supposes such a monstrous degree of wickedness, that charity forbids us to conclude him guilty of so black a villainy. But, admitting this to have beeen his aim (as it is known that tyrannical ministers have, at some time, embraced even this hellish measure to accomplish their cursed designs), should he not have considered that every power in Europe looks with envy on the colonies which Great Britain enjoys in America? Could he suppose that the powerful and politic France would be restrained by treaties, when so fair an opportunity offered for the recovery of their ancient possessions? At least, was he so ignorant of nature as not to know, that, when the rage of the people is raised by oppression to such a height as to break out in rebellion, any new alliance would be preferred to the miseries which a conquered country must necessarily expect to suffer? And would no power in Europe take advantage of such an occasion? And, above all, did he not know that his royal benevolent master, when he discovered his views, would detest and punish him? But, whatever was proposed by the Stamp Act, of this I am certain, that the regard which the colonies still bear to His Majesty arises more from an exalted idea of His Majesty's integrity and goodness of heart than from any prudent conduct of his late minister.

I have written, sir, much more than I intended, when I first sat down; but I hope you will pardon my prolixity upon so important a subject.

I am, sir, your most sincere friend and humble servant,

JOSEPH WARREN.

To MR. EDMUND DANA.

P.S.—I hope for the favor of a line from you the first opportunity.

The simple way in which Warren, in this letter, deals with vital principles, indicates that they had been so wrought into his mind as to have become the mould and guide of his life. He tested the absorbing measure of the day, the Stamp Act, not only by the abstract idea of justice, but by its adaptation to the condition of the people of the colonies, showing with bold strokes of theory a practical turn of mind. He evinced clear insight into causes, and accurate judgment as to effects. His remark, that freedom and equality is a state of nature, indicates, that with him the French dogma of the equality of man was joined to the English dogma of the freedom of man; and that he grasped the principle which has most thoroughly leavened modern opinion, and promises to modify most deeply the constitution of society and the politics of States:[1] while the strain of sentiment on the division of property shows an appreciation of the fact of the equality of condition which modern philosophy pronounces to be the central point of American society.[2] His letter is a representation of the enthusiasm and resoluteness with which the young men welcomed the principles of the Revolution, and which led Hutchinson to say, that independence had entered into the heart of America.

With these comprehensive views and high aims, Warren engaged in public life by enrolling himself in the band of popular leaders whose service to the country associated Faneuil Hall with the idea of civil freedom, and fixed it in the public mind and affection as the cradle of American liberty. "In this hall," it has been said, "was first heard the eloquence of a Hancock, the two Adamses, a Bowdoin, a Molineux,

---

[1] Maine's Ancient Law, 92. [2] De Tocqueville's Democracy in America.

and a Warren."[1] This band were mostly young men, or men of middle age. Jonathan Mayhew, a celebrated divine, and Oxenbridge Thacher, a distinguished lawyer, both pioneer patriots, had recently died at forty-three; Samuel Adams, and William Cooper, the faithful and intrepid town-clerk, were forty-six; James Otis, who, six years before, made the great freedom-plea on the question of writs of assistance, and Thomas Cushing and Samuel Cooper, were forty-three; John Adams, the future president, ambitious to be a great lawyer, was thirty-three; Paul Revere, a representative of the patriotic mechanics, was thirty-two; John Hancock, a wealthy merchant, who threw a powerful social influence in favor of the cause, was thirty-one; Josiah Quincy, jun., who had become a lawyer of great oratorical power, was twenty-five; and others, like Molineux, a stirring business-man, Thomas Young, a physician, and William Phillips, a merchant, who took a prominent part in the action of the patriots, were in the prime of life. James Bowdoin was the oldest, being sixty-one. This band of leaders engaged in the contests of party with as much freedom from sinister motives, and with purposes as elevated, as are ordinarily seen in the guidance of public affairs. They were Warren's friends or associates, with whom, down to the close of his life, he communed in the

---

[1] In this hall was first heard the eloquence of a Hancock, the two Adamses, a Bowdoin, a Molineux, and a Warren. In this hall was first kindled that divine spark of liberty, which, like an unconquerable flame, has pervaded the continent, — a flame, which, while it proved a cloud of darkness to the enemies of America, has appeared like a pillar of fire to the votaries of freedom, and happily lighted them to empire and independence. — *Massachusetts Magazine*, March, 1789.

social circle, counselled in the political club, acted in the public meeting, and served on important committees.

His relations were of the most confidential nature with one of this band, Samuel Adams, who, of all the patriots, had the most radical love of liberty, and was a universally good character.[1] He was educated at Harvard College, where he was distinguished for proficiency in logic and the classics. He was trained for the ministry; but, after he was graduated, he went into business as a small trader, and soon accepted the office of collector of taxes. He evinced a decided inclination for politics, spent much time in talking with people about their rights, and, as he grew in years, his reputation increased for a just appreciation of public questions, firmness of principle, and sagacious leadership. He was known also as a contributor to the journals, and the framer of able State papers. He moved before the community with a morality that was instinctive, a love of country that was undying, and a faith that rose to the sublime; and these inspirations mingled with and guided his public and private life. As a party leader, he was prudent; and yet, when it was necessary, he was bold. He was keen in penetrating the designs of his opponents, and was inflexible in carrying out his purposes. He had confidence in the virtue and intelligence of the people; believed they had a high destiny; and, passionately loving the republicanism that was so firmly embedded in his native soil, he regarded this element as vital to individual, communal, and national progress.

[1] John Adams's Works, vol. ii.

It was the custom of this patriot to watch the rise of every brilliant genius, seek his acquaintance, court his friendship, and enlist him as a co-worker in the common cause;[1] and there were two characters in Boston, who, John Adams said, after he had served in congress, were as great, in proportion to their age, as he had ever known in America. One was Josiah Quincy, jun., and the other was Warren. "They were both my intimate friends," Adams says, "with whom I lived and conversed with pleasure and advantage. I was animated by them in the painful, dangerous course of opposition to the oppressions brought upon our country."[2] Warren was "a young man whom nature had adorned with grace and manly beauty, and a courage that would have been rash absurdity, had it not been tempered by self-control."[3] Samuel Adams found in him a kindred spirit. Both respected the common capacity, estimated alike the greatness of the political issues, embraced similar vital principles, and strove for the same object. Both, with faith in an ultimate triumph of the right, had the moral courage that bears up in the day of weakness, and the patience in labor that waits for the day of strength. Both acted fearlessly on their convictions. Both were representative men, — one personifying more a peculiar theological element; and the other, more a passionate nationality. What though Warren had the fascination that marks the true man of the world, and Adams had the rigid inflexibility that has caused him to be regarded as the last of the Puritans; and what though one was naturally inclined

---

[1] John Adams's Works, x. 364. [2] John Adams's Letter, July 29, 1775.
[3] Bancroft, v. 441.

to cultivate the things that charm in social life, and the other was moved to shun, if not to despise, luxury and display: both were gentle, kind, and generous; both were sincere and self-sacrificing; the hearts of both beat in unison for a common cause; and both were inspired by visions of the future glory of their country. They became bosom friends. "Their kindred souls were so closely twined that they both felt one joy, both one affection."[1] Warren proved a trustworthy counsellor, on whom Adams ever leaned, and could always rely; and they labored lovingly together in the great revolutionary action of Boston and Massachusetts, until Warren sealed his work with his blood, and the heart of Adams poured itself out like water over the early grave of his friend.

[1] Perez Morton's Eulogy.

CHAPTER III.

CONNECTION WITH THE PRESS.

THE TOWNSHEND REVENUE ACTS. — FRANCIS BERNARD. — WARREN OPPOSES THE ADMINISTRATION. — HIS CONNECTION WITH THE PRESS. A TRUE PATRIOT. — PROCEEDINGS AGAINST THE "BOSTON GAZETTE."

1767 TO MARCH 1768.

IT has been remarked, that the great authority and influence which Warren exercised over his fellow-citizens, in the latter part of his life, evidently show that he had taken an active part in political affairs from the commencement of his residence in Boston; though, as the foreground of the stage was occupied by the great men who were the fathers of the Revolution, his activity must have been confined to a secondary sphere.[1]

There was an intermission in the controversy between Great Britain and her colonies, on the repeal of the Stamp Act; and at this period Warren's name does not occur in connection with public affairs. In 1767, the Townshend Revenue Acts were passed, which imposed duties on paper, glass, painter's colors, and tea; created a Board of Customs; and legalized Writs of Assistance. These measures, with the doings of crown-officials, who acted under royal instructions, which were declared to have the force of law, constituted a system of arbitrary power.

[1] Everett's Warren, 106.

At this time, Francis Bernard was the Governor of Massachusetts. He was born in England, educated at Oxford, and, with the knowledge and training in civil affairs acquired as a solicitor at Doctors' Commons, was appointed Governor of New Jersey; and, after two years of service in that colony, was transferred to Massachusetts. He was a scholar, and kept fresh his memory of *Alma Mater*. He loved literature and science, could write elegies in Latin and Greek, used to say that he could repeat the whole of Shakspeare, and had gifts of conversation which charmed the social circle. His politics were of the Oxford school. He was a good hater of republican institutions; habitually spoke of the local government, with its recognition of popular rights, as a trained mob; and deemed it a marvel that Charles II. had not made a clean sweep of the little New-England republics, as he characterized these provinces, and had not supplied their place with more aristocratic governments, with executives having vice-regal powers, moulded, as nearly as possible, like that of England. He thought, that though people might bluster a little when such reform was proposed, yet they never would resist by force; and, if they did, a demonstration of British power, such as the presence of the king's troops in a few coast-towns, and the occupation of a few harbors by the royal navy, would soon settle the contest.[1]

Bernard, in September, 1767, before receiving officially the new Revenue Acts, sketched the state of things in Boston, in the following terms in one of his letters: "Never were people more divided in opin-

[1] Letter, Aug. 30, 1767.

ions, hopes, and fears, than those of Boston now are. Men of a timid complexion give up the town, and expect greater disturbances than have been hitherto; and at the same time wish for troops to protect them, and are afraid of their coming here. Others persuade themselves that the gentlemen of the town will be able to keep it quiet, and defeat the purposes of the faction. I believe there is a great deal of pains taken to prevent mischief. On the other hand, the faction is as indefatigable in promoting it. The minds of the common people are poisoned to a great degree; so that (to use an expression of one of their own partisans) their bloods are set on boiling. It is a melancholic consideration that this rich and populous town should be thus distracted and disgraced by a set of desperadoes (perhaps not a dozen), whose own ruined or insignificant fortunes make the distraction of their country a matter of indifference to them; who, having themselves little to lose, are unconcerned at the consequences of a contest which they are desirous of bringing about, and must be fatal to persons of real worth and property."[1] This letter supplies a glimpse of the British official, as well as a view of opinion in Boston; and shows how little he appreciated the men or the spirit of his time. To him, a band of enlightened patriots, who represented not merely the aims of a town, but of a great and free people, appeared but a criminal faction advocating a ruinous cause. A few months later, he named Warren as one of the chiefs of the faction which he described.

The divisions in the popular ranks, which were noticed by Bernard, had their origin in the different

[1] Bernard to Lord Shelburne, Sept. 21, 1767.

views that were taken of public questions. Some, in their political theory, accepted a shadowy line, which had been marked out by Lord Chatham, between internal and external taxation; while others rejected it. "The claim," Hutchinson says, "to an independence of parliament, in whole or in part, is now become most universal. When they [the patriots] are most moderate, Lord Chatham's distinction is admitted: others say it is but reasonable we should be restrained in our trade; but the true heroes for freedom say, that if we are to be under restraint at all, by any authority without us, we are but slaves."[1] Warren was of the class who rejected the distinction between internal and external taxes, and uniformly held that every kind of taxation was tyranny.[2] Their theory, however, was not stated accurately by Hutchinson. They did not claim to be exempted from authority which they considered to be national, but only claimed the right to make the local law. When it was urged, on the side of the Administration, that the right of parliament to make laws for the American colonies remained indisputable at Westminster;[3] it was replied, on the side of the colonies, that their right to make laws for their own internal government and to tax themselves had never been questioned.[4] They regarded the colonies and Great Britain as members of one great empire, — each under the constitution having independent legislatures; the parlia-

---

[1] Letter, March 23, 1768.   [2] Eliot's Biographical Dictionary.
[3] Bernard's Message, Sept. 25, 1765.
[4] Answer of the House of Representatives, Oct. 28, 1765, which says: "The charter of this province invests the General Assembly with the power of making laws for its internal government and taxation. . . . The parliament has a right to make all laws within the limits of their own constitution."

ment having the right to make the laws for England, and the local assemblies to make the laws for America, with the king as the common chief-magistrate, whose rightful prerogative was in force in each colony as it was in England. There was this difference between the two parties: the theory set up for parliament was regarded by the Whigs as an abstraction of the British lawyers, which, though dangerous, had lain dormant; while the claim urged for the local government was for customs which were a part of their daily life, and by the exercise of which they had attained and now enjoyed a high degree of individual and communal freedom.

The popular leaders were united in the determination to avoid such riotous excesses as had disgraced the uprising against the Stamp Act, to confine their action to constitutional methods, and to build up their cause on the foundation of an enlightened public opinion. It was now said in the press, and probably by Warren, "Let the persons and properties of our most inveterate enemies be safe. Let not a hair of their scalps be touched. Let this be the language of all, — no mobs, no confusions, no tumults. Save your money and save your country"[1] A call from a Southern colony, printed in the journals, had the same injunction: "The liberties of our common country are exposed to imminent danger; and Massachusetts must first kindle the sacred flame that must warm and illuminate the continent. The cause is nothing less than to maintain the liberty with which Heaven itself has made us free; and let it not be disgraced by a single rash step, for constitutional methods are

[1] Boston Gazette, Nov. 9 and 14, 1767.

the best methods."[1] This indicates the fixed resolution of the patriots, that social order should be the base-line of worthy political action in behalf of a common country.

Warren shared in the indignation of his countrymen as the plan of establishing arbitrary power in the colonies developed. He was, at twenty-six, as settled in principle, and as firm in the purpose of devoting himself to the patriot cause (as his letter already printed shows), as his whole past career proves him to have been at thirty-four. A few of his sentences will attest his life-long ruling passion: "We eye the hand of Heaven in the wonderful union of the colonies." "The mistress we court is Liberty, and it is better to die than not to obtain her." "America must and will be free; the contest may be severe, the end will be glorious." These words reveal his inward impulse, his purpose, and his faith; and he ever appeared earnest to impress his views on others. It is related by John Adams,[2] that when, as the President of the Provincial Congress, he addressed, in the form of a charge, every military officer, on delivering his commission, "he never failed to make the officers, as well as all the assembly, shudder." This indicates, that, when his spirit was roused, there came from beneath his native amiableness a burning energy of soul that was magnetic and irresistible. This may account for the personal influence which he exercised.

Warren now began to appear in the foreground of the public stage in connection with the great popular

[1] Letter in the Boston Gazette, "from a gentleman of fortune, family, and great abilities, in a remote southern colony, to his friend in this town," dated Dec. 5, 1765. It was by John Dickinson, and is printed in Tudor's Otis.

[2] John Adams's Works, iii. 277.

leaders. "Neither resentment," Dr. Gordon, who knew him, says, "nor interested views, but a regard to the liberties of his country, induced him to oppose the measures of the Government. He stepped forward into public view, not that he might be, noted and admired for a patriotic spirit, but because he *was* a patriot. He was a gentleman of integrity, in whom the friends of liberty could confide. The soundness of his judgment enabled him to give good advice in private consultations."[1] And his eulogist, Perez Morton, remarking on his public service, says, "*Amor patriæ* was the spring of his actions, and *mens conscia recti* was his guide. And on this security he was, on every occasion, ready to sacrifice his health, his interest, and his ease, to the sacred calls of his country.'

The earliest identification of Warren with political affairs, and in opposition to the measures of the Administration, is his connection with the press. He began to contribute to the journals in the time of the Stamp Act, and he continued to supply matter to them down to the close of his life.

The newspaper had been established sixty-three years in Boston; but, at first, it was little more than a chronicle of the passing time, and left the discussion of political affairs to the pamphlets. The earliest paper established in the town and the country ("The News Letter"), after continuing twenty years, announced that it would publish those transactions only that had no relation to the quarrels of the day. The "New-England Courant," however, a contemporary journal, criticised so sharply the Administration and the theology of the day, as to draw upon it the

[1] Gordon's History, ii. 49.

indignation of the general court. In 1748, Samuel Adams and other popular leaders, to arouse the people to maintain their rights, established the "Independent Advertiser," which was printed but two years. In 1755 the same politicians encouraged the printing of "The Boston Gazette and Country Journal," a weekly paper. Its publishers, Benjamin Edes and John Gill, were men of probity and enterprise, and zealous Whigs; but the influence that moulded public opinion proceeded from the Adamses, Otis, Thacher, Quincy, Warren, and their associates, who wrote elaborate editorials and communications in the faith and inspiration "that Providence had set them to defend the rights and liberties of mankind." Their record in this journal warrants the generous judgment of Isaiah Thomas, a patriotic co-worker in the same field, that "no paper on the continent took a more active part in defence of the country, or more ably supported its rights, than the 'Boston Gazette:' its patrons were alert, and ever at their posts; and they had a primary agency in events which led to our national independence."[1]

The popular leaders employed with great effect the press, in exposing the system of arbitrary power. Warren, who was now a frequent contributor to it, used his pen, not to win a literary reputation, but, as the farmer uses his spade, to do his work. "He sought not," Perez Morton says, "the airy honors of a name; else many of those publications, which, in the early period of the controversy, served to open the minds of the people, had not appeared anonymous." He had the talent of seizing the pith of a

[1] Thomas's History of Printing, ii. 236.

subject, making salient points, imparting his own spirit, and with clearness, precision, and force, saying much in a few words. His vein of the poetic and his nervous style were calculated to strike the public mind. His productions contain many pointed sentences. Dr. Eliot calls him a fine writer. Many of his articles appeared in the "Gazette." A Tory informer, after mousing about Edes and Gill's printing-office, in search of matter to use in court, in the case of the arrest of the popular leaders, made affidavit that Warren had burned his manuscripts.

Governor Bernard watched the newspapers narrowly, and represented in his official letters that they teemed with matter against the new revenue laws precisely of the same nature as that which preceded the former insurrection, meaning the popular action against the Stamp Act; and that they were calculated and designed to raise the mob against the new establishment. Six years later, he prepared an elaborate narrative of the transactions in Boston, which begins as follows: "The success which had attended the flagitious publications in the Boston newspapers, on the subject of the Stamp Act, in exciting the popular tumults which followed the promulgation of that law, was too obvious to escape the attention of those who wished to see the same opposition given to the subsequent revenue laws; and therefore, when it became known that such laws were proposed, at least as soon as they were published, and the concomitant establishment of the commissioners of the customs had taken place, the press again teemed with publications of the most daring nature, denying the authority of the supreme legislature, and tending to excite the people to opposition to its laws."[1]

Bernard advised Lord Shelburne, Oct. 15, 1767, that he had received the new revenue acts, and that they had been printed in the journals; and he persistently represented that the patriots designed to oppose them by an insurrection. He specified the occasions on which he expected the insurrection to begin, as when the commissioners of the customs should land, or when the revenue acts should go into effect; but he had no proofs of the existence of the disloyal designs which he denounced; and it is difficult not to believe that he feigned the fear which it suited his purposes to express. A town-meeting was held in Faneuil Hall, Oct. 28, when the passive mode of meeting the acts by a non-importation and non-consumption agreement was adopted. At the adjournment of this meeting, Nov. 20, the day on which the new revenue laws went into effect, there was a seditious hand-bill posted under Liberty Tree. "Under the tree," Bernard wrote, "was stuck up a paper so highly seditious, that it would be undoubtedly deemed in England an overt act of high treason. It contained an exhortation to the Sons of Liberty to rise on that day, and fight for their rights; stating, 'that, if they assembled, they would be joined by legions; that, if they neglected this opportunity, they

---

[1] Governor Bernard's Letter Books, vol. viii. In 1774, by command of the king, he laid before the privy council, for their use, an elaborate narrative, entitled, "State of the Disorders, Confusion, and Misgovernment which have prevailed, and do still continue to prevail, in his Majesty's Province of Massachusetts Bay in America," since the repeal of the Stamp Act. This narrative was accompanied by a list of three hundred and sixteen documents; the date of the last one being a letter of Thomas Hutchinson, of Jan. 28, 1774.

would be cursed by all posterity.'"[1] This circumstance drew from James Otis, who was the moderator, an *extempore* speech, strongly denunciatory of mobs, in which he urged that the opposition to burdensome measures should be strictly constitutional;[2] and, in the course of it, he reminded the people that their forefathers of the reign of Charles I., for fifteen years, offered prayers to their God and petitions to the king, for a redress of grievances, before they resorted to force; and, in closing, he exhorted all good citizens to assist the civil magistrate in preserving the peace. The speech was received by all parties with great applause; the obnoxious paper was removed and disavowed by the patriots, who said that it was the device of their enemies; and the meeting voted,

---

[1] Bernard to Lord Shelburne, Nov. 21, 1767.

[2] This important speech is not mentioned in Tudor's "Life of James Otis." There is a report of it in the "Evening Post," Nov. 23, 1767. After stating that a resolution was offered in support of good order, the "Post" proceeds: "On this occasion, the moderator made a speech to the following purpose: —

"That many people seemed to have blended two things together in their minds which were totally distinct, — that is, the duties laid upon many articles imported, and the office of the commissioners of the customs, — as though the commissioners had occasioned those duties, and that we must get rid of the latter in order to avoid the former; that it was absurd to suppose that the commissioners had the least hand or influence in laying or procuring those duties; that we had from the first, and for a long course of time, acknowledged the authority of the custom-house officers appointed by the Crown, and sent among us; that we had often desired the establishment of a board of commissioners in the plantations, and complained that, for want of it, we were deprived of many advantages which our fellow-subjects in Great Britain enjoyed, who, if oppressed by any undue severities of the subordinate officers, might have immediate redress by application to that board, which we could not by reason of our distance; that we ought, therefore, to consider the establishment of that board here as a favor and a great advantage, and treat the commissioners with all due respect; that if the duties were thought burthensome, and we had just reason to complain of them, we ought to behave like men, and use the proper and legal measures to obtain redress; that the means were in our power; access to the throne was always open; that there was no doubt but our humble and dutiful petitions and remonstrances would, sooner or later, be heard, and meet with success, if supported by justice and reason, — but, let our burthens be ever so heavy, or our

unanimously, a resolution against mobs. But this did not stop the flow of Bernard's misrepresentation. In January, 1768, he wrote: "It seems to me unavoidable that the whole power of the Government must be in the hands of the people before June next, unless some relief, I know not what, comes from England. I can't stand in the gap again, unless I am assured of being supported from home. If I am left to myself, I must deliver up the fort, and make the best terms I can."[1] He said that the memorable "Circular Letter," in which Massachusetts, in February, proposed united action to the colonies, was designed to raise a general flame.

In the mean time, he kept on complaining of the

grievances ever so great, no possible circumstances, though ever so oppressive, could be supposed sufficient to justify private tumults and disorders, either to our consciences before God or legally before men; that our forefathers, in the beginning of the reign of Charles I., for fifteen years together, were continually offering up prayers to their God, and petitions to their king, for redress of grievances, before they would betake themselves to any forcible measures; that to insult and tear each other in pieces was to act like madmen, and would have no tendency to obtain redress of any of our grievances, if we had any to complain of; that it was observable, that, during the course of the revolution which placed King William on the throne, there were no tumults or disorder; and, when the whole city of London was in motion, only a single silver spoon was stolen, and that they showed such resentment to this as immediately to hang up the person who was guilty of the theft.

"Upon the whole, he concluded by recommending a quiet and proper behavior, and that the inhabitants of the town would show their dislike and abhorrence of all tumults and disorders, and do all in their power to assist the civil magistrates in preserving peace and good order.

"This speech was much to his honor, and greatly applauded; and is thought would have a very good effect. The conduct of the gentlemen selectmen, on this occasion, was also greatly applauded."

This report elicited from Otis a card in the "Boston Gazette" of Nov. 30, 1767, in which, with explanations as to what he said as to the commissioners, he renews with emphasis his detestation of mobs. This speech and an extract from the speech made by Josiah Quincy, jun., in the Old South Church, Dec. 16, 1773, on the Tea Question, are the only reports, of any length, of all the speeches made in the Boston public meetings from 1768 to 1775.

[1] Letter, Jan. 14, 1768.

work of the press. He sent cuttings from it to the ministry, and sometimes files of the "Gazette;" and he suggested that legal proceedings should be commenced against the profligate and flagitious popular printers.[1] Lord Shelburne received the suggestion of a prosecution of the journals with great coldness; and in allusion to an observation of Bernard, that their mischievous matter was contemptible in ability and impotent in influence, Lord Shelburne said, with singular good sense, that contemptible writings were rendered more abortive by being left to oblivion; and he gave sound advice in relation to appearing as his majesty's governor in any case as the prosecutor.[2]

The popular leaders had accurate information of the course of Bernard; and the following article, written by Warren, appeared in the "Boston Gazette," on the twenty-ninth day of February, 1768:[3]—

"MESSRS. EDES AND GILL, — Please insert the following: —

"MAY IT PLEASE YOUR ——, We have for a long time known your enmity to this province. We have had full proof of your cruelty to a loyal people. No age has, perhaps, furnished a more glaring instance of obstinate perseverance in the path of malice than is now exhibited in your.—— Could you have reaped any advantage from injuring this people, there would have been some excuse for the manifold abuses with which you have loaded them. But, when a diabolical thirst for mischief is the alone motive of your conduct, you must not wonder if you are treated with open dislike; for it is impossible, how much soever we endeavor it, to feel any esteem for a man like you.—— Bad as the world may be, there is yet in every breast something which points out the good man as an object worthy

---

[1] Letter, Jan. 30, 1768.   [2] Shelburne to Bernard.
[3] This article is marked "Dr. Warren," in Harbottle Dorr's file of the "Boston Gazette," in the possession of the Massachusetts Historical Society; and it is ascribed to him in "Rees's Cyclopædia" and Loring's "Boston Hundred Orators."

of respect, and marks the guileful, treacherous man-hater for disgust and infamy. —— Nothing has ever been more intolerable than your insolence upon a late occasion, when you had, by your jesuitical insinuations, induced a worthy minister of state to form a most unfavorable opinion of the province in general, and some of the most respectable inhabitants in particular. You had the effrontery to produce a letter from his lordship, as a proof of your success in calumniating us. Surely you must suppose we have lost all feeling, or you would not dare thus tauntingly to display the trophies of your slanders, and upbraidingly to make us sensible of the inexpressible misfortunes which you have brought upon us. But I refrain, lest a full representation of the hardships suffered by this too-long insulted people should lead them to an unwarrantable revenge. We never can treat good and patriotic rulers with too great reverence. But it is certain that men totally abandoned to wickedness can never merit our regard, be their stations ever so high.

"'If such men are by God appointed,
The devil may be the Lord's anointed.'
"A TRUE PATRIOT."[1]

The governor said that he could not, with safety to the Government, let this article pass unnoticed.[2] He first consulted, informally, several members of the council, who advised him to lay it officially before that body and the House of Representatives, which was then in session; which he did, by sending a similar message (March 1, 1768) to each. He said that he usually treated the "Boston Gazette" with the

[1] On this day, Feb. 29, 1768, the "Boston Chronicle," an Administration journal, stated that articles printed in Boston, in August, September, and October last, "had lately occasioned much conversation in a certain place;" and that, "soon after the meeting of the P——t, Mr. G—— G——, when the house was sitting, produced some American newspapers, which, he said, contained doctrine of a dangerous and alarming tendency; and proposed that the printer should be sent for and the author inquired after. Upon this, Mr. C——y replied, that the gentleman's motion was contrary to the order of the house; that, beside, it was only reasonable, before they sent for printers and authors from such a distance, they should make reformation at home among those who were just at hand. It was then put off for six months."

[2] Bernard to Lord Shelburne, March 5, 1768.

contempt which it deserved, but that he felt bound to notice it, when its publications were carried to such an extent as to endanger the existence of the Government; that this paper was of this character, and he presented it to them for their serious consideration, that they might act as the majesty of the king, the honor of the general court, and the interest of the province, might require.

The council received this message, Bernard says, "at a very full board, — there being twenty present the whole number but three," — who appointed a committee to prepare an answer, which was "unanimously agreed upon by the same number."[1] The council (March 3, 1768) remarked, that the article gave the board a real concern, and characterized it as a false, scandalous, and impudent libel on His Excellency. They said it was an insolent and licentious attack on the king's representative; involved an attack on Government itself; was subversive of all order and decorum; an insult on the general court, on the king's authority, on the King of kings; and worthy only of the utmost abhorrence and indignation: and the reply closed with the assurance, that the council would always support the dignity of the king's governor. It is questionable whether the council, in this reply, preserved its own dignity; for, while it affected to be shocked by the licentiousness of the press, it showed itself a master of the vocabulary of invective. The governor (March 3) returned his most hearty thanks for so decided an address, by a message, in which he said that he should not have taken notice of the libel, if he had not apprehended it to be pregnant with danger to the Government.

[1] Bernard to Lord Shelburne, March 5, 1768.

The house also considered the governor's message. Bernard says:[1] "In the house, which was grown thin, and evacuated by the friends of Government in greater proportion than [by] the opponents, it had not the same success. The faction labored with all their might to prevent the paper being considered. It was debated a whole afternoon, and adjourned to the next morning." The house, after such deliberation, agreed (39 to 30) upon an answer to the message. They said (March 3) that they had given due attention to the communication of the governor; had examined the paper which he had transmitted; and expressed sorrow, that any publication in a newspaper, or any other cause, should give His Excellency an apprehension of danger to the being or dignity of His Majesty's Government here. The house, however, could not see reason to admit of such conclusion from that paper. No person was named in it; and as there was nothing contained in it that could affect the majesty of the king, or the honor of the general court, the house thought they were justified in taking no further notice of it; remarking, "The liberty of the press is a great bulwark of the liberty of the people: it is, therefore, the incumbent duty of those who are constituted the guardians of the people's rights, to defend and maintain it." The answer closed by an expression of the opinion, that the provision already made for the punishment of abuses by the press, in the common course of the law, was sufficient in the present case. "The house," Hutchinson says, "rather justified the libel than condemned it." The criticism would have been more just, had it

[1] Bernard's Letter, March 5, 1768.

read, — The house rather condemned the action of the governor than justified the contents of the paper. In truth, the house understood its position; and its admirable answer is a calm and strong word for the freedom of the press.

The governor, with reason, now asked the council to prosecute the printers of "A True Patriot;" but this body declined to proceed farther in the affair. "This," Bernard wrote, "is one of the consequences of the fatal ingredient in this constitution, — the election of the council," which he termed "the cankerworm of the Government." He next directed the attorney-general to commence proceedings against the printers in the courts; and the article was brought before the grand jury. Hutchinson, as the chief-justice, delivered on this occasion a charge, in which he says, "I told them in almost plain words, that they might depend on being damned, if they did not find a bill." This charge received from his friends great praise for its legal ability. But the grand jury, which sympathized with the House of Representatives, braved the penalty named by the chief-justice, and refused to find a bill against the printers.[1]

[1] It appears from the following communication in the "Gazette" of March 27, 1769, written probably by Warren, that the article, "A True Patriot," was again before the grand jury.

"MESSRS. EDES AND GILL, — Please to insert the following: —

"I am informed of what passed with the grand jury last week, relative to a paper signed 'A True Patriot,' published in the supplement to your 'Gazette' of Feb. 29, 1768. I imagined nothing more would have been said upon a subject which has so ridiculously taken up the time of many persons, who might have been more wisely employed. However, I know the motives of those who have again brought it upon the *tapis*. It is to be represented to the ministry as an instance of disregard to law and good order. What success plotters will have, time must discover. In the mean time, it may be depended on that their representations will not, as in time past, be suffered to go without company.

"T. N. MONUMENT-MAKER."

Warren, in two communications printed in the "Boston Gazette," under the signature of "A True Patriot," reviewed with scathing severity these proceedings. While he disavowed any intention to destroy the dignity of authority, and remarked with contempt on the doctrines of divine right and passive obedience, he expressed the pleasure with which he heard the voice of "all orders of unplaced and independent men," who were determined to support their rights and the liberty of the press. He said that the House of Representatives showed themselves resolute in the cause of justice; and the grand jurors demonstrated by their action that influence was not able to overcome their attachment to sacred honor, a free constitution, and their country. He remarked of the people, that, when they knew their true interest, they would distinguish their friends from their enemies, and would protect from tyrannic violence generous defenders in the cause of justice and humanity; but, should a mistaken complaisance lead to a sacrifice of their privileges, or to a desertion of their well-meant supporters, they would deserve bondage, and soon find themselves in chains. He said that the authors of some of the misfortunes under which the province groaned, had been detected; and he closed in the following words· "We will strip the serpents of their stings, and consign to disgrace all those guileful betrayers of their country. There is only one way for men to avoid being set up as objects of general contempt, which is — not to deserve it."[1]

The result of this affair caused great chagrin to the

[1] One of these papers is in the "Boston Gazette" of March 7; and the other, in that of March 14.

Tories. Hutchinson said it convinced him as much as any thing which had occurred, that the laws had lost their force; Bernard said it proved that the Government could not regain its authority without aid from superior powers; Lord Hillsborough said it was "but too striking an evidence of the influence of those who sought to disturb the public peace, and persisted with so much obstinacy and malevolence in sowing the seeds of disorder and discomfort."[1] The patriots, on the other hand, appreciated a triumph that assured freedom of utterance in behalf of their cause. They had grasped the idea that the liberty of the press and the liberty of the land must stand or fall together. "I am no friend to licentiousness," Andrew Eliot said, "but the liberty of the press must be preserved sacred, or all is over;"[2] and the exulting voice of the people found expression, on festive occasions, in toasts to the honest and independent grand jurors.

Bernard did not allege that his individual character had been injured in the article signed "A True Patriot," but based his action on the ground, that it tended to bring the Government into contempt. It was not until a later period that the distinction was practically recognized between attacks on private character, to gratify a malicious intent, and an exposure of official wrongs, to promote the common welfare. In ordinary times, there can be no abridgment

---

[1] Lord Hillsborough to Bernard, June 11, 1768.
[2] April 18, 1768, in Mass. Hist. Society "Collections," 4th series, iv. 425. He wrote, May 13, 1767: "Nothing is of greater importance than to secure the entire freedom of publishing, without fear, any censures upon public measures. The liberty of the press is the palladium of English liberty. If this is gone, all is gone."

of a right to arraign measures of Administration; for it must be unrestrained, or it is no right:[1] it is a necessity to insure publicity, that great safeguard against corruption; and, if acts are detrimental to the general welfare, their originators ought to be brought into contempt. The House of Representatives and the grand jury, with an American instinct, proceeded on the rule which is now widely recognized; for the common-law offence of libelling a Government is ignored, in constitutional systems, as inconsistent with the genius of free institutions. Political comment, in this country and in England, severer than that which, in the article entitled "A True Patriot," disturbed the royal governor, now passes unnoticed; and he would be regarded as quite an indifferent observer, who should from this draw the inference that the Government, in permitting this freedom, compromised its authority, or that the people, in countenancing it, wavered in their loyalty.

The first great duty of the press — that of collecting intelligence of passing events, and making it common property — was an invaluable service rendered to the popular cause. In addition, during the preparatory struggle, when public opinion was forming and a thinking community achieved our Revolution, before a battle had been fought,[2] the press, assuming as of right to be free, was keen in the exposure of error and injustice, and noble in the presentation of truth and right. The popular leaders did not veil the Temple of Liberty, but arraigned corrupt officials and

---

[1] Livingston's System of Penal Law, 176.

[2] "Be it remembered," Daniel Webster remarks, "it was a thinking community that achieved our Revolution before a battle had been fought."

dangerous measures with a power, which, though to Toryism it seemed to be the seed of disorder, was really the kernel of national life. It was a standing marvel to the royal governor, that the Administration would not prosecute a band of printers, who, he said,[1] were continually directing daggers to the heart of their mother country and sovereign State, and to whom was very applicable the fable of the trumpeter, who was told, on being taken prisoner, that he was answerable for all the mischief done by the soldiery.[2]

[1] Letter, Nov. 25, 1769.

[2] Bernard advised Lord Hillsborough, June 25, 1769, that Messrs. Edes and Gill, the printers of the "Boston Gazette," had been made "the apparent instruments of raising that flame in America which has given so much trouble;" and recommended their arrest, as the first step towards calling the chiefs of the faction to an account.

CHAPTER IV

CONNECTION WITH PUBLIC MEETINGS.

PUBLIC MEETINGS. — WARREN AND THE CLUBS. — THE COMMISSIONERS OF THE CUSTOMS. — A RIOT IN BOSTON. — WARREN IN TOWN-MEETING. — PUBLIC OPINION.

1768. MARCH TO JUNE.

WARREN, in 1768, took a leading part in the public meetings that were held in Boston to remonstrate against the acts of the Administration. The people had been so long in the habit of assembling to discuss political questions, that the custom was looked upon as a right, and really was a part of American law, written and unwritten. The officers of the Crown, however, held that town-meetings for such objects were illegal. The political education of the people of England had been so backward, that, in times of excitement, they still resorted to tumultuous and riotous assemblages, in order to overawe the deliberations of Parliament. The institution of public meetings, as a regular mode of popular influence, forms a new era in constitutional government.[1]

There was a quiet direction given to the public meetings of Boston by political clubs, which were of several years' standing. Warren was accustomed

---

[1] May's Constitutional History, ii. 125. Parliament was overawed, in 1765, by a riot. In Albemarle's "Life of Rockingham," ii. 92, 93, 94, is an account of public meetings, in which it is stated, "From the summer of 1769 is to be dated the establishment of public meetings in England."

to say that nothing contributed more to promote the great end of society than a frequent interchange of sentiment in friendly meetings; and, as a member of some of the clubs and the adviser of others, he continued to be connected with them down to the close of his life, and their ruling spirits relied much on his judgment.

The largest of these clubs consisted of mechanics, traders, and others, and were named "The North End Caucus" "The South End Caucus," and "The Middle District Caucus."[1] A smaller club consisted of lawyers, clergymen, and the popular leaders. "From 1768," Eliot says, "a number of politicians met at each other's houses, to discuss public affairs, and to settle upon the best methods of serving the town and the country. Many of these filled public offices. But the meetings were private, and had a silent influence on the public body."[2] Warren was a member of this club, and also of the North End Caucus. Hutchinson, in his history, says that a circle, consisting of a number of the inhabitants, and members of the general court, met at least once a week in the evening; and at these meetings, besides determining what should be done at town-meetings, and agreeing upon other measures, they generally furnished the newspapers with speculations and compositions for the service of the cause in which they were engaged;[3] and he says, in a letter, that he

---

[1] In the records of one of these caucuses, the word is spelt caucos ("Siege of Boston," 30). In the "Boston Gazette" of 1760 are the following sentences: "Nothing of the least significance was transacted at a late meeting of the New and Grand Corcas." — "Votes are to be given away by the delicate hands of the New and Grand Corcas."

[2] Eliot's Biographical Dictionary.   [3] Hutchinson's Massachusetts, iii. 167.

could fill his sheet with acts of Government, come into by the town, the Cadet Company, and the clubs, remarking, "We have no sort of companies but which look upon it they have a right to do something or other in public affairs."[1] A Tory writer, in tracing the origin of the popular movement in Boston, says, "Garrets were crowded with patriots; mechanics and lawyers, porters and clergymen, huddled promiscuously into them; their decisions were oracular; and from thence they poured out their midnight reveries. They soon determined to form an independent empire."[2]

Warren's influence in the clubs is noticed by Dr. Eliot, in his biographical sketch, and by Paul Revere, in his well-known military narrative; and his zeal in promoting public meetings is seen in a relation in the Diary of John Adams, who writes, of 1768: "I was solicited to go to the town-meetings, and harangue there. My friend, Dr. Warren, most frequently urged me to do this. My answer to him always was, 'That way madness lies.' The symptoms of our great friend Otis, at that time, suggested to Warren a sufficient comment on those words, at which he always smiled, and said it was true."

Warren is named in the proceedings of a town-meeting that was held in March, when he was appointed a member of a committee to prepare a letter of thanks to the author of "The Farmer's Letters." The town recognized the service rendered by the farmer, John Dickinson, in his "most seasonable, sensible, loyal, and vigorous vindication of the rights and liberties of America;" and promised "warmly to

---

[1] Letter, June 7, 1768.   [2] News Letter, Jan. 11, 1776.

recommend and industriously to promote that union among the several colonies, which is so indispensably necessary for the security of the whole." The farmer, in a reply, complimented "the rank of Boston," the wisdom of her counsels, and the spirit of her conduct.

Warren appeared before the public as a popular leader in a memorable town-meeting, that was occasioned by the proceedings of the new commissioners of the customs. This board consisted of Charles Paxton, Henry Hulton, William Burch, John Robinson, and John Temple. Not much is said of Hulton or Burch, who were simply placemen; Robinson is remembered by a savage assault on James Otis; Temple, who was not in favor of the creation of the board, incurred the enmity of the other members, by disapproving of some of its doings; Paxton, its ruling spirit, was a bland, courtier-like, greedy partisan, who was very obnoxious to the people. The members were appointed to reside in Boston, and to superintend the collection of the revenue on the line of coast extending from Labrador to the Gulf of Mexico. They held their first board in Mr. Deblois's great room, in Hanover Street, and soon surpassed Bernard in misrepresentations of the designs of the patriots.

The revenue was duly paid; and the members had not been injured, though Burch had been frightened by a collection of boys and others about his house: yet they asserted that their persons were in danger of violence from a mob, and that British sovereignty was threatened with an insurrection of the colonies. They would ask the governor what support he could give them in case of an insurrection. "I answer," Bernard says (March 3, 1768), "none at all. They desire me to apply to the general for troops. I tell them I cannot do it; for I am directed to consult the council about requiring troops, and they will never advise it, let the case be ever so desperate. Indeed, I no more dare apply for troops than the council dare advise me to it. Ever since I have perceived that the wickedness of some and the folly of others will, in the end, bring troops here, I have conducted myself so as to be able to say, and swear to it, if the Sons of Liberty shall require it, that I have never applied for troops; and therefore, my Lord, I beg that nothing I now write may be considered such an application." The commissioners were very desirous to have a British force stationed in the town. "About a fortnight ago," Hutchinson writes (March 28, 1768), "I was in consultation with the commissioners. They were very desirous the governor should —— for a R—— If he had done it, by some means or other it would have transpired; and there is no saying to what lengths the people would have gone in their resentment." The commissioners carried themselves so arrogantly in collecting a revenue which was held to be oppressive, that their conduct excited odium in Boston, and elicited censure in England. They were, Samuel Adams said, extremely disgustful to the people, were neglected by men of fortune and character, and were viewed, in general, in no better light than the late stamp commissioners. Expressions of the public feeling are seen in the vote of the Independent Cadets, to the effect that they would not escort the governor, on the day of the election of councillors, if the commissioners were invited to dine with the governor and council; and also by the vote of the town, refusing the royal governor the use of Faneuil Hall to dine in, unless the commissioners were excluded.[1]

The commissioners, soon after the consultation just named, obtained a naval force in Boston harbor, by misrepresenting what occurred on the 18th of March, which was the anniversary of the repeal of the Stamp Act, and was celebrated as a holiday. There were, at daylight, hanging on Liberty Tree, effigies of Commissioner Paxton and Inspector Williams, — the last being a cabinet-maker, had a glue-pot by his side; but the popular leaders soon had these removed. During the day, cannon were discharged in the principal streets; public-spirited citizens decorated their residences with flags, and received their friends; a very respectable company had a festive season at the British Coffee House, where one of the toasts was, "The 'Boston Gazette' and the worthy members of the house who vindicated the freedom of the press:" in the evening, sailors and apprentices went through the streets, giving hearty huzzas; and as they passed by the Province House, where Bernard lived, he said they disturbed him and his family by their noise. At ten o'clock, a Whig report says, "The town was quiet, without there having been riot or rumpus; and the whole conduct of the day was a complete exhibition of a decent and rational

---

[1] May 4, 1768. Upon a motion made and seconded, voted, that the selectmen be directed to refuse the use of Faneuil Hall to His Excellency, the governor, and council, on the ensuing election-day, unless it shall be ascertained that the commissioners of the board of customs, or their attendants, are not to be invited to dine there on said day. The town almost unanimously, on the 23d of May, refused to reconsider this vote. — *Boston Records.*

joy."[1] The commissioners officially represented, that the mob certainly intended, on this day, to oblige them to resign their commissions under Liberty Tree; that the governor and magistrates had not the least authority in the town; and they made a demand on Commodore Hood, who was at Halifax, for immediate aid to secure the revenue and save the honor of the Government. "The moment," this officer says, "application was made to me by the commissioners for assistance from the king's ships, I ordered the 'Romney,' of fifty guns, to Boston, — a lucky event for those gentlemen, as she proved an asylum to them in a time of need; and from time to time I continued to throw in additional force, till they said no more was wanted."[2] Two tenders accompanied the "Romney." Hyperion (Josiah Quincy, jun.) said, in the "Gazette," that the Tories had threatened the defenders of America with halters, fire, and fagots; but there was nothing more serious than threats, or more authentic than rumors, until this appearance of the "Romney" and her tenders. As they lay in the harbor, a press-gang from them seized several Massachusetts citizens; a practice, which, though defended even later by Junius, was repudiated in the colonies as a relic of barbarism.

---

[1] The "Boston Post Boy" of March 21 had only the following as to this celebration: "Friday last, being the anniversary of the repeal of the Stamp Act, a number of gentlemen met on the occasion, and dined together at the Bunch of Grapes and British Coffee House in this town." And "The Chronicle," Tory, says the anniversary "was celebrated by a large company, who met at the British Coffee House and Colonel Ingersoll's, in King Street. A numerous body of the people assembled in the evening, and attempted to kindle a bonfire, but were prevented by a number of gentlemen, who at length persuaded them to retire peaceably."

[2] Grenville Papers," iv. 362.

Meantime the journals contained reports, that the ministry were determined to maintain the powers claimed for parliament; and they printed eulogies from abroad on the people of New England for the spirit with which these claims had been denied.[1] In May, Governor Bernard negatived the choice, by the House of Representatives, of Hancock and Otis as councillors. It was the talk of the town, that the colonists were to be taxed, in order to maintain a race of sycophants, court favorites, and hungry dependants; that needy lawyers from abroad, or tools of power at home, would be their judges; and that their governors, if natives, would be partisans rewarded for mercenary service, or, if foreigners, would be nobles of wasted fortunes, and greedy for salaries to replenish them. The people, who were sincere in their loyalty, felt that they were ill-treated; and were sullen.[2] This was a time of great excitement on popular rights in England; the Boston journals, after an arrival from London, abounded in matter relative to the Wilkes controversy; and, if "London[3] resounded the word 'liberty' from every corner and every voice," there was an echo in every home and street in Boston.

The officers of the Crown regarded this temper of the public mind as affording fresh proof of the necessity of a British force to preserve the public peace. "Our politicians," Hutchinson said, "are the most

---

[1] "It is with peculiar satisfaction, I can assure you, the New-England spirit of patriotism and economy is greatly approved of; and I am not alone in opinion, that, if America is saved from its impending danger, your country will be its acknowledged guardian." — *Phil. Letter in Boston Gazette, Feb. 22,* 1768.

[2] Andrew Eliot, 4 Mass. Hist. Soc. Coll., iv. 420.

[3] Boston paper, June 6, 1768.

wrong-headed people in the world. Every step they take for relief has a direct tendency to increase our distress. Their threats can never intimidate, but certainly must incense, the parliament; and they are determined to provoke a power they cannot resist:"[1] and Bernard advised the ministry, that he was "well assured that it was the intention of the faction in Boston to raise an insurrection against the Crown officials."[2]. The popular leaders in vain averred that it was their object to procure, by constitutional methods, a repeal of acts which they held to be illegal, and that they desired to preserve the union between the colonies and Great Britain.

Information was now laid before the commissioners of the customs, of a violation of the revenue laws, in the case of the sloop "Liberty," owned by John Hancock; and the solicitor-general, Mr. Lisle, on the 10th of June, advised her seizure. On hearing of this intention, Warren said to the comptroller, Mr. Hallowell, "that, if the seizure were made, there would be a great uproar, and that he could not be answerable for the consequences."[3] The commissioners, however, gave directions for the seizure. The sloop lay at Hancock's Wharf; and near the hour of sunset on this day, as the laborers of the town were going from their day's work, the revenue officials put upon her the broad arrow; and, as though the people would not respect the law, a boat's crew from the "Romney" cut her fastenings from the wharf, and moored her under the guns of the man-of-war. No official warrant was produced; and, in doing this, the British

---

[1] Letter, April 19, 1768.   [2] Letter, May 9, 1768.
[3] Hallowell's Examination, July 21, 1768.

captain and his officers used vulgar and threatening words to the bystanders. This was the beginning of a war of epithets, in the usual way of brawls, between the crowd, which kept increasing, and the custom-house officers; and, by a sort of natural law of mobs, grew into a riot, in which the offending officials were pelted with dirt and stones, the windows of the houses of the comptroller and inspector, Mr. Irving, were broken, and the pleasure-boat of the collector, Mr. Harrison, was drawn out of the water, and carried to the common, where above a thousand people gathered. One of them, in a harangue, exclaimed, "We will support our liberties, depending upon the strength of our arms." The boat was set on fire. Hancock, Samuel Adams, and Warren had been in consultation; and as it is said that Hancock, and others of influence, came on to the Common while the boat was burning, the inference is a fair one, that the three came together. Through their exertions, the riot ceased; the word was passed round, "Each man to his tent;" and the town, at about eleven o'clock, was as quiet as usual. Outrages had been committed which the popular leaders never attempted to justify, but alleged that they were provoked by the brutal language of the commander of the "Romney," Captain Corner, and the arbitrary conduct of the officers of the Crown. This was a slight affair, in comparison with the contemporary terrific mobs of London; and Colonel Barré said, in the House of Commons, that, in this riot, "Boston was only mimicking the mother-country."

On Saturday, there was great excitement among the people. Bernard says, that "the riot was followed by papers, stuck upon Liberty Tree, containing an invitation to rise, and clear the country of the commissioners and their officers;"[1] and that one of them was doomed to death. These were the words of the rash spirits. The commissioners, who had not been harmed, were the most violent of all the officials. As they had fancied signs of an insurrection in the hilarity of a holiday, they had neither difficulty nor scruple in magnifying a riot into a rebellion; and it was in vain that Bernard, on this day, entreated them to change their measures. He also laid the state of the town before the council, who advised such of the members as were justices of the peace to make inquiry into the facts, and report at a future meeting. Warren, on this day, exerted himself to allay the excitement; and, in Hancock's name, he proposed to Hallowell, whose bruises confined him to his house, "that, if the vessel were brought back to the shore, he (Hancock) would give his bond that he would have her forthcoming on the trial;" but no agreement was concluded.

On Sunday, Warren acted again as mediator between the parties. Mr. Harrison, in a note to Hancock, said, that, if he (Hancock) would agree that the "Liberty" should be forthcoming on the trial, she should be returned to the shore; and, in the morning, Warren informed Hallowell that matters were so far settled, that, on the next day, the "Liberty" would be

---

[1] The reports of this riot, in the papers, were very brief. The "Boston Gazette" of June 13, 1768, had the following: "Last Friday evening, some commotions happened in this town, in which a few windows were broke, and a boat was drawn through the streets, and burnt on the Common; since which, things have been tolerably quiet, it being expected that the cause of the disturbance will be speedily removed."

restored. During the day, the commissioners kept quiet, though Bernard still urged them to be conciliatory, while they spoke of going to the castle. There was a consultation of the popular leaders, in the evening, at Hancock's house, which was filled with the patriots; those named as present being Warren, Samuel Adams, and Otis. Here the affair of the "Liberty" was fully considered, and the course of the patriots was determined. At twelve o'clock at night, Warren went to Hallowell's house, and said to him, "that he had been at Hancock's, and was extremely sorry that matters could not be settled as he told him in the morning; for Mr. Hancock had taken the advice of his counsel and friends, and would have nothing to do with the business, but would let it take its course, and would give nothing under his hand." It was held by the patriots, that the seizure, as no legal process had been filed, was illegal.

On Monday morning, labor throughout the town was mostly suspended; the inhabitants gathered in various places under their leaders; and things wore a threatening aspect, as the outrage committed by the press-gang was connected in the public mind with the seizure of the "Liberty." The name of the sloop, the popularity of her owner, and the aversion to the board of commissioners, contributed to inflame the people.[1] There were reports, that, on certain contingencies, the country was coming into Boston to begin an insurrection; though Hutchinson, characterizing this as madness, said he could not bring himself to believe that any number of people worth regarding had a serious thought of this sort, or would dare

[1] Gordon's History, i. 232.

to fire on the king's representatives. Early in the day, four of the commissioners, on the pretext that their persons were not safe, notified the governor, by a card, that they were going on board the "Romney," and asked for orders for their admission to the castle, whither they soon went, with their families. Temple and several of the chief officers remained in the town.[1] In the afternoon, by a hand-bill, the Sons of Liberty requested those who, in this time of distraction and oppression, wished well to the town and the province, and who would promote peace, good order, and security, to assemble on the next day (Tuesday), at ten o'clock in the forenoon, at Liberty Hall, under Liberty Tree; and the journals say, that the expectation of this meeting kept the town in peace. A red flag was now hoisted above Liberty Tree.

On Tuesday morning, though it rained, so many people flocked into Boston from the neighboring towns, that there was a larger assemblage at Liberty Tree, over which still waved the red flag, than had ever been seen in the town. The senior member of the board of selectmen was the moderator, who was surrounded by the popular leaders; but, it being uncomfortable in the streets, the meeting, before passing any votes, adjourned to Faneuil Hall. On re-assembling here, it was resolved, as the call had been informal and there was not a legal town-meeting, to adjourn, to meet at the same place, at three o'clock in

[1] It is stated in the "Boston Evening Post," March 20, 1769, that, when the four commissioners retired to the castle, "the following gentlemen did not fall in with their plan, but resided safely in Boston, and went daily to the castle to do business: the Hon. Mr. Temple, a commissioner; Samuel Venner, Esq., secretary; Charles Stuart, Esq., receiver-general; John Williams, Esq., inspector-general; William Wooten, Esq., inspector-general; David Lysle, Esq., solicitor-general; Messrs. McDonald and Lloyd, principal clerks.

the afternoon; and accordingly the selectmen issued a warrant for a meeting. Meantime the governor, at his country-seat, Jamaica Plain, Roxbury, received such startling advices from his friends, as to the doings of the Sons of Liberty, that he sent one of his own sons into town, to desire the immediate attendance of the Lieutenant-governor, Hutchinson, as he (Bernard) was in expectation of very important news from town, and of such a nature that he would be obliged to withdraw to the castle.

Faneuil Hall, at three o'clock, could not contain the people who assembled. It was the largest town-meeting ever known. Those inside the hall organized by choosing James Otis for moderator. The patriot, since the argument on the question on writs of assistance, had been the popular idol. The Tories affected to consider his manly word, in the November meeting,[1] against mobs and for social order, as in favor of the measures of the Administration; and he had met the ordeal of being eulogized by his political opponents. On entering the hall, the meeting gave him a warm reception; there being " great clapping of hands" as he passed through the crowd to take the chair. No other business was transacted here; a motion being carried to adjourn, for the better accommodation of the people, to the Old South Church.

In the church, the moderator spoke from the pulpit on the questions of the day. Hutchinson says, that, after haranguing the people some time, he suffered them to harangue one another; and Bernard says, that some "made wild and violent proposals, but were warded off;" one being, that every captain of a

[1] See page 38.

man-of-war who came into the harbor should be under the command of the general court. A petition, to be presented to the governor, was submitted to the meeting. It averred that a people had the fundamental right to make their own laws; that the late acts of parliament were in direct violation of this right; that menaces had been thrown out fit only for barbarians; that the state of the town was as though war had been declared against it. It expressed the hope that, as the commissioners had relinquished their office of their own motion, they would not renew it; and it requested the governor to order the "Romney" to be removed from the harbor. "To contend with our parent-state," are its words, "is, in our idea, the most shocking and dreadful extremity; but tamely to relinquish the only security we and our posterity retain of the enjoyment of our lives and properties is so humiliating and base, that we cannot support the reflection." And it expressed the opinion, that it was in the power of the governor to prevent the distressed and justly incensed people "from effecting too much, and from the shame and reproach of attempting too little." It is related, in the town-records, that the petition was adopted, "after very cool and deliberate debates upon the distressed circumstances of the town and critical condition of affairs." A committee was now appointed, consisting of John Rowe, John Hancock, and Warren, to ascertain when the governor would receive the petition; and, on their reporting that he was at his country-seat, a committee of twenty-one, Warren being one, was directed to wait on him immediately. A committee, of which Warren was a member, was chosen to prepare a letter to the Massachusetts agent in London, Mr. De Berdt;[1] another committee, consisting of Warren, Benjamin Church, and Samuel Adams, was appointed to prepare resolves expressing the feeling that was excited by the removal of the "Liberty" from Hancock's Wharf, and characterizing the ill consequences that would follow the introduction of the troops into Boston. The moderator, on adjourning the meeting until the next afternoon at four o'clock, earnestly enjoined an adherence to peace and order. "The grievance the people labor under," James Otis said, "might in time be removed; if not, and we are called on to defend our liberty and privileges, I hope and believe we shall, one and all, resist unto blood; but, at the same time, pray Almighty God it may never so happen."

The reports of these transactions that were carried to the governor, at Jamaica Plain, strengthened his impression that an insurrection was at hand; and as he was awaiting, in the afternoon, the arrival of his confidential adviser (Hutchinson), he must have been surprised to see on the road, moving towards his house, not a noisy populace, pell-mell, flourishing pikes and liberty caps, but a train of eleven chaises, from which alighted at his door the respectable committee[2] from the meeting; among whom were Otis, Samuel Adams, and Warren. "I received them," Bernard says, "with all possible civility; and, having

---

[1] This was the same committee who presented the petition to the governor.

[2] The committee were James Otis, John Hancock, John Rowe, Joshua Henshaw, John Ruddock, Joseph Jackson, Samuel Pemberton, Henderson Inches, Thomas Young, Joseph Warren, Thomas Cushing, Samuel Adams, Benjamin Church, Samuel Quincy, Edward Payne, Daniel Malcolm, Richard Dana, Melatiah Bourne, Benjamin Kent, Royal Tyler, Josiah Quincy.

heard their petition, I talked very freely with them, but postponed giving a formal answer till the next day, as it should be in writing. I then had wine handed round; and they left me highly pleased with their reception, especially that part of them which had not been used to an interview with me." Considering the governor's state of mind, the committee could not have been more highly pleased when they left than he was when they arrived; but his perturbation was over when Hutchinson, soon after this interview, came in, and the governor was convinced that there was no insurrection, and that there was no occasion for him to take the awkward step of retiring to the castle, or, indeed, for any unusual political action.

On the next day, Wednesday, at the adjournment of the meeting, at four o'clock in the afternoon, in the Old South Church, the answer of the governor to the town's petition was read. He said that his official station made him a very incompetent judge of the rights which the people claimed as set against the acts of parliament; and on this subject he expressed no opinion. He stated, that he had no control over the board of customs, and was bound to support their authority; but he promised to remove the inconveniences of impressments. He said that he should think himself most highly honored, if, in the lowest degree, he could be an instrument in promoting a perfect conciliation between the colonies and Great Britain. This answer, on the face of it proper and reasonable and conciliatory throughout, was unusually satisfactory to the patriots. The moderator, Otis, made it still more acceptable, by acknowledging the polite treatment which the committee received from the governor, and by declaring that he believed Bernard was a well-wisher to the province. An elaborate report was now read from the committee appointed to prepare a letter to be sent to the agent in England, Mr. De Berdt, which is a spirited paper, and bears Warren's ardent impress. It went over the whole question of the public grievances; gave full details of the recent stirring events; and put, as the groundwork of the whole difficulty, an unconstitutional imposition of taxes for raising a revenue. This, the letter says, was oppression; and it came down on the people like an armed man, though they were the subjects of an empire which was the toast of nations for freedom and liberty. It severely arraigned the commissioners of the customs, and the swarm of placemen under them, who were supported out of this pilfered revenue, which it characterized as booty drained from the merchant, the mariner, the farmer, and the tradesman. The meeting, having accepted this spirited letter, and appointed a committee,[1] with Warren as the chairman, to prepare instructions to the representatives, adjourned, to meet on the 17th of June, in Faneuil Hall.

This meeting was viewed with great interest by the officers of the Crown. Bernard immediately sent an elaborate narrative of what had occurred to Lord Hillsborough,[2] and again urged the council to adopt measures to prevent an insurrection; Hutchinson declared, that the petition to the governor was the most

[1] The committee were Joseph Warren, Richard Dana, Benjamin Church, John Adams, John Rowe, Henderson Inches, Edward Payne.
[2] Letter, June 16, 1768.

extraordinary thing that had appeared;[1] the commissioners represented, in a letter to the lords of the treasury, that there had been matured, by a correspondence carried on between the local assemblies, an extensive plan of resistance to the authority of Great Britain, and nothing but a military force could prevent a revolt of the town, which might spread through the provinces; and Paxton wrote, that, unless two or three regiments were sent to Boston, it was the opinion of all the friends of the Administration that the town would be in rebellion.[2] On this day, the patriots, in a hand-bill, urged a general attendance of the citizens at the adjourned meeting, as "the fate of the province and of all America depended on the measures to be adopted."[3]

On the 17th of June, the people again met in town-meeting, in Faneuil Hall. Warren, chairman of the committee, reported instructions to the representatives,[4] which declared that the principle of the Stamp Act was revived in the Revenue Act; proclaimed the unalterable resolution to vindicate invaluable rights at the hazard of fortune and life; expressed the determination to maintain loyalty and duty to their most gracious sovereign, a reverence and due subordination to the British Parliament as the supreme legislature, in all cases of necessity, for the preserva-

---

[1] Letter, June 16, 1768. [2] Letter, June 20, 1768.
[3] The citation is from Hutchinson's letter. This is one of the hand-bills:

BOSTON, June 16, 1768.

It is thought by the real friends to liberty, that the fate of America depends on the steady and firm resolution of the town of Boston, at the adjournment of their meeting to-morrow. It is earnestly wished and instructed, that the well-disposed inhabitants would excite each other to give their punctual attendance at so important a crisis. A THOUSAND.

[4] This paper was drawn up by John Adams.

tion of the whole empire, and a sincere and cordial affection for their parent-country. The representatives were instructed to propose action in the legislature against impressments; to urge an inquiry into the authors of the rumors, that troops were to be ordered to Boston; and to recommend for adoption a resolution to the effect, "That any such person who shall solicit or promote the importation of any troops at this time is an enemy to the town and province, and a disturber of the peace and good order of both." These instructions were unanimously adopted. It is related by Hutchinson, that a much higher toned resolve was introduced, which was to the effect, that whoever had, by any means, promoted the introduction of troops, "was a tyrant in his heart, a traitor, and an open enemy to his country;" but this motion, though supported by William Cooper, the town-clerk, and others, was rejected. The meeting on this day was dissolved.

In the transactions that occasioned this town-meeting, and in the whole of its proceedings, Warren appears by the side of Otis, Hancock, and Samuel Adams. He was a member of all its committees, was the chairman of three of them, and, probably, prepared some of the documents which it issued. This indicates the public confidence he had gained.

The petition which the town presented to the governor was regarded as the most important action of the meeting. Its author is not named. It contains the principle as to the inherent right of taxation, and of internal government in the local legislatures, which was held by Warren and Samuel Adams. If the governor saw the reach of this principle, he evaded a discussion of it in his reply. This was so conciliatory that it was used against him in British political circles, where he was accused of giving way to a popular clamor; and it required explanation by his friends to remove the unfavorable impression. Six years later, he said, in his narrative prepared for the privy council, "Whether proceedings of this nature, in a town-meeting, legal only to the purposes of the election of officers and the management of the prudential concerns of the town, are or are not criminal, or, if criminal, what is the criminality, must be submitted." In an elaborate report, the same year (1774), in the House of Lords, it was singled out of the accumulated matter; and it was said, "In this petition the town disavowed the legislative authority of this country, and asserted that it would be better for them to struggle against it than tamely to relinquish their rights."

A contemporary judgment on this meeting, in commending the heartiness with which the citizens came forth to give their presence to the support of the patriot cause, lamented the necessity of their action. "Unhappy for families," are the words, "unhappy for towns, unhappy for the province, that so many valuable freeholders, honest tradesmen, and husbandmen, of every kind and denomination, should be laid under a necessity, by the laws of nature and the ties of duty, to future generations, to quit their useful operations and turn politicians."[1] But happy was it when pub-

[1] American Gazetteer, 1768, p. 123. A letter, dated London, Aug. 5, 1768, addressed to a person in Philadelphia, and copied into the "Boston Post Boy" of Oct. 24, gives an idea of the impression which the popular action, in opposition to arbitrary power, was now making on the friends of liberty in England. "The conduct of the Boston people has raised a fresh cry against the

lic liberty was in danger, that its possessors, animated by such motives, turned politicians to protect it. Their movement derived dignity and importance from the idea of freedom at its base and its wide relations. It was in harmony, in principle and in object, with the views of a great people. It was an illustration of an intelligent American opinion, appearing as an actor on the public stage. And hence it indicated, not a mere ripple on the top of shallow waters, but the ground-swell of an ocean-tide of irresistible and providential power.

Americans. . . . For my own part, I know not of any people, since the ruin of the Roman Commonwealth, that seem to me to entertain more just ideas of liberty, or breathe forth a more true spirit of independence, than what the brave sons of North America do. The petitions of her merchants, the remonstrances and resolves of their assemblies, and, in a word, all their public transactions display a manly resolution, a quick discerning, that is not to be equalled by any body of people in the world. This cannot but engage my good wishes for their preservation and prosperity, whatever extremities things may be pushed to."

CHAPTER V.

PROTEST AGAINST A STANDING ARMY.

TOWN-MEETINGS. — THE MASSACHUSETTS CIRCULAR LETTER. — BRITIS. TROOPS ORDERED TO BOSTON. — THE PUBLIC FEELING. — A TOWN-MEETING. — A CONVENTION. — EFFECT OF THE POPULAR MOVEMENT.

1768. JUNE TO OCTOBER.

WARREN took a prominent part in the town-meeting that was occasioned by the decision of the ministry to station a British force in Boston. So marked was the effect of the regular action of popular power, in the formation of public opinion, that Hutchinson wrote, June 18, " Ignorant as they be, yet the heads of a Boston town-meeting influence all public measures." Ignorance had no such power. The band of popular leaders, who were guiding the patriot cause so discreetly, were of such character and intelligence, that, besides members of congress, judges, and state officers, they supplied four governors of Massachusetts and one president of the United States; and among them were names honorably connected with literature and science.

An event now occurred which increased the excitement in the town, and strengthened the popular cause. The Circular Letter, which the House of Representatives sent to the assemblies of the other colonies, proposing unity of action, was said by the Tories to have been designed to raise a general flame and to organize a confederacy; and, on the allegation that it was dangerous to the king's prerogative, Governor Bernard was instructed by Lord Hillsborough to demand the house to rescind it. This was an exciting period. "Our people," Hutchinson said, June 19, "seem to be more infatuated than ever; and I cannot say what further extravagance they may rule." As Governor Bernard imagined what might occur when he should execute the order which he had in hand, he said, June 18, "I don't know whether I shan't be obliged to act like the captain of a fire-ship, — provide for my retreat before I light my fuse. There seems at present a determination to resist Great Britain." In this mood, he sent in the royal order. But the patriots, in their circular, simply invited their brother patriots to join in a petition for a redress of grievances; and, this being clearly constitutional, the house refused, by the vote of ninety-two to seventeen, to rescind the circular, when, as the penalty, the governor first prorogued and then dissolved the legislature. This question was declared to have been the most important which an American assembly had ever acted on. As this magnificent "No" of Massachusetts resounded through the colonies, it elicited a response which filled the hearts of the Boston patriots with joy. It showed a spirit of unity in the colonies in support of common rights. "The action of the other colonies," Hutchinson wrote, "keeps up the spirit of our demagogues. I am told Adams and Cooper say it is the most glorious day they ever saw.'

The decision of the ministry to station a British force in Boston was made before the June riot. On the 8th of this month, Lord Hillsborough ordered General Gage, who commanded the king's forces in America, to send at least one regiment to Boston, and to garrison Castle William; and, on the 11th, Lord Hillsborough advised Bernard of this measure, saying it had been done "upon the most mature consideration of what had been represented by himself (Bernard) and the commissioners of the customs." In an elaborate despatch, dated the 30th of July, Lord Hillsborough directed Bernard to institute an inquiry into the conduct of any persons who had committed any act of overt resistance to the laws, with the view of arresting them, and transporting them to England for trial in the King's Bench.

Meantime the commissioners had made the June riot the occasion of a demand on General Gage for the protection of troops, and on Commodore Hood for additional men-of-war. The general was evidently surprised at the silence of the governor, but immediately tendered to him all the force for which he (Bernard) might make a requisition. But the governor declined to make such requisition, and wrote to Gage, "My not applying for troops is no argument that they are not wanted. It is above three months ago since I informed the secretary of state of my situation, and utter inability to preserve the peace of the town, or support the authority of Government; but the letter went too late to expect an answer by this mail. I must beg that you will keep this letter to yourself as much as you can; that is, wholly so on this side of the water, for obvious reasons." The commissioners succeeded better with Hood, who immediately, on receiving their request, sent two more ships to Boston. This prompt action, he said, secured the castle from all attempts at a surprise, though Hutchinson thought there would have been no danger of such a consummate piece of Quixotism, if there had not been a man-of-war in America.[1]

As additional ships appeared in the harbor, and reports multiplied that military power was to be used to enforce the new revenue laws and the violations of the right of internal Government, there was roused the traditionary English hatred of standing armies, which had ever been mercenary instruments of despotic power; and the people were very bitter and suspicious towards all whom they supposed to be concerned in the applications for troops. There is no report of any saying of Warren in this hour of passion. A like fiery spirit, his friend Josiah Quincy, jun., said, "Before all the freeborn sons of the North will yield a general and united submission to any tyrannic power on earth, fire and sword, famine and slaughter, desolation and ruin, will ravage the land."[2] The intrepid Samuel Adams said, "Before the king and parliament shall dragoon us, and we become

---

[1] Hutchinson wrote, July 27, 1768, "Four of the commissioners of the customs thought themselves in danger, and took shelter in the castle. Some people were so foolish as to say that they might be taken from thence, and we have had the castle surrounded ever since with men-of-war. We have such people among us: but an attempt upon the castle would be the most consummate piece of Quixotism; and, mad as we are, I cannot think we are mad enough for it, if there had not been a man-of-war in America. Mobs, a sort of them at least, are constitutional, and we have reason enough to fear mobs; and our misfortune is, that the authority of Government is so weak, that we are not able to check them when they rise, but are forced to leave them to their natural course. We cannot continue a great while in this state. Government must be aided from without, or else it must entirely subside."

[2] Life of Josiah Quincy, jun., 16.

slaves, we will take up arms, and spend our last drop of blood." The calm Andrew Eliot said, "You cannot conceive of our distress, — to have a standing army! What can be worse to a people who have tasted the sweets of liberty?" In a letter it was said, "We are frequently threatened with a naval and military force to execute the late acts of parliament; but fifty thousand troops, with fifty men-of-war, will never be able to oblige us to import, buy, or consume English goods."[1] Hutchinson said, "Many of the common people were in a frenzy, and talked of dying in defence of their liberties," while "too many above the vulgar countenanced and encouraged them."

It is a curious coincidence, that, at the time (July 30), Lord Hillsborough was justifying this use of force, on the ground that "Boston was in the possession of a licentious and unrestrained mob," so that neither the council nor the House of Representatives could proceed in their deliberations with the freedom that was incident to their constitution, the council, containing friends of the Administration, unanimously decided against making any application for troops, on the ground that the civil power did not need them. This decision was made in July, when the governor, first enjoining an oath of secrecy, laid before a very full council a formal tender, by General Gage, of troops, when they should be called for. Bernard, in advising Lord Barrington of this vote, says (July 30), "Though I was prepared for this answer, I was not for the high strain of the present popularity with which this question was treated; from whence I am convinced that I am no longer to de-

[1] American Gazette, 127, in a letter, dated Boston, Aug. 18, 1768.

pend upon the council for the support of the small remains' of royal and parliamentary power now left; the whole of which has been gradually impeached, arraigned, and condemned under my eye."

There was a brilliant celebration of the 14th of August, which was the third anniversary of the uprising against the Stamp Act, when the appearance of the town was not unlike that of Boston on a Fourth of July. Bernard did not fail to extract out of this celebration additional signs of a riotous spirit in the town. There was a great procession, and Bernard (Aug. 29) said that one person in it had been the foremost man in a riot, who was celebrating his mob exploits; and two of the principal merchants rode in the foremost chariots, who in this way were countenancing mobs. If these merchants were John Hancock and Thomas Cushing, or James Bowdoin and William Phillips, they were the last persons who would have countenanced riots. Candid observers saw the truth, and said, in the British press, that the popular leaders were much more concerned at any riots than the friends of the Administration, who seem pleased with them, because they sustained their representation that troops were a necessity to keep the people in order.[1]

A long correspondence between civil and military officials, relative to the introduction of troops, came to a result in August. The representations of the state of the town, by Bernard, Hutchinson, and others,

[1] London Chronicle, April 22, 1769, has a letter which says: "I was at Boston last October, and found that the patriot leaders of the opposition were much more concerned at any mobs that happened than the Government people. These last seemed pleased with them, as countenancing their representations, — the necessity of sending soldiers to keep them in order."

were direct to the point, that it was under the dominion of a mob. But William Knox, of London, a keen observer, after looking closely into American affairs down to the 24th of this month, wrote to his friend, Mr. Grenville, that all was quiet at Boston, and that the non-importation agreement went no further than to avoid importing articles on which duties had been laid. He says, "I looked over all the Boston newspapers, and did not find one rash or violent expression; and the entries, inwards and outwards, at the custom-house, were as many as usual. There are advertisements also for the sale of English goods and Madeira wines, and notices of the meeting of county courts, and such sort of things as are commonly transacted in times of tranquillity."[1] On the 31st of August, General Gage, at New York, sent his aide-de-camp, Captain Sheriff, to Boston, on the pretence of private business, bearing a letter addressed to Bernard, stating that one regiment, the Fourteenth, had been ordered from Halifax to Boston, but that it would be left for him to say whether the order made out for the Twenty-ninth regiment should be withheld or transmitted. General Gage, in requesting a reply to this letter, said, "The contents of this, as well as of your answer, and every thing I now transact with you, will be kept a profound secret, at least on this side of the Atlantic." Bernard received this letter on Saturday evening, September Third.

When the public had nothing but rumors as to the coming of troops, there appeared in the "Boston Gazette" of Sept. 5, a communication with the cap-

[1] The Grenville Papers, iv. 367.

tion of "READER, ATTEND!" which, under a series of queries, urged that in theory the acts of the Administration, by breaking the compact between the colonies and the mother country, had dissolved their union. It arraigned with great severity the course of the Crown officials. As the governor had dissolved the legislature, it was proposed that the towns of the province should be invited to elect delegates authorized to meet and consider public affairs, remonstrate to the king, and declare that there was nothing this side of eternity which they dreaded more than being broken off from his Government. "If an army," it read, "should be sent to reduce us to slavery, we will tell them that we are willing and desirous to be their fellow-subjects. We are Englishmen, and claim the privileges of Englishmen; but we are never willing to be slaves to our fellow-subjects; and, if this will not satisfy them, we will put our lives in our hands, and cry to the Judge of all the earth, who will do right."

This communication caused a great sensation in official circles, and led to important action. Bernard says, in a letter to Lord Hillsborough, "In the 'Boston Gazette' of the 5th instant appeared a paper, containing a system of politics exceeding all former exceedings. Some took it for the casual ravings of an occasional enthusiast. But I persuaded myself that it came out of the cabinet of the faction, and was preparatory to some actual operations against the Government. In this persuasion, I considered, that, if the troops from Halifax were to come here on a sudden, there would be no avoiding an insurrection, which would at least fall upon the Crown officers, if it did not not amount to an opposition to the troops. I therefore thought it would be best that the expectation of the troops should be gradually communicated, that the heads of the faction might have time to consider well what they were about, and prudent men opportunity to interpose their advice." Accordingly he says that he "took an occasion to mention to one of the council, in the way of discourse, that he had private advice that troops were ordered to Boston, but had no public orders about it."

When passion was moving a community so powerfully, and when this community was a type of the indignant feeling, in all the colonies, at the encroachments of arbitrary power, Warren again appeared on the public stage as a popular leader. The question in reality to be met and decided was, whether the American cause was to be wrecked on the rock of a premature insurrection, or whether it was to be led on by cautious and wise steps, under the dominion of law, until it should develop into the majesty of a successful revolution.[1]

Before Thursday night, Bernard says, the intelligence which he communicated to a member of the council spread all over the town. A petition to the selectmen was now numerously signed, praying for a town-meeting. "Your petitioners," it says, after reciting the governor's declaration, "apprehensive that the landing of troops in the town, at this particular

---

[1] Bernard, July 11, 1768, wrote to John Pownal, for years under-secretary of state to Lord Hillsborough, "We are now just entering into the critical situation which I have long ago foreseen must come sooner or later; that is, the time of trial, whether this town, &c., will or will not submit to Great Britain, when she is in earnest in requiring submission. Hitherto the Sons of Liberty have triumphed."

juncture, will be a matter of great uneasiness, and perhaps be attended with consequences much to be dreaded, humbly beg the town may be forthwith legally convened to request of His Excellency the grounds of such declaration, and to consider the most wise and prudent, and most considerate, loyal, and salutary measures to be adopted on such an occasion." The selectmen issued the usual warrant for a meeting, to be held on the following Monday, in Faneuil Hall "A town-meeting," Bernard promptly advised Hillsborough, "is appointed for Monday. I hope it will be for the best; but I can't be answerable for events in so precarious a body as a popular assembly."

On Saturday, the governor and his friends were much disturbed by signs and reports which they judged indicated an insurrection. Somebody had put a turpentine barrel in the skillet that hung at the top of the beacon-pole on Beacon Hill, which was alleged to be the signal for a rising; and it was reported that Samuel Adams said, "On lighting the beacon, the people of the town would be joined by thirty thousand men from the country, with bayonets fixed." Bernard subsequently said that the plan was for five hundred men, who had been enrolled for this purpose, to capture the castle, to seize the governor and lieutenant-governor, take possession of the treasury, set up their standard, and put in force the old charter.[1] The belief in this plan explains the haste of members of the council in asking the governor to call a meet-

---

[1] "It is now known," Bernard wrote, Dec. 23, 1768, "that the plan was to seize the governor and lieutenant-governor, and take possession of the treasury, and then set up their standard."

ing of that body, which was held before night, at a private residence, half-way between Boston and Jamaica Plain. Here, after grave debate, it was voted to request the selectmen to cause the tar barrel to be taken down. On the evening of this day, several of the popular leaders met at Warren's house, — James Otis and Samuel Adams being named as present, — where resolutions were drawn up and other preparation was made for Monday's meeting. This was reported to Bernard, who advised Lord Hillsborough, that, " at this very small private meeting at the house of one of the chiefs of the faction, it was resolved to surprise and take the castle on the Monday night following;" and he also named " a large private meeting" of the patriots, on the night before, at which, he says, it was " the general opinion that they should raise the country and oppose the troops." In stating these as reports, Bernard indicated doubts of their accuracy, in which he was more just to the popular leaders than he was in his subsequent positive averment, that there was a deep-laid plot; for, whatever may have been the gasconade of the rash in the patriot ranks, it was certainly the object of the wise among them to guide the deep and general indignation at the prospect of a standing army into a safe channel of action, and to turn this insult, offered to their loyalty, to the benefit of the common cause.

On Sunday, the selectmen were called together to consider the request of the council, in the matter of the tar barrel; but it was regarded as too trivial an affair to be acted upon. When the council directed Sheriff Greenleaf to take the barrel down, Hutchinson says, that, " in the most private manner he could, he executed his order, taking six or seven men with him, just at dinner-time; and in about ten minutes, luckily as he thought, effected his purpose."[1] This transaction was the subject of several affidavits in the papers.

On Monday, the journals called the attention of the freeholders and other inhabitants to the notification for the town to assemble at nine o'clock, A.M., in Faneuil Hall, and desired a universal and punctual attendance.[2] At this hour, the gathering was so large that Bernard said the faction appeared with all its forces; by which he meant the people. He also said that very few of the principal gentlemen attended, and only as anxious and curious spectators; by whom he meant the Tory party. James Otis was chosen the moderator, and the Rev. Dr. Cooper opened the meeting with prayer. The petition of the citizens was read, when it was voted, that, as the governor had intimated his apprehensions that troops were daily expected, Thomas Cushing, Richard Dana, Samuel Adams, Joseph Warren, John Rowe, John Hancock, and Benjamin Kent, be a committee to wait on him, and humbly request that he would be pleased to communicate to the town the grounds he might have for expecting the arrival of troops. The meeting now adopted a petition, praying that he would issue pre-

---

[1] Hutchinson's Massachusetts, iii. 203.

[2] The freeholders and other inhabitants of this town, qualified as the law directs, are to meet at Faneuil Hall, at nine o'clock this day, to take into consideration what measures are most proper to be adopted under the present critical aspect of the times, agreeable to a petition of a number of the inhabitants for that purpose; and 'tis desired there may be a universal and punctual attendance. — *Boston Gazette, Sept.* 12.

cepts forthwith for a general assembly, in order that measures might be taken to preserve their rights and privileges; and it asked the favor of an immediate answer. A large committee, of which Warren was a member,[1] was then appointed to consider public affairs, and to recommend suitable measures to meet the present emergency. The town records say, that " a vote of the honorable board (the council), respecting a tar barrel, which was the other night placed on the skillet on Beacon Hill, by persons unknown, was communicated to the town, but not acted on." The meeting was then adjourned to the next day. Bernard says that the speeches of this meeting were much of the same purport as the sentiment of the communication already noticed in the " Gazette " of the 5th instant.

At the adjournment of the meeting, on Tuesday, the committee appointed to wait on the governor reported his reply; in which, in spite of his file of official letters on the subject of troops, he coolly stated that his apprehensions of an arrival of some of his majesty's troops arose from information of a private nature, and that he had received no public letters notifying him of their coming, or asking quarters for them; and that, the business of calling another assembly being before the king, he could not act in the matter until he received the royal commands. The committee on public affairs now reported a declaration and a series of resolves. They aver, as a principle of society founded in nature and reason, that consent,

[1] The committee consisted of James Otis, Samuel Adams, John Ruddock, Thomas Cushing, John Hancock, Richard Dana, John Rowe, Samuel Quincy, Joseph Warren, William Molineux, John Bradford, Daniel Malcom, William Greenleaf, Adino Paddock, Thomas Boylston, Arnold Wells. — *Town Records.*

either by the individual or by his representative, through his own free election, should be the basis of law; they cite, in support of their position, the precedent of 1688, which gave the crown to William and Mary; they claim, that, by charter and birthright, the fathers held certain rights and customs to as great an extent as though they were born in England; and they declare the purpose, by all legal and constitutional means, to defend these immunities at the utmost peril of their lives and fortunes. They affirm that these rights were violated when money was levied within the province, for the use of the Crown, in any other way than by the general court, and when a standing army, unauthorized by the assembly, should be kept among them to enforce laws which the people had not made. This paper, the town records say, was several times distinctly read; and a glimpse of the scenes in Faneuil Hall, as it was considered, is supplied in the official letters of Bernard. He had friends in the meeting, who reported to him some of the words that were uttered. He says that the reading of the report was followed by a set of speeches by the chiefs of the faction, and no one else, who succeeded one another in such method, that it appeared as if they were acting a play; every thing, as to matter and order, seeming to have been preconcerted beforehand, — which was a compliment to the foresight of the patriots, who met on the previous Saturday evening at the house of Warren, and to the good sense of the people, in coinciding with these wise exponents and champions of their cause.

It is not strange, that, where speech was free, some of the speakers exhibited a zeal and indignation which outran discretion, and which had to be met and checked. The Tory observers did not fail to report to Bernard the bitter terms which embodied the chafings of such spirits; nor did Bernard scruple to transmit them to the ministry as the real exponents of the meeting. One man cried out, "The people wanted a head;" but he was overruled. An old man protested against every thing but the people's rising immediately, and taking power into their own hands; but he was soon silenced. One man, very profligate and abandoned, Bernard says, and, if so, could be of little account with the Bostonians, argued, in a short, startling argument, in favor of massacring enemies. "Liberty," he said, "is as precious as life: if a man attempts to take away my liberty, I have a right to take his life;" and he argued, that, when a people's liberties were threatened, they were in a state of war, and had a right to defend themselves. Bernard adds, that he carried these arguments so far, that his own party were obliged to stop him. The position was taken, that the people had a right to oppose with arms a military force sent to compel them to submit to unconstitutional acts; and it was urged that both town and country ought to arm against their enemies. There had been in England some talk of a war with France;[1] and Bernard says this fact was not only used as a cover for the frequent use of the word "enemy," but as an argument for the immediate delivery of four hundred muskets that lay in

[1] London, July 13. "One day last week, a wager of a thousand guineas to twenty was laid, that war would be declared between Great Britain, on the one part, and France and Genoa on the other, before the 3d of August." Another paragraph says, "There was great talk in England of a war with France." — *Boston News Letter*, Sept. 8, 1768.

boxes on the floor of the hall. It was said "the enemy might be here before the convention met;" and a motion was made that these muskets be delivered at once. The moderator, James Otis, skilfully parried this plausible proposition, as, pointing to the boxes, he said, "There are the arms; when an attempt is made against your liberties, they will be delivered: our declaration wants no explication." On the question being put on the acceptance of the report, the vote was unanimous in the affirmative; and the record remains to the honor of Boston among all posterity.[1]

It was judged that the crisis required other measures. The people, deprived of their general court, were on the eve of military rule; to submit tamely, they said, was to consent to be slaves, and to bring upon themselves the curses of posterity; while to act rashly would imperil a common cause, and create a justification for the presence of a standing army. Hence the meeting adopted, unanimously, a preamble and resolutions, declaring that, — as the parliament of William and Mary enacted, that, for the redress of grievances and the preservation of the laws, parliaments ought to be held frequently; and as present grievances threatened the destruction of their natural and charter rights, and as the governor was unable to convene the general court, which was an assembly of the States of the province,— therefore the town would make choice of a "committee" to act with such committees as might be joined from the other towns, "in order that such measures might be consulted and advised as His Majesty's service and the peace and safety of his subjects in this province might require."

[1] Bancroft, vi. 198.

The four representatives elect, James Otis, John Hancock, Thomas Cushing, and Samuel Adams, were named as this committee. The selectmen were directed to write to the selectmen of the several towns within the province, inform them of the above vote, and propose that a convention be held in Faneuil Hall, on the 22d of the same month, at ten o'clock before noon.

The remainder of the proceedings of the meeting may be briefly stated. It recommended the citizens to observe a good and wholesome law of the province, requiring each to have a well-fixed firelock, musket, accoutrements, and ammunition; listened with high satisfaction to the reading of a letter from the New-York merchants, on their agreement relative to a non-importation of British goods; directed the selectmen to request the ministers to set apart the succeeding Tuesday as a day of fasting and prayer; ordered the proceedings to be printed in the news papers, and copies to be sent by express to the several towns of the province; and it then dissolved.

The journals contain no comments on this meeting. Strangers in town said that it was "one of the most regular they ever attended; for every thing was conducted with the utmost good order and decorum." Hutchinson, in his history, says of the movement, " It must be allowed by all that its proceedings had a greater tendency towards a revolution in Government than any preceding measure in any of the colonies. The inhabitants of one town alone took upon them to convene an assembly from all the towns, that, in every thing but in name, would be a House of Representatives, which, by the charter, the governor had the sole authority of convening. The projectors of the plan depended upon their influence over this assembly to keep it under such restraints as they judged proper."

It happened that there had been a fresh arrival from London; and, when the meeting dissolved, the Boston journals abounded in details, taken from the British press, of the sensation which the June meeting occasioned in England; the fall in the price of stocks, the indignation in court circles, the midnight cabinet councils, the despatch of additional ships and troops to Boston, and all the varied expression of the public anger. The truthful memorial[1] presented to the ministry, in behalf of the inhabitants of Boston, containing a touching expression of loyalty to the Crown, made no impression in the court circles or on the public mind; and the ministry determined

---

[1] "A memorial in behalf of the inhabitants of Boston, showeth: —

"That they bear the same sentiments of loyalty and duty towards our gracious king, and the same reverence for the great council of the nation, the British parliament, as ever; and therefore are not willing their conduct should appear in an odious light to the ministry. The principal occasion of the late tumults arose from the haughty conduct of the commissioners, and other officers appointed by them. The 'Romney' man-of-war, having moored before the town, intimidated the coasting vessels bringing provisions, firewood, &c.; committed many acts of violence and outrage; and, in particular, by cutting away a vessel from Mr. Hancock's wharf, detaining her several days, without any legal process being filed against her, &c. This irritated the people, who patrolled the streets in a tumultuous manner, broke several windows to the value of about £5 sterling, burnt a pleasure-boat belonging to the collector, and then dispersed about eleven o'clock at night. All which will more fully appear by twelve affidavits of different persons who were eye-witnesses of the proceedings hereunto annexed. Three days after this, the commissioners made a voluntary abdication of their office, and went on board the 'Romney' man-of-war. And, from all the affidavits, it does appear, that the cause of such tumult was entirely from the imprudent and violent proceedings of the officers, particularly from the master of the 'Romney,' who frequently ordered the marines to fire, and abused everybody who advised a cooler conduct."

The above memorial was presented to the Administration, with the twelve affidavits (immediately upon hearing the reports which were so prejudicial to the town), by Dennis De Berdt, Esq., agent for the assembly. — *Amer. Gazette*, 1768.

to proceed with severity against Boston, and to endeavor to divide the colonies.

This threatening tone occasioned no change in the purposes of the popular leaders of Boston. On the 14th, the selectmen issued circulars to the towns, and invited them to send delegates to the proposed "Committee of Convention." They briefly described the melancholy and very alarming circumstances to which the province and all America were reduced, and urged the expediency of assembling gentlemen, having the greatest public confidence, to give sound and wholesome advice, and thus happily prevent any sudden and unconnected measures which the people, in their anxiety and even agony of mind, might be in danger of falling into. The Crown officials pronounced this proceeding to be treasonable, and collected some of the circulars having the autographs of the selectmen, to be used in case of arrests. Bernard (Sept. 16) wrote to Lord Hillsborough, "How large their meeting will be, and what they will do at present, can only be guessed at. But, as they have hitherto pursued the dictates of the paper in the "Boston Gazette," it is supposed they will go through with them, and exclude the Crown officers, and resume the first original charter, which has no ingredient of royalty in it. It certainly will be so, if it is not prevented by power from without; and I much doubt whether the force already ordered by General Gage, namely, two regiments, will be sufficient. For my own part, if I had any place of protection to resort to, I would publish a proclamation against the assembling of the convention; but I dare not take so spirited a step, without first securing my retreat."

The circular of the selectmen stated, that the February circular of the House of Representatives "implied nothing more than a right in the American subjects to unite in humble and dutiful petitions to their gracious sovereign, when they found themselves aggrieved;" and they now proposed only to act in a constitutional way. The manner in which this circular was received served to show the temper of the country. As the people met in town-meetings to choose "committees," they, in some places, dedicated, with enthusiasm, trees to liberty; and, in others, they listened to the reading of Cato's Letters, to Magna Charta, to Dissertations on Liberty, and the Bill of Rights. This order of facts shows how clearly the American Revolution was the child of the English Revolution, which was guided by the great politics of Eliot, Pym, and Hampden.

On the day fixed for the convention, Sept. 22, this novel election was going on. It was Coronation Day, when Boston was accustomed to be resonant with royalty. On this legal holiday, there were salutes from Castle William and the town batteries; the militia and the Ancient and Honorable Artillery had their parades and fired their volleys in the capital streets; and at noon, by invitation of the governor, the principal citizens went to the council chamber, in the Town House, to drink the king's health. It is not mentioned that committees elected to the convention were invited to this festivity, or were present; but, at the dedication of liberty trees, the first toast was "The king:" and there was no inconsistency between the purposes entertained by the patriots and this pledge of fidelity to the flag of their country; for the king, or the sovereignty which they cheerfully recognized, was looked upon as the constitutional protector of the rights and liberties which they enjoyed and meant to preserve.

On this day, above seventy delegates, from sixty six towns, assembled in Faneuil Hall, as a "Com mittee of Convention." It was a fine representation of the intelligence and patriotism of the province, and was really but a mode of popular action now of every-day occurrence, and indispensable in carrying on self-government. Thomas Cushing, the speaker of the house, a citizen of great weight of personal character, and ever temperate in speech and action, was elected chairman; and Samuel Adams, the clerk of the house, was made the secretary. The first day's business was mainly the adoption of a petition to the governor, in which, disclaiming any pretence of being a law-making body, they prayed for a meeting of the general court. But the Crown officials saw in this novel spectacle a dangerous phase of popular action, and the governor declined to receive the petition. On the second day of the session of the convention, the governor, through the chairman, sent to it a proclamation, in which he assumed, that the organization was, to all intents and purposes, a law-making body; charged the Boston selectmen with ignorance of the law, and with committing a grave offence in issuing the call; and warned the members to disperse, as the king was determined to maintain his sovereignty over the province; and the usurper of any of its rights would repent of his rashness. The intrepid Samuel Adams, holding this untruthful and irritating paper in his hand, read and commented upon each paragraph with great severity; and, after he had finished, he threw it from him in a manner strongly expressive of his indignation and contempt.[1] On the third day, the convention, by a well-timed message in reply to this proclamation, calmly assured the governor, that neither the delegates nor their constituents proposed to do, or to consent to, any thing oppugnant to or inconsistent with the regular execution of Government in the province; and this was urged earnestly and truthfully. The governor, however, declined to receive this communication. Having sat with open doors three days, the convention adjourned until Monday. Thus far Otis had been absent.

Monday's journals were laden with matter which must have been of the deepest interest to the distressed population. They contained a report of the three days' sessions of the convention, and the papers that had passed between it and the governor. They stated that the number of members had increased daily since Thursday, and that towns were still holding meetings to choose delegates. They printed the letters of officials relative to the introduction of troops, and the menacing street-talk of the rash among the Tories, who threatened the patriots, when a standing army should arrive, with the pillory and the whipping-post, and the loss of their ears or their heads. And why? "Hyperion" (Josiah Quincy, jun.) gloriously said on that morning, in the press, "An ill timed oppugnation of the commissioners' authority; a manly boldness in delivering patriotic sentiments to

[1] Samuel Adams Wells, MS. Life of Adams, i. 162.

the world; and an open daring to discuss the rights of mankind, the liberty of the press, and freedom of speech, — are those unpardonable crimes for which the scaffold alone can work an expiation."

The convention, on re-assembling this day, sat with closed doors, Otis being present; and it continued its deliberations, by successive adjournments, three days. It received so many additions, that, before dissolving, it contained delegates from ninety-six towns and six districts. According to Dr. Eliot, there were three parties in the convention: one party, fearful of the legality of the meeting, would gladly have done nothing; another party would have laid no restraint on the people, but left them to act for themselves; a third party desired to await the arrival of the troops, and then assume the direction of affairs. Fortunately, the same discretion that controlled the town-meetings guided the deliberations of the convention. As a result, it agreed upon an address, which briefly restated the rights of the colonists; earnestly disclaimed any intention to assume the work of Government; and avowed a firm adherence to the principles of the constitution, and the peace and good order of society. The convention then dissolved. The rash were undoubtedly disappointed; but the wise regarded the result as salutary. "By the mere act of assembling," Bancroft remarks, "the object of the convention was accomplished. It was a bold and successful attempt to show, that, if the policy of suppressing the legislature should be persisted in, a way was discovered by which legislative Government could still be instituted, and a general expression of opinion and concentration of power be obtained."

Warren, though not a delegate to this convention, was a member of all the committees of the town-meeting which determined to call it; and probably the plan was carried out that was matured at the consultation of the popular leaders, at his residence, on the evening of the Tenth of September.

The assertion, by the municipality and by the provincial assembly, of their constitutional rights, in the transactions which have been described, greatly moved the public mind of the colonies, " awakened an attention in the very soul of the British empire,"[1] and even occupied the time of continental cabinets. Though the judgment passed on this popular action by the conservative and the progressive schools was as opposite as the poles, yet they agreed in ascribing to it a marked effect on the progress of events. Both recognized the appearance of a new agency in the formation of public opinion. The Tory said that it was in the town-meeting that the flame of discord and rebellion was first lighted up and disseminated over the colonies; the Whig said that the spark in the breast of the individual American, that blazed more conspicuously in the public meeting, was that almost divine spirit which evidenced the approach of an independent and free republic.[2]

---

[1] Samuel Adams, in the Boston Gazette, 1769.

[2] A Tory judgment reads, " The town-meeting at Boston is the hot-bed of sedition. It is there that all their dangerous insurrections are engendered; it is there that the flame of discord and rebellion was first lighted up, and disseminated over all the provinces." — *Sagittarius's Letters*, 1774, p. 58.

A Whig judgment reads, " That almost divine spirit which evidenced the approach of an independent and free republic in America blazed from a small spark, kindled by heaven in the breast of every American individually, to a more conspicuous blaze in the meeting of town inhabitants. Thence it kindled into conventions, and finally collected itself in that luminous body called the Con-

I have not the space to present in detail the consequences of the popular proceedings. They were the subject of cabinet consultations, severe comment by the British press, exciting debates in both houses of parliament, and threatening resolves. Lord North then made the memorable declaration, "Whatever prudence or policy might hereafter induce us to repeal the paper and glass act, I hope we shall never think of it till we see America prostrate at our feet,"[1] — words that sunk deep into the popular heart, and will be transmitted from age to age as an embodiment of a spirit of arbitrary power.

This "September rebellion," as British officials termed it, was declared to have given the Government great advantage, because it enabled it to separate the case of Boston and Massachusetts from all the other towns and colonies.[2] Bernard now urged, in letter upon letter, that this occasion should be seized on to justify a forfeiture of the charter of Massachusetts and a re-organization of the local Government;

gress; from whence light and firmness are diffused to every State and senate on the continent." — *Boston Gazette,* Jan. 27, 1777.

[1] This famous remark of Lord North was printed in the "Massachusetts Gazette," Feb. 9, 1769, in a letter from London, dated Nov. 10, 1768, giving an account of the proceedings in the House of Commons. "Lord N***h, the c***c**l*r of the e*c**q**r, said that whatever prudence or policy might hereafter induce us to repeal the late paper and glass act, he hoped we should never think of it *till we saw America prostrate at our feet.* These were his very words."

[2] A letter from London, Nov. 19, 1768, says, "The news of the last defiance of the king's authority came just before the meeting of the parliament, to open the eyes of the nation, and to let them see the desperate lengths which your incendiaries would lead your people into. Nothing could have been done to give the Government here such an advantage over the colony, as their separating and distinguishing their case from that of all the other colonies, and the town of B   n from all other places, as none but the B   n s   ct   n have assumed to themselves the royal prerogative of calling a convention, and none but the province of M   ts have dared to meet in direct contradiction to the king's authority." — *Mass. Gazette,* Jan. 26, 1769.

and even Lord Camden, of the cabinet, suggested "as there was no pretence for violence anywhere but in Boston," that Massachusetts should be selected out from the other colonies, and that punishment should be levelled against it as "the ringleading province;" while British lords urged in parliament the necessity of altering the law fundamentally as to jurors, the council, and the municipality, — avowals that were marked by the patriots; and they foreshadowed the measures which, seven years later, were the occasion of the morning guns of Lexington and Concord.

The ministry determined to use force in the colonies, in order to check the rising popular power. "I am convinced," Lord Barrington wrote to Bernard, Feb. 12, 1769, "the town-meeting in Boston, which assembled the States of the province against the king's authority, and armed the people to resist his forces, was guilty of high crimes and misdemeanors, if not of treason; and that Mr. Otis, the moderator (as he is improperly called) of that meeting, together with the selectmen of Boston, who signed the letters convoking the convention, should be impeached. This would carry terror to the wicked and factious spirits all over the continent, and would show that the subjects of Great Britain must not rebel with impunity anywhere. Five or six examples are sufficient; and it is right they should be made in Boston, the only place where there has been actual crime." In the spirit of this citation, the Duke of Bedford moved and carried in parliament an address to the king, urging His Majesty to put in force against the men of Boston a statute of Henry VIII.; take them to

England, and try them before a special commission. "Thus was it designed," Lord Mahon says, "to draw forth the mouldering edict of a tyrant from the dust where it had long lain, and where it ever deserved to lie, and to fling it — instead of bread, a stone — not merely at the guilty, but also at the innocent, whom it equally despoiled of their rightful native juries Such a proposal, made at such a time, to me appears at least utterly unjustifiable."[1]

The popular leaders understood their position. They did not intend to create a rebellion, and aimed only to preserve their constitutional rights. The truth was seen and expressed by candid observers; and it was precisely said of this period, "The American colonies aspire not to independence, but to equality of rights with the mother country."[2] The men of Boston were neither thrown off their balance by the eulogies of friends, nor cowed by the threats of their enemies. They averred in the press, that there was not "a person, either in or out of parliament, who has justly stated or proved one single act of that town, as a public body, to be, I will not say treasonable and seditious, but even at all illegal; nor is it in the power of any man, either on this or the other side of the Atlantic, to do it." And they said, "It is the part this town has taken on the side of liberty, and its noble exertions in favor of the rights of America, that has rendered it so obnoxious to the tools of power."[3]

When Samuel Adams, Warren, and their associates

---

[1] Lord Mahon's History of England, v. 241.
[2] The French diplomatist, Durand, said this to Choiseul. — *Bancroft*, vi. 96.
[3] Boston Gazette, January, 1769.

were guiding popular action, freedom had hardly begun to achieve its modern civic triumphs. England, which had supplied a grand armory of principles in the republican school of patriots and statesmen of her Revolution, had not attained a just municipal life,[1] or the public meeting, or practical freedom of the press, or publicity in the law-making body; and more citizens gathered in the largest public meetings in Boston than had a voice in all Great Britain in the choice of a majority of the members of parliament. In France, a few citizens in each town, by virtue of money paid by their ancestors by some one of the old kings, held the right of governing the other citizens for ever;[2] and the people, for a hundred and forty years, had not appeared for a single instant on the public stage.[3] In Germany, serfdom had not been abolished,[4] and there was but a feeble glimmer, here and there, of an open verbal discussion of public measures, an unfettered press, or of political freedom.[5] The spirit of progress was active in all these countries; but it is no more than simple justice to the popular leaders and the people of America to recollect the status of the political world in their day, in order to be properly grateful for their pioneer stand in behalf of customs and principles so vital as to underlie all free institutions, and as wide in their application as our common humanity.

---

[1] The Municipal Reform Bill was passed in 1836.
De Tocqueville's Old Regime, 61.   [3] *Ib.*, 218.   [4] *Ib.*, 38.
[5] Schlosser's Eighteenth Century.

CHAPTER VI.

THE BOSTON MASSACRE AND A CIVIC TRIUMPH.

AN ARMY IN BOSTON. — THE QUESTION OF REMOVAL. — TOWN-MEETINGS. — THOMAS HUTCHINSON. — THE CITIZENS AND THE TROOPS. — THE BOSTON MASSACRE. — THE SIXTH OF MARCH. — THE REMOVAL OF THE TROOPS.

OCTOBER, 1768, TO MARCH, 1770.

WARREN took a part in all the town-meetings that were held during the seventeen months[1] that succeeded the September convention. This was an interesting period, when arbitrary power, true to its threat, used a standing army as an instrument to overawe the inhabitants of a single town, with the hope of intimidating the free people of the colonies.

A fleet of British men-of-war arrived in the harbor, and were moored around Boston. They were prepared for action on the first day of October, by having their guns loaded and springs put on their cables; and the two regiments which were on board, — the Fourteenth and the Twenty-ninth, — and a portion of the Fifty-ninth, with a train of artillery, were supplied with sixteen rounds of powder and ball. About eleven o'clock, the commander of these troops,

---

[1] An account of the events in Boston during this period of seventeen months will be found in the "Atlantic Monthly" for June and August, 1862, and November, 1863.

Lieutenant-colonel Dalrymple, went privately on shore, walked over the peaceful town, sought in vain Governor Bernard, who had gone to Jamaica Plain, and, much disappointed at the appearance of things, returned to the fleet. At noon, he landed his force on the Long Wharf, marched up King Street, and then to the Common. If the unusual spectacle occasioned no scene of war, it inspired no feeling of terror. "Our harbor is full of ships and our town full of troops," Hutchinson wrote; "the red-coats make a formidable appearance, and there is a profound silence among the Sons of Liberty." The Sons chose to labor and to wait, and the troops could not attack the liberty of silence.

A long and irritating controversy now occurred between the Crown officials and the municipal and provincial authorities, relative to providing quarters for these troops, in which the patriots, by standing on the terms of the law, won a great victory. Warren's name does not occur in connection with this contest. Bernard, in a letter (Oct. 30), gives an idea of it, and of his own mortification at its result "The account, up to this time," he says, "will end in my having employed myself from Sept. 19 to Oct. 26, that is, thirty-eight days, in endeavoring to procure quarters for the two regiments here to no purpose. For, having during this time been bandied about from one to another, I at length got positive refusals from every one I could apply to; that is, the council, the selectmen, and the justices of the peace; upon which the general (Gage), who came here on purpose, has found himself obliged to hire and fit up buildings at the expense of the Crown."

General Gage came from New York on a visit. In a short time, two regiments, — the Sixty-fourth and Sixty-fifth, — direct from Ireland, landed in the town; Commodore Hood, the commander of the naval forces in the American seas, came from Halifax; and General Pomeroy, colonel of the Sixty-fourth, arrived in December, and took the command of the land-force. He was an excellent officer, and became popular with the citizens. The two regiments that last arrived were quartered in commodious stores on Wheelwright's Wharf: a portion of the troops that first arrived were quartered in a house owned by James Murray, and hence the name "Murray's Barracks," which, from its connection with the massacre, became historic. The main guard was located in King Street, directly opposite the Town House; and here were planted two field-pieces pointing towards this building, in which the courts met and the legislature held its sessions. Detachments were posted at the land avenue into the town and at the ferryways. "Our town is now a perfect garrison," the patriots said, as this rough experiment on their free municipal life began.

This presence of force created a local issue of the deepest interest, in which Warren entered with his accustomed zeal. The popular leaders, disclaiming any scheme of rebellion, held that to quarter among them in time of peace a standing army, without the consent of the general court, was as violative of the constitution of Massachusetts, and as harrowing to the feelings of the people, as it would be contrary to the Bill of Rights and the English Constitution, and irritating to the British people, if an army were posted in London without the consent of parliament. They therefore opposed a continuance of the troops in the town, as being against constitutional right and an impeachment of their loyalty. The question of their removal entered largely into the politics of the day; and a steady pursuit of this object from October, 1768, to March, 1770, gave unity, directness, and an ever-painful foreboding to the local politics, until the flow of blood created a crisis. The House of Representatives, in reviewing this period, declared that there resulted from the quartering of this military force in Boston a scene of confusion and distress which ended in the blood and slaughter of His Majesty's good subjects.

I have only space to glance at the meetings in which Warren took a part, and to refer generally to the aspect of the town, until the crisis, which was brought on by the event known as the " The Boston Massacre." Warren mingled with his fellow-citizens on the memorable evening of the Fifth of March, and took a part in the great town-meeting on the following day. He also delivered two of the commemorative discourses on the massacre. He became in this way identified with these scenes.

Warren was a member of an important committee, appointed at the annual March meeting of 1769 which adopted a petition to the king, praying for a removal of the troops. This paper, with the strongest declarations of attachment to constitutional rights, expressed the warmest loyalty to the Crown; and it pronounced those relations ill-grounded which represented the town as held to its allegiance and duty to the best of sovereigns only by the bond of terror and the force of arms. The meeting appointed a noble committee to consider the expediency of vindicating the town from the misrepresentations to which it had been exposed; the members being James Otis, Samuel Adams, Thomas Cushing, Richard Dana, Joseph Warren, John Adams, and Samuel Quincy.

Governor Bernard now received (April 20) from Lord Hillsborough,[1] who had recently been appointed first lord of trade, a letter, enclosing the address of the House of Lords to the king, in relation to the proceedings of the town, with the king's severe answer. The minister instructed the governor to take the most effectual methods for procuring the fullest information that could be obtained, "touching all treasons or misprision of treason," committed in the province since the 30th of December, 1767, and to transmit the same, together with the names of the persons who were the most active in the commission of such offences. Thus the governor was clothed with all the power for which he applied, to inflict censure on, as he said, the heads of the faction which had harassed the province for three years.

Warren, at the May town-meeting, was one of the committee appointed to prepare the customary instructions to the representatives. This paper, besides delineating the public grievances, claimed for each subject in America equality of political rights with

[1] The appointment of the Earl of Hillsborough to the post of the first lord of trade is an event much to the satisfaction of those concerned in our colonies, as well as to the mother-country in general; being universally acknowledged a judicious choice in the ministry, as that amiable nobleman's character and abilities will add lustre to their recommendation.

John Pownall, Esq., secretary to the lords of trade, is appointed undersecretary of state to the Earl of Hillsborough. — *Boston Evening Post*, Sept. 5, 1768.

each subject in England, and for the general court the dignity of a free assembly. It averred that the first labors of the assembly ought to be an endeavor to procure a removal of " those cannon and guards, and that clamorous parade, that had been daily about the Court House since the arrival of His Majesty's troops."

Warren took part in a town-meeting in June, which was called to consider the subject of the removal of the troops, and was held under peculiar circumstances. The military force was now under the command of Hon. Alexander Mackay, colonel of the Sixty-fifth Regiment, and a member of parliament. He was a major-general; and, on his arrival (April 30), it was announced that "the command of the troops of the eastern district of America" devolved on him. The ministry, without consulting Governor Bernard, authorized General Gage, if he should think it best, to withdraw the troops from Boston; when General Mackay was ordered to remove the Sixty-fourth and Sixty-fifth Regiments from the town. The first notice Bernard had of this order was the reception (June 10) of a letter from General Gage, advising him of the order, and asking him (Bernard) whether even the remainder were necessary to preserve the public peace. The report of this order, at which Bernard expressed great surprise, and other reports, he says, exalted the Sons of Liberty as though the bells had rung for a triumph; while there was consternation among the Crown officials and adherents of the Administration, who strongly urged a retention of the troops. Warren was one of the leading petitioners, a hundred and forty-two in number, for a town-meeting, to urge a removal of the troops. This meeting declared that the law of the land made ample provision for life and property, and that the presence of the troops was an insult. This availed nothing. The governor, who was much embarrassed by the request of General Gage, replied, after some hesitation, that to remove a portion of the two regiments would be detrimental to His Majesty's service; to remove both of them would be quite ruinous to the cause of the Crown; but that one regiment in the town and one at the castle might be sufficient. Of course, General Gage, if he paid any respect to the governor's advice, could do no less than order both regiments to remain.

Governor Bernard received (June 10) the king's command to repair to England, and lay before him the state of the province. He now said that "the Boston faction" had taken possession of the general court in such a manner that there were not ten members in both branches who dared to contradict it. As he left Boston (July 31, 1769), the general joy was manifested by congratulations among the people, salutes from Hancock's Wharf, the Union flag flying above Liberty Tree, and bonfires kindled on the hills.[1] He had been a bad governor, but not worse than the cause which he was required to uphold. He had been arbitrary, but was not so imperious as were his instructions. He had been vascillating, but not to

[1] The Union flag was displayed from Liberty Tree, where it was kept flying till Friday. Colors were also flung out from most of the vessels in the harbor, and from the tops of the houses in town. The bells were rung and cannon were incessantly fired until sunset. In the evening, there was a bonfire on Fort Hill, and another on the heights of Charlestown. The general joy in this city was soon diffused through the neighboring towns, who gave similar demonstrations of it. — *Boston Gazette, Aug.* 7, 1769.

the extent of the vascillation of the ministry, who, in line upon line, approved of all his proceedings, with the exception of the conciliatory reply to the June town-meeting. As in England he reviewed his career, he wrote, with an increase of wisdom, but with evident chagrin, "I was obliged to give up, a victim to the bad policy and irresolution of the Supreme Government."

It was now semi-officially announced,[1] that the lieutenant-governor would administer the functions of the executive office until the return of the chief magistrate to his post. These officials had been personal friends and political associates. Indeed, so close had been their private and public relations, that Bernard ascribed the origin of his administrative difficulties to his adoption of the quarrels of Hutchinson. The governor, in urging his friend as his successor in office, represented that Hutchinson was well versed in the local affairs; knew the motives of the governor; warmly approved of the policy of the ministry; had been, on critical occasions, a trusted confidential adviser; and, in fact, had become so thoroughly identified with public affairs, that, of the two officials, he (Hutchinson) was the most hated by the faction. The governor favored this appointment as a measure that would be equivalent to an indorsement of his own Administration. "It would be," he said, "a peculiarly happy stroke; for, while it would dis-

---

[1] We are assured that the order for Sir Francis Bernard, Bart., to return to England, is expressed to be, to attend the king as governor, to report to him the present state of the province; that it contains directions for the administration of the Government during his absence; and that there is no intimation of any intention at present of superseding his commission. We hear that he proposes to embark about the end of July. — *Boston Post Boy, June* 19, 1768.

courage the Sons of Liberty, it would afford another great instance of rewarding faithful servants to the Crown."

Thomas Hutchinson, descended from one of the most respected families of New England, and the son of an honored merchant of Boston, was now fifty-seven years of age. He was a pupil at the Old North Grammar School, and was graduated at Harvard College. He then entered upon a mercantile life. He was not successful as a merchant. Thus early, however, he evinced the untiring industry that marked his whole career. He had a decided political turn, and, with uncommon natural talent, had the capacity and the ambition for public life. An irreproachable private character, pleasing manners, common-sense views of things, and politics rather adroit than high-toned, secured him a run of popular favor and executive confidence so long, that he had now (1769) been thirty-three years uninterruptedly engaged in public affairs; and he confessed to his friends that this concern in politics had created a hankering for them which a return to business-pursuits could not overcome.

His fame at the beginning of the Revolutionary controversy was at its zenith; for, according to John Adams, "he had been admired, revered, rewarded, and almost adored; and the idea was common, that he was the greatest and best man in America." He had reason to be gratified at the tokens of public approbation which he had received. He had been so faithful to the municipal interests as a selectman, that the town had intrusted him with an important mission to England, which he satisfactorily executed; his wide commercial knowledge, familiarity with constitutional law and history, decided ability in debate, and reputed disinterestedness, had given him large influence as a representative in the general court; he had evinced as councillor an ever-ready zeal for the prerogative, and won the most confidential relations with so obsequious a courtier as Bernard; as judge of probate, he was attentive, accurate, kind to the widow, and won general commendation; and, as a member of the superior court, he administered the law, in the main, satisfactorily. He had been chief justice for nine years, and for eleven years the lieutenant-governor. He had also prepared two volumes of his History, which, though rough in narrative, is a valuable authority; and his volume of "Collections" was now announced.

He was, and had been for years, the master-spirit of the Tory party. It is an anomaly that he should have attained to this position. He knew, from practical knowledge as a merchant, the intolerable injustice of the old mercantile system; and yet he sided with its friends. He had dealt, as a politician, to a greater degree than most men, with the rights and privileges which the people prized, conceded that they had made no ill use of them, and yet urged that they ought to be abridged. As a patriot, when he loved his native land wisely, he remonstrated against the imposition of the Stamp Tax; and yet he grew into one of the sturdiest of the defenders of the supremacy of parliament in all cases whatsoever. He exhibited the usual characteristics of public men, who, from unworthy considerations, change their principles and desert their party. No man urged a more arbitrary course; no man passed more discreditable judgments on his patriot contemporaries; and if, in this way, he won the smiles of the court which he was swift to serve, he earned the hatred of the land which he professed to love. The more his political career is studied, the greater will be the wonder that one who was reared on republican soil, and had antecedents so honorable, should have become so complete an exponent of arbitrary power.

Hutchinson was not so blinded by party spirit, or by love of money or of place, as not to see the living realities of his time: for he wrote that a thirst for liberty seemed to be the ruling passion, not only of America, but of the age; and that a mighty empire was rising on this continent, the progress of which would be a theme for speculative and ingenious minds in distant ages. It was the vision of the cold and clear intellect distrusting the march of events and the capacity and intelligence of the people. He had no heart to admire, he had not even the justice to recognize, the greatness around him that was making an immortal record; the sublime faith, the divine enthusiasm, the dauntless resolve, the priceless consciousness of being in the right, that were the life and inspiration of the lovers of freedom. He conceded, however, that the body of the people were honest, and said they acted on the belief, inspired by wrong-headed leaders, that their liberties were in danger. While, with the calculation of the man of the world, he dreaded, and endeavored to stem, still, with a statesman's foresight, he appreciated, and held in respect, the mysterious element of public opinion. He felt that it was rising as a power. He saw this power already intrenched in the impregnable lines of free institutions. He desired to know its springs, and was a close and at times a shrewd observer, as well from a habit of research in tracing the currents of the past, as from occupying a position which made it a duty to watch the growth of the present. His letters, very voluminous, deal with causes as well as with facts, and are often fine recognitions of the life-giving power of vital political ideas, from the pen of a subtle and determined enemy.

One of these ideas was local self-government. He defined its basis to be, "The opinion, that every colony has a legislature within itself, the acts and doings of which are not to be controlled by parliament, and that no legislative power ought to be exercised over the colonies except by their respective legislatures."[1] He said that this opinion was the Alpha and Omega of the troubles between Great Britain and her colonies. He termed it a grave political error, detrimental to the public peace, and equivalent to a denial of the authority of parliament. He averred that it was a principle of independence that was fatal to the integrity of the empire. He stated that "this false opinion was broached at the time of the Stamp Act,"[2] and that it had spread so rapidly that it bid fair to be as generally received as the maxim of no taxation without representation; and he urged, that, unless this doctrine was checked, the dependence of the colonies on England would

---

[1] Letter, Aug. 27, 1772. He wrote, in a letter, March 27, 1768, "The authority of parliament to make laws of any nature whatsoever, to have force in the colonies, is denied with the same freedom their authority to tax the colonies has been for two or three years past. This is a new doctrine; but it spreads every day, and bids fair to be as generally received as the other."

[2] Letter, Oct. 23, 1772.

cease. He suggested, as the remedial policy, a prosecution of its champions, and their punishment by fines, imprisonments, and disqualifications for public trusts. He proposed that parliament should adopt this course towards communities who enjoyed a free municipal life, provincial legislatures, the public meeting, and a free press, in the vain hope of rooting out a custom which liberal thinkers recognize as the basis of free government.

Another vital idea was the Union. The patriots now held "that the whole force of American politics was collected in this line. By uniting, we stand; by dividing, we fall." This doctrine was regarded by Hutchinson as fatal to a continuance of the connection with England; and, to counteract it, he advocated the policy of forming several unions. He suggested one union for the Canadas, one for the New-England provinces, one for the middle colonies from New York to Virginia, and one for the Carolinas, with separate governments for each. In his view, the formation, in this way, of several unions would tend to diminish the political strength of the colonies, and to incline them to retain their dependence on England, which he regarded to be the best for their permanent welfare; while one solid union tended directly to independence. Holding these views, he closely watched and commented freely on any signs of disunion. When the Tory partisans said that the Sons of Liberty of Boston were despised by the Sons of Liberty of the other colonies, he would write in a hopeful strain. He had a better basis for his prophecies in the criminations and divisions that grew out of the non-importation scheme, when he would exultingly say that the Union was broken, and express the hope that it would never be restored. His reasonings and prophecies on this theme, seen for years in his letters, are solid compliments to the foresight and statesmanship which kept the popular movement true to the idea, as a kindling guiding-star, that the American people, though cast by circumstances into the forms of separate communities, were destined by the law of geographical affinity and of material interests, to be infolded in one Union, to live under one constitution, and to have but one national flag.

Warren had much political intercourse with Hutchinson during the succeeding five years. Their aims were as divergent as their principles were antagonistical, and their career presents striking contrasts. Indeed, seldom are seen more marked exhibitions of wisdom in youth, and folly in age, than are supplied in the views of Warren, as, at twenty-five, he analyzed the genius of his countrymen, and labored with the steady aim of preserving their rights; and the utterances of Hutchinson, as, at threescore, he aimed at preserving the colonies in a state of dependence on England, and urged the necessity of an abridgment of colonial liberties. Warren's thought was suited to the condition of the people, and in harmony with the progressive spirit of the age; Hutchinson, siding more and more with the principles and designs of a cold and selfish British aristocracy, urged, as applicable to communities enjoying well-nigh the entire cluster of the liberties, a policy that must be judged incompatible with the spirit of a free Government.

When Hutchinson became the acting governor, the ministry had announced that they intended to propose, at the next session of parliament, a repeal of a portion of the revenue acts wholly on commercial considerations; and the popular leaders in the colonies were pressing with great zeal an adherence to the non-importation agreement, in the hope of obtaining a repeal of the whole act, on the ground of constitutional right. In pursuance of these objects, the merchants of Boston had held a public meeting in Faneuil Hall, which, after passing spirited resolves, adjourned to meet on a future day. Hutchinson was now asked to employ the troops to disperse this meeting. He had urged their introduction; had predicted that their presence would make the Boston saints as tame as lambs; had ascribed to their timely landing the service of preventing a great catastrophe; and considered them to be necessary for the future vindication of the national authority. Though he said that "the confederacy of the merchants was certainly a very high offence,"[1] he shrunk from the arbitrary work of directing foreign bayonets against the right of public meeting. The patriotic merchants were not interrupted in their proceedings. "I am very sensible," Hutchinson wrote to Lord Hillsborough, "that the whole proceeding is unwarrantable; but it is so generally countenanced in this and in several of the colonies, and the authority of Government is so feeble, that an attempt to put a stop to it would have no other effect than still further to inflame the minds of the people. I can do no more than

[1] Letter to Jackson, Oct. 4, 1769. On the 6th, he suggested an act of parliament, disqualifying all officials who had been concerned in these combinations from holding any public office.

represent to your lordship, and wait for such instructions as may be thought proper."

Warren, I have stated, was a member of a committee that was appointed to consider the expediency of vindicating the town from the misrepresentations of the Crown officials, which reported at a town-meeting in October. The town then made an "Appeal to the World," which was drawn up mostly by Samuel Adams, and was a candid and manly State paper. The committee who were appointed to circulate this appeal consisted of Thomas Cushing, Samuel Adams, Joseph Warren, Richard Dana, Joshua Henshaw, Joseph Jackson, and Benjamin Kent; names that have shed lustre on the country. They said, in their Circular Letter which accompanied the Appeal, that "the people will never think their grievances redressed till every revenue act is repealed, the board of commissioners dissolved, and the troops removed." Reason and truth, imbued with the cardinal quality of sincerity, uttered in this way, exerted a marked influence in the formation of public opinion. Hutchinson felt the force of this consideration. "We find, my lord, by experience," he wrote to Lord Hillsborough, Oct. 19, 1769, "that associations and assemblies, pretending to be legal and constitutional, assuming powers that belong only to established authority, prove more fatal to this authority than mobs, riots, or the most tumultuous disorders; for such assemblies, from erroneous or imperfect notions of the nature of Government, very often meet with the approbation of the body of the people; and, in such case, there is no internal power which can be exerted to suppress them. Such case we are in at present, and shall probably continue in it until the wisdom of parliament delivers us from it." This is a significant recognition of the effect of the regular action of popular power as it was guided by the leading patriots.

Warren this year (1769) was one of a committee to transmit the thanks of the town to Colonel Barré, and one of the signers of the letters which the patriots sent to Franklin and Wilkes.

The next mention of Warren, besides an appearance in a law-case,[1] is in connection with the masonic order. This year the St. Andrew's Lodge, of which he was a member, united with two lodges, which consisted of members who belonged to the British regiments then in Boston, in sending a petition to the Earl of Dalhousie, Grand Master of Masons in Scotland, for a grand lodge; and they received from him a commission, "appointing Joseph Warren, Esq., Grand Master of Masons of Boston, New England, and within one hundred miles of the same."[2] He was installed (Dec. 27) at the Masons' Hall, in the Green Dragon Tavern, which was in Union Street; and among the grand officers of this second Grand Lodge on the American continent were Thomas Crafts and Paul Revere, two zealous patriots; and Captains French and Molesworth, two officers of the Twenty-ninth Regiment.[3] There was on this occasion

[1] The "Boston Gazette" of Dec. 18, 1769, has the following paragraph: "Last week an interesting trial came on before the supreme court, now sitting here; wherein Dr. Joseph Warren, administrator on the estate of Nathaniel Wheelwright, Esq., late of Boston, deceased, was plaintiff, for the recovery of part of the estate which the said Nathaniel had made over to Charles W. Apthorp, Esq. The trial lasted four days, and we hear the jury brought in their verdict in favor of the administrator."

[2] Moore's Masonic Memoir of Joseph Warren, 109.

[3] By virtue of a commission lately received from the Right Honorable and Most Worshipful, the Earl of Dalhousie, Grand Master of Ancient, Free, and

"an elegant oration," of course by the Grand Master, and a joyous, festive season.

Soon after this masonic promotion, Warren took part in the great town-meeting which was occasioned by the firing of the troops on the citizens, when the sixteen-months' question of their removal was forced to a conclusion.

I have mentioned the departure from the town of the Sixty-fourth and Sixty-fifth Regiments, leaving the Fourteenth and the Twenty-ninth. Their general Mackay, soon after, left for England; when the command devolved on Lieutentant-colonel Dalrymple, under whom they landed. He said that the arrival of the land and naval forces was the most seasonable thing that was ever known. "Had we not," he wrote to Commodore Hood, "arrived so critically, the worst that could be apprehended must have happened." Hood, who had returned to Halifax, characterized Dalrymple as a very excellent officer, quite the gentleman, knowing the world, having a good address and with all the fire, judgment, coolness, integrity, and firmness that a man could possess.

This military force was sufficiently large to be a perpetual fret to the citizens, but too small to render essential service in case of an insurrection; and the Crown officials thought it best to refrain from making arrests. The popular leaders, with touching declarations of loyalty to the king, averred that they aimed

---

Accepted Masons in Scotland, on Wednesday, was solemnized, at a Grand Lodge of Ancient, Free, and Accepted Masons in this town, held at Masons' Hall, the instalment of the Most Worshipful Joseph Warren, Esq., provincial Grand Master of Ancient, Free, and Accepted Masons in North America. On the occasion, there was an elegant oration. After the instalment, there was a grand entertainment. — *Boston Gazette, Jan.* 1, 1770.

only at a change of the measures of the Administration. The Tories, however, continued to represent the town to be a nest of disorder and rebellion. Hutchinson, when the executive responsibility rested upon him, seems to have felt that this misrepresentation had been carried to a suicidal extent; for he now advised Lord Hillsborough, that, "in matters that had no relation to the dispute between the kingdom and the colonies, Government retained its vigor, and the administration of it was attended by no unusual difficulty." This is high authority, and the evidence is to the point and conclusive. The same truth was urged by the popular leaders in calm and candid reasonings. In appeals to public opinion, made through the board of selectmen, the town-meeting, the legislature, and the council, they analyzed the events of the Eighteenth of March, to show that they were trivial; and held that the riots of the Tenth of June and other tumults were exceptional: they also pointed to the good order of the town as habitual and general; and claimed that, in their political action, they had not taken a single unconstitutional step. It was a marvel to them, that the ministry, to use the words of Samuel Adams, should employ troops only "to parade the streets of Boston, and, by their ridiculous merry-andrew tricks, to become the objects of contempt of the women and children."

Much had occurred, for sixteen months, in connection with the troops, to irritate the inhabitants. Horse-racing on the Common, by the soldiers on Sundays, and military parades in the streets, grated on the feelings of a church-going people; and formal complaints were made to the commanders, on one occasion, that the Yankee tune, "Yankee Doodle," and, on another, "Nancy Dawson," was played by the band, about meeting-time, by order of officers. These practices, however, were stopped. High-spirited citizens, on being challenged in their walks by the sentinels, could not control their temper; the violent would have their say; there were many personal quarrels; yet, in all the brawls between the citizens and the soldiers, fist had been met with fist, and club with club, and not a gun had been fired in an affray. Often cases were carried into the courts. The presence of this force was deplored on purely local grounds. "The troops," Dr. Cooper said (Jan. 1, 1770), "greatly corrupt our morals, and are in every sense an oppression. May Heaven soon deliver us from this great evil!"

During this period, the exigency that would justify the troops in firing on the people was acutely discussed in the journals. "What shall I say?" runs an article in the "Gazette." "I shudder at the thought. Surely no provincial magistrate could be found so steeled against the sensations of humanity and justice as wantonly to order troops to fire on an unarmed populace, and more than repeat in Boston the tragic scene exhibited in St. George's Fields." Hutchinson, in a letter, states the conclusions that were reached: "Our heroes for liberty say that no troops dare to fire on the people without the order of the civil magistrate, and that no civil magistrate would dare to give such orders. In the first part of their opinion, they may be right; in the second, they cannot be sure until they have made the trial." It was feared that such a step would produce a collision between the citizens and the troops. "I have been in constant panic," Franklin wrote to Dr. Cooper, "since I heard of troops assembling in Boston, lest the madness of mobs, or the interference of soldiers, or both, when too near each other, might occasion some mischief difficult to be prevented or repaired, and which might spread far and wide."

Hutchinson had the same fears, and repeatedly refused to use the troops to repress popular agitation. On one occasion, when the merchants were holding a public meeting in Faneuil Hall, on matters connected with the non-importation agreement, prominent Tories urged that it was best to bring things to a crisis; and that chronic local irritant, the commissioners of the customs, now more odious than ever by the assault of one of them on Otis, said, that "there could not be a better time to try the strength of the Government." The nature of the assembly may be inferred from the high character of its presiding officer, William Phillips, of educational fame as well as revolutionary renown. Hutchinson shrunk from directing the foreign bayonet against such a public meeting. He said that many of the civil magistrates made a part of the body that was to be suppressed, and that there could not have been a worse occasion to call out the troops. "I think," are his words, "any thing tragical would have set the whole province in a flame, and may be spread farther."

The fears expressed by Franklin and Hutchinson, of a general movement, show that the events which were transpiring in Boston had more than a local bearing. When the king, in a speech from the throne, repeated the calumny as to disobedience to law, that was uttered by the local Crown officials, in their letters, it is not strange that the patriots in the colonies regarded the town as a type of their cause, and that all eyes were turned on this question of a removal of the troops. "In this day of constitutional light," a New-York essay, reprinted in a Boston journal, runs, "it is monstrous that troops should be kept, not to protect the right, but to enslave the continent."

During the last portion of February and the first days of March, the Boston journals contained an uncommon quantity of inflammatory matter: among it, relations of the cutting-down the Liberty Pole in New York by the military, and its replacement by the people; of McDougal's imprisonment there, for free comment in the press, on the New-York assembly, because it voted supplies for the British troops; the funeral, in Boston, of the boy Snider, who was killed by an informer; and the great letter of Junius to the king. The bitterness between the citizens and soldiers was now very great. The feeling also was strong against Tory importers, who feared an assault in their houses, and slept with loaded guns by their bedsides. Some of them were allowed a file of soldiers to protect them. These facts show the inflamed state of the public mind, when the leaders of both political parties were called on to meet a paroxysm without a parallel in the former history of the colonies.

The Fourteenth Regiment was quartered in Murray's Barracks, which were but a short distance north of King Street, and near the Brattle-street Church; the Twenty-ninth Regiment was quartered in Water and Atkinson Streets, which were a little south of King (State) Street. The main guard was located directly opposite the door, on the south side of the Town House, in this street, where the two field-pieces were planted on the landing of the troops. There is much said about this main guard. Its location had been very galling to the people. Hutchinson, in January, 1770, when he expected the general court would meet, obtained permission of General Gage to remove this guard to another place; but, as this body did not then convene, they remained. The soldiers detailed for daily guard-duty were regularly brought here, and thence marched to their posts.

It was said, in the "Boston Gazette," that soldiers had pricked the citizens with bayonets, and had rescued offenders against the laws by force from the hands of the magistrates. There was, in February, an increase of personal quarrels. None, however, were of importance. But, on Friday, the 2d of March, as two soldiers were at Gray's ropewalk, which was not far from the quarters of the Twenty-ninth Regiment, they were insulted by one of the workmen. Sharp altercation followed, and the soldiers went off, but soon returned with a party of their comrades, when there was a challenge to a boxing-match; which grew into a fight, the ropemakers using their woulding-sticks; and the soldiers, clubs and cutlasses. It proved to be the most serious quarrel that had occurred. Lieutenant-colonel Carr, commander of the Twenty-ninth, which, Hutchinson said, was composed of such bad fellows that discipline could not restrain them, made a complaint to the lieutenant-governor relative to the provoking conduct of the ropemaker which brought on the affray; and thus this affair became the occasion of political consultation, which tended to intensify the animosity between the parties.

On Saturday, the report was circulated, that the parties engaged in this affray would renew the fight on Monday evening. On Sunday, Carr and other officers went into the ropewalk, giving out that they were searching for a sergeant of their regiment. Though on these days there was much irritation, the town was comparatively quiet.

On Monday, the lieutenant-governor laid the complaint of Carr before the council, and asked the advice of this body, which gave rise to debate about the removal of the troops; members freely expressing the opinion, that the way to prevent collisions between the military and the people was to withdraw the two regiments to the castle. No important action was taken by the council, although the apprehension was expressed that the affair at the ropewalk might grow into a general quarrel. And it is worthy of remark, that, ominous as the signs were, the lieutenant-governor took no precautionary measures, not even the obvious step of having the troops kept in their barracks. His letters, and, indeed, his whole course, up to the eventful evening of this day, indicate confidence in the opinion, that there was no intention, on the part of the popular leaders, to molest the troops; and that the troops, without an order from the civil authority, would not fire on the citizens.

Nor was there now, as zealous Tories alleged, any plan formed by the popular leaders, or by any persons of consideration, to expel the troops by force from the town, much less the obnoxious commissioners of the customs. Nor is there any evidence to support the allegation on the other side, that the Crown officials, civil or military, meditated or stimulated an attack on the inhabitants. The patriots regarded what had occurred, and what was threatened, like much that had taken place during the last seventeen months, as the motions of a rod of power needlessly held over the people to overawe them, serving no earthly good, but souring their minds and imbittering their passions; while the Crown officials represented this chafing of the free spirits at the incidents of military rule as a sign of the lost authority of Government, and of a desire for independence. Among the fiery spirits on both sides constituting the mob-element, the ropewalk affair was regarded as a drawn game; and a renewal of the fight was desired, on the ground that honor was at stake. To inspirit the Whigs, to use Dr. Gordon's words, " The newspapers had a pompous account of a victory obtained by the inhabitants of New York over the soldiers there in an affray; while the Boston newspapers could present but a tame relation of the result of the affray here." These facts account satisfactorily for the intimations and warnings given during the day to prominent characters on both sides, and for the hand-bill that was circulated by the soldiers in the afternoon, proposing concert of action between the Fourteenth and the Twenty-ninth Regiments.[1] The course things

[1] Hand-bill, in writing, posted up by the soldiers in the afternoon:

"Boston March ye 5, 1770.

"This is to Inform ye Rebellious People in Boston that ye Soldjers in ye 14th and 29th Regiments are determined to Joine together and defend themselves against all who shall Opose them   Signd Y^e Soldjers of ye 14th & 29th

"Regiments."

took fully justifies the remark of Gordon, that "every thing tended to a crisis; and it is rather wonderful that it did not exist sooner, when so many circumstances united to hasten its approach."

There was a layer of ice on the ground, a slight fall of snow during the day, and a young moon in the evening. At an early hour, as though something uncommon was expected, parties of boys, apprentices, and soldiers, strolled through the streets; and neither side was sparing of insult. Ten or twelve soldiers went from the main guard, in King Street, across this street to Murray's Barracks, in Brattle Street, about three hundred yards from King Street; and another party came out of these barracks, armed with clubs and cutlasses, bent on a stroll. A little after eight o'clock, quite a crowd collected near the Brattle-street Church, many of whom had canes and sticks. After wretched abuse was bantered on both sides, things grew into a fight. As it became more and more threatening, a few Northenders ran to the Old Brick Meeting-house, on what is now Washington Street, at the head of King Street, and lifted a boy into a window, who rang the bell. About the same time, Captain Goldfinch, of the army, who was on his way to Murray's Barracks, crossed King Street, near the Custom House, at the corner of Exchange Lane (now Exchange Street), where a sentinel had long been stationed. The captain, as he was passing, was taunted by a barber's apprentice, as a mean fellow, for not paying for dressing his hair; when the sentinel ran after the boy, and gave him a severe blow with his musket. The boy went away crying, and told several persons of the assault; while the captain went on towards

Murray's Barracks, but found the passage into the yard obstructed by the affray going on there; the crowd pelting the soldiers with snowballs, and the latter defending themselves. Being the senior officer, he ordered the men into the barracks: the gate of the yard was then shut, and the promise made, that no more men should be let out that evening. In this way, the affray here was effectually stopped.

For a little time, perhaps twenty minutes, there was nothing to attract to a centre the people who were drawn by the alarm-bell out of their homes on this frosty, moonlit, memorable evening; and, in various places, individuals were asking where the fire was. King Street — then, as now, the commercial centre of Boston — was quiet. A group was standing before the main guard with fire bags and buckets in their hands; a few persons were moving along in other parts of the street; and White, the sentinel at the Custom House, with his firelock on his shoulder, was pacing his beat quite unmolested. In Dock Square, a small gathering, mostly of participants in the affair just over, were harangued by a large, tall man, who wore a red cloak and a white wig; and, as he closed, there was a hurrah, and the cry, "To the main guard!" In another street, a similar cry was raised, "To the main guard!—that is the nest!" But no assault was made on the guard. The word went round that there was no fire, "only a rumpus with the soldiers," who had been driven to their quarters; and well-disposed citizens, as they withdrew, were saying, "Every man to his home!"

But, at about fifteen minutes past nine, an excited party passed up Royal Exchange Lane, leading into

King Street; and as they came near the Custom House, on the corner, one of the number, who knew of the assault on the apprentice-boy, said, "Here is the soldier who did it!" when they gathered round the sentinel. The barber's boy now came up, and said, "This is the soldier who knocked me down with the butt-end of his musket." Some now said, "Kill him! knock him down!" The sentinel moved back up the steps of the Custom House, and loaded his gun. Missiles were thrown at him; when he presented his musket, warned the party to keep off, and called for help. Some one ran to Captain Preston, the officer of the day, and informed him that the people were about to assault the sentinel; when he hastened to the main guard, on the opposite side of the street, about forty rods from the Custom House, and sent a sergeant, a very young officer, with a file of seven men, to protect the sentinel. They went over in a kind of trot, using rough words and actions towards those who went with them, and, coming near the party round the sentinel, rudely pushed them aside, pricking some with their bayonets, and formed in a half-circle near the sentry-box. The sentinel now came down the steps, and fell in with the file, when they were ordered to prime and load. Captain Preston almost immediately joined his men. The file now numbered nine.

The number of people here at this time is variously stated from thirty to a hundred; "between fifty and sixty" being the most common enumeration. Some of them were fresh from the affray at the barracks, and some of the soldiers had been in the affair at the ropewalk. There was aggravation on both sides.

The crowd were unarmed, or had but sticks, which they struck defiantly against each other; having no definite object, and doing no greater mischief than, in retaliation of uncalled-for military roughness, to throw snowballs, hurrah, whistle through their fingers, use oaths and foul language, call the soldiers names, hustle them, and dare them to fire. One of the file was struck with a stick. There were good men trying to prevent a riot, and some assured the soldiers that they would not be hurt. Among others, Henry Knox, subsequently the general, was present, who saw nothing to justify the use of fire-arms, and, with others, remonstrated against their employment; but Captain Preston, as he was talking with Knox, saw his men pressing the people with their bayonets, when, in great agitation, he rushed among them. Then, with or without orders, but certainly without any legal form or warning, seven of the file, one after another, discharged their muskets upon the citizens;[1] and the result indicates the malignity and precision of their aim. Crispus Attucks, an intrepid mulatto, who was a leader in the affair at Murray's Barracks, was killed

---

[1] I have constructed his narrative by a careful collation of the evidence that appears to be authentic; but it will be vain to attempt to reconcile all the statements in relation to this transaction. An illustration of the necessity of weighing the authorities is seen in the case of the affidavit of "Charlotte Bourgate," No. 58, in the report of the trial; who testified that guns were fired from the Custom-House windows. In 1771, in the case of The King *vs.* Bourgate, a jury convicted him of perjury for false swearing in relation to this firing. "The court ordered, that the said Charles Bourgate be set in the pillory for the space of one hour; that he be whipped twenty-five stripes upon his naked back, at the public whipping-post; and that he pay costs of prosecution, — standing committed until this sentence be performed." Hutchinson, in a letter dated July 27, 1770, says: "I do not believe Preston intended his men should fire. I do not know he is not to be justified in ordering his men to charge; but they are in general such bad fellows in that regiment, that it seems impossible to restrain them from firing upon an insult or provocation given them."

as he stood leaning with his breast resting on a stout cord-wood stick; Samuel Gray, one of the rope-makers, was shot as he stood with his hands in his bosom, and just as he had said, "My lads, they will not fire;" Patrick Carr left his house on hearing the alarm-bell, and was mortally wounded as he was crossing the street; James Caldwell, in like manner summoned from his home, was killed as he was standing in the middle of the street; Samuel Maverick, a lad of seventeen, ran out of the house at the alarm of fire, and was shot as he was crossing the street; six others were wounded. But fifteen or twenty minutes had elapsed from the time the sergeant went from the main guard to the time of the firing. The people, on the report of the guns, fell back, but instinctively and instantly returned for the killed and wounded; when the infuriated soldiers prepared to fire again, but, checked by Captain Preston, were withdrawn across the street to the main guard. The drums beat: several companies of the Twenty-Ninth Regiment, under Colonel Carr, promptly appeared, and were formed in three divisions before the main guard; the front division near the north-east corner of the Town House, in the kneeling posture for street firing. The Fourteenth Regiment was ordered under arms, but remained at their barracks.

The report now spread that "the troops had risen on the people;" and the beat of drums, the church-bells, and the cry of fire, summoned from their homes the inhabitants, who hastened to the place of alarm. In a few minutes, thousands collected; and the cry was, "To arms! to arms!" The whole town was in confusion; while, in King Street, there was now what the patriots had so long predicted, dreaded, and endeavored to avert, — an indignant population and an exasperated soldiery face to face. The excitement was terrible. The care of the popular leaders for their cause, since the mob-days of the Stamp Act, had been like the care of their personal honor: it drew them forth as the prompt and brave controlling power in every crisis; and they were among the concourse on this "night of consternation." Warren, early on the ground to act the good physician as well as the fearless patriot, gives the impression produced on himself and his co-laborers as they saw the first blood flowing that was shed for American liberty "The horrors," he says, "of that dreadful night are but too deeply impressed on our hearts. Language is too feeble to paint the emotions of our souls, when our streets were stained with the blood of our brethren, when our ears were wounded by the groans of the dying, and our eyes were tormented by the sight of the mangled bodies of the dead... Our hearts beat 'To arms!' we snatched our weapons, almost resolved, by one decisive stroke, to avenge the death of our slaughtered brethren, and to secure from future danger all that we held most dear."[1]

Meantime, the lieutenant-governor, at his residence in North Square, heard the sound of the church-bell near by, and supposed it was an alarm of fire. But soon, at nearly ten o'clock, a number of the inhabitants came running into his house, entreating him to go to King Street immediately; "otherwise," they said, "the town would be all in blood." He immediately started for the scene of danger. On his way, in the

[1] Oration, 1772.

Market Place (Dock Square), he found himself amidst a great body of people, some armed with clubs, others with cutlasses, and all calling for fire-arms. He made himself known to them, but pleaded in vain for a hearing; and, to insure his safety, he retreated into a dwelling-house, and thence went by a private way into King Street, where he found an excited multitude anxiously awaiting his arrival. He first called for Captain Preston; and a natural indignation at a high-handed act is expressed in the stern and searching questions which the civilian put to the soldier, bearing on the vital point of the subordination of the military to the civil power. "Are you the commanding officer?"—"Yes, sir."—"Do you know, sir, you have no power to fire on any body of people collected together, except you have a civil magistrate with you to give orders?" Captain Preston replied, "I was obliged to, to save the sentry." So great was the confusion, that Preston's reply was heard but by few. The cry was raised, "To the Town House! to the Town House!" when Hutchinson, by the irresistible violence of the crowd, was forced into the building, and up to the council chamber; and, in a few minutes, he appeared on the balcony. Near him were prominent citizens, both Tories and Whigs; below him, on the one side, were his indignant townsmen, who had conferred on him every honor in their power; and, on the other side, the soldiers in defiant attitude. He could speak with eloquence and power: throughout this strange and trying scene, he bore himself with dignity and self-possession; and as in the stillness of night he expressed great concern at the unhappy event, and made solemn pledges to the people, his tone must have been uncommonly earnest. "The law," he averred, "should have its course: he would live and die by the law." He promised to order an inquiry in the morning, and requested all to retire to their homes. But words now were not satisfactory to the people; and those near him urged, that the course of justice had always been evaded or obstructed in favor of the soldiery, and that the people were determined not to disperse until Captain Preston was arrested. In consequence, Hutchinson immediately ordered a court of inquiry. The patriots also entreated the lieutenant-governor to order the troops to their barracks. He replied, that it was not in his power to give such an order; but he would consult the officers. They now came upon the balcony, — Dalrymple of the Fourteenth Regiment being present; and, after an interview with Hutchinson, he returned to the troops. The men now rose from their kneeling posture; the order to "Shoulder arms!" was heard; and the people were greatly relieved by seeing the troops move towards their barracks.

The people now began slowly and sullenly to disperse. Meanwhile, the court of inquiry on Captain Preston was in session; and, after an examination that lasted three hours, he was bound over for trial. Later, the soldiers were also arrested. It was three o'clock in the morning before the lieutenant-governor left the scene of the massacre. And now all, exceptcepting about a hundred of the people, who formed themselves into a watch, left the streets. Thus wise action by the Crown officials, the activity of the popular leaders, and the habitual respect for law in the people, proved successful in preventing further carnage. "Propitious Heaven," are Warren's words, "forbade the bloody carnage, and saved the threatened victims of our too keen resentment: not by their discipline, not by their regular array; no, it was Royal George's livery that proved their shield; it was that which turned the pointed engines from their breasts."[1] Hence a contemporary versifier and participater in these scenes was able to write, —

> "No sudden rage the ruffian soldier bore,
> Or drenched the pavements with his vital gore:
> Deliberate thought did all our souls compose,
> Till, veiled in gloom, the lowery morning rose."

During the night, the popular leaders sent expresses to the neighboring towns, bearing intelligence of what had occurred, and summoning people from their beds to come to the aid of Boston; but, as the efforts to restore quiet were proving successful, the summons was countermanded. This action accounts for the numbers, who, very early in the morning of the 6th of March, flocked into the town. They could learn details of the tragedy from the actors in it, could see the blood of the slaughtered inhabitants, could hear the groans of the wounded, could view the bodies of the dead; and this revelation of the work of arbitrary power, to a people habitually tender of regard for human life, shocked their sensibilities. The temper of the public mind was again wrought up to a fearful state of indigna-

[1] Warren has the following note, in his oration of 1772, under this sentence: "I have the strongest reason to believe that I have mentioned the only circumstance which saved the troops from destruction. It was then, and now is, the opinion of those who were best acquainted with the state of affairs at that time, that, had thrice that number of troops, belonging to any power at open war with us, been in this town, in the same exposed position, scarce a man would have lived to see the morning light."

tion; and it required the strongest moral influence to keep the terrific demand for a redress of grievance and future security within the bounds of moderation and in the safe channel of the law.

The lieutenant-governor, during the night, had summoned such members of the council as were within reach, to meet in their chamber in the morning; and, on joining them, he found the selectmen, with most of the justices of the county, waiting for him, to represent, as he says, "their opinion of the absolute necessity of the troops being at a distance, that there might be no intercourse between the inhabitants and them, in order to prevent a further effusion of blood." Such was the logic of events which now forced the seventeen months' question of the removal of the troops on the civil and military authorities with an imperativeness that could not be resisted.

The question, however, came up in a new shape. To put it in the simplest way, and in the words used on that day, the people were so excited by the shedding of blood on the preceding night, that they were resolved no longer to acquiesce in the decision of the constituted authorities as to the troops; but, failing in other means, they were determined to effect their removal by force, let the act be deemed rebellion or otherwise. Not that any conspiracy existed, not that any plan had been matured to do this; but circumstances had transferred the question from the domain of reason to that of physical force; and the only point with the Crown officials, during the whole of this day's deliberations, was, whether they would be justified in what appeared to them to be lowering the national standard at the demand of a power which they called "the faction," or whether they might venture to take the responsibility of resisting the demand, and of meeting the consequences.

The selectmen expressed to the lieutenant-governor the opinion, that "the inhabitants would be under no restraint whilst the troops were in town." — "I let them know," Hutchinson says, "that I had no power to remove the troops." They also informed him that they had been requested to call a town-meeting, which was the special dread of Hutchinson. As the fixed determination of the people became more manifest, the anxiety of the lieutenant-governor deepened as to what the day might bring forth; and he sent for Colonels Dalrymple and Carr to be present in the council, and act as military advisers. But the discussions in this body were interrupted by the entrance of a messenger from another assembly, bearing a request for the immediate presence of the selectmen in Faneuil Hall.

This summons invites attention to the movements of the people, who had been constantly coming in from the neighboring towns, and had gathered in great numbers "in a perfect frenzy," Hutchinson says, around Faneuil Hall. It was, however, the general disposition, volcanic as were the elements, to act with caution, deliberation, and in a spirit of unity, and doubtless with the consideration, that the eyes of the friends of their cause were upon them. Hours passed without the appearance of a warrant calling a town-meeting. Nor was there any organization to which the people could look in this crisis; for the general court stood prorogued by the arbitrary decision of the ministry. At eleven o'clock, the town-records say, "the freeholders and other inhabitants" held a meeting, "occasioned by the massacre made in King Street by the soldiery." The town-clerk, William Cooper, acted as the chairman. This intrepid patriot held that office forty-nine years; a fact which speaks for his fidelity to duty, intelligence, devotion to principle, and moral worth. "The selectmen," his clear, round record reads, "not being present, and the inhabitants being informed that they were in the council chamber, it was voted that Mr. William Greenleaf be desired to proceed there, and acquaint the selectmen that the inhabitants desire and expect their attendance at the hall." This was virtually a command, and the selectmen immediately repaired to the hall. Thomas Cushing was chosen the moderator. He was now the speaker of the House of Representatives, and by urbanity of manner, a high personal character, diligent public service, and fidelity to the patriot cause, exercised large influence. It was voted that Constable Wallace wait upon the Rev. Dr. Cooper, and acquaint him that the inhabitants desired him to open the meeting with prayer. He was a brother of the town-clerk, was on confidential terms with the popular leaders, and a devoted friend to the patriot cause. He was rich in genius and learning, Dr. Eliot says, with a gift in prayer peculiar and very excellent. He complied with the request of the town; but no reporter transmitted the words of this righteous man, or described this solemn assembly, as fervent prayer now went up for the country.

The meeting voted to invite any citizen to give information of the massacre of the preceding evening, "that the same might be minuted by the town-clerk;" whereupon several persons related details of the tragedy, which the clerk inscribed in the town-records. John S. Copley stated, that Mr. Pelham and his wife, and some persons of Mr. Samuel Winthrop's family, heard a soldier say, after the firing, "that the Devil might give quarters: he should give them none." John Scott stated, that a lad of Mr. Piermont's said at Mr. Chardon's, that a soldier was heard to say, his officer had acquainted them, "if they went abroad at nights, they should go armed and in companies." Mr. Piermont informed the meeting, "that, before the firing last night, he had disarmed a soldier, who had struck down one of the inhabitants." Pool Spear related, "that last week he heard one Kilson, a soldier of Pharras's company, say that he did not know what the inhabitants were after; for they had broken an officer's windows (meaning Nathaniel Roger's windows), but that they had a scheme on foot which would soon put a stop to our (the people's) procedure; that parties of soldiers were ordered (to go) with pistols in their pockets, and to fire upon those who should assault said house again; and that ten pounds sterling were to be given as a reward for their killing one of these persons, and fifty pounds sterling for a prisoner." These homely relations are life-like glimpses of the spirit of the hour. No speech could have been more eloquent, because none could have been better calculated to deepen the general conviction and minister to the common emotion. However, so many witnesses were ready to testify, that it was found to be impracticable to hear all; and a committee was appointed to receive and digest the evidence.[1]

[1] I have taken these minutes from the town-records.

Samuel Adams addressed this remarkable meeting. He spoke with a pathos peculiar to himself. His manner, naturally impressive, was rendered more so by the solemnity of the occasion; and every heart was moved.[1] The great hour demanded dignity and discretion in unison with firmness, and they were combined in the action of the meeting. It resolved that the inhabitants would submit no longer to the insult of military rule. A committee of fifteen[2] was chosen to wait on the lieutenant-governor, and acquaint him that it was the unanimous opinion of the meeting that the inhabitants and soldiery could no longer dwell together in safety, and that nothing could be rationally expected to restore the peace of the town, and prevent additional scenes of blood and carnage, but the immediate removal of the troops; and to say, further, that they most fervently prayed His Honor that his power and influence might be exerted, in order that this removal might be instantly effected. This committee well represented the intelligence, the patriotism, the interests, and the true greatness of Boston. The meeting now dissolved; when the selectmen issued a warrant for a regular town-meeting, to convene at the same place, at three o'clock in the afternoon, to consider what measures were most proper to be taken to preserve the peace of the town at that alarming and important period.[3]

[1] S. A. Wells's MS.

[2] This committee consisted of Thomas Cushing, John Hancock, Henderson Inches, Joshua Henshaw, Samuel Adams, William Phillips, Samuel Pemberton, Samuel Austin, Benjamin Austin, Joseph Jackson, William Molineux, Benjamin Church, Jonathan Mason, Ezekiel Goldthwait, John Ruddock.

[3] The following was the selectmen's warrant for this meeting : —

"Boston, *ss.* To the constables of the town of Boston, and each and every of them greeting:

About noon, the lieutenant-governor received the committee of the town, in a session of the council, at their chamber. I have found no details of what was said by the committee at this interview, in urging a compliance with the demand. Hutchinson said he was not prepared to reply, but would give an answer in writing, when the committee withdrew into another room. He gives glimpses of what then occurred. "I told the council," he says, "that a removal of the troops was not with me; and I desired them to consider what answer I could give to this application of the town, whilst Colonel Dalrymple, who had the command, was present." Some of the members, who were among the truest patriots, urged a compliance; when the lieutenant-governor declared, that "he would, upon no consideration whatever, give orders for their removal." The council advised the removal of one regiment. Dalrymple concurred in this result. As Hutchinson rose from this sitting, he declared that "he meant to receive no further application on the subject."

Things wore a gloomy aspect during the interval between the session of the council and the time of the

"In His Majesty's name, you are required forthwith to warn all the freeholders and other inhabitants of the town of Boston, legally qualified, ratable at twenty pounds' estate to a single rate (beside the poll), to convene at Faneuil Hall, on Tuesday the sixth instant, three o'clock afternoon, to consider what measures are most proper to be taken to preserve the peace of the town at this alarming and important period.

"Hereof fail not, and make return of this warrant, with your doings thereon, unto myself as soon as may be before the time of said meeting.

"Dated at Boston, the sixth day of March, in the tenth year of His Majesty's reign, annoque Domini, 1770. — By order of the Selectmen, WILLIAM COOPER, Town-clerk."

On the back of the warrant is the return of the twelve constables for the twelve wards, dated March 6, to the effect that they had duly warned the inhabitants.

afternoon meeting; for the action of the Crown officials tended to increase the spirit of the people. The men who had been long branded as incendiaries and traitors, now earnestly endeavored to prevent a catastrophe. There were consultations between the leaders of the two parties: it was intimated to members of the council, that though Dalrymple might receive no formal order to remove all the troops, yet he would do it if the lieutenant-governor and council expressed a desire to have it done. With a view to further action, Hutchinson was prevailed upon to meet the council in the afternoon. This was a great point gained for the popular cause.

At three o'clock, Faneuil Hall was filled with the excited population assembled in town-meeting. Thomas Cushing again was chosen the moderator; but the place would hold only about thirteen hundred, and the record reads, "The hall not being spacious enough to receive the inhabitants who attended, it was voted to adjourn to Dr. Sewall's meeting-house," — the Old South. The most convenient way for the people would be to pass from Faneuil Hall into King Street, up by the council chamber, and along what is now Washington Street, to the church. No mention is made of mottoes or banners or flags, of cheers or of jeers. Thomas Cushing said his countrymen " were, like the old British commoners, grave and sad men;" and it was said in the council to Hutchinson, " This multitude are not such as pulled down your house;" but they are " men of the best characters," " men of estates and men of religion," " men who pray over what they do." They were (Hutchinson's words) "warmed with a persuasion that what they were doing was right, and that they were struggling for the liberties of America;" and that the other colonies were deeply interested in their action.

As Hutchinson looked out on this scene, perhaps scanned the concourse who passed from Faneuil Hall to the Old South, an analogy from history forced itself on his mind. With like determined men, who feared God and were devoted to public liberty, Cromwell won at Marston Moor; and, as Hutchinson read in the countenances before him the signs of resolute hearts, he judged "their spirit to be as high as was the spirit of their ancestors when they imprisoned Andros, while they were four times as numerous." As the burden of responsibility pressed on him heavily, he realized that he had to deal with an element far more potent than "the faction" which officials had long represented as composing the patriot party, and that much depended on dealing with it wisely. This was not a dependent and starved host, wildly urging the terrible demand of "Bread or blood;" nor was it fanaticism in a season of social discontent, claiming impossibilities at the hand of power: the craving was moral and intellectual; it was an intelligent public opinion, a people, with well-grounded and settled convictions, making a just demand on arbitrary power. Was such public opinion about to be scorned as though it were but a faction, and by officials who bore high the party-standard? And were men of such resoluteness of character and purpose about to be involved in a work of carnage that might extend far and wide? or would the wielders of British power avoid the extremity by concession? Boston, indeed America, had seen no hour of intenser interest, of deeper solemnity, of more instant peril, or of truer moral sublimity. As this assembly deliberated with the sounds of the fife and drum in their ears, and with the soldiery in their sight, questions like these must have been on every lip; and they are of the civil-war questions that cause an involuntary shudder in every home.

The Old South was not large enough to hold the people; and they stood in the street, and near the Town House, awaiting the report of the committee of fifteen, chosen in the morning, who were now in the Town House. The lieutenant-governor was at the council chamber, where, in addition to Colonels Dalrymple and Carr, there had been summoned Captain Caldwell, of the "Rose" frigate; and Hutchinson would, he says, have summoned other Crown officers, but he knew the council would not consent to it. He took care to repeat to the committee, he says, the declaration which he had made in the morning to the selectmen, the justices, and the council, "that the ordering of the troops did not lie with him." As the committee, with Samuel Adams at their head, appeared on the Town-house steps, the people were in motion; and the word passed, "Make way for the committee!" Adams uncovered his head; and, as he went towards the church, he bowed alternately to those on each side of the lane that was formed, and repeated the words, "Both regiments or none."[1] The answer of the lieutenant-governor to the demand made in the morning, for a total removal of the troops, was read to the meeting in the church. It was to the effect, that he had conferred with the com-

[1] S. A. Wells's MSS.

manders of the two regiments, who received orders from the general in New York, and it was not in his power to countermand these orders: but the council desired their removal, and Colonel Dalrymple had signified, that, because of the part which the Twenty-ninth Regiment had taken in the differences, it should be placed, without delay, in the barracks at the castle; and also that the main guard should be removed; while the Fourteenth Regiment should be so disposed, and laid under such restraint, that all occasion for future differences might be prevented. There now resounded through the excited assembly, from a thousand tongues, " Both regiments or none!"

A short debate occurred, when the answer was voted to be unsatisfactory. Then another committee was chosen. It was resolved, that John Hancock, Samuel Adams, William Molineux, William Phillips, Joseph Warren, Joshua Henshaw, and Samuel Pemberton, be a committee to inform the lieutenant-governor it was the unanimous opinion of the people, that the reply was by no means satisfactory, and that nothing less would satisfy them than a total and immediate removal of the troops. This committee was one worthy of a great occasion. Hancock, Henshaw, and Pemberton, besides being individually of large influence from their ability, patriotism, worth, and wealth, were members of the board of selectmen, and therefore represented the municipality; Phillips, who had served on this board, was a type of the upright and liberal merchant; Molineux was one of the most determined and zealous of the patriots, and a stirring business-man; Warren, ardent and bold, of rising fame as a leader, personified the generous devotion and noble enthusiasm of the young men; Adams, though not the first-named on the committee, played so prominent a part in its doings, that he appears as its chairman. He was so widely and favorably known that he was now addressed as "The Father of America." Of middling stature, plain in dress, quiet in manner, unpretending in deportment, he exhibited nothing extraordinary in common affairs; but on great occasions, when his deeper nature was called into action, he rose, without the smallest affectation, into an upright dignity of figure and bearing, with a harmony of voice and a power of speech which made a strong impression, — the more lasting from the purity and nervous eloquence of his style and the logical consistency of his argument.[1] Such were the men selected to speak and act for Boston in this hour of deep passion and of high resolve.

The committee, about four o'clock, repaired to the council chamber. It was a room respectable in size, and not without ornament or historic memorials. On its walls were representatives of the two elements now in conflict, — of the Absolutism that was passing away, in full-length portraits of Charles II. and James II., robed in the royal ermine; and of a Republicanism which had grown robust and self-reliant, in the heads of Endicott and Winthrop and Bradstreet and Belcher. Around a long table were seated the lieutenant-governor and the members of the council, with the military officers; the scrupulous and sumptuous costumes of civilians in authority, — gold and silver lace, scarlet cloaks, and large wigs, mingling with the brilliant uniforms of the British army and navy. Into

[1] John Adams.

such imposing presence was now ushered the plainly attired committee of the town.[1]

At this time, the lieutenant-governor, a portion of the council, the military officers, the secretary of the province, and other officials in the Town House, were sternly resolved to refuse compliance with the demand of the people. When the vote of the meeting was presented to the lieutenant-governor, Adams remarked at length on the illegality of quartering troops on the inhabitants in time of peace, and without the consent of the legislature; urged that the public service did not require them; adverted with sensibility and warmth to the late tragedy; painted the misery in which the town would be involved, if the troops were suffered to remain; and urged the necessity of an immediate compliance with the vote of the people. The lieutenant-governor, in a brief reply, defended both the legality and the necessity of the troops, and renewed his old assertion, that they were not subject to his authority. Adams again rose; and attention was riveted on him, as he paused and gave a searching look at Hutchinson. There was in his countenance and attitude a silent eloquence that words could not express; his manner showed that the energies of his soul were roused; and in a tone not loud, but deep and earnest, he again addressed himself to Hutchinson. "It is well known," he said, "that, acting as governor of the province, you are, by its charter, the commander-in-chief of the military forces within it; and, as such, the troops now in the capital are subject to your orders. If you, or Colonel Dalrymple under you, have the power to remove one regiment, you

---

[1] John Adams's letter.

have the power to remove both; and nothing short of their total removal will satisfy the people or preserve the peace of the province. A multitude, highly incensed, now wait the result of this application. The voice of ten thousand freemen demands that both regiments be forthwith removed. Their voice must be respected, — their demand obeyed. Fail, then, at your peril, to comply with this requisition! On you alone rests the responsibility of the decision; and, if the just expectations of the people are disappointed, you must be answerable to God and your country for the fatal consequences that must ensue. The committee have discharged their duty, and it is for you to discharge yours. They wait your final determination."[1] As Adams, while speaking, intently eyed Hutchinson, he says, "I observed his knees to tremble; I saw his face grow pale; and I enjoyed the sight."[1]

[1] Hutchinson, in a letter dated March 18, 1770, addressed to Sir Francis Bernard, says, "The calling of the council the next day could not be avoided, though I knew no good could come from it; for the people, high and low, a few only who you will easily guess, and who chose to keep their houses, were up in a body, heated and ready to take force, and were impatient waiting for the c—— (council) meeting. If the c—— would have joined with me, and disclaimed all authority over the troops, and encouraged the people to wait until there could be an order from the general, they might have been appeased; but, instead of that, the major part encouraged them in their demand. They first urged me to give orders to the troops, or said if I would do it by their advice, they knew they would immediately remove. I told them nothing should ever induce me to such a measure; and, upon D. (Dalrymple) coming in, I let him know I had nothing to do with it, and it lay with him only. Upon the representation made of this state of the people by Tyler backed by S——, Pitts, and Dexter, he told them he would remove the 29th till he could hear from the general. When the committee of the town were informed of this, Adams immediately told him if he could remove one he could remove both, and he would be amenable for the consequence of not doing it, or to that effect, I think in stronger words. I wished to have been clear of the council in the afternoon, but it was not possible. When they pressed me to comply with their advice, it was immediately known among the people that D. was ready to remove them if I would only join in desiring it. Upon consulting

An interval of silence followed this appeal. Then there was low conversation, to a whisper, between the lieutenant-governor and Colonel Dalrymple, who, in the spirit of the unbending soldier, was for resisting this demand, as he had been for summary proceedings in the case of other meetings. "It is impossible for me," he had said this afternoon, "to go any further lengths in this matter. The information given of the intended rebellion is sufficient reason against the removal of His Majesty's troops." But he now said, in a loud tone, "I am ready to obey your orders;" which threw the responsibility on Hutchinson. All the members of the committee urged the demand. "Every one of them," Hutchinson says, "deliberately gave his opinion at large, and generally gave this reason to

the secretary (Oliver) in the beginning of the afternoon, he agreed with me, that it was best finally to stand out, and leave it to D. and the council; but, when he saw how artfully it was steered, he whispered to me that I must either comply, or determine to leave the province."

In this letter, Samuel Adams is represented as addressing Dalrymple; but, from Adams's contemporary letter (1771), cited in the text, it is certain that he also addressed Hutchinson. Bancroft, vi. 344, prints the traditionary relation by John Quincy Adams. I copy from S. A. Wells's MS. James Allen, who participated in these scenes, thus described this town-meeting in his poem, printed in 1772:

"No mob then furious urg'd the impassion'd fray,
Nor clamorous tumults dinn'd the solemn day;
In full convene the city senate sat,
Our fathers' spirit rul'd the firm debate:
The freeborn soul no reptile tyrant checks,
'T is heaven that dictates when the people speaks;
Loud from their tongues the awful mandate broke,
And thus, inspir'd the sacred senate spoke;
Ye miscreant troops, begone! our presence fly;
Stay, if ye dare, but if ye dare, ye die!
Ah, too severe, the fearful chief* replies,
Permit one half, the other, instant, flies.
No parle, avaunt! or by our fathers' shades,
Your reeking lives shall glut our vengeful blades.
Ere morning's light, begone, — or else we swear
Each slaughter'd corse shall feed the birds of air!'"

* Hutchinson.

support it, — that the people would most certainly drive out the troops, and that the inhabitants of the other towns would join in it: and several of the gentlemen declared that they did not judge from the general temper of the people only, but they knew it to be the determination, not of a mob, but of the generality of the principal inhabitants; and they added, that all the blood would be charged to me alone for refusing to follow their unanimous advice, in desiring that the quarters of a single regiment might be changed, in order to put an end to the animosities between the troops and the inhabitants, seeing Colonel Dalrymple would consent to it."

After the committee withdrew, the debates of the council were long and earnest; and, as they went on, Hutchinson asked, " What protection would there be for the commissioners, if both regiments were ordered to the castle?" Several said, " They would be safe, and always had been safe." — "As safe," said Gray, " without the troops as with them." And Irving said, " They never had been in danger, and he would pawn his life that they should receive no injury." — " Unless the troops were removed," it was said, " before evening there would be ten thousand men on the Common." — " The people in general," Tyler said, " were resolved to have the troops removed, without which they would not be satisfied; that, failing of other means, they were determined to effect their removal by force, let the act be deemed rebellion or otherwise." As the council deliberated, the people were impatient; and the members were repeatedly called out to give information as to the result. There was at length unanimity. This body resolved, that, to preserve the peace, it was absolutely necessary that the troops should be removed; and they advised the lieutenant-governor to communicate this conclusion to Dalrymple, and to request that he would order his whole command to Castle William.

The remark of Dalrymple, as well as the decision of the council, became known to the people, and the word passed round, "that Colonel Dalrymple had yielded, and that the lieutenant-governor only held out." This circumstance was communicated to Hutchinson; and he says, "It now lay upon me to choose that side which had the fewest and least difficulties; and I weighed and compared them as well as the time I had for them would permit. I knew it was most regular for me to leave this matter entire to the commanding officer. I was sensible the troops were designed to be, upon occasion, employed under the direction of the civil magistrate; and that at the castle they would be too remote, in most cases, to answer that purpose. But then I considered they never had been used for that purpose, and there was no probability they ever would be, because no civil magistrate could be found under whose directions they might act; and they could be considered only as having a tendency to keep the inhabitants in some degree of awe, and even this was every day lessening; and the affronts the troops received were such, that there was no avoiding quarrels and slaughter." Still he hesitated substantially to retract his word; for now a request from him, he knew, was equivalent to an order; and, before he determined, he consulted three officers of the Crown, who, though not present in the council, were in the building, and the secretary, Oliver. All agreed that he ought to comply with the advice of the council. He then formally recommended Dalrymple to remove all the troops, who gave his word of honor that he would commence preparations in the morning for a removal, and that there should be no unnecessary delay in quartering both regiments at the castle.[1]

It was dark when the committee bore back to the meeting the great report of their success. It was received with expressions of the highest satisfaction. What a burden was lifted from the hearts of the patriots! They did not, however, regard their work as done. They voted that a strong watch was necessary through the night, when the committee who had waited on the lieutenant-governor tendered their services to make a part of the watch; and the whole matter was placed in their hands as a "committee of safety." They were authorized to accept the service of such inhabitants as they might deem proper; and arrangements were made for a general muster of the people in case of necessity. The meeting then dissolved.

Warren, being a member of this "committee of safety," was one of the watch. The duties of the committee continued until the troops left the town. "From the time of this fatal tragedy," a letter of March 12 says, " a military guard of town militia has been constantly kept in the Town House and Town

[1] The "Boston Gazette" has the following: "London, April 30. A letter from Colonel Dalrymple, at Boston, to a general officer, his friend in England, mentions, that, if the troops had not retired out of the town of Boston at the time they did, the most terrible and fatal consequences would most certainly have happened, as the inhabitants had absolutely determined to risk their lives in an attack upon the military, in order to revenge the cruel and wanton massacre of their countrymen."

Prison, at which some of the most respectable citizens have done duty as common soldiers." In a short time, the two regiments were removed to Castle William, where they continued under the command of Colonel Dalrymple.

These events produced a deep impression on Warren's sensitive nature. Years after, he spoke of the slaughter of the citizens as an unequalled scene of horror, the sad remembrance of which took full possession of his soul. "The sanguinary theatre," he said, "again opens itself to view. The baleful images of terror crowd around me; and discontented ghosts, with hollow groans, appear to solemnize the anniversary of the Fifth of March." And the mark made on John Adams's mind was not less indelible. It is not necessary to accept strong expressions by ardent natures as literal facts, but they often vividly recall the spirit of an era; and this is seen in a few sentences from Adams's letters: "On that night, the foundation of American independence was laid." — " Not the Battle of Lexington or Bunker's Hill, not the Surrender of Burgoyne or Cornwallis, were more important events in American history than the Battle of King Street, on the 5th of March, 1770." — " The death of four or five persons, the most obscure and inconsiderable that could have been found upon the continent, on the 5th of March, 1770, has never yet been forgiven by any part of America."[1]

Warren ascribed the great civic triumph in the removal of the troops to the union of the people. He said, "With united efforts, you urged an immediate departure of the troops from the town; you urged it

---

[1] John Adams's Works, viii. 384, ix. 352; x. 203.

with a resolution which insured success; you obtained your wishes; and the removal of the troops was effected without one drop of their blood being shed by the inhabitants." John Adams estimated the number who took part in the meeting on this day " at ten or twelve thousand," which is probably too high an estimate.

The withdrawal of the troops caused great surprise in England; and there were consultations in the cabinet, and angry crimination in parliament. The opposition characterized it as an indignity put upon Great Britain, and called on the ministry to resent it, or resign their places. The expectation was general, that General Gage, without waiting for the Government, would send a re-enforcement to Boston, and order the whole of the troops into town. "Every one," Governor Bernard wrote, "without exception, says it must be immediately done. Those in opposition are as loud as any. Lord Shelburne told a gentleman, who reported it to me, that it was now high time for Great Britain to act with spirit." The governor advised Hutchinson, that, should it turn out that he had been successful in preventing Captain Preston from being murdered by the mob, "Government might be reconciled to the removal of the troops." There was much outside clamor; and those who indulged in it could not overlook the fact of "six hundred regular troops giving way to two or three thousand common people, who, they say, would not have dared to attack them, if they had stood their ground;" and this class regarded the affair " as a successful bully." Colonel Barré, in the House of Commons, disposed of the question in a few words: "The

officers agreed in sending the soldiers to Castle William: what minister will dare to send them back to Boston?"

The prudent conduct of the people of Boston on the landing of the troops, and their moderation and forbearance on the occasion of the firing upon the people, with their uniform and spirited support of the general cause, elicited the warmest encomiums from the friends of liberty; and, as these encomiums appeared in the press, they were copied into the Boston journals. A few sentences will suffice to show their tone· "Your Bostonians shine with renewed lustre." — "So much wisdom and virtue as hath been conspicuous in Bostonians will not go unrewarded." — "The patriotism of Boston will be revered through every age." — "The noble conduct of the representatives, selectmen, and principal merchants of Boston, in defending and supporting the rights of America and the British Constitution, cannot fail to excite love and gratitude in the heart of every worthy person in the British Empire. They discover a dignity of soul worthy the human mind, which is the true glory of man, and merits the applause of all rational beings. Their names will shine unsullied in the bright records of fame to the latest ages; and unborn millions will rise up, and call them blessed."[1]

Some of the towns now passed resolves expressing similar admiration of the conduct of Boston, which were transmitted under the signature of their officials, and are among the Boston archives. One citation will show their character. The town of Medford

---

[1] These sentences are copied from the Boston papers. The last is reprinted from a Southern journal in a Boston paper of Dec. 18, 1769.

(March 14, 1770), in a letter to the town of Boston, said it was greatly rejoiced that the metropolis had acted with such unexampled moderation as to proceed against the perpetrators of the massacre "according to the common course of justice, and, at the same time, with a laudable and unconquerable firmness of resolution becoming the character of free British subjects, insisting upon the immediate removal of the troops;" and then the letter says, "With joy and gratitude, this town embrace this opportunity also to declare their opinion, that the brave and patriotic spirit which the town of Boston has often shown in the common cause of liberty, and also the laudable, generous, and spirited behavior of its respectable merchants, in these times of trouble, justly merit the thanks of all British America, and of this province and town in particular. And this town do assure them, that they are fully determined to assist the town of Boston, at all times, in every salutary measure they shall adopt for the preservation of our inalienable rights and privileges."

This strain of eulogy on Boston constitutes an interesting feature of these times, and therefore ought to have a place in history. It was not of a local cast, for it appears in several colonies and in England; it was not manufactured by politicians, for it is seen in the private letters of the friends of constitutional liberty which have come to light subsequently to the events; it was not a transient enthusiasm, for the same strain was continued during the years preceding the war. The praise was bestowed on a town small in territory, and comparatively small in population. Such were the cities of Greece in the era of their renown.

"The territories of Athens, Sparta, and their allies," remarks Gibbon, "do not exceed a moderate province of France or England; but, after the trophies of Salamis or Platæa, they expand in our fancy to the gigantic size of Asia, which had been trampled under the feet of the victorious Greeks." No trophies had been gathered in an American Platæa; there was no hero upon whom public affection centered; there was, indeed, little that common constructors of history would consider to be history. Yet it was now written and made common thought by an unfettered press, — "Nobler days nor deeds were never seen than at this time."[1] This was an instinctive appreciation of a great truth; for the real American Revolution was going on in the tidal flow of thought and feeling, and in the formation of public opinion. A people, inspired by visions of better days for humanity, luxuriating in the emotions of hope and faith, yearning for the right, mastering the reasoning on which it was based, were steadily taking their fit place on the national stage, in the belief of the nearness of a mighty historic hour. And their spontaneous praise was for a community heroically acting on national principles and for a national cause. Because of this did they predict that unborn millions would hold up the men of Boston as worthy to be enrolled in the shining record of fame.

---

[1] These words occur in a warm Southern eulogy on Boston, printed in the "Gazette" of Feb. 12, 1770.

CHAPTER VII.

ORATION ON THE MASSACRE.

An Interval of two Years. — The Repeal of the Townsend Act. Apathy of the Community. — Hutchinson and Adams. — Differences between the Popular Leaders. — Warren's Oration. Its Effect.

March, 1770, to March, 1772.

I HAVE traced the career of Warren, as, animated by the ruling passion of the love of country, he sought the press, the club, and the town-meeting as instrumentalities to promote the patriot cause. He appears on the public stage, for the most part, in company with his seniors in years; but, when he rendered his next salient service, he stood alone: it was the delivery of a discourse in commemoration of the massacre. In order to do this utterance justice, it may be well to glance at the state of affairs during an interval of two years.

Much interesting local history succeeded the Sixth of March, as the funeral of the slaughtered inhabitants, the departure of the obnoxious troops, and the trials of the accused soldiers. The superior court wisely decided to postpone the trials for a season: the public, however, were impatient; and Hutchinson relates (March 23, 1770), that " Samuel Adams, William Cooper, Warren, and others, came from Mr. Jones's, where they had dined that day, and a vast concourse of people after them, into the superior court, and harangued the judges," in order to induce them to alter their decision. These occurrences were marked by intense feeling, and the details are quite voluminous; but they were but the sequel of the important events which have been described, and are of the order of facts that make no special impress on public opinion.

Warren took a part in the town-meetings this year. He was a member of a committee appointed to prepare a narrative of the massacre; and, with James Bowdoin and Samuel Pemberton, was selected to send this narrative to prominent characters in England. He was one of a committee to wait on Colonel Dalrymple, and urge a speedy departure of the troops. At the May meeting, he was on the committee to prepare the instructions to the representatives, which deserve a passing remark. These instructions averred that the idea of a lasting union of the colonies lay deep in the heart of every sensible and honest American as one of the most weighty matters; declared there was no one point which ought more to engage their affectionate zeal; inculcated a cordial intercolonial intercourse; and urged that, as the interests of the colonies were so inseparable, nothing was required to cement their political and natural attachment but an intimate communion. This paper was drawn up by Josiah Quincy, jun. Its union sentiment is calculated for all time. To Hutchinson, however, who watched this idea closely, it was poison. He says (May 22, 1770), "Nothing can be more infamous than the Boston instructions. Is it possible they should pass without notice? Young Quincy, who goes by the name of Wilkes Quincy, penned them. He bids fair to be a successor to Otis, and it is much if he does not run mad also." According to a Tory writer, Warren, a like enthusiast for union, had a touch of the same sort of madness; for it was said, "One of our most bawling[1] demagogues and voluminous writers is a crazy doctor."

Warren, in July, was appointed on a committee to consider the state of the town, and transmit a report to England: the same month he was appointed, at a meeting of merchants and others, one of a committee "to consider what might be proper to be done to strengthen the union of the colonies," and to give efficiency to the non-importation agreement; and, in September, he was placed by the town on a committee to devise measures for the promotion of arts, agriculture, and commerce in the province. Interesting as these subjects are, I am unable to give any detail of Warren's special agency in them.

The Townsend Revenue Act was now repealed, it was alleged, on the petition of British merchants, and for the convenience of England, excepting the preamble, asserting a right in parliament to legislate for the colonies in all cases whatsoever, which was retained to save this principle, and the tax on tea, kept to secure its acknowledgment. "I know not what reason," Hutchinson wrote (Oct. 15, 1770), "may make it necessary to continue the duty on tea; but I

---

[1] I cite this from that compilation of the lowest sort of politics, "Sagittarius's Letters (page 9); in which the errors of the patriots, to use an expression of James Lovell, "were written with gall by the pen of malice." This Tory writer does not name Warren, and may refer to Dr. Young.

think the repeal of it, or making the same duty payable in England, is necessary to prevent disorders in the colonies." The idea of making the duty payable in England may have been original with Hutchinson; but the credit of carrying it out by the East-India Company is ascribed to King George.

The non-importation agreement, about which there is a world of matter, now came to an end; and the quantity of tea imported from England was so small, that the tax was virtually a nullity. There was a lull in political affairs: the community became apathetic; and this continued through the year 1771. The town records are brief and tame. The only political matters acted on this year, in public meeting, were a commemoration of the Fifth of March, an answer to a patriotic letter of Dr. Lucas, of Ireland, on the massacre, and a reply to the false publications about the town; and Warren was a member of all the committees that matured the action. Hutchinson wrote (May 24, 1771), — "The faction in this province against the Government is dying; but it dies hard. I have waived all dispute with them upon the general points between the kingdom and the colonies, and have obtained the victory in all the controversy upon points confined to our particular constitution. They are now reduced to personalities, and those of a general nature, — hypocrisy, ambition, [and a] tyrannical disposition."

It was now said that the people of the colonies were weary of their altercations with the mother country, and that a little discreet conduct on both sides would perfectly establish the warm affection felt towards Great Britain.[1] But two good observers,

---

[1] Bancroft, vi. 406.

Hutchinson and Samuel Adams, looked beneath this deceitful surface, and formed a different judgment. Their measure of each other, at this time, is at least curious. Hutchinson doubted whether there was a greater incendiary in the king's dominions than Adams; and Adams wrote of Hutchinson, "It has been his principle from a boy, that mankind are to be governed by the discerning few; and it has ever since been his ambition to be the hero of the few."[1] Hutchinson was a type of conservatism, clinging with sturdy fidelity to the past; Adams, of the spirit of progress, with a noble faith in the future of the race.

Hutchinson saw what he called "the spread of levelling principles," the growing importance of "the commonality," and the tenacity with which the people held on to the right of making their local or municipal law. He continued to misrepresent this right as a claim for exemption from all parliamentary authority; and he now urged, that "parliament must give up its claim to a supreme authority over the colonies, or the colonies must cease from asserting a supreme legislature within themselves." As he saw also such union sentiment as was as common as the day in the press, and was embodied in Quincy's instructions, he wrote that "something must be done, or the colonies will be riveting their principles of independence on parliament, until it will be too late to break them off; the wound might be skinned over, but could never be healed until it was laid open to the bone;" and he wrote, "I dare not trust to pen and ink my thought upon some provisions which might be made by parliament for preventing an unwarrantable combination

[1] Letter to Stephen Sayre, Nov 23. 1770

between the colonies. Ever since the congress in New York, a regular correspondence has been kept up by demagogues in each colony."[1] While he urged that parliament should deal with the union idea, he bent himself to one single point, that of curtailing the popular power as to the local Government, by taking from it, under the authority of royal instructions, functions that had been enjoyed uninterruptedly above a century, and transferring them to the Crown.

Samuel Adams saw this deadly warfare waged on the two primordial ideas of our country's life, — local government and the union, — as clearly as though he had before him the letter-book of Hutchinson, or knew the secret counsels of the ministry; and he felt that there was no peace. The arbitrary dealing of the executive with the general court, in proroguing and dissolving it, and in summoning it to meet at Cambridge, all at the pleasure of His Majesty; the veto of bills concerning local taxation, a thing never before known; and the new doctrines avowed of the right of interference by parliament and by the Crown, — were to him so many proofs of a design to curtail the rights of the people. His eye was fixed on the fountain of this aggression. "The minister," he wrote, "has taken a method, which, in my opinion, has a direct tendency to set up a despotism here, or rather is the thing itself; and that is, by sending instructions to the governor, to be the rule of his Administration, and forbidding him, as the governor

---

[1] Stephen Sayre wrote to S. Adams, Sept. 11, 1770, that Hutchinson's letters were not allowed to be seen by anybody except Lord Hillsborough and his confidential secretary, John Pownal.

declares, to make them known to us; the design of which may be to prevent his ever being made responsible for any measures he may advise, in order to introduce and establish arbitrary power over the colonies." He never was more a moral hero than when a cloud hung over the cause to which his life was devoted; and he never was more active in the press and in private correspondence than he was now. On the failure of the non-importation agreement, he wrote to the patriots of Charleston, S.C., "Let us forget there ever was such a futile combination, and awaken attention to our first grand object, — union in support of constitutional principles." It is related that, on some occasion, probably in the House of Representatives, — the anecdote is fixed in this period, — he wrapped his cloak around him, and exclaimed with vehemence, "I will stand alone: I will oppose this tyranny at the threshold, though the fabric of liberty fall, and I perish in its ruins!"[1]

Though these statesmen saw ideas working on society with the certainty of law, yet they had seasons of hopes and fears, which rose and declined with the things of the hour. Hutchinson, observing the apathy of the people and the divisions of the Whigs, was much encouraged; while Adams judged that "there never was a time when the political affairs of America were in a more dangerous state." There was this difference between these political leaders: Hutchinson's letters show doubt, hesitancy, and vacillation; Adams writes with the confidence, decision, and firmness of one inspired by faith in the ultimate triumph of the right. "I have a firm persuasion,"

[1] S. A. Wells's MSS.

are his words, "that, in every struggle, this country will approve herself as glorious in defending and maintaining her freedom, as she has been heretofore happy in enjoying it."[1]

A few citations from the letters of Hutchinson, who became governor in March, 1771, will show his view of parties and men. "There is now a general appearance of contentment throughout the province; and even here the persons who have made the most disturbance have become of less importance." — "At present, Hancock and Adams are at variance. Some of my friends blow the coals, and I hope to see a good effect." He wrote to the under-secretary of Lord Hillsborough (Oct. 17, 1771), "Your intimation what measures would be approved of by the highest authority, I take very kind, and shall remember that it is in confidence. To answer the purpose proposed, I must have from Hancock some assurance of breaking his connection, before I can give my consent to his election. He is quiet at present, and so are most of the party. All of them, except Adams, abate of their virulence. Adams is the writer in the incendiary newspaper, and would push the continent into a rebellion to-morrow, if it was in his power." And he represents Otis as being subject to a temporary frenzy.

Eliot, on the Whig side, states, as the cause of the collision between the popular leaders, the question of the removal of the general court from Cambridge to Boston; it having refused to proceed with the ordinary business on account of the arbitrary summons

---

[1] Letter to John Wilkes, Dec. 27, 1770. Stephen Sayre wrote to Samuel Adams, Sept. 18, 1770, "I have already done myself the honor of addressing you as the Father of America."

of it by the governor to Cambridge. Hutchinson offered to convene the court at its old place of meeting, the Town House in Boston, "upon certain conditions, which the majority of members saw fit to comply with. Mr. Hancock voted with them. Adams was against the measure, and expressed sentiments in opposition to his friend and colleague. Mr. Hancock was a man impatient of contradiction, and, upon some occasions, indulged in a petulant humor. He could not bear the opposition of even Adams on this question. It was one cause of the alienation between them. That gentleman was cool and determined, hard and unyielding, as well as bold in his argument. He sometimes was sarcastic in his replies; but, upon the subject that then divided the house, he observed the utmost delicacy, and seemed to dread the consequence of this political difference."

Hancock, who was now the idol of the people, was serving on the board of selectmen. "His generosity," Eliot says, "upon all public occasions, and kindness to individuals, were the theme of continued and loud applause. It was said that his heart was as open as the day to acts of beneficence, and that he sunk his fortune in the cause of his country. This was the prevailing idea, and it gave a perfume to the sacrifice." Hancock might have been vain, but he was ever true to the cause; and Hutchinson never obtained from him the assurance that would warrant a bestowal on him of court favor.

Otis's health was declining. A short time after the assault on him by Commissioner Robinson, Otis was asked to appear in a case in the superior court. On refusing, he said that his constitution was gone;

that he had but a little while to live, and must quit business; saying, "I have done much more mischief to my country than can ever be repaired. I meant well, but am now convinced that I was mistaken. Cursed be the day I was born!" This incident is related in an official letter by Hutchinson, who adds the unfeeling remark, that, when Otis found " such talk would hurt his interest, he would be more wicked than ever to recover his character." His mind was impaired, and for this reason he had been left off the representative ticket; but one of the representatives, John Adams, having removed to Braintree, Otis, who seemed to be in better health, was elected in Adams's place, and served his last session in the general court. At times, he was calm and natural; but it soon appeared that his lucid intervals were but flickerings of the expiring lamp. John Adams, at Braintree, relates this incident: "John Chandler, Esq., of Petersham, came into P.'s, in the evening, from Boston, yesterday, and gave us an account of Mr. Otis's conversion to Toryism. Adams was going on in the old road; and Otis started up, and said they had gone far enough in that way, the governor had an undoubted right to carry the court where he pleased, and moved for a committee to represent the inconveniences of sitting there, and for an address to the governor. He was a good man: the ministers said so, the justices said so, and it must be so, and moved to go on with the business; and the house voted every thing he moved for. Boston people say he is distracted." During this session, his friends were obliged to bear him, worse than ever, into the country; and his career was substantially ended.

John Adams, after residing three years in Boston, during which, he avers, he cheerfully sacrificed interest, health, ease, and pleasure in serving the people, and stood by them "much longer than they would stand by themselves," said that he had learned wisdom from experience, meant certainly to become more retired and cautious, and to mind his farm and his office. Exclaiming, "Farewell, politics!" he removed to Braintree to gain strength for subsequent years of noble service to his country. "I was asked," Bernard wrote to Hutchinson, "by one of the ministry, to-day, who that *John* Adams was? I gave as favorable an answer as I could, but not such as would have justified the appointment to him of an office of trust." Adams became a looker-on in politics, keeping his office in Boston; and his diary supplies glimpses of men and things in the town. He mentions meeting, at clubs and parties, Otis, Hancock, and Adams, which shows that the political differences did not interrupt social intercourse. As Adams was one day taking a pipe with Judge Trowbridge, the judge remarked, Adams relates, "You will never get your health till your mind is at ease. If you tire yourself with business, but especially with politics, you won't get well." Adams said, "I don't meddle with politics nor think about them."—"Except," said the judge, "by writing in the papers."—"I'll be sworn," replied Adams, "I have not wrote one line in the newspapers these two years!"

Thomas Cushing, speaker of the House of Representatives, was now widely known in England by his name being signed to the public papers, and was spoken of there as the leader of the Whigs in this country; but though his character and position gave him influence, yet, Dr. Eliot says, he had less political zeal than Otis or Adams or Hancock, and was not esteemed the leader here. He is represented at this time, by John Adams, as inclined to temporize;[1] but an incident shows that he could be spirited. "Cushing, last night," Hutchinson says,[2] "on being asked if he was not afraid of a *quo warranto* against the charter, on account of a refusal of the house to do business, answered, "There had been none since the reign of the Stuarts, and they dared not send one here."

Warren, at thirty, moved in the circle formed by these characters, and others not less worthy, enjoying their friendship and respect. He rented the house on Hanover Street, on the site of the present American House, which he occupied during the remainder of his life; and he was a member of the Congregational Church in Brattle Street, of which Dr. Cooper was the pastor. He had (1772) two sons and two daughters. A negro slave made a part of his household, who was perhaps a family servant, whom he took when he hired the house.[3] He was

---

[1] John Adams's Works, ii. 278. [2] Aug. 4, 1770.

[3] I am indebted to Dr. S. A. Green for two papers which have the autograph of Warren. Joshua Green owned the house which Warren rented.

"Boston, June 28th, 1770. I the Subscriber having this day purchas'd a Negro Boy of Joshua Green have made the follow[gs:] conditions with him vizt. That I will add Ten pounds Lawfull money to be paid in Potter's Ware manufactur'd in this Town, in three years to the Thirty pounds first agreed for if in 3 months from this date I shall think the negro worth the money & if I do not think him worth the additional ten pounds I will reconvey him to s[d] Green he return[s] the two notes I gave him for the negro, one for 17£ & the other for 13£, both of them bearing date herewith.   JOSEPH WARREN."

"It is also further agreed that in case of my decease that the withinmention'd negro shall become the property of said Green he delivering up my two notes.
JOSEPH WARREN."

in the full circle of medical practice, as is attested by his bills and a portion of his day-book extant.[1] His brother John, who had just graduated from Harvard College, was with him as a medical student; and a number of young men pursued their professional studies under his direction.[2]

In the Ewer Papers, in the archives of the New-England Historic-Genealogical Society, is the following paper, illustrative of the times.

"Boston, April 3, 1770. Received this day from Thomas Fayerweather, Esq., five black men-servants, — Cato, Charleston, Jack, Prince, and Boston, — upon the terms following: We agree to find them meat, drink, clothing, washing, and lodging, &c., and to pay the doctor's bill in case of sickness; as also to make good the loss of either or all of the above-named black men-servants in case of death; and, farther, we agree to allow and pay to the said Thomas Fayerweather, Esq., one shilling l. money per week for hire of the above-named servants.

"Wit. Josh Carnes. Witness our hands,
"BENJ. & JOHN GUDLY."

At this period, there was effort made not merely to abolish the slave-trade, but slavery. The following letter, from Governor Hutchinson to Lord Hillsborough, is instructive and suggestive: —

"BOSTON, May, 1771.

"MY LORD, — The bill which prohibits the importation of negro slaves appeared to me to come within His Majesty's instructions to Sir Francis Bernard, which restrains the governor from assenting to any laws of a new and unusual nature. I doubted beside whether the chief motive to this bill, which, it is said, was a scruple upon the minds of the people, in many parts of the province, of the lawfulness, in a merely moral respect, of so great a restraint of liberty, was well founded; slavery, by the provincial laws, giving no right to the life of the servant: and a slave here is considered as a servant would be who had bound himself for a term of years exceeding the ordinary term of human life; and I do not know that it has been determined he may not have a property in goods, notwithstanding he is called a slave.

"I have reason to think these three bills will be again offered to me in another session, I having intimated that I would transmit them to England, to know His Majesty's pleasure concerning them

"THO. HUTCHINSON.

" The Rt. Hon. the Earl of HILLSBOROUGH."

[1] The town of Boston paid Warren a bill, in 1771, for service rendered from May 3, 1770, to May, 1771; one item of which is seven hundred and thirty visits during this period. Ellis Ames, Esq., loaned to me fragments of Warren's daybook, the earliest date in which is Jan. 13, 1771; and the last is Jan. 31, 1775.

[2] Dr. Joseph Warren, memorable for patriotism and public virtue, was in full circle of medical practice, and educated a number of young gentlemen to the profession. — *Thacher's Medical Biography*, 24.

Though of marked amiability of character, he was naturally high-tempered, impulsive, and quick to resent an insult: at times he was passionate. One evening, when the British troops were quartered in the town, he was challenged in a burly way by a sentinel, when Warren knocked him down. He could be vehement in the expressions of feeling. On an occasion when his spirit was stirred by the taunts that British officers were uttering on the Americans, he said to William Eustis, subsequently the Governor of Massachusetts, "These fellows say we won't fight: by heavens, I hope I shall die up to my knees in blood!"

I have met with no criticisms on Warren's public conduct, or any accounts of differences between him and the patriots; and the manner in which all his contemporaries refer to him warrants the remark, that those who knew him the best were the most attached to him. Biography is something more than a strain of panegyric; but a warm contemporary panegyric, when supported by the tenor of a life, may be used in making up an estimate of character. The following strain, in an elegy printed about a fortnight after Warren's death, indicates that he attained an enviable reputation as a man and a physician: —

> "Sure, godlike Warren, on thy natal hour,
> Some star propitious shed its brightest power;
> By Nature's hand with taste and genius formed;
> Thy generous breast with every virtue warmed;
> Thy mind imbued with sense, thy form with grace,
> And all thy virtues pencilled in thy face.
> Grave Wisdom marked thee as his favorite child,
> And on thy youth indulgent Science smiled;
> Well pleased, she led thee to her sacred bower,
> And to thy hands consigned her healing power."

In the life-like diary of John Adams, there are glimpses of Warren, as he mingled with his friends, during these two years, in the joys of social life, loving and beloved. Here Warren is seen receiving the future president of the United States at his own table; dining in the historic Hancock House, on Beacon Street, with Cooper, Adams, and others, when they were treated with green tea, which Adams hoped was imported from Holland, but did not know; making one of a party at Samuel Adams's house, where Otis was more than usually social, steady, and rational; meeting with "the Club," a brilliant circle of politicians and divines, among whom were the two Coopers and the Adamses, where he doubtless enjoyed the dispute that arose about wit, in which Dr. Cooper cited the proverb, that "an ounce of mother wit was worth a pound of clergy," and Otis repeated another, — perhaps with feeling, — that "an ounce of prudence was worth a pound of wit;" and dining with "The Merchants' Club," at the Coffee House, who had met here for twenty years.[1]

I have stated that Warren was a member of two of the political clubs, a select circle of the prominent politicians, and the North-end Caucus. Dr. Eliot says that one of these clubs, "in 1772, agreed to increase their number, and to meet in a large room, invite a number of substantial mechanics to join them, and hold a kind of caucus *pro bono publico*. They met in a house near the North Battery, and more than sixty

---

[1] When Josiah Quincy, jun., was requested to defend the British soldiers arrested for firing on the people, he says he refused, "until advised and urged to undertake it by an Adams, a Hancock, a Molineux, a Cushing, a Henshaw, a Pemberton, a Warren, a Cooper, and a Phillips." — *Life of Josiah Quincy, jun.*, 37.

were present at the first meeting. Their regulations were drawn up by Dr. Warren and another gentleman, and they never did any thing important without consulting him and his particular friends. It answered a good purpose to get such a number of mechanics together; and, though a number of Whigs of the first character in the town were present, they always had a mechanic for moderator, generally one who could carry many votes by his influence. By this body of men, the most important matters were decided. They agreed who should be in town offices, in the general court, in provincial congress, from Boston." This caucus met about two years in the house near the North Battery, and then at the Green Dragon Tavern in Union Street. Dr. Eliot was "assured, by some of the most prominent characters of this caucus, that they were guided by the prudence and skilful management of Dr. Warren, who, with all his zeal and irritability, was a man calculated to carry on any secret business; and that no man ever did manifest more vigilance, circumspection, and care." In this way, the useful instrumentality of the club was organized for more efficient service than ever.

The press continued its high-toned course, though the public mind continued calm. "We have been free from disturbance this winter," Hutchinson wrote in March. "The scurrility of the newspapers has been much as it used to be, and about as much regarded." This apathy in the people, with the divisions among the Whig leaders, led him at times to ignore the steady setting of the current towards doctrines which he held to be fatal, and to build up a hope on things that were really transient. "I am apt enough," he now wrote (Feb. 12, 1772), "to look on the dark side of the prospect; but at present I have more spirits to encounter what is before me, or else really there is a better prospect than there has been of some good degree of peace and order, without giving up any part of the prerogative." It seemed hardly possible that the community, now so quiet, was the same, which, two years before, had been stirred on the waves of a fearful passion by the baptismal flow of innocent blood for American liberty.

The town had determined to have an annual commemoration of the massacre. An influential committee[1] chosen to select the orator, unanimously selected Warren, who was thus called upon to become the exponent of the community, when the Whig cause was far from being hopeful. On the anniversary morning (March 5, 1772), with his mind filled with the thought he was to utter, he might have read in the Tory organ, the "News Letter," an able communication, filling one side and a half, which commenced in the following strain: "Among the many novel doc-

---

[1] This committee, chosen at a town-meeting, April 2, 1771, were Thomas Cushing, Richard Dana, John Hancock, Ebenezer Story, Samuel Adams, Benjamin Church, Samuel Pemberton. At this time, Church was playing a treacherous game (Bancroft, vi. 409). When Bernard was governor, he says in his letters that he had authentic sources of information, which he was under obligations to keep secret, but gives no names.

On the 2d of March, 1772, there was a petition to the selectmen for a town-meeting on the 5th. William Phillips's name is at its head, and it was numerously signed. It stated that the committee on the selection of the orator had unanimously chosen Dr. Joseph Warren, but had made no report to the town; and the subscribers conceived "it of high importance that the proceedings of the committee should be ratified by the town with as much union and formality as they were originated, as well as that the town should take some order touching the regulations of said affair," and asked for a legal town-meeting. The selectmen, on the same day, issued a warrant for a meeting, to be held in Faneuil Hall, at nine o'clock, to receive the report of the committee.

trines broached by our newspaper-politicians, there is none more wild and chimerical, or big with greater mischiefs to the colonies, than this, — that the king, with each and every of the colonial assemblies, form so many complete and entire separate governments, independent of the realm of England." This was partisan misrepresentation, made in the face of constant denials by the Whigs, that they entertained such ideas of independence. The just division line between the purely colonial and the imperial was not precisely defined in written law, and because political science had not reached a sufficiently advanced point to define it; but it was practically understood in America. The colonists had grasped that idea of local self-government which is now pronounced to be the basis of constitutional freedom,[1] and which that admirable statesman, Sir William Molesworth, fifteen years ago, advocated for the British colonies with such a signal triumph, that the "London Times" called him the liberator and regenerator of the colonial empire of Great Britain.

On this anniversary, the town met in legal meeting, in Faneuil Hall, at nine o'clock, when Richard Dana was chosen the moderator. He was an eminent lawyer, of unblemished private character and large public spirit, whose name often occurs in connection with the proceedings of the patriots. It happened to be the

[1] May, in his excellent "Constitutional History of England," ii. 460, says, "That Englishmen have been qualified for the enjoyment of political freedom, is mainly due to those ancient local institutions by which they have been trained to self-government. . . . England alone among the nations of the earth has maintained a constitutional polity ; and her liberties may be ascribed, above all things, to her free local institutions. . . . Thousands of small communities have been separately trained to self-government; taxing themselves, through themselves, for local objects."

forenoon of the ancient "Thursday Lecture;" and, when the town voted to adjourn to the Old South, it fixed half past twelve to assemble again. At this hour, the town was called to order in the church. The pulpit was covered with black cloth. "That capacious house," the "Gazette" says, "was thronged with a very respectable assembly, consisting of the inhabitants and many of the clergy, not only of this, but of the neighboring towns." The "News Letter" says "the vast concourse was composed of both sexes." The object which the popular leaders had in view was to rouse public attention to danger, when aggression was insidious and the aggressors were adroit.

The orator, after a remark on the causes of the mighty revolutions in the rise and fall of States, which strike the mind with solemn surprise, paid a tribute to civil government. When it had for its object the strength and security of all, it was one of the richest blessings to mankind and ought to be held in the highest veneration. In new-formed communities, the grand design of this institution is most generally understood, because that equality which prevailed among them is remembered, and every one feels it to be his interest and duty to preserve inviolate a constitution founded on free principles, on which the public safety depends. It was a noble fidelity to such a free constitution that raised Rome to her summit of glory, gave her peace at home, and extended her dominion abroad; but, when this fidelity decayed, she became the scorn and derision of nations, "and a monument of this eternal truth, that public happiness depends on a virtuous and unshaken attachment to a free constitution."

The orator next urged that it was this noble attachment to a free constitution that inspired the first settlers of this country, who, rather than carry on a civil war to obtain it, left their native land, and landed on this barren soil, which they cultivated and defended. At length, after the struggles between liberty and slavery, during the tyrannic reign of the Stuarts, the connection between this colony and Great Britain was settled by the compact of the charter, which secured to this province, as absolutely as any human instrument could do it, all the liberties and immunities of British subjects. "And it is undeniably true, that the greatest and most important right of a British subject is, that he shall be governed by no laws but those to which, either in person or by his representative, he hath given his consent. This is the grand basis of British freedom; it is interwoven with the constitution; and, whenever this is lost, the constitution must be destroyed.'

The orator then considered the division of this constitution copied here into three branches, with the characteristics of monarchy, aristocracy, and democracy, composing the law-making power, — the governor representing the king; the council, the lords; and the House of Representatives, the House of Commons, in which only a tax can originate: and only when the consent of these branches was obtained was taxation legal. In the name of justice, how could the late acts of parliament taxing America be constitutionally binding? Are the members of the House of Commons the democracy of the province? If not, can they originate a bill taxing the people here? Are the lords the peers of America? If not, no act of theirs can be said to be that of our aristocratic branch. "The power of the monarchic branch, we with pleasure acknowledge, resides in the king, who may act either in person or by his representative." A proclamation for raising money in America, issued by the king's sole authority, would be equally consistent with the constitution, and therefore equally binding with the late acts of parliament imposing a revenue; for all their validity arose from his approval. "By what figure of rhetoric can the inhabitants of Massachusetts be called free subjects, when they are obliged to obey implicitly such laws as are made for them by men three thousand miles off, whom they know not and whom they never have empowered to act for them." Or how can they be said to have property, if such a foreign body can oblige them to deliver a part or the whole of their substance without their consent. If in this way they may be taxed, "even in the smallest trifle, they may also, without their consent, be deprived of every thing they possess, although never so valuable, never so dear."

The orator then dwelt on the means used to enforce these acts, — a standing army, with the intention to overawe the inhabitants, — and portrayed its baneful influences. He dwelt on the massacre, the removal of the troops, and the trial of the soldiers. He commented on the astonishing infatuation in the British councils, which dictated the repeated attacks on the freedom of the colonies, and, even from the point of interest, could see no gains from the policy which they might not secure by the smooth channel of commerce. The trade of the colonies contributed to the amazing increase of the riches of Britain; and it was the earnest desire of people here that "she might continue to enjoy the same emoluments until her streets were paved with American gold."

The orator closed in a fervent strain on liberty. He expressed a confidence that the justice of the American cause would finally open the eyes of the British nation to their true interest, and not suffer their honor to be sported away by a capricious ministry. "They nourish in their own breasts a noble love of Liberty; they hold her dear; and they know that all who have once possessed her charms had rather die than suffer her to be torn from their embraces." The orator expressed confidence that his countrymen had a like love of liberty, and had the spirit to defend it. There is so much of the ruling passion of his life — his own lofty spirit — in the closing strain, that I refrain from making an abstract, but cite it entire: —

"I am confident that you never will betray the least want of spirit, when called upon to guard your freedom. None but they who set a just value upon the blessings of Liberty are worthy to enjoy her. Your illustrious fathers were her zealous votaries. When the blasting frowns of Tyranny drove her from public view, they clasped her in their arms, they cherished her in their generous bosoms, they brought her safe over the rough ocean, and fixed her seat in this then dreary wilderness; they nursed her infant age with the most tender care; for her sake they patiently bore the severest hardships; for her support they underwent the most rugged toils; in her defence they boldly encountered the most alarming dangers; neither the ravenous beasts that ranged the woods for prey, nor the more furious savages of the wilderness, could damp their ardor! Whilst with one hand they broke the stubborn glebe, with the other they grasped their weapons, ever ready to protect her from danger. No sacrifice, not even their own blood, was esteemed too rich a libation for her altar! God prospered their valor; they preserved her brilliancy unsullied; they enjoyed her whilst they lived, and, dying, bequeathed the dear inheritance to your care. And, as they left you this glorious legacy, they have undoubtedly transmitted to you some portion of their noble spirit, to inspire you with virtue to merit her, and courage to preserve her: you surely cannot, with such examples before your eyes as every page of the history of this country affords,[1] suffer your liberties to be ravished from you by lawless force, or cajoled away by flattery and fraud.

"The voice of your fathers' blood cries to you from the ground, 'My sons, scorn to be slaves! In vain we met the frowns of tyrants; in vain we left our native land; in vain we crossed the boisterous ocean, found a new world, and prepared it for the happy residence of Liberty. In vain we toiled, in vain we fought, we bled in vain, if you, our offspring, want valor to repel the assaults of her invaders!' Stain not the glory of your worthy ancestors; but, like them, resolve never to part with your birthright: be wise in your deliberations, and determined in your exertions for the preservation of your liberties. Follow not the dictates of passion, but enlist yourselves under the sacred banner of reason; use every method in your power to secure your rights; at least prevent the curses of posterity from being heaped upon your memories.

"If you, with united zeal and fortitude, oppose the torrent of oppression; if you feel the true fire of patriotism burning in your breasts; if you from your souls despise the most gaudy dress that slavery can wear; if you really prefer the lonely cottage (whilst blessed with liberty) to gilded palaces, surrounded with the ensigns of slavery, — you may have the fullest assurance that Tyranny, with her whole accursed train, will hide their hideous heads in confusion, shame, and despair. If you perform your part, you must have the strongest confidence that the same Almighty Being who protected your pious and venerable forefathers, who enabled them to turn a barren wilderness into a fruitful field, who so often made bare his arm for their salvation, will still be mindful of you their offspring.

"May this Almighty Being graciously preside in all our councils! May he direct us to such measures as he himself shall approve and be pleased to bless! May we ever be a people favored of God! May our land be a land of Liberty, the seat of virtue, the asylum of the oppressed, a name and a praise in the whole earth, until the last shock of time shall bury the empires of the world in one common undistinguished ruin!"

[1] "At simul heroum laudes, et facta parentis
Jam legere et quæ sit poteris cognoscere virtus." — VIRG.

In this effort, the orator met the expectations of his friends. Hutchinson, on remarking on the increase of the popularity of Warren, says, "Though he gained no great applause for his oratorical abilities, yet the fervor, which is the most essential part of such compositions, could not fail in its effect on the minds of the great concourse of people present."[1] The press was more generous in its praise. "The orator," the "Gazette" says, "had the unanimous applause of his audience;" and the "News Letter" (Tory) adopted these words. The town voted him their thanks, and requested a copy of his oration for the press.[2] It was printed, and in this form contributed to the formation of public opinion.

It will be observed, that it was Warren's main purpose to develop and defend the doctrine as to the power of the colonial legislatures, or of internal government, which Hutchinson regarded to be of so dangerous a tendency, that he urged that its advocates should be made subject, by a special act of par-

[1] History, iii. 348.
[2] "At a meeting of the freeholders and other inhabitants of the town of Boston, duly qualified and legally assembled in Faneuil Hall, and from thence adjourned to the Old South Meeting-house, on Thursday, the 5th day of March, Anno Domini 1772, —

"*Voted unanimously*, That the moderator, Richard Dana, Esq., the Honorable John Hancock, Esq., Mr. Samuel Adams, Joseph Jackson, Esq., Mr. Henderson Inches, Mr. Daniel Jeffries, and Mr. William Molineux, be and hereby are appointed a committee to return the thanks of this town to Joseph Warren, Esq., for the oration just now delivered by him, at their request, in commemoration of the horrid massacre perpetrated on the evening of the 5th of March, 1770, by a party of soldiers of the Twenty-ninth Regiment, and to desire a copy thereof for the press.

"Attest: WILLIAM COOPER, *Town-clerk.*"

"GENTLEMEN, — The generous candor of my fellow-citizens prevails on me to give a copy of what was yesterday delivered, for the press.

"I am, gentlemen, with much respect, your most humble servant,
"JOSEPH WARREN."

liament, to fines, imprisonment and disqualification for office. Underlying the ornate style, the fervor, and at times extravagant metaphor, there were frankness, clearness of thought, sincerity, strength of argument, and, as was seen in his early Letter,[1] the ruling passion of his life,—a warm love of country. Behind the oration was the man. Warren *was* a patriot, and he spoke the timely word of a patriot.

[1] See page 20.

CHAPTER VIII.

COMMITTEES OF CORRESPONDENCE.

WARREN IN TOWN-MEETINGS. — THE PROGRESS OF EVENTS. — HUTCHINSON AND ADAMS. — THE POPULAR LEADERS. — THE QUESTION OF THE JUDGES' SALARIES. — A TOWN-MEETING. — COMMITTEE OF CORRESPONDENCE. — REPORT ON THE RIGHTS OF THE PEOPLE. — ITS EFFECTS.

MARCH, 1772, TO JANUARY, 1773.

WARREN rendered his next great service in company with his brother patriots. They continued on the defensive. It was the steady purpose of the political party who now ruled England, and for sixty years "maintained all that was bigoted, and persecuted all that was liberal,"[1] to establish an imperial despotism in America: it was the object of the patriots to protect

---

[1] Earl Russell, in his valuable introduction to the last edition (1865) of his "Essay on the English Government and Constitution," writing of 1829, says: "The political party which for sixty years had swayed, with very brief intervals, the destinies of the State; which had led the nation to the American and the French wars; which had resisted all reform and protected all abuse; which had maintained all that was bigoted, and persecuted all that was liberal, — broke down." Cooke, in his "History of Party," says (iii. 588) of the Whigs, "They came into office determined to clear away the foul deposits of nearly seventy years of Toryism." In writing of 1830, he says (iii. 578), "Within a very few years, the daily journals have sprung from mere chronicles of robberies upon Hounslow Heath . . . to powerful and thoroughly organized engines for the dissemination of party principles and the universal distribution of political knowledge." In a note he says, "The Tories heard the wind approaching," and cites the following as a groan from the Tory "Quarterly Review:" — "We cannot help expressing our apprehension, that both education and reading have been pushed too far among the lower classes." These things ought to be remembered by Americans in justice to their own statesmen.

and perpetuate their republican institutions. "Americans," it was said precisely and truly in the press, "though represented by their enemies to be in a state of insurrection, mean nothing more than to support those constitutional rights to which the laws of God and nature entitle them." For this the popular leaders now sought union. As they labored in this cause, they did not expect to reap the fruit on the day they sowed the seed, but watched and waited for the growth of public opinion; and, when this had ripened, they aimed to clothe the union sentiment with power by the organization of committees of correspondence. Warren, by going hand in hand with Samuel Adams, identified his name with this vital measure.

Warren was on the usual committee, at the May town-meeting, to instruct the representatives, the election canvass of whom had been uncommonly spirited, on account of an attempt made to prevent the return of Samuel Adams, which was unsuccessful; and the circumstance rendered the patriot dearer to the people. Warren was also on a large committee, raised to consider the tenure of the judges' salaries, which was now much agitated, and in which a vital principle was involved. It was proposed to make the compensation of these officials depend on the Crown, and through the alarming mode of royal instructions, instead of keeping on in the old custom of having this matter determined by the legislature. The committee reported, "that they could not agree upon any set of instructions." Nor could the town agree, after long debate, to raise a new committee; and it voted to postpone the whole subject.

The patriots, in the conviction that unity was their

strength and glory, were urging in the press a mutual free correspondence and a union of the colonies, preparatory to another convention and congress.[1] There were differences of opinion among the popular leaders, as was indicated in the action of the town-meeting. The Tories used the failure of the non-importation scheme to foment these divisions. The session of the general court, which Hutchinson adjourned from Cambridge to Boston, did not improve the situation of the popular cause. "The session is at length over," Samuel Adams writes.[2] "I have been, as I expected, plagued almost to death with the dubitations of Whigs, and the advantages the Tories constantly make of them. As we have been adherents of each other, and I believe ever shall, you have shared with me the curses of Tories on the Commencement Day, when confusion to me and my adherents was given as a toast." And the patriot added, "This will appear the greater honor done me, as it succeeded the health of Bute, North, Hillsborough, and Bernard." Warren was certainly one of the adherents of Samuel Adams; for, whoever may have doubted and hesitated, he was never undecided, and was ever ready for action.

Months passed on, however, and no exigency seemed to require a town-meeting. The press, under the control of the popular leaders, teemed with proofs

[1] Fervidus, in the "Boston Gazette," May 18, 1772, addressing "all true English American patriots," says, "The important things which are humbly recommended to your attention are exemplary union, mutual free correspondence, invariable steadiness, and constant endeavors, in the circles of your respective stations, to illuminate and excite the people." — "Thus prepare the way for another con———n (when requisite), and a con———ss too, in which, it is hoped, the pr———nt will not betray his trust and his country. . . Unity is always our strength and glory."

[2] Samuel Adams to James Warren, July 16, 1772.

of their intelligent judgment of passing events; so that much of their speculation reads now like fulfilled prophecy. They boldly pushed evil principles to their legitimate results, and sounded the alarm of fresh aggressions on popular rights. They said, "This country must do something more than either reason or write, or it will soon be the most miserable and ignominious of the earth"[1] It was urged in ringing tones, that, after all, the only solid guaranty for the security of public liberty was a union of the colonies. I have no means of specifying Warren's share of this service of the press, in rousing the spirit of the people up to the mark of a national movement.

Still, the most spirited appeals in the press failed to excite the public mind and produce unusual action.[2] The Administration had managed its side so adroitly as to have lulled the people into a false security, and the tameness seemed to be well nigh insurmountable. "The grand design of our adversaries is," Samuel Adams wrote, "to lull us into security, and make us easy while the acts remain in force which would prove fatal to us." An event was needed to rouse the people. It was now reported that the Fourteenth Regiment, which had remained in Castle William, was soon to be removed to Boston and encamped on the Common, when petitions were presented to the selectmen for a town-meeting; the name of Samuel Adams being at the head of one, and that of Warren near it. The selectmen issued a warrant for a meeting; but,

[1] Boston Gazette, July 6, 1772.
[2] There was a similar lull of parties in England. Burke wrote, July 31, 1771, "After the violent ferment in the nation, a deadness and vapidity has succeeded." Lord Mahon (v. 301) says this lull may be said to have continued nearly three years.

as the report was contradicted, the warrant was revoked.[1]

In spite of the steady aggression of arbitrary power, town and country remained tranquil. However the commissioners of the customs might have irritated the commercial world, by the use of writs of assistance, when smuggling was pronounced patriotism, no great general grievance stirred the body of the people of Massachusetts, to say nothing of the other colonies. The statutes interdicting trade and prohibiting domestic manufacture were dead letters; customs and laws, in other countries arbitrary and oppressive, had no foothold in America; no tenth of the product of labor was exacted as a tax; no secret process, as in France, abducted idolized leaders; no attempt had been made to carry the popular champions to London

---

[1] The petition which was headed by Samuel Adams and Warren is dated June 26, and is as follows:—

"GENTLEMEN,—A report has been propagated in this town, within a few days past, that the Fourteenth Regiment, now in garrison in Castle William, is soon to be encamped on Boston Common.

"This report is alarming to us, and must be so to every man who recollects with just indignation the horrors of the evening of the 5th of March, 1770. If the report is well grounded, it requires the immediate attention of the inhabitants of the town; or, if we are to suppose the design is only to try the temper of the town, it is of the greatest importance that it may appear to the world that the same spirit prevails which actuated the town the day following that fatal evening. In either case, we think a meeting of the town is necessary; and therefore earnestly request that you, gentlemen, would call one with all speed, that the minds of the inhabitants may be known concerning the measures proper to be taken on this occasion."

Another petition is dated June 28, and is as follows:—

"To the Selectmen of the Town of Boston.

"GENTLEMEN,—Inasmuch as we are informed that Mr. James Forrest and others have reported that the Fourteenth Regiment, now at Castle William, is soon to encamp upon the Common in this town,—

"We desire you would, without delay, call a meeting of the town, to know what is to be done on this matter; for we shall not like to see again our streets stained with the blood of our brethren."

Tower; there had been no arrests; each colony had met, for the most part, with success, the strain on its local government; the action in the spirit of tyranny was insidious; and the people, especially the yeomanry, who were unmolested in their individual and communal freedom, were enjoying a season of rare material prosperity. Experience shows, that, however thoroughly vital principles may be grasped, or however tenaciously they may be held, mankind do not risk the solid blessings of peace, practical liberty, and good government, for the sake of a principle however sound, or to put down an abstraction however false, but are rather disposed to suffer while evils are sufferable. The state of things in the colonies illustrates the correctness of this sentence of the Declaration. The policy of the ministry was judged to be fatal to popular rights; yet it needed sharper aggressions on them to stir the popular depths and justify measures that might affect life, fortune, and honor.

A change was now made in the American department of the ministry. Lord Hillsborough was forced by his colleagues to resign, and Lord Dartmouth was appointed to his place. Hutchinson said, "No minister ever went out of office with greater honor." Adams said, "He has the curses of the disinterested and better part of the colonists." His insult to Franklin shows meanness, and his haughty exercise of arbitrary power proves that he deserved the scathing contemporary criticism. Lord Dartmouth, amiable and of high personal character, had been friendly to the colonies, which, in reality, meant nothing more in his class than to concede that they had a claim to be well governed. The hope, however, was indulged that he would recognize their right to govern themselves. But it was the purpose of the king and the Tory party to consolidate power in the colonies at the expense of the popular element; and arbitrary royal instructions soon made it plain that the ministry had no intention of yielding the principle of parliamentary supremacy, and that the king's prerogative was not to be held as an abstraction. A feature, which, on Hutchinson's appointment, was termed a novelty,[1] it became evident was the settled purpose of the ministry.

Lord Dartmouth now advised Governor Hutchinson that the king, in order to secure the real dependence of local officials on the Crown, had the right to provide for their salaries; and that the compensation of the judges of the superior court was placed on a footing which made them independent of grants by the general court. This instruction was regarded as fresh proof that the party in power intended to persist in aggression on republican customs and laws with the consistency of system. Still, this aggression was not of a nature to rouse the public mind; nor were the popular leaders agreed on the action which the exigency required. The divisions indicated in the May town-meeting, already referred to, continued. These, however, rather touched matters of expediency than of principle; for there do not appear to have been

---

[1] In "Captain Robson," from London, arrived His Majesty's several commissions, appointing the Hon. Thomas Hutchinson, Esq., governor and commander-in-chief in and over this province; the Hon. Andrew Oliver, Esq., lieutenant-governor; and the Hon. Thomas Flucker, Esq., secretary. It is said that the two former of these gentlemen are to have salaries annually paid to them out of the American revenue, independent of the people of the province; which, if it be true, is a novelty which claims the serious attention of this and the other colonies. — *Boston Gazette, March* 11, 1771.

radical differences among the friends of the popular cause. It is not difficult to state with a good degree of precision the relations of the more prominent actors at this time to passing events. Otis had substantially completed the service which makes his fame so rich and his name so dear to his country; Hancock, still at variance with Samuel Adams, was averse to taking unusual action; Cushing, who was not of the class of positive men, was in favor of trusting to an increase of population — the masterly inactivity policy — for an ultimate solution of the question in favor of the colonies; John Adams, thirsty for learning, and bent on achieving triumphs at the bar, still kept aloof from politics, and had so planned his future, that he hoped, though vainly, to avoid even thinking of them; Molineux, though zealous, reliable, and bold, does not rank in the class of leaders; and the selectmen, — Austin, Marshall, Scollay, and Newell, all but Oliver Wendell — shared in Hancock's hesitancy. Others, however, were for decisive measures. Josiah Quincy, jun., was urging, through the press, the necessity of immediate action; Warren[1] heartily sym-

[1] Wednesday last being the festival of St. John the Baptist, the Most Worshipful Joseph Warren, Esq., Provincial Grand Master of Ancient, Free, and Accepted Masons, attended by his grand officers, and the masters, wardens, and brethren of the Lodges under his jurisdiction, — viz., St. Andrew's and Massachusetts Lodges, held in this town, the Tyrian Lodge, held at Gloucester, and St. Peter's Lodge, held at Newburyport, clothed in the jewels and badges of their several offices, — marched in procession from Concert Hall to Christ Church, where a very suitable and pertinent discourse was delivered by the Rev. Brother Fayerweather, of Narragansett, from 1 Cor. v. 11, which was received with universal approbation by a numerous and polite audience.

When the service was ended, they proceeded to Masons' Hall, where an elegant entertainment was provided in the garden adjoining said house, under a large canopy erected for that purpose; and the remainder of the day was dedicated to the purposes of benevolence and social festivity. — *Boston Gazette, June* 29, 1772.

pathized with this view, and was soon to show that his whole soul was bent on politics; Samuel Adams lived in the contemplation of public affairs; and, down to the Declaration of Independence, by his weight of character, bore a relation to the American cause like that which Pym, with his massive strength, sustained in the English Revolution. He was one of those rare men in whom theory is so thoroughly rooted, that they stand as a type, and yet in whom practical sense is so predominant, that they apprehend and reflect the paramount want of a time. His vigilance was sleepless. His efforts were untiring. His soul was energized with the purpose of saving the liberties of his country. He viewed the proposed change in the judicial tenure as another violation of vital constitutional principles, and as designed to aid in the subjugation of " a people," he said, "who, of all the people on the earth, deserved most to be free." He urged, as the pressing want, a union of the colonies for the support of their constitutional rights. For this his spirit hungered and thirsted, and only in this could he see strength and future triumph.

Meantime Governor Hutchinson watched with an anxious eye the progress of events. The divisions in the popular ranks and the recriminations in the press were his warrant for writing (June 22, 1772), "The union of the colonies is pretty well broke. I hope I shall never see it renewed. Indeed, our Sons of Liberty, for their illiberal treatment of all in authority as for their shuffling in the late non-importation project, are hated and despised by their former brethren in New York and Pennsylvania; and it must be something very extraordinary ever to reconcile them."

Hutchinson saw the doctrine as to the power of the local legislatures, affecting, he said, all the executive parts of the administration of affairs, and constantly gaining ground; and he looked upon this doctrine as being fatal to the theory of the supremacy of parliament, which, he says, was the all-in-all of his own politics. If he was often a shrewd observer of the progress of ideas, he proved but an indifferent prophet on the signs of the times. Circumstances had so warped his judgment as to the habit and genius of his countrymen, that he predicted they would discard this doctrine, if the British nation, with one voice, would condemn it, or, if parliament, at every hazard, would maintain its supremacy. "For then," he says, "all this new doctrine of independence would be disavowed, and the first inventors or broachers of it would be sacrificed to the rage of the people who had been deluded by them."

Intelligence now came of the final determination of the ministry as to the tenure of the judges' salaries, which made them independent of the local and fundamental law. "The last vessels from England, Josiah Quincy, jun., said in the "Boston Gazette" of Sept. 28, "tell us the judges and the subalterns have got salaries from Great Britain! Is it possible this last movement should not move us, and drive us, not to desperation, but to our duty? The blind may see, the callous must feel, the spirited will act;" and the words of the noble man were not too strong, when the people's rights were to be subjected to the will of one man. It was now proposed to consolidate the popular party by an organization to be known as committees of correspondence, to constitute an authentic medium for an interchange of views, and for promoting concert of action. Samuel Adams had long mused on the feasibility of this scheme; and the more he mused on it, the stronger grew his desire to realize it. If the towns of Massachusetts, he now wrote, would begin this work, it would, in his opinion, extend from colony to colony; and, thus united, the people would be enabled to resist successfully the measures of the ministry. The idea of a union of the colonies was nearly as old as their foundation; the mode of committees of correspondence had often been suggested; but the fame of a statesman consists in an embodiment, at the right time, of a great thought into a wise measure. Let the authentic record attest how large a credit is due for the inauguration of committees of correspondence, and hence for a movement towards the first national party in this country, to Samuel Adams and Joseph Warren.

Hutchinson was now greatly disturbed at the tone of the press. He did not resign his place on the bench when he became the governor. In a trial in Worcester, where he presided as chief-justice, there was tampering in the selection of the jury; and he said, in an opinion, that the non-importation agreement was against the laws of God and man. This case was elaborately and severely criticised in the journals. In one of the articles, Josiah Quincy, jun., asked the salient question, whether, under the cover of the law, it was not "the policy of the times, from Mansfield to the lowest subaltern in office, to eradicate and render worthless the trial by jury"? Hutchinson, as he now urged a prosecution of the printers, wrote, "There is a great clamor about the judges' salaries; the town is full of cabals; the papers are more treasonable than ever; and the leaders of the people make every new measure subserve their purpose to promote discontent and rekindle a flame among them."

Some of the popular leaders regarded the exigency so alarming as to require extraordinary measures. They were of the class of minds who believe that God works in the courses of history; and they said that union was the only method which Providence pointed out for the preservation of their rights.[1] They represented the feeling of reverence and the growing Americanism of the time. Two of this class were Samuel Adams and Joseph Warren. It was their aim to rouse the public mind from its lethargy, into political action worthy of a great cause; and they are seen working together not only in the initial movement of the town-meeting, but in the steady and arduous labors of which this meeting was the parent.

Petitions were now circulated for a town-meeting. One of them (Oct. 14, 1772), which had more than a hundred signatures, stated as the object of the meeting, an inquiry into the truth of the report, " that stipends were affixed, by order of the Crown, to the offices of the justices of the superior court of judicature of this province "[2] It declared, that a judiciary wholly dependent on the Crown would not be suffered by the people of Great Britain, and ought not to be tolerated by any free people; and that the establish-

[1] In a communication in the "Boston Gazette," Nov. 2, 1772, urging united action by the people of all the colonies, it is said, "This is the plan that wisdom and Providence point out to preserve our rights; and this alone. . . . Every consideration that animates a free and noble mind urges our putting the plan above mentioned into execution. It is practicable, safe, and easy; and, if not pursued, slavery will be our inevitable portion."   [2] There were 198 petitioners.

ment would poison the streams of justice, and complete the ruin of the liberties of the people. The selectmen[1] received the petition on the 20th, and, on the next day, issued a warrant for the meeting. The petition was printed (Oct. 26) in the " Gazette."

The patriots were of one mind as to the dangerous nature of the last aggression, but differed as to the best way of meeting it. One of the petitioners for the meeting says in the " Gazette," " I should esteem myself happy, should it be a full one. I wish the people would lay the axe to the root of the tree, and sleep no longer on the bosom of destruction. The influence of your example, my brethren, may produce a glorious effect. Our situation is indeed critical. May wisdom, and a proper portion of spirit, govern the debates of the town; and may the Province, which shares in the distress, be seasonably awakened! What language can possibly express our complaints? What would the English say, if the king of France should come, at the head of a hundred thousand men, to impose laws upon England?"

The official now enjoying the honors and emoluments of governor and chief-justice was moved by the circulation of these petitions to enlighten his new superior in office on the cause of this expression of feeling in the press, and movement among the people. " The source, my lord," he wrote, Oct. 23, to Lord Dartmouth, " of all this irregularity, is a false opinion, broached at the time of the Stamp Act, and ever since cultivated, until it has become general, that the

---

[1] Hutchinson, in his "History" (iii. 361), says that the petition was first rejected. The tone of the " Gazette " shows that there was hesitancy; but the records of the selectmen do not warrant this statement.

people of the colonies are subject to no authority but their own legislatures; and that the acts of the parliament of Great Britain, which is every day, in print, termed a foreign state, are not obligatory. All attempts to punish the public assertors of this doctrine, and other seditious and treasonable tenets deduced from it, have failed; and, whilst this opinion prevails, there seems but little reason to hope that a grand jury will present, or a petty jury convict. Until this opinion prevailed, the people of this province saw the necessity of Government, and were disposed to support its authority. Could it be eradicated, I doubt not the disposition would again take place. I know the cause of the disease, but am at a loss for a proper remedy."

The town-meeting in Faneuil Hall, on the Twenty-eighth day of October, in spite of the urgent appeals in the press, was not large, though there was a respectable attendance. This was ascribed to the busy season of the year, to differences as to points of policy in the popular ranks, to the dexterity of the Tories in fomenting these divisions, and to the opinion of some that the town was not the most appropriate organization to consider the question at issue. The presence of John Hancock[1] as the moderator must have dashed all Hutchinson's hope of detaching him

---

[1] When Hancock declined to take a seat in the council, the "Gazette" said: "Mr. Hancock's declining a seat at the council-board is very satisfactory to the friends of liberty among his constituents. This gentleman had been chosen five years successively, and as often negatived. Whatever may have been the motive for his being approbated at last, his own determination now shows that he had rather be a representative of the people, since he has had so repeatedly their election and confidence. Their approbation is always a mark of sincere respect, which, in virtuous times, a man in public character seldom fails of having while he continues to merit it." — *Boston Gazette, June 1, 1772.*

from his party; and, if he were opposed to the creation of committees of correspondence, which was the understood object of the meeting, his service showed that his love of the cause, and a desire to see unity in its ranks, predominated over any small pride of opinion.

There was, the report of the meeting reads, "the coolest and most candid debate and deliberation;" but not a word that was uttered is preserved. Samuel Adams read a cheering letter from Marblehead, written by Elbridge Gerry,[1] — who subsequently was the Governor of Massachusetts and Vice-president of the United States, — averring that it was no longer matter of doubt that the ministry were determined to deprive the colonies of their constitutional rights; expressing the hope that the people would have virtue enough to withstand the attempt; and pledging that town to be ever ready, in attention to the great subject, with interest or life.[2] This was received with great satisfaction. "The town," the "Gazette" says, "came into a very full vote; there being only one hand held up against it, and that through inattention, as the person assures us, to prepare a decent and respectful message to the governor." Samuel Adams, Joseph Warren, and Benjamin Church were chosen to frame it; when the meeting adjourned till the afternoon.

The committee, in the afternoon, reported the draft of a brief message, to be presented to the governor. It stated as the nature of the report, believed to be well grounded, "that stipends were affixed to the offices of the judges, contrary to ancient and invaria-

---

[1] Austin's Life of Gerry, i. 81.   [2] Ib., 82.

ble usage;" that it spread alarm among all considerate persons who had heard of it, in town or country; that the measure was viewed as tending to complete the system of their slavery; and, as the judges held their places during pleasure, that establishment appeared big with fatal evils. The message requested the governor to inform the town, whether he had received such advice as to create the assurance in his mind that such establishment had been or was likely to be made. This draft, the "Gazette" says, "was freely canvassed, and finally accepted by a very full vote, *nemine contradicente;* and thereupon William Phillips, Esq., the Hon. James Otis, Esq., Mr. Samuel Adams, Dr. Joseph Warren, Dr. Benjamin Church, Mr. Timothy Newell, and Col. Thomas Marshall, were appointed to wait on His Excellency with the same."[1]

[1] The names of two distinguished patriots no longer appear on the committees, — Richard Dana, a justice, and John Ruddock, a selectman. On their decease, the "Gazette" contained the following obituary notices: —

On Sunday, the 17th of May last, died at his house in Boston, Richard Dana, Esq., barrister at law, seventy-two years of age. He was a gentleman of unblemished morals. By his liberal education, very good natural powers, and diligence in the study of the law, he was eminent in his profession. He was faithful to his clients and unjust to no man. Ever since he came into business, he was exemplary in carefulness, diligence, and frugality, whereby he has left to his widow (only sister of the Honorable Judge Trowbridge) and to his children, two sons and one daughter, a handsome fortune. He hated flattery. Agreeably to the natural but honest severity of his manners, he was a most inveterate enemy to luxury and prodigality. A very steady and strenuous, and, it must be confessed, many times a passionate opposer of all those (even from the highest to the lowest, but especially the former), who, in his judgment, were enemies to the civil and religious rights of his country; and he very well understood what those rights were. In short, to Mr. Dana may be applied with great justice Horace's —

"Justum ac tenacem propositi virum,
Non vultus instantis tyranni,
Mente quatit solida." *Boston Gazette, June* 1.

Wednesday last, died very suddenly of a lethargic disorder, in the sixtieth year of his age, Major John Ruddock, commander of the North Battery. This gentleman, having passed through town-offices with reputation, and being well

Two of the committee were of the board of selectmen. The meeting now adjourned for two days.

The committee, on the next day, waited on the governor, to present the message of the town. Samuel Adams, just before going, wrote a letter to Elbridge Gerry; and, having penned these words, "This country must shake off their intolerable burdens at all events; every day strengthens our oppressors and weakens us; if each town would declare its sense of these matters, I am persuaded our enemies would not have it in their power to divide us,"[1] — he made a dash with his pen, and closed by saying he was going, with the committee, to His Excellency. Adams expected a negative reply; still, he says, it was his object to prefer requests which could not be justly branded as unconstitutional, but which every friend of the popular cause would pronounce to be reasonable; while the executive, in refusing to com-

---

acquainted with the affairs of the town, he has for about ten years past been annually chosen a selectman; which trust he discharged, in these days of trial and danger, with resolution and fidelity. As a justice of the peace and quorum, he delivered his opinion on the bench, respecting men and things, with integrity and a manly fortitude; and, when trifling complaints were brought before him as a magistrate, he endeavored to compose differences rather than profit by them. In his large dealings, he discovered that he had the feelings of humanity; and few persons in trade have suffered more by their lenity. In his domestic connections he was affectionate and tender, and in his friendships sincere and steady. As a good member of society, always ready not only to patronize the oppressed and relieve the needy, but to encourage necessary and charitable undertakings with his subscriptions; he was a true friend to the constitution of the churches of New England as stated and set forth in their excellent platform, and firmly adhered to the doctrines of the first reformers; and he honored his profession as a Christian, not only by always giving his influence on the side of virtue and religion, but by exerting himself in the defence of our violated civil rights. Five sons and a daughter survive to mourn their loss. His remains were on Friday evening attended to the grave by a very respectable number of his friends and townsmen. During the procession, minute guns were fired from the North Battery. — *Gazette, Sept.* 7, 1772.

[1] Samuel Adams to Elbridge Gerry, Oct. 29, 1772.

ply with them, must necessarily put himself in the wrong in the opinion of honest and sensible men. As a consequence, such reasonable and manly measures as the people might adopt for their security would be more reconcilable to timid minds, and thus the vital point would be reached of harmony and unanimity.[1] This explanation is a key to the whole of a movement which resulted in a great revolutionary deed, of which this action was, as it were, the threshold.

At the adjournment of the meeting (Oct. 30), an answer of the governor to the message of the town was read, in which he said it was not proper for him to lay before the inhabitants any part of his correspondence as governor; and he declined to say whether he had or had not received advices relative to the public officers of the Government, but said he was ready to gratify the inhabitants, "upon every regular application to him on business of public concernment to the town," consistently with fidelity to the trust which His Majesty had reposed in him. A committee — James Otis, Samuel Adams, and Thomas Cushing — was now appointed to draft a petition for presentation to the governor. They framed a compact and admirable paper. "It represented that the new measure as to the judges' salaries was contrary, not only to the plain and obvious sense of the charter, but also to some of the fundamental principles of the common law, to the benefit of which all British subjects, wherever dispersed throughout the British Empire, were indubitably entitled;" that the judges should hold their commissions, not at the pleasure of the Crown, but during good behavior; and that the

---

[1] Samuel Adams to Elbridge Gerry, Nov. 5, 1772.

change appeared fraught with such fatal evils, that the most distant thought of its taking effect filled the public mind with dread; and the petition asked that the governor would be pleased "to allow the general assembly to meet at the time to which it stood prorogued, in order that, in that constitutional body with whom it is to inquire into grievances and redress them, the joint wisdom of the province may be employed in deliberating and determining on a matter so important and alarming." Their draft was accepted; and the committee appointed to carry the message of the town, Warren being a member, was directed to wait on His Excellency with this petition. The town then adjourned to meet on the second day of November, at three o'clock in the afternoon, at Faneuil Hall, the "Gazette" says, "to receive an answer to the petition, and take such further measures as this most important affair may require."

On the morning of the Second day of November, the day on which the town was to meet, the "Boston Gazette" had seven columns of matter on politics, and shone in the glory of a free press, endeavoring to kindle an influence in favor of a just cause. One of the communications is addressed "to the people of America." The writer said, that "tyranny, like time and death, was creeping on unperceived;" and, full of the central thought of a union, he urged that the only method that promised any prospect of a preservation of freedom, was for the people to unite in remonstrance to the king, and to say that, unless their liberties were restored whole and entire, they would form an independent commonwealth, after the example of the Dutch provinces, secure their ports, and offer a free trade to all nations. "My brethren," the patriot says, " our present situation is dangerous, but not desperate: let us now unite like a band of brothers in the noblest cause, look to Heaven for assistance, and He who made us free will crown our labors with success." The style and sentiment are like the oration of Warren: the reverence and spirit of nationality reflected the spirit of the time.

The meeting in the afternoon, at Faneuil Hall, was not large, though it was respectable in numbers and character; showing that there needed a fresh impulse to rouse the public mind. The governor, in an answer, declined to allow the assembly to meet at the time to which it stood prorogued, saying that he had determined, before receiving the address of the town, to prorogue it to a further time; that the reasons presented had not altered his opinion; and, if he should meet the assembly contrary to his own judgment, he should yield to the town the exercise of this part of the prerogative, and should be unable to justify his conduct to the king. In the closing paragraph, he remarked, "There would, moreover, be danger of encouraging the inhabitants of the other towns in the province to assemble, from time to time, in order to consider the necessity or expediency of a session of the general assembly, or to debate and transact other matters which the law that authorizes towns to assemble does not make the business of a town-meeting." This high-toned paper was read several times; and, after considering it and voting it to be unsatisfactory, the meeting resolved, "That they have, ever had, and ought to have, a right to petition the king or his representative for the redress of such grievances as they feel, or for preventing of such as they have reason to apprehend, and to communicate their sentiments to other towns." Hutchinson pleads, in his history, that this was waiving the point; that he had taken no exception to the right of petition, nor to the communication of sentiment from one town to another; but that his exception had been to the assumption by towns, as corporations, to act beyond limits defined by the law. But he does not define the legal limit nor the illegal assumption. Had towns a right to petition, and yet no right to meet for the purpose of determining by debate what their petition should contain? The truth is, that Hutchinson, in accordance with his private correspondence, denied indirectly, and meant to deny, the right of the towns to hold meetings to consider political questions; and his special plea, in the court of history, is an after-thought and a subterfuge.

Samuel Adams,[1] after the passage of this resolve, made the motion which the Tories termed " the source

[1] John Adams, in "Novanglus," printed Feb. 6, 1775, asks, "When a certain masterly statesman invented a committee of correspondence in Boston, . . . did not every colony, nay, every county, city, hundred, and town upon the whole continent, adopt the measure, I had almost said as if it had been a revelation from above, as the happiest means of cementing the union and acting in concert?" The antagonist of Adams, "Massachusettensis," in the "Massachusetts Gazette" (Tory), said, Jan. 2, 1775, "A new, unheard-of mode of opposition had been devised, said to be the invention of the fertile brain of one of our party agents, called a committee of correspondence. This is the foulest, subtlest, and most venomous serpent that ever issued from the eggs of sedition." The "Continental Journal," of May 7, 1778, has a report of a dinner which was given to Samuel Adams, when he was on his way from Boston to attend a session of congress. Two of the toasts were, "Our worthy friend and patriot, Mr. Samuel Adams;"—"In memory of the first committee of correspondence in America, and all those who dared to support our glorious cause in times of danger." There were committees of correspondence before 1772; but it was the mode, through the channel of the law and its extension through the colonies, that constituted the peculiarity.

of the rebellion," and which Bancroft says "included the whole revolution." He moved, "That a committee of correspondence be appointed, to consist of twenty-one persons, to state "the rights of the colonists, and of this province in particular, as men, as Christians, and as subjects; to communicate and publish the same to the several towns in this province and to the world, as the sense of this town, with the infringements and violations thereof that have been, or from time to time may be made; also requesting of each town a free communication of their sentiments on this subject." — "This motion was carried, *nemine contradicente.*" When the names of Hancock, Cushing, and Phillips, representatives, and Austin and Scollay, selectmen, with others, were announced as members of this committee, they declined; not because they were opposed to the measure, but on the ground that their private business would not admit of their acceptance. The committee are recorded in the following order: James Otis, Samuel Adams Joseph Warren, Benjamin Church, William Dennie, William Greenleaf, Joseph Greenleaf, Thomas Young William Powell, Nathaniel Appleton, Oliver Wendell, John Sweetser, Josiah Quincy, John Bradford, Richard Boynton, William Mackay, Nathaniel Barber, Caleb Davis, Alexander Hill, William Molineux, Robert Pierpont. The committee were requested "to report to the town as soon as may be;" when the meeting adjourned.

Bancroft says of the three first names, "The name of James Otis, who was now but a wreck of himself, appears first on the list, as a tribute to former services. The two most important members were Samuel

Adams and Joseph Warren: the first now recognized as a masterly statesman and the ablest political writer in New England; the second, a rare combination of gentleness with daring courage, of respect for law with the all-controlling love of liberty. The two men never failed each other, — the one growing old, the other in youthful manhood; thinking one set of thoughts; having one heart for their country; joining in one career of policy and action; differing only in this, that, while Warren still clung to the hope of conciliation, Adams ardently desired, as well as clearly foresaw, the conflict for independence."

This committee, until it was in a measure superseded by the committee of safety, was the executive power of the popular party of Boston, and, indeed, virtually of the whole province. It proceeded with a vigor and efficiency, and yet with a caution, rarely witnessed in political action. It organized, at its first meeting (Nov. 3), by choosing James Otis chairman, and William Cooper clerk. Its members gave to each other the pledge of honor, " not to divulge any part of their conversation at their meetings to any person whatsoever, excepting what the committee itself should make known." It immediately arranged for the preparation of the report which it was instructed to make to the town; assigning to Adams the general exposition of the rights of the colonies, to Warren the specification of the violation of these rights, and to Church the framing of a circular letter, to be addressed to the towns.[1]

Governor Hutchinson informed Lord Dartmouth of the appointment of the committee, on the day it

[1] Bancroft's History, vi. 431.

entered upon its labors, and stated the objects of the town-meeting that created it; and, ten days later, he expressed further views relative to the meeting and the character of the committee. The reckless faction in the town, he said, had pleased themselves with hopes of fresh disturbances out of the question of the judges' salaries; they had taken the usual first step, of a town-meeting, which was brought on with an intent to raise a general flame. On the 3d of November, he was not apprehensive that this design would succeed; and, on the 13th, he expressed still more pointedly the opinion that the movement would fail. "Hitherto," he says of the popular leaders, "they have fallen much short of their expectation, and, even in this town, have not been able to revive the old spirit of mobbing; and the only dependence left is to keep up a correspondence through the province, by committees of the several towns, which is such a foolish scheme that they must make themselves ridiculous." He thus laid out his own course. In common times, he said, he should have refused any other answer to the town's petition than to acquaint it, that the purpose for which it assembled was not lawful; but he thought it best not to irritate "I immediately," he says, "prorogued the court (the journals say to the 6th of January), and sooner than I otherwise should have done, to show them that I would not give the least encouragement to their unwarrantable doings, there being no law to support towns in transacting any other business than what is of public concernment to the towns; but the inhabitants of Boston, like the livery of London, have been for a long time used to concern themselves with all the affairs of Government."[1] The governor ought to have remembered, that the customs of a people are a part of their liberties. On the 13th, he indulged in a strain of disparaging remark on the members of the committee. "Strange," he says, "that a Government, which, within a century, was so pure as to suffer no person to be free of their commonwealth who was not one of their church-members, should now take for their leaders men who openly contemn all religion, and should join deacons and atheists in one trust, and that they should be instigated to this by some of the clergy who make the highest pretence to devotion; and yet the spirit of political party produces all this." Strange that Hutchinson could write apparently unconscious that the spirit of party was shading his pen-drawing; and strange, too, that representations similar to what this letter contained should have been read to the king, and made the basis of cabinet action.

On this day (Nov. 3), Samuel Adams sent to Arthur Lee, who was in London, his view of Hutchinson's course. Adams gave an assurance that the body of a long-insulted people would bear insult and oppression no longer than until they felt in themselves strength to shake off the yoke; and, if they had not gathered so fully as formerly in town-meet-

---

[1] Hutchinson wrote to Lord Hillsborough, May 29, 1772, "The meetings of that town (Boston) being constituted of the lowest class of the people, under the influence of a few of the higher class, but of intemperate and furious dispositions and of desperate fortunes, men of property and of the best characters have deserted these meetings, where they are sure of being affronted. By the constitution, forty pounds sterling, which they say may be in clothes, household furniture, or any sort of property, is qualification enough; and even into that there is scarce any inquiry, and every thing with the appearance of a man is admitted without scrutiny."

ings, it was "partly from the opinion of some that there was no method left to be taken but the last: which was also the opinion of many in the country." And he characterized the leading Tories around him as "the most artful, plausible, and insinuating men, and some of them the most malicious enemies of the common rights of mankind." His thought ran on the nature of free governments, and the indignity of submission to arbitrary power; and his maledictions were upon those who were plotting the ruin of American liberties. On the next day (Nov. 4), in a letter to James Warren, besides hoping "that Mother Plymouth would see her way clear to have a meeting to second Boston," which "had thought proper to take what the Tories apprehend to be leading steps," he said, he had neither time nor inclination to take up his thoughts in complaining of tyrants or tyranny; for it was more than time this country was rid of both. His words are, "We have long had it thrown in our faces, that the country in general is under no such fears of slavery, but are well pleased with the measures of administration." — "Whenever the friends of the country shall be assured of each other's sentiments, that spirit which is necessary will not be wanting."

As the sub-committee were at work on their report, Adams received (Nov. 10) a letter from Elbridge Gerry, who said, "The steps taken by our vigilant metropolis, I am well assured, will succeed; but, should they fail, the merit of those worthies who oppose the strides of tyranny will not be diminished; neither would their being overpowered by numbers alter the heroism of their conduct." The reply of

Adams is not less high-toned. He expressed great satisfaction that the friends of liberty in Marblehead were active; that the pulse of the people of Plymouth beat high; that a great number in Cambridge petitioned for a town-meeting; that Roxbury was to act on Monday; and said, "May God grant that the love of liberty, and a zeal to support it, may enkindle in every town!"

The town, on the Twentieth of November, on the warrant of the selectmen, met in Faneuil Hall, to receive the report of the committee of correspondence. It was first read by the chairman, James Otis, and afterwards by the moderator, John Hancock. It consisted of three divisions, entitled, first, "A State of the Rights of the Colonists and of this Province in particular," which was the portion allotted to Adams, and makes twelve pages of the pamphlet; second, "A List of the Infringements and Violations of those Rights," which was the part assigned to Warren, and makes sixteen pages; third, "A Letter of Correspondence with the other Towns," of six pages, and was Church's portion. The "Gazette" says the report was "thoroughly examined and amended by the town, when it was accepted by a full vote, *nemine contradicente*. The town then voted that these proceedings be printed, and ordered the town-clerk to sign printed copies of the same, in the name and behalf of the town, to be sent to the selectmen of each town and district in the province, and to such other gentlemen as the committee shall direct. Thus this matter is left to the candid consideration of our brethren and fellow-subjects in general." The town-meeting, about ten o'clock, P.M., was dissolved.

Six hundred copies of the report which had been adopted were printed, and sent out to the towns and to prominent Whigs in other colonies.

The first portion of this report consists mostly of a statement of abstract principles. The rights of the colonists are classified under three heads, entitled, "Rights as men, as Christians, and as subjects." Here are announced the right of expatriation in the face of the English maxim, "Once a subject, always a subject;" of just and true liberty, equal and impartial in matters spiritual and temporal, when the Dissenter in the mother-country was the subject of a penal code and civil disabilities; of the equality of all before the law; so that the report says, citing Locke, "There should be one rule of justice for rich and poor; for the favorite at court and the countryman at the plough." It developed the idea at length, that consent is the true basis of law; it affirmed that the legislature had no right to absolute, arbitrary power over the lives and fortunes of the people, and could not justly assume to itself a power to rule by extemporary, arbitrary decrees; but was bound to see justice dispensed and rightly decided "by promulgated, standing, and known laws," interpreted by a judiciary as independent as far as possible of prince or people. The statement of the basis of personal freedom is radical: "If men, through fear, fraud, or mistake, should in terms renounce or give up any essential, natural right, the eternal law of reason and the grand end of society would absolutely vacate such renunciation: the right to freedom being the gift of God Almighty, it is not in the power of man to alienate this gift, and voluntarily to become a slave." The argument on taxation was re-iterated with great force; and it was denied that there could be any representation in parliament that would render taxation of the colonies by that body legal. It characterized Magna Charta as a constrained declaration of original, inherent, indefeasible, natural rights. It says, "That great author, that great jurist, and even that court-writer, Mr. Justice Blackstone, holds that this recognition was justly obtained, sword in hand; and peradventure it must be one day, sword in hand, again rescued and preserved from total oblivion."

The second portion of the report, which was assigned to Warren, enumerated, under ten heads, the "infringements and violations of rights;" and began with the remark, that they "would not fail to excite the attention of all who consider themselves interested in the happiness and freedom of mankind in general, and of this continent and province in particular." To frame an abstract of these ten counts of this indictment of the British Administration would be to repeat the instances already related of their violation. Three of the counts, however, show so strikingly the grasp there was in the public mind of great ideas, as to require comment.

The report says that parliament "assumed the powers of legislation, in all cases whatsoever, without obtaining the consent of the inhabitants, which is ever essentially necessary to the rightful establishment of such a legislature;" and it affirmed, in relation to a religious establishment, that "no power on earth can justly give either temporal or spiritual jurisdiction within this province, except the great and general court." It instanced, among the rankest violations of this principle, the royal instructions, interfering with the tenure of the judiciary, rendering one branch of the legislature merely a ministerial engine, and threatening an entire destruction of the liberties of the people. "The province," it says, "has already felt such effects from these instructions, as, we think, justly entitle us to say, that they threaten an entire destruction of our liberties; and must soon, if not checked, render every branch of our Government a useless burden upon the people." This was the idea of local government on which Hutchinson so continuously dwelt.

The report presents as an indictment, "the extending the power of the courts of vice-admiralty to so enormous a degree, as deprives the people of the colonies, in a great measure, of their inestimable right to trials by juries; which has ever been justly considered as the grand bulwark and security of English property." It alleged that this right was also infringed in the acts for preserving His Majesty's dock-yards, and in a revival of an obsolete statute of Henry VIII. The British statute is commented on, wherein, while the estates and properties of the people of Great Britain are expressly guarded, those of the colonists are given up to the decision of one dependent, interested judge of admiralty. "Thus our birthrights are taken from us, and that, too, with every mark of indignity, insult, and contempt. We may be harassed and dragged from one part of the continent to another, and finally be deprived of our whole property, by the arbitrary determination of one biassed, capricious judge of admiralty."

The report says, "The restraining us from erecting

slitting-mills, for manufacturing our iron, the natural produce of this country, is an infringement of that right with which God and nature have invested us, to make use of our skill and industry in procuring the necessaries and conveniences of life." The acts were cited which restrained the manufacture of hats, the carrying wool even over a ferry, as oppression; and it is said that inhabitants "have often been put to the expense of carrying a bag of wool near a hundred miles by land," when the trouble might have been saved by passing over a river. Here is a manly protest against those trammels on colonial enterprise, which the great British economist pronounced a manifest violation of the most sacred rights of mankind.[1]

Here, too, is a demand, not for a government to supply work to those who live under it, but for the recognition of the right of each individual to select his field of work, to reap its fruits, and enjoy them in security. In a word, here freedom is asked for that industrial energy which has contributed so largely to the growth and glory of the country; and it was asked at a time when arbitrary restrictions on business and labor disgraced the legislation of civilized nations!

The last portion of the report, which was assigned to Church, was a brief but spirited "Letter of Corre-

---

[1] Adam Smith, in the "Wealth of Nations," printed in 1775, in alluding to the restrictions imposed on the colonies, says, "She prohibits the exportation from one province to another by water, and even the carriage by land, upon horseback or in a cart, of hats, of wools, and woollen goods, of the produce of America." He remarks, "To prohibit a great people from making all they can of every part of their own produce, or from employing their stock and industry in the way that they judge most advantageous to themselves, is a manifest violation of the most sacred rights of mankind." These words were written in October, 1773. — *McCulloch's Smith*, 261.

spondence to the other Towns;" which contained a short epitome of the ideas of the two previous portions of the report, a reference to the official papers that passed between the town and the governor, and invited a free communication of sentiment to Boston. "If," the letter says, "you concur with us in opinion, that our rights are properly stated, and measures of administration pointed out by us are subversive of these rights, you will doubtless think it of the utmost importance that we stand firm as one man to recover and support them."[1]

This report was the boldest and most comprehensive summary of the American cause that had appeared. It is remarkably free from passion; and, stating principles and their violation with simplicity, it calmly addressed the reason. It may not, in a literary point of view, rank with the great state-papers of congress, which Lord Chatham subsequently eulogized; but it had the qualities of other Boston state papers, which he now (1772) perused with avidity, as " genuine fruits of unsophisticated good sense and of virtue uncorrupted;"[2] and, being grandly American, it well supplied the wants of the people on a theme — its own words — " of such great and lasting moment as to involve in it the fate of all their posterity."

[1] This report is entitled, " The Votes and Proceedings of the Freeholders and other Inhabitants of the Town of Boston, in town-meeting assembled according to Law. Published by order of the Town. To which is prefixed, as introductory, an Attested Copy of a Vote of the Town at a Preceding Meeting. Boston: printed by Edes and Gill in Queen Street, and T. and J. Fleet in Cornhill."

[2] Thomas Hollis, Nov. 26, 1772, sent to Lord Chatham three publications of Boston, " which," he wrote, " tend to show a people of strong sense and virtue, in the rough, on the rise: " to which Lord Chatham replied, on the same day, "Lord Chatham will peruse with avidity the publications of the honest New Englanders, — genuine fruits of unsophisticated, masculine good sense, and of virtue uncorrupted."

The public mind, however, was so calm, — its surface appearing even glassy to earnest souls, — that it was feared a failure of the towns to respond to the call of the metropolis would prejudice the cause which it was designed to promote. "I wish the measure would take a general run," a zealous patriot, James Warren, of Plymouth, wrote (Dec. 8, 1772) to Samuel Adams. "I shall not fail to exert myself to have as many towns as possible meet, but fear the bigger part of them will not. They are dead, and the dead can't be raised without a miracle. I am sensible that the Tories spare no pains (as you say) to disparage the measures; which, with their other conduct, shows their apprehension. They are nettled much." Adams was prompt to reply, "I am very sorry to find in your letter any thing that discovers the least approach towards despair. *Nil desperandum.* That is a motto for you and for me. All are not dead; and, where there is a spark of patriotic fire, we will rekindle it. Say you that the Tories spare no pains to disparage our measures? I knew they would, and should have greatly doubted of the importance of the measures, if they had not been nettled."[1] Anxious, however, as

[1] John Adams, at this time, owing to his health and professional practice, was averse to political life. His Diary (Life and Works of John Adams, ii. 298), of the year 1772, supplies interesting glimpses of political men. He says, Sept. 22, "I will devote myself wholly to my private business;" Nov. 21, "I must avoid politics, political clubs, town-meetings;" Nov. 28 (he had removed his family to Boston), "I am disengaged from public affairs;" Dec. 16, he dined with Warren, at Rev. Mr. Howard's: Captain Phillips was of the party, who said, "they (the people) were all still and quiet at the southward, and at New York they laugh at us." Dec. 29, Samuel Pemberton and Samuel Adams invited him to deliver the next oration, which he declined to do. Dec. 30, "Spent the evening with Mr. Samuel Adams, at his house. Had much conversation about the state of affairs, Cushing, Phillips, Hancock, Hawley, Gerry, Hutchinson, Sewall, Quincy, &c. Adams was more cool, genteel, and agreeable than common; concealed and restrained his passions, &c. He affects to despise riches, and not to dread pov-

the originators of the measure were for its success, they did not follow the report into the country, and speak there in public meetings in its favor. I have not seen the mention of a single address, delivered by a Boston orator to a political gathering in the other towns, during the ten years' controversy before the war;[1] nor of a speech, delivered by a patriot from the country, at a Boston public meeting. The popular leaders relied on correspondence and the press, in the promotion of their objects.

The report was its own orator. In a few weeks after it was sent out on its mission, the fears of the timid were dispelled, and the faith of the confident was justified. When the selectmen of the towns read it[2] in their legal meetings, it reached communities which were planted under Christian influences,

erty; but no man is more ambitious of entertaining his friends handsomely, or of making a decent, an elegant, appearance than he. He has lately new covered and glazed his house, and painted it very neatly, and has new papered, painted, and furnished his rooms; so that you visit at a very genteel house, and are very politely received and entertained. Mr. Adams corresponds with Hawley, Gerry, and others. He corresponds in England, and in several of the other provinces. His time is all employed in the public service."

[1] In one instance, application was made to Josiah Quincy, jun., to prepare resolutions for the town of Petersham, which Gordon (i. 316) incorporates into his text. The introduction, and several resolutions which are marked with an asterisk, were not supplied by Quincy.

[2] The "Boston Gazette," Dec. 28, 1772, has the proceedings of the town of Marblehead, on the 15th inst. It is said the debates lasted through the day, and that the meeting was composed of the greatest number of inhabitants ever known to attend a town-meeting in this place. One resolve provides that one of the pamphlets be preserved in the clerk's office, and read annually; and, —

"Further: To inform posterity, should their rights and liberties be preserved, how much they are indebted to many eminent patriots of the present day: that the names of the Hon. John Hancock, Esq., moderator of the meeting that originated the state of rights; of the Hon. James Otis, Esq., Mr. Samuel Adams, Esq., Dr. Warren, and other members of the committee which reported them, — be recorded in the book of this town, as great supporters of the rights and liberties of this province, and gentlemen who do much honor and service to their country."

fixed in habits of personal independence, and invigorated by the customs of freedom; whose youth were nurtured in the common schools, and whose young men were trained in civil affairs in the town-meeting. These communities were and are, all over the country, fountains of public spirit that never failed in a crisis to supply a noble conservatism on the side of law and liberty. It was instinctively felt that the report dealt with precious heirlooms which were prized and cherished. As the people mused on its thought,— each community kindling its own fires, — patriotism warmed; and the flow of sentiment from every quarter, to the Boston committee, had the power of an intelligent public opinion.

The journals, those photographs of passing time, preserved a picture of this great scene for the admiration of posterity. Their record of the communing of the towns with the metropolis, by addresses, letters, and resolves, often elaborate, ever fresh, and always soul-stirring, is an authentic manifestation of the spirit of the time. They embrace the names of the chief men of the place as the local committee, indorse the sentiment of the report, pledge to support the metropolis as the exponent of the general cause, and express a desire for union. "May every town in this province," are the words of Cambridge, "and every colony upon the continent, be awakened to a sense of danger, and unite in the glorious cause of liberty!"[1] "It becomes us," a town resolved in the

---

[1] The "Boston Gazette" of Dec. 28, 1772, has the "following letter, lately received from Cambridge," which will give an idea of this political communion : —
"To the Committee of Communication and Correspondence at Boston : —
"The committee appointed by the town of Cambridge to write to the committee of communication and correspondence at Boston, gladly embrace this oppor-

heart of the province, "to rely no longer on an arm of flesh, but on the arm of that All-powerful God who is able to unite the numerous inhabitants of this extensive country as a band of brothers in one common cause." In a month, forty-five towns, out of two hundred and fifty in the province, heartily indorsed the report. A week later, it was stated that the number had increased to eighty. The announcement was then made that it would be impossible to print the proceedings of all the towns, and to make selections would be to show impartiality; and for this reason the journals stopped entirely the publication of them; but a card,[1] from authority, appeared in the journals,

tunity. In the name and behalf of the said town of Cambridge, and with the most sincere respect, they acknowledge the vigilance and care, discovered by the town of Boston, of the public rights and liberties; acquainting you that this town will heartily concur in all salutary, proper, and constitutional measures for the redress of those intolerable grievances which threaten, and, if continued, must overthrow the happy civil constitution of this province.

"It is with the greatest pleasure we now inform you, that we think the meeting was as full as it has been, for the choice of a representative, for a number of years, if not fuller; and that the people discovered a glorious spirit, like men determined to be free. We have here enclosed you a copy of the votes and proceedings of this town, at their meetings, so far as they have gone.

"We would add, may the town of Boston, the capital of this province, rejoice in perpetual prosperity! May wisdom direct her in all her consultations! May her spirited and prudent conduct render her a terror to tyrants! May every town in this province, and every colony upon the continent, be awakened to a sense of danger, and unite in the glorious cause of liberty. Then shall we be able effectually to disappoint the machinations of our enemies. To conclude, that this land may be purged from those sins which are a reproach to a people, and be exalted by righteousness; that God Almighty may be our God, as he was the God of our fathers; and that we may be possessed of the same principles of virtue, religion, and public spirit which warmed and animated the hearts of our renowned ancestors, — is the sincere prayer of your friends in the common cause of our country, the committee of the town of Cambridge.

"EBENEZER STEDMAN, *per order.*"

[1] To the Public. — It is proposed that all the proceedings of the towns in the Massachusetts province, for the preservation of the rights of America, be collected and published in a volume, that posterity may know what their ancestors have done in the cause of freedom; it is expected that the inhabitants of every

recommending that the whole of this action in behalf of the rights of America be collected in a volume, in order that posterity may know what their ancestors did in the cause of freedom; and each town, however small, was desired and expected to publish its sentiments to the world, in order that its name, with the names already printed, might be included in this catalogue of fame, and handed down to future ages! So firm in the faith were this generation, that the rising in the horizon was not a rushlight, but a sun, destined to illumine the political heavens; and that future ages would hail with acclaim the early gleams of its dawn.

The blindness of Toryism was remarkable. Its leaders piled ridicule on the origin of this movement, its object, and its execution. They said there were not twenty men in Faneuil Hall when the "Circular Letter" was voted upon, when the selectmen deemed it necessary to certificate three hundred; they discharged volleys of rhetorical criticism on portions of the phraseology of the report; and they scornfully asked what the band of corresponding committees could do: Hutchinson, unusually obtuse, declaring the plan to be foolish; Franklin, of New Jersey, saying it was only a scheme to keep the party alive; and not one of them seeing the national power that was germinating. But, in after years, Hutchinson says in his history, "Such principles in government were avowed as would be sufficient to justify the colonies in revolting, and forming an independent state; and such in-

---

town, however small, will at this time publish their sentiments to the world, that their names, with those who have already published, may be recorded in this catalogue of fame, and handed down to future ages. — *Boston Gazette, Jan.* 18, 1773.

stances are given of the infringement of their rights by the exercise of parliamentary authority, as, upon like reasons, would justify an exception to the authority in all cases whatsoever: nevertheless, there was color for alleging that it was not expressly denied in every case. The whole frame of it, however, was calculated to strike the colonists with a just claim to independence, and to stimulate them to assert it."

The closer the story of our national life is studied, the greater must be the attention which the formation and direction of public opinion will command. This appeal of Boston reached the body of the people, and revealed the thought that was in their minds, prior to their doing a great revolutionary deed. Before this appeal, there were apathy and a feeling of false security; after it, there was a general sense of danger: before this movement, there was no party organization; after it, the Whigs became connected by a trustworthy representation throughout the province, which widened until it became colonial, and each local committee felt the inspiration of being co-workers with a national party. The scheme found the ball of revolution moving sluggishly: it imparted an irresistible momentum. The report was to the American cause what the Grand Remonstrance was to the English Revolution. A step had been taken, in inaugurating the regular action of popular power, towards that Union which was destined to place on Public Liberty the most beautiful face that ever adorned that angel-form.[1]

[1] Daniel Webster's Works, vi. 226

CHAPTER IX.

DESTRUCTION OF THE TEA.

WARREN ON NEW-YEAR'S DAY. — THE PATRIOTS AND UNION. — HUTCHINSON'S SPEECH. — DEATH OF ELIZABETH WARREN. — THE CALL FOR A CONGRESS. — TEA IMPORTATION. — ACTION OF PHILADELPHIA. — PROCEEDINGS OF BOSTON. — THE DESTRUCTION OF THE TEA. — CONTEMPORARY VINDICATION.

1773. JANUARY TO DECEMBER.

WARREN was required to devote himself still more to the public service, by being a member of the committee of correspondence. Its records attest his continuous labors in the patriot cause. This committee, as the executive power of the Whigs, took the lead in the measures that resulted in the destruction of the tea in Boston harbor; and Warren was in the foreground of the whole action in this great crisis. I know of no revolutionary deed more worthy of a careful analysis and a grateful remembrance. It brought into requisition the press, the club, the public meeting, and the new party organization. This act of self-preservation, like a decisive battle, influenced the course of events.[1]

---

[1] It is said, in a political review in the "Independent Chronicle," Dec. 25, 1777, that it is "certain the consequences of the destruction of the tea" were "a dissolution of civil government, the seizure of the capital, the commerce of it interdicted, and a military government, supported by a formidable armament, both by sea and land." William C. Rives ("Life of James Madison," i. 40), says, "This memorable occurrence was undoubtedly, in the immediate sequence of the events which it produced, the proximate cause of the American Revolution." The late Joseph T. Buckingham ("Annals of Mass. Charitable Associa-

Warren passed the evening of New-year's Day with a circle of kindred spirits, among whom were Cushing, Pemberton, and John Adams, whose diary supplies a glimpse of this social occasion. The conversation, mostly political, turned on matters in Rhode Island, the judges' salaries, the town-meetings, and recent lucubrations by General Brattle, a Tory; and there was good-natured badinage on each other's characters. Adams remarked of Cushing, that he never knew a pendulum to swing so clear; Warren repeated a remark of Pemberton, that John Adams was the proudest and cunningest fellow he ever knew, — adding, "that he (Adams) was rather a cautious man, but he could not say he ever trimmed: when he spoke at all, he spoke his sentiments." Adams, in his diary of this day, renewed his determination to devote himself to the pleasures and duties of private life. In another place he writes, "I have never known a period in which the seeds of great events have been so plentifully sown as this winter. A providence is visible in that concurrence of causes which produced the debates and controversies."

The political horizon, aglow with the harbingers of a new American day, seemed to the learned and the unlettered the sign of a providence beckoning them on. This feeling is seen in every great step towards the goal of nationality. I state a fact as certain as the Revolution.[1] What was then faith is now sight.

tion," 19), says, "It is an event which has never yet been so copiously described, nor so elaborately considered in its effects, as it deserves by the philosophical historian."

[1] Washington, on taking the oath as President of the United States, said: "No people can be bound to acknowledge and adore the invisible hand which conducts the affairs of men, more than the people of the United States. Every step by which they have advanced to the character of an independent nation seems to have been distinguished by some token of providential agency."

It is plain that these signs were indications of the under-current that was setting towards independence. Still, it was a tendency rather than an aim, — the working of ideas rather than the plan of man. The immediate object of the Whigs, as they formed themselves into a national party, whether they acted in Virginia or in Massachusetts, was, in the common expression of their great thought, a union of all the colonies on the continent. They saw in this union not merely the unconquerable arm of America, but a blessing to mankind.[1] It became a part of their religion to promote it. They yearned for it as though they appreciated what it would be in its development; as though they felt there was hanging on it —

> "Humanity, with all its fears,
> With all the hopes of future years."

The declarations of the towns, in answer to the Boston November meeting, manifested great similarity of political sentiment; and, besides zeal for union, they showed a determination to hold on to their local government. The Boston committee of

---

[1] The national sentiment found in the press, during the eight months preceding the destruction of the tea, is remarkable. I copy from an article in the "Boston Gazette" of June 14, 1773, Supplement, to show the feeling of the time:

"Messrs. Printers, — I have lived ten years in America, and I am fully convinced from history, that no people since the world has been inhabited ever equalled the Americans in the progress they have made in settlement, manufactures, learning, &c.; and it is evident that they will soon surpass all nations in those things which constitute the dignity and happiness of mankind. The UNION of the colonies, which now is the grand object the Americans are pursuing, will fix their rights and liberties upon an immovable basis, and at once secure them against all their designing enemies, foreign and domestic, British, French, Spanish, and all others. The unconquered and unconquerable arm of America, whenever it is lifted up, will make its foes tremble. . . . Americans, your sources of wealth and power are boundless; be sensible of your dignity, feel your true importance, act in character, and you will be for ever free."

correspondence say, in one of their replies, "A large number show that a uniformity of sentiment, though expressed in a variety of language, runs through them all: freedom from every legislation on earth but that of this province is the general claim." And the committee, as if to meet a growing ultraism, wrote, "We do not aim at freedom from law and lawful authority, but from the tyrannical edicts of a British parliament and ministry." The movement received warm commendation in the press, and in other colonies; and the members, cheered by the uprising and the union, placed on their records an expression of the faith, "that Providence would crown the efforts of the colonies with success, and thus their generation would furnish the example of public virtue worthy of the imitation of all posterity."[1]

The Tories took a different view of the signs of the times. Hutchinson, keenly sensitive to any supposed invasion of the national sovereignty, but extremely dull to any violations of constitutional rights, saw in the Boston report a culmination of the theory as to local powers, which he characterized as a total independence of parliament; and regarded the movement "as tending to sedition and mutiny." He said, "The contagion which had begun in Boston was spreading through the towns." — "They succeed in their unwearied endeavors to propagate the doctrine

[1] The same faith is seen in the press. The "Boston Gazette" of Jan. 11, 1773, says, "It must afford the greatest pleasure to the friends of liberty and the constitution, to perceive the country so thoroughly awakened to a sense of their danger; that almost every town have or are about calling meetings, to express their sentiments at this alarming crisis; that union and good sense, patriotism and spirit, already manifested in all parts of this province, must, under Providence, work out our political salvation, in spite of all the efforts of our enemies to prevent it."

of independence upon parliament, and the mischiefs of it every day increase." — " What can be more insolent than the resolves passing every day in the province." — " Every day, through the unwearied pains of the leaders of the opposition, made proselytes to these new opinions of government." He wrote (Jan. 7, 1773), that " he had discovered that the same persons who laid this dangerous plot of drawing in all the towns in the province" meant, when this was done, to issue a circular from the House of Representatives, and to endeavor to effect the same thing in all the assemblies on the continent. He said that, since he had been governor, he had avoided, as far as it was possible, the points of controversy between the kingdom and the colonies; but a measure had been entered upon, which, if pursued, must work a total separation from Great Britain; and, were he to do nothing, he might be charged with conniving at proceedings which he ought to have opposed with all the means at hand. He therefore determined, in a consultation with his confidential friends, though not with the advice of his council, to present the Administration side to the general court. Though it might not have the effect he could wish on the assembly, still he hoped it might change the minds of the people. In brief, the governor, in this official way, resolved to make an appeal to public opinion.

Hutchinson accordingly (Jan. 6, 1773) opened the session of the general court with a speech, containing an elaborate defence of the theory of the supremacy of parliament in all cases whatsoever, and an arraignment of the towns which had denied this theory. He reached the conclusion, that, in consequence, the bonds of government were weakened, and its authority was made contemptible. It was a subtle and thorough presentation of the Tory side of the controversy, which was much praised by the friends of the author, though deeply regretted in England. The House returned a keen, searching, triumphant reply, which was an uncommonly able exposition of the Whig side, and elicited the warmest eulogies from the patriots. John Adams related, years afterwards, that the committee charged with framing this reply invited him to aid them; and that, at their first meeting, they exhibited a draft, neatly and elegantly prepared, which, at the instance of Samuel Adams, had been drawn up by Warren. "It was," Adams says, "full of those elementary principles of liberty, equality, and fraternity which have since made a figure in the world, — principles which are founded in nature, and eternal, unchangeable truth, but which must be well understood and cautiously applied." It contained, however, no answer to the governor's constitutional points. Adams criticised it freely; and, by request, revised it. He drew a line over the eloquent parts of "the oration," introduced legal and constitutional authorities, and met with the committee several evenings until the reply was completed. He says, "The effect on public opinion was beyond expectation." There is undoubtedly a certain correctness in the long relation of Adams. Warren probably, on some occasion, prepared such an "oration," and Adams rendered the critical service which he described; but he attributes to this reply an effect on public opinion that can only be ascribed to the Boston town-meeting of November; and, according to Bancroft, this masterly answer of the House was from the pen of Samuel Adams.[1]

"I have stopped the progress of the towns for the present," Hutchinson wrote (Feb. 18, 1773), "and I think I have stopped the prosecution of another part of the scheme, which was for the assembly to invite every other assembly on the continent to assent to the same principles. This part has been acknowledged to me by the speaker [Cushing], who is in all these measures." The quietness that continued in other colonies favored this view. "A general state of quiescence," Arthur Lee wrote to Joseph Reed (Feb. 18, 1773), "seems to prevail over the whole empire, Boston only excepted. I admire the perseverance with which they pursue the object of having

---

[1] The relation of John Adams may be seen in his Works (ii. 311, 318). Bancroft (vi. 448), says that Samuel Adams had the aid of Joseph Hawley. Hutchinson addressed two elaborate speeches to the House on the question of legislative supremacy, and the House returned answers to both: the last answer was on the 2d of March. The *fac-simile*, in Adams's Works, of a note of Samuel Adams, shows that John Adams was consulted on both occasions. This note was written when Samuel Adams was preparing the second reply, and relates to a statement which he made in the first reply, on the authority of John Adams. Hutchinson, on the 10th of March, said that the replies to the House were written by Samuel Adams, "with the aid of Hawley and the lawyer Adams." — "They have," he says, "such an opinion of them, that they have ordered the whole controversy to be printed in a pamphlet for the benefit of posterity." Lord Dartmouth disapproved of the governor's course. In a letter of June 14, 1773, Hutchinson wrote to Lord Dartmouth, "It gives me pain that any step which I have taken with the most sincere intention to promote His Majesty's service should be judged to have a contrary effect." On the same day he wrote to the under-secretary, J. Pownall, "I had the fullest evidence of a plan to engage the colonies in a confederacy against the authority of parliament. The towns of this province were to begin; the assemblies to confirm their doings, and to invite the other colonies to join."

The controversy was elicited by the Boston town-meeting of November. The town also, in March, replied to Hutchinson. Samuel Adams was the chairman of the committee, and Warren was a member of it. Perhaps it was on this occasion that Warren composed "the oration," and John Adams sat with the committee from evening to evening until an answer to Hutchinson was prepared.

their violated rights redressed."[1] Hutchinson had neither intimidated the metropolis, nor stopped the meetings in the country. Boston had its usual annual commemoration of the massacre,[2] when Warren was on the committee that matured the business; and, three days later (March 8), he was appointed a member of an able committee, Samuel Adams being the chairman, to vindicate the November town-meeting from the aspersions of Hutchinson. This committee, in an elaborate paper, advocated the right of the towns to assemble to consider political matters, went

---

[1] Samuel H. Parsons, of Providence, R.I., in a letter to Samuel Adams, March 3, 1773, says, "When the spirit of patriotism seems expiring in America in general, it must afford a very sensible pleasure to the friends of American liberty to see the noble efforts of our Boston friends in the support of the rights of America, as well as their unshaken resolution in opposing any, the least invasion of their charter privileges." He suggested an annual meeting of commissioners of the colonies, and dwells on the New-England Confederacy of 1643.

[2] The oration on this anniversary was delivered by Dr. Benjamin Church, who was a member of the committee of correspondence, became subsequently a member of the provincial congress and the general court, and, in October, 1775, was convicted of holding a secret correspondence with the enemy.

Hutchinson (see note on p. 224) says, that he had, as early as the 6th of January, 1773, the fullest evidence of the plans of the patriots. Later, he sent (Oct. 19, 1773) to Lord Dartmouth a copy of a letter, written by the Massachusetts agent in London (Franklin) to Speaker Cushing, elaborately urging the necessity of a congress; probably the letter dated July 7, 1773, printed in Sparks's "Franklin," viii. 60. Hutchinson not only did not name the person who supplied him with the copy of this letter, but asked Lord Dartmouth not to let it be known that he (Hutchinson) supplied the copy, saying, if it were known, that "it might be the means of preventing any further useful intelligence which he might otherwise have from the same person."

Who was this person? It is stated by Dr. Cooper, in a letter, that Church had an understanding with Hutchinson as to the delivery of the 5th of March oration; and that Church did this service to throw the patriots off their guard. Paul Revere says (1 Mass. Hist. Coll., v. 106), that words uttered on an evening in 1774, at a caucus at the Green Dragon, were reported to him the next day, through a Tory channel, and by a Whig at heart, though of Tory connections. Revere relates other circumstances connected with Church, and says, "I know that Dr. Warren had not the greatest affection for him."

There is little doubt that the person who supplied Hutchinson with information was Dr. Church.

at length into the subject of the meeting, and treated briefly the question of parliamentary supremacy; urging that it was impossible for parliament to legislate for the colonies in all cases whatsoever, without violating rights belonging to the people as men, as Christians, and as subjects, or without destroying the foundation of its own constitution. They said it was an unspeakable satisfaction that so many towns, and so many "gentlemen of figure in other colonies," had indorsed the November movement. "It adds a dignity to our proceedings," are their words, "that the House of Representatives, when called upon by the governor to bear their testimony against them, saw reason to declare that they had not discovered that the principles advanced by the town of Boston were unwarrantable by the constitution." An expression of this feeling — that the town was acting in harmony with all friends of the cause — is frequently seen.

The proceedings of the November town-meeting were sent by the Boston committee to leading Whigs of Virginia and other colonies.[1] Meantime the burning of the "Gaspee," in Rhode Island, occasioned fresh legislation by parliament affecting personal rights. When the Virginia assembly came together, in March, Dabney Carr moved the memorable resolutions that formed a colonial committee of correspondence for that colony, and invited all the assemblies on the continent to join them. This

---

[1] The report was sent to Franklin, who had it printed in London, and wrote a preface for this edition, in which he said it was "not the production of a private writer, but the unanimous act of a large American city." Sparks ("Works of Franklin," iv. 381) says of this report, "It was the boldest exposition of American grievances which had hitherto been made public, and was drawn up with as much ability as freedom."

was another great step. It was the organization of a national party. It filled the hearts of the Boston patriots with joy. "The reception of the truly patriotic resolves," Samuel Adams wrote to Richard Henry Lee, "of the House of Burgesses of Virginia, gladden the hearts of all who are friends of liberty. Our committee of correspondence had a special meeting on the occasion, and determined to circulate immediately printed copies of them in every town in the province.[1] . . . I am desired by them to assure you of their veneration for your most ancient colony, and their unfeigned esteem for the gentlemen of your committee. . . . I hope you will have the hearty concurrence of every assembly on the continent." And the patriot gave an assurance of the hearty co-operation of Massachusetts. Hutchinson, when he saw the action of Virginia, abandoned the futile claim of having thwarted the patriots; urged that their triumph would be greater than ever, if their doings were allowed to pass unnoticed by the ministry; said

---

[1] The "Boston Gazette," May 17, 1773, has a letter by the Woburn committee, addressed to the Boston committee, which shows the manner in which the action of Virginia was responded to by the towns. Woburn is about ten miles from Boston.

"WOBURN, April 24, 1773.

"GENTLEMEN, — We have just received your letter, dated the 9th inst., wherein are contained not only the spirited proceedings of the town of Boston of the 8th of March last, but an extract of the noble and patriotic resolves of the Honorable House of Burgesses in Virginia, which, in our esteem, are worthy the imitation of every house of general assembly on this continent; and may they all follow the example which that virtuous province hath set, whose name was given to it in honor of a virgin!

"We are with respect, gentlemen, your obedient and humble servants,

"SAMUEL WYMAN,
ROBERT DOUGLASS,
SAMUEL BLODGET,
LOAMMI BALDWIN,
TIMOTHY WINN,
Committee of Correspondence for Woburn."

that something should be done, though he was at a loss to say what it should be; and endeavored to rouse his party to decisive action. He complained that, after the delivery of his last address, the Government was deserted, and alleged that a dozen of the best men on his side had left the general court when it was in their power to have given affairs a turn in favor of the Tory cause.

While engaged in the labors of the committee, and doubtless sharing the general joy, Warren's home became a house of mourning by the death of his wife. She left four children. The "Boston Gazette" (May 3, 1773) has the following notice and tribute: —

"On Tuesday last, Mrs. Elizabeth Warren, the amiable and virtuous consort of Dr. Joseph Warren, in the twenty-sixth year of her age. Her remains were decently interred last Friday afternoon.

"If fading lilies, when they droop and die,
Robbed of each charm that pleased the gazing eye,
With sad regret the grieving mind inspire,
What then when virtue's brightest lamps expire?
Ethereal spirits see the system's right,
But mortal minds demand a clearer sight.
In spite of reason's philosophic art,
A tear must fall to indicate the heart.
Could reason's force disarm the tyrant foe,
Or calm the mind that feels the fatal blow,
No clouded thought had discomposed the mind
Of him whom Heaven ordained her dearest friend.
Good sense and modesty with virtue crowned
A sober mind, when fortune smiled or frowned;
So keen a feeling for a friend distressed,
She could not bear to see a worm oppressed.
These virtues fallen enhance the scene of woe,
Swell the big drops that scarce confinement know,
And force them down in copious showers to flow.
But know, thou tyrant, Death, thy force is spent, —
Thine arm is weakened, and thy bow unbent.
Secured from insults from your grisly train
Of marshalled slaves t' inflict disease and pain,

> She rides triumphant in the aërial course,
> To land at pleasure's inexhausted Source.
> Celestial Genii, line the heavenly way,
> And guard her passage to the realms of day."

The "Massachusetts Gazette" of May 20, 1773 has the following: —

> "Epitaphium Dominæ Elizsæ* War * * *."
>
> "Et tumulum facite, et tumulo superaddite carmen." — VIRG.
>
> "Omnes, flete, dolete, cari virtutes amici!
> Heu! nostras terras dulcis Eliza fugit.
> Quisnam novit eam, gemitusque negare profundos
> Posset? permagni est criminis ille reus." — D*****.

About this time, Samuel Adams was requested to name one or more persons for membership of the London "Society for Supporting the Bill of Rights," the main object of which was the preservation of the English constitution as it had been established at the Revolution. In reply, Adams wrote to Arthur Lee, a member, as follows: "I can with the greatest integrity nominate my two worthy and intimate friends, John Adams and Joseph Warren, Esqs.; the one eminent in the profession of law, and the other equally so in that of physic; both of them men of an unblemished moral character, and zealous advocates of the common rights of mankind."

At the election of representatives in May, Thomas Cushing, Samuel Adams, John Hancock, and William Phillips, received nearly all the votes; the largest number being four hundred and eighteen, and the lowest being only five less. The committee chosen by the town to prepare the customary instructions to them consisted of Warren as the chairman, Benjamin Church, Joseph Greenleaf, Nathaniel Appleton, and William Cooper. The draft probably was by Warren. It regarded the unanimity of the election, at the important juncture, as evidence of the confidence which the people reposed in the ability of these patriots and their inflexible attachment to constitutional rights; and of the general conviction that they would vigorously oppose encroachments on their ancient privileges, and never betray their constituents by surrendering the powers "of framing laws and taxes for the people to any usurper under heaven." These terms indicate the ardent character of this paper. It was quite elaborate. It dwelt on political grievances, and claimed that the privileges and powers of the commons of the colony as to legislation were as uncontrollable within the colony as were the commons of England within the realm, but that both were subject "to the revision of the king." It closed by warmly commending the plan proposed by "the noble, patriotic sister colony of Virginia," with the most sanguine expectation, that a union of counsels and conduct among the colonies, by the smiles of Heaven, would assuredly fix their rights on a solid basis.

The legislature, which met in May, promptly responded to the union action of Virginia, by choosing a legislative committee of correspondence. It was soon announced, that Connecticut, Rhode Island, and New Hampshire had joined in this action; and it was said (June 14) in the press, —

> "The day, the important day, is come, of old
> By our prophetic ancestors foretold," —

of a union of the colonies. Under this couplet, which heads an article, is the following: "Things are moving with a rapid progress to complete the triumph of freedom in America: the hand of Providence is evidently working out our political salvation. Experience has taught Americans their strength and importance among the nations, and wisdom has now led them to adopt a plan of union." One nationality was the inspiring and elevating thought. "No people," it was said, "that ever trod the stage of the world have had so glorious a prospect as rises before the Americans. There is nothing good or great but their wisdom may acquire; and to what heights they will arrive in the progress of time no one can conceive."

The demand for a congress of all the colonies was frequently made in the press and on festive occasions. An elaborate essay, by a Philadelphian, is reprinted in the "Gazette" of the 15th of March, filling a side and a half, which recommends a congress, in order to form a court like that of the Amphictyons of Greece. A spirited appeal in this paper of the 2d of August urges a meeting of American States. "Britons, attend! Americans, give ear!" are its words: "the people of this continent are awakened by the cause of liberty, and are now forming plans to preserve it in perfection to future ages. There should be a meeting of American States, composed of members chosen by the several houses of representatives in the colonies, to consider what measures will most effectually preserve the liberties and promote the prosperity of America. Let every man of sentiment and patriotism rouse up his genius."

The Fourteenth of August, the anniversary of the uprising against the Stamp Act, was celebrated with great spirit, when a large procession marched from Boston to Roxbury. A "union flag" floated over the tent in which the company had their entertainment; and among the toasts were, " The patriotic House of Burgesses of our ancient sister colony of Virginia." — " A constitutional and permanent union of the colonies in North America." — " The Sons of Liberty throughout America."

I have nothing to relate of Warren especially, until he acted with his brother patriots on the tea-question. His name is not connected with the publication of the letters of Hutchinson and others, supplying proofs of their agency in introducing arbitrary power, which created great excitement. Nor is there any identification of his contributions to the press, though there is much matter written in his style. For instance, a communication in the "Gazette" (Sept. 27), signed W., is in the same elevated tone of citations already made. "It must awaken," are the words, "all the feelings of humanity to behold a prospect of liberty for the many millions who compose our growing empire, and entail it to future ages: this is a blessing for which we cannot too long and too earnestly contend; and I trust all future generations will bless the present for their manly exertions in so noble a cause. We long wandered in uncertainty, and our motions were eccentric; but we have now reduced American policy to a system (first formed by our vigilant brethren of Virginia), the grand principles of which are, that a constant correspondence shall be maintained between the colonies, and nothing important be transacted without consulting the whole."

Hutchinson's letters of this period are very voluminous. He had much to say of "the grand incendiary," Samuel Adams. "Our principal incendiary," he wrote, "has a great deal of low art and cunning;" and he related the success of the scheme of forming committees of correspondence. He said (July 10), "We have now subsisting in this province, committees of correspondence in most of the towns of the province; committees of the house and council to correspond with their respective agents, to effect the removal of the governor and lieutenant-governor, and for other purposes; a committee of correspondence of the house to concert with committees of correspondence, with other assemblies, and to give information." He was in hopes the colonies would not unite in the proposed measure of a congress; was much cheered, after a trip into the country, to find the excitement which the publication of his letters occasioned had subsided; and he wrote (Sept. 6), "In a late journey to the remote parts of the province, I was surprised to find the flame, which had spread so universally, so soon and so generally extinguished."

Soon after the statement in the press, just cited, of a general understanding that the patriots of one colony would transact nothing important without consulting the patriots of the other colonies, reached through inter-colonial committees of correspondence, or a national party organization, it was announced that there was to be an insidious importation of tea, on which the duty had been retained. I need go no further into general history than to state, that the king re solved to try the question with America by this tax; and, at his suggestion, an act was passed by parlia ment, authorizing the East-India Company to export tea to America, duty free in England, but subject to the existing threepence tax in America, which was to be paid into the national treasury by the company's agents. It was designed in this way to collect the duty, and obtain a recognition of the supremacy of parliament.

The fact was announced in a Philadelphia journal (Sept. 29), in a letter from London, (dated Aug. 4), as follows: "The East-India Company have come to a resolution to send six hundred chests of tea to Philadelphia, and the like quantity to New York and Boston; and their intention, I understand, is to have warehouses, and sell by public sale four times a year, as they do here." The company, on receiving the requisite license, made consignments of teas simultaneously to Charleston, Philadelphia, New York, and Boston; and selected certain persons in each of these ports to act as consignees, or, as they were called, tea commissioners. This new, practical issue turned discussion at once from questions having mainly a local bearing, as that of the judges' salaries, royal instructions, and the star-chamber commission in Rhode Island, to the original question of taxation, which bore directly on all the colonies.

All America was in a flame about this insidious tea importation.[1] The political matter in the press now

[1] A British officer at New York, in a letter to a person in London, dated Nov. 1, 1773, says, "All America is in a flame on account of the tea exportation. The New Yorkers, as well as the Bostonians and Philadelphians, are, it seems, determined that no tea shall be landed. They have published a paper, in numbers, called the "Alarm." It begins first with "dear countrymen," and then goes on exhorting them to open their eyes, and, like sons of Liberty, throw off all connection with the tyrant, their mother-country. They have, on this occasion, raised a company of artillery, and every day almost are practising at a target.

became more abundant than ever. Differences of opinion are seen as to the way the duty on the tea was to be paid. "We know," it was said, "that on a certificate of its being landed here, the tribute is, by an agreement, to be paid in London. Landing, therefore, is the point in view; and every nerve will be strained to obtain it." It was asked in New York, "Are the Americans such blockheads as to care whether it be a hot red poker or a red hot poker which they are to swallow, provided Lord North forces them to swallow one of the two?" At that time, political science had not devised written constitutions creating tribunals with powers like the supreme courts of the States, and the United States, to relieve the people from the operation of palpably unconstitutional acts;[1] and the only thing practicable was to follow in popular action, the irregular mode, which had been so long customary in England. In this way it was determined to thwart the designs of the East-India Company.

Public opinion was first brought to bear on the consignees. An able hand-bill was circulated in Philadelphia, headed, "By uniting we stand; by dividing

Their independent companies are out at exercise every day. The minds of the lower people are inflamed by the examples of some of their principals. They swear that they will burn every ship that comes in; but I believe our six and twelve-pounders, with the Royal Welsh Fusiliers, will prevent any thing of that kind." This was printed in the newspapers.

[1] James Otis, in his "Rights of the British Colonies of 1764," says that the courts had this power. "The equity and justice of a bill," he says, p. 41, "may be questioned with perfect submission to the legislature. Reasons may be given why an act ought to be repealed, and yet obedience must be yielded to it till that repeal takes place. If the reasons that can be given against an act are such as plainly demonstrate that it is against *natural* equity, the executive courts will adjudge such act void. It may be questioned by some, though I make no doubt of it, whether they are not obliged by their oaths to adjudge such act void."

we fall;" signed Scævola, and addressed "To the commissioners appointed by the East-India Company for the sale of teas in America." They were characterized as "political bombardiers to demolish the fair structure of American liberty;" it was said that all eyes were fixed on them, and they were urged to refuse to act. This was followed by a great public meeting, held "at the State House," which passed a series of resolves against this tea importation, and requested the tea consignees to resign. They soon bowed to public opinion, and relinquished their trust. The hand-bill just referred to was reprinted in the journals of New-York, where the merchants assembled, and thanked the captains and owners of the ships belonging to that port, for declining to take the East-India Company tea on freight.

The towns of Massachusetts were still responding to the Boston town-meeting of November, and choosing committees of correspondence; and their proceedings appeared from time to time in the journals.[1] The Boston committee of correspondence, keeping a vigilant eye on public affairs, said, in a circular to the towns (Sept. 21), that their enemies were alarmed "at the union which they see is already established in this province, and the confederacy into which they expect the whole continent of America will soon be drawn;" urged that the talk of conciliatory measures by the

[1] The Boston town-meeting of November, 1772, continued to provoke comment from the Tories; and this undoubtedly stimulated the Whigs to keep up their action. Though the editors of the "Boston Gazette" said (Jan. 21, 1773), that they should insert no more reports of the proceedings of the towns in answer to Boston, "unless by particular request, especially as they were to be printed in a volume," yet these reports continued to appear in the paper. The whole first side of its issue of the 30th of August, 1773, is filled with the resolves and letter of the town of Harvard, in answer to the Boston report of November.

ministry was insidious; and averred that the cause demanded the greatest wisdom, vigilance, and fortitude.[1] The committee appointed by the House of Representatives, in a letter (Oct. 21) addressed to the committees of the other colonies, represented that the ministerial measures could only "end in absolute despotism," and dwelt on the importance of union; "so that, in whichsoever of the colonies any infringements were made on the common rights of all, that colony might have the united efforts of all for its support." "We are far," are its words, "from desiring that the connection between Great Britain and America should be broken. *Esto perpetua* is our ardent wish, but upon the terms only of equal liberty." The letter closed by urging the necessity that each colony

[1] The committee received spirited replies to this circular. The following was from Charlestown, where the Bunker-hill Battle was fought. The original is indorsed in Cooper's handwriting, "Received Oct. 12, 1773; not to be printed:

"*Seth Sweetser, Clerk of Committee of Charlestown, to William Cooper, Clerk of Committee of Boston.*

"CHARLESTOWN, Oct. 11, 1773.

"SIR,—Last Saturday I received a letter from you, purporting to be the just remarks of the worthy and watchful committee of correspondence for the town of Boston, upon the present situation of our public affairs, highly fit to be well considered of by every friend to his country. I am proud of the good opinion the committee have of me; and they may depend upon my using my utmost endeavors that the salutary ends they aim at may be answered; and, were my power and influence equal to my wishes, there would not be one enemy to our happy constitution left on this continent; and I believe here are our greatest. Those that are inimical to us, finding that violent measures do not answer their designs, will try what flattery can do (a more dangerous method), by insinuating, that, if we will desist from asserting our claim of rights, we shall soon be eased of the grievances we complain of. A rattle this, fit only to lull a crying child to rest. If this new scheme should take, (which God forbid!) tyranny and bondage will soon follow, which are more terrifying to a generous mind than the sound of the trumpet summoning to fight for liberty in the most bloody field of battle.

"I am, with all possible respects, the committee's most obedient and very humble servant, SETH SWEETSER.

"WILLIAM COOPER, as clerk of the committee of correspondence for the town of Boston, to be communicated to said committee."

should take effectual methods to counteract the design of the ministry in the shipment of the teas by the East-India Company.¹

There was nowhere a more general or a deeper feeling on the subject of the teas than in Boston. The consignees were either relatives or hearty sympathizers with the governor. Two of them were his sons Elisha and Thomas, the latter subsequently one of the mandamus counsellors. The others were Richard Clarke and Sons, Benjamin Faneuil, jun., and Joshua Winslow, persons of great respectability. The elder Clarke, a Harvard graduate, was a merchant of high standing, one of whose daughters married J. S. Copley, the artist, who was the father of the late Lord Lyndhurst. All the consignees subsequently went to England, and some had their property confiscated.

All eyes were now fixed on the consignees, who saw reflected in the press, in excited language, the tone of public opinion, and could see that it was similar to what it was in other places. The hand-bill that was circulated in Philadelphia was printed in all the Boston papers, even in the Tory paper, Draper's, (Oct. 25); and also the proceedings of the people, both of New York and Philadelphia. Still there was no resignation of the consignees. As the time approached when the tea ships might be expected, the subject was considered in the North-end Caucus, which was composed mostly of mechanics, many of whom lived in this part of the town; and its ses-

---

[1] This remarkable letter is in the Massachusetts archives. The following is the postscript: "It is desired you would not make the contents of this letter public, as it will give our enemies opportunity to counteract the design of it."

sions, at which a mechanic always presided, were miniature town-meetings. Warren was one of the members in whose judgment they had great confidence. This body voted (Oct. 23), that they "would oppose with their lives and fortunes the vending of any tea" that might be sent to the town for sale by the East-India Company. These proceedings were secret.

There is no evidence to connect this caucus with a hand-bill[1] that appeared a few days after, inviting the freemen of Boston and the neighboring towns to meet at Liberty Tree, to hear the consignees make a public resignation of their office, and to swear to re-ship to London any teas that might be consigned to them; or with the notice, on the night of the 1st of November, served on the consignees, who were roused from their sleep, and, by letter, warned to appear at the same place, and not to fail at their peril. No names were attached to the hand-bill or the letter. The governor and the consignees, however, regarded both as proceeding from the popular leaders, and looked forward to the proposed meeting with deep concern. Hutchinson advised his sons not to be out of town on the day appointed for it.

The North-end Caucus was again called together

[1] Draper's "Gazette" says, hand-bills were stuck up all over the town on Tuesday morning; but gives only the following, dated on the day of the meeting: —

" To the Freemen of this and the neighboring towns.

"GENTLEMEN, — You are desired to meet at Liberty Tree, this day, at twelve o'clock at noon; then and there to hear the persons to whom the tea shipped by the East-India Company is consigned, make a public resignation of their office as consigners upon oath; and also swear that they will re-ship any teas that may be consigned to them by said company by the first vessel sailing for London.

"O. C., *Secretary*.

"BOSTON, Nov. 3, 1773.

" ☞ Show us the man that dare take down this."

(Nov. 2) for deliberation on this subject; when one committee was sent to invite the committee of correspondence to meet with them, and another committee invited John Hancock; and thus were assembled the choice Whig spirits of the town. This action indicates good sense, and the importance attached to the occasion. The proceedings cannot be related in detail. The official record of this session is brief; but the action was to the point, and significant: " Voted that the tea shipped by the East-India Company shall not be landed."

On Wednesday morning (Nov. 3), a large flag was raised above the Liberty Tree: the town-crier summoned the people to meet at this place, and the bells rang from eleven to twelve o'clock. About five hundred assembled, among whom were three of the representatives, — Adams, Hancock, and Phillips, — the selectmen, the town-clerk and treasurer, Warren, Molineux, and several other of the prominent patriots; making a fair representation of the character, intelligence, and wealth of the town. The consignees, Hutchinson says, "agreed they would be together, that they might all fare alike;" and were at the warehouse of Richard Clarke, at the lower end of King Street, with a few of their friends and a justice of the peace. The governor was at the Town House, at the head of the same street.

The presiding officer of the meeting is not named. It is related, that, the consignees not appearing, a select number went into Liberty Hall, and made choice of seven or nine,[1] to wait on the consignees,

---

[1] The names of eight are William Molineux, William Dennie, Joseph Warren, Benjamin Church, Major Barber, Gabriel Johonnot, —— Proctor, and Ezekiel Cheever.

and request their resignation of their trust; and, in case they refused, or declined to give a pledge not to land the tea or to pay the duty on it, to present a resolve to them, declaring them to be enemies to their country. The committee immediately proceeded in their duty; those named as acting, being Messrs. Molineux, Warren, Dennie, Church, and Johonnot,[1] who were followed by a portion of the meeting. Hutchinson saw the procession, — it might have been as it passed the Town House, — and says there were on the committee, citizens of considerable popularity, who were accompanied by a large body of the people, many of them not of the lowest rank. On arriving at the warehouse, some entered the lower story, the doors of which had been left open, while the committee went up the stairs leading to the counting-room in which were the consignees, but found the doors closed. A parley was carried on between these parties through an open window, Molineux acting as the spokesman. "From whom are you a committee?" asked Clarke. "From the whole people" was the reply. The names of the committee were then read, and the demand of the meeting was stated. "I shall have nothing to do with you," Clarke said. The consignees declined to resign their trust. The resolve was now read, declaring them to be enemies of their country. When the committee returned to the lower story of the building and reported the result, the cry arose, "Out with them! out with them!" and some pushed up stairs. A slight disturbance had occurred, from an attempt by Mr. Clarke's friends, on a request from the counting-room, to close the doors of the

---

[1] These are named in Bernard's narrative as acting at Clarke's warehouse.

warehouse This was resisted; and the doors were unhinged, and carried to another street. The justice, who, in the king's name, now commanded the peace, was hooted at and struck, when the people were persuaded to refrain from further violence. One of the Hutchinsons, with a friend, soon came out of the counting-room, passed quite unmolested through the crowd, and joined his father in the council chamber at the head of the street. He had with him less than a quorum of the council, and did not act. The committee soon returned to Liberty Tree, where they reported in form to the meeting; when the people dispersed. The character of the citizens who gave countenance to this meeting attested its respectability: it reflected the general sentiment; and the rough denial of a demand, which in other places had been complied with, was ominous of the future.[1]

It was said by the Tories, that the meeting at Liberty Tree was irregular, and of no account. Petitioners for a town-meeting now represented (Nov. 4) the common alarm at the report that the East-India Company were shipping cargoes of tea to America; that they had reason to fear, what more than any thing in life was to be dreaded, the tribute would be established, and thus, by this political plan, the liberties for which they had so long contended would be lost to them and their posterity; and they prayed for a town-meeting to take such steps as their safety and well-being required. The selectmen issued

[1] Bancroft, vi. 484, gives the conversation at Clarke's warehouse. Bernard says that it was Mr. Hatch, the justice, who was struck. The "Gazette" and "News Letter" say that the whole body of the people went from Liberty Tree to King Street. Hutchinson's letters are voluminous on the proceedings relating to the tea.

a notification for a meeting, to be held the next day at ten o'clock in the morning.

The meeting on the fifth of November was largely attended, and John Hancock was the moderator. After earnest debates, it was decided that the sense of the town could not be better expressed than in the words of a series of resolves which had been passed at a meeting convened (Oct. 18) for the same object in Philadelphia; and these resolves, temperate in tone but clear in principle and decided in terms, were adopted. They declare that freemen have an inherent right to dispose of their property; that the tea tax was levying contributions on them without their consent; that the purpose of it tended to render assemblies useless, and to introduce arbitrary government; that a steady opposition to this ministerial plan was a duty which every freeman owed to himself, his country, and posterity; that the East-India Company importation was an attempt to enforce this plan; and that whoever countenanced the unloading, vending, or receiving the tea, was an enemy to his country. They requested the consignees, out of regard to their character and to the peace of the province, immediately to resign their appointment. The meeting chose a committee[1] to present these resolves to the consignees; it voted that the town expected the merchants, under no pretext whatever, would import any tea liable to duty; and it then adjourned until three o'clock. At this hour there was again a full meeting, when the committee reported that the consignees gave as a reason why a definite answer could not be

---

[1] This committee consisted of the moderator, Henderson Inches, Benjamin Austin, and the selectmen.

given until Monday, that two of their number, the Hutchinsons, were at Milton; and, as they chose to have a consultation, they could not agree upon an answer until that day. Samuel Adams, Warren, and Molineux were then desired to acquaint the Messrs. Clarke and Mr. Faneuil that the town expected an immediate answer from them; and the committee soon reported that a reply might be expected in half an hour. These consignees, in a letter, gave the reasons why they regarded it as impossible for them to comply with the request of the town; but the meeting voted the letter to be unsatisfactory. A committee,[1] Warren being a member, was directed to wait on the Hutchinsons, and request an immediate resignation; and then the meeting adjourned until the next day. One of the Hutchinsons was at the governor's house, at Milton; and the other was at the house of the lieutenant-governor, in Boston.

Faneuil Hall, on the next day, was crowded. The committee to wait on the Hutchinsons reported that they sought them in vain at Milton, but found Thomas Hutchinson in town, who, in a letter, stated that, when he and his brother knew definitely that they had been appointed factors, they would be sufficiently informed to answer the request of the inhabitants. This cool reply caused great excitement in the meeting; there were cries, "To arms! to arms!" and the ominous words were responded to by clapping of hands, and general applause. As usual, good sense predominated; and the meeting simply voted that the obnoxious letter was daringly affrontive to the town,

---

[1] This committee consisted of John Hancock, John Pitts, Samuel Adams, Samuel Abbot, Joseph Warren, William Powell, and Nathaniel Appleton.

and then dissolved. Hutchinson (Nov. 8) said that he was trying to collect evidence of the inflammatory speeches that had been uttered, but could find no person willing to give it.

Nothing material, in relation to the tea question, occurred for a week. No person, it was said, attempted the smallest affront to the tea commissioners. The town was quiet. It was believed that the tea ships were near the harbor; and the journals were full of political speculation, some of it inflammatory, but, in the main, strong, well put, statesmanlike, and of an elevating character. There is significance even in the names selected for signatures. They are not of the school of Rousseau, but of Milton. "Sydney"[1] says, "America seems to be reserved by Providence for a land of real freedom, that the world may see in these latter days the true glory of liberty. "Locke" says, "It will be considered by Americans, whether the dernier resort and only asylum for their liberties is not an American commonwealth."[2] It was evident to the leaders on both sides, that things were drifting to the pass of a great exigency; nor did they disagree in the view which they took of the principle at stake.

---

[1] Massachusetts Spy, Nov. 11, 1773.

[2] Ib., Nov. 26. Z., in the "Boston Gazette," Oct. 11, 1773, writes: "How shall the colonies force their oppressors to proper terms? This question has been often answered by our politicians; viz., 'Form an independent State, — an American commonwealth.' This plan has been proposed, and I can't find that any other is likely to answer the great purpose of preserving our liberties: I hope, therefore, it will be well digested and forwarded, to be in due time put into execution, unless our political fathers can secure American liberties in some other way. As the population, wealth, and power of this continent are swiftly increasing, we certainly have no cause to doubt of our success in maintaining liberty, by forming a commonwealth, or whatever measures wisdom may point out for the preservation of the rights of America."

Hutchinson says that he "foresaw that this would prove a more difficult affair than any which had preceded it."[1] He regarded the principle of the supremacy of parliament to be in issue: with his ideas of the prerogative of the Crown, and British sovereignty, he could not think of yielding the point of the whole controversy, and he determined to make no concession. He described (Nov. 15), with much particularity, the state of affairs, in a letter to Lord Dartmouth. After remarking that the people of the town were in a great ferment, and that he had done all that he could to preserve the peace without the aid of the council, he says, "They [the council] profess to disapprove of the tumultuous, violent proceedings of the people: but they wish to see the professed end of the people in such proceedings attained in a regular way; and, instead of joining with me in proper measures to discourage an opposition to the landing and sale of the teas expected, one and another of the gentlemen of the greatest influence intimate, that the best thing that can be done to quiet the people would be the refusal of the gentlemen to whom the teas are consigned to execute the trust; and they declare they would do it, if it was their case, and would advise all their connections to do it. Nor will they ever countenance a measure which shall tend to carry into execution an act of parliament which lays taxes upon the colonies for the purpose of raising revenue. The same principle prevails with by far the greater part of the merchants, who, though in general they declare against mobs and violence, yet they as generally wish the teas may not be import-

[1] Hutchinson's History, iii. 425.

ed." Hutchinson repeatedly concedes in his letters that the mass of the people acted in the conviction that their rights were invaded. This citation presents the merchants in an honorable light; the action of the North-end Caucus speaks for the mechanics; and the proceedings of the towns attest the spirit of the yeomanry. It is worthy of remark, that Hutchinson, in his unbending course, stood almost alone; for his political friends advised concession. In this he exactly represented his royal master George IH. At this time, Lord North was accustomed to reply to remonstrances, that His Majesty was resolved to try the question. In the words of an English writer, the hazardous experiment was to be attempted on men, many of whose ancestors had fled to the desert from the tyranny of that martyred sovereign, who had the same imprudent propensity for trying questions with his subjects;[1] and the Bostonians stood forth, like their native rocks, sharp, angular, and defiant.[2]

Samuel Adams, like the royal governor, believed that he was engaged in an extraordinary work. He wrote (Nov. 9) to Arthur Lee, "One cannot foresee events; but, from all the observation I am able to make, my next letter will not be upon a trifling subject;" and in that next letter he characterized the event which he dwelt upon "as remarkable as had happened since the commencement of the struggle for American liberty." Though there was a presentiment that an event of great moment was at hand, yet the popular leaders at the helm — Adams, Warren, Hancock, Molineux, and Young were subsequently named to the privy council as the most prominent —

[1] Macknight's Life of Burke, ii. 38.   [2] *Ib.*, ii. 40.

were not moved by the desire to force the town to do a deed for the sake of the name; but they simply aimed to meet honorably a great exigency. They asked of power no greater concession than had been made elsewhere. A failure to obtain the resignation of the consignees had already created suspicion; and fears[1] began to be expressed abroad that Boston would not meet the expectations of the patriots of other colonies. When the cautious or the timid of the town questioned whether it were not premature to push matters in this case to extremities, it was replied by the bold and determined, that, if fidelity to the common cause were likely to bring on a quarrel with Great Britain, it was the best time for it to come. "Our credit," it was said, "also is at stake: we must venture; and, unless we do, we shall be discarded by the Sons of Liberty in the other colonies, whose assistance we may expect upon emergencies, in case they find us steady, resolute, and faithful"[2] The union of the colonies, inchoate as it was, had become a moral power.

In this way, by the force of circumstances, there were engaged face to face the actors on this public and even national stage. The "Post Boy" (Nov. 15), in a semi-official tone, said, "We learn that His Majesty has declared his intention of supporting the

---

[1] Gordon (i. 331) relates, that, before these events, Thomas Mifflin, of Philadelphia, subsequently the governor, being in Boston, said to the Boston patriots, in relation to the teas, "Will you engage that they shall not be landed? If so, I will answer for Philadelphia." The patriots pledged their honor to resist the landing. In all the Boston journals of Nov. 11, 1773, there is printed a letter from Philadelphia, in which are the following sentences: "There are many fears respecting Boston. . . . It is to be hoped the town of Boston will appear on the present occasion with their usual spirit." — *Massachusetts Spy, Nov.* 10.

[2] Gordon, i. 336.

supreme authority and right of the British parliament to make laws binding on the colonies;" which agrees so precisely with Hutchinson's views of his duty, that he might have penned it. He did pen on this day, in the letter to Lord Dartmouth already cited, these words: "The persons to whom the teas are intrusted declare, that, whilst they can be protected from violence to their persons, they will not give way to the unreasonable demands which have been made upon them." When Power was thus clinging to every inch of its formal authority and a determined people were standing firmly on their rights, there could be no compromise; and so events moved steadily on to the consummation of an act which, in its consequences, proved second only to the Declaration of Independence.[1]

A fresh fact, now freely commented on in the press, deepened the interest of the hour. Hutchinson, under his own hand, issued an order[2] to Colonel John

[1] The storage or detention of a few cargoes of teas is not an object in itself sufficient to justify a detail of several pages; but, as the subsequent severities towards the Massachusetts were grounded on what the ministry termed their refractory behavior on this occasion, and as those measures were followed by consequences of the highest magnitude both to Great Britain and the colonies, a particular narration of the transactions of the town of Boston is indispensable. — *Mrs. Warren's History of the American Revolution*, i. 105.

[2] I am indebted to Colonel James W. Sever for a copy of this order. He has the original, which is in Hutchinson's handwriting: —

"MASSACHUSETTS BAY.   BY THE GOVERNOR.
"*To Colonel John Hancock, Captain of the Governor's Company of Cadets, &c.*

"The Cadet Company under your command having signalized itself heretofore upon a very necessary occasion, and the late tumultuous proceedings in the town of Boston requiring that more than usual caution should be taken at this time for the preservation of the peace, I think it proper that you should forthwith summon each person belonging to the company to be ready, and to appear in arms, at such place of parade as you think fit, whensoever there may be a tumultuous assembling of the people in violation of the laws, in order to their being aiding and assisting to the civil magistrate, as occasion may require.

"Dated at Boston, the 11th day of November, 1773.

"TH. HUTCHINSON."

Hancock, "the Captain of the Governor's Company of Cadets," to summon forthwith each member to hold himself ready to appear in arms whenever there might be "a tumultuous assembling of the people in violation of the laws," which showed an intention to use military force to suppress public meetings. This company took its orders directly from the governor. It rendered service in the riots of the 26th of August, 1765; was accustomed to parade on holidays, such as coronation and election days; and was often complimented for its discipline. It occasioned also uneasiness, that companies of the British troops stationed at Castle William were now marched into the neighboring towns. There was now quite a respectable naval force in the harbor, under the command of Admiral Montague.

On the seventeenth, a vessel arrived from London with the news that three ships for Boston, under Captains Bruce, Hall, and Coffin, and having the East-India Company's teas on board, had sailed down the channel, and that other tea vessels had cleared for Philadelphia: when petitioners to the selectmen — the fourth name being Warren's — stated that the town was alarmed at the hourly expectation of the arrival of the teas; and, apprehending that the consignees might be sufficiently informed on the terms of its consignment as to be able to give their promised answer to the town, they asked for a town-meeting; when the selectmen appointed one for the next day. On the same day, one of the firm of the Clarke's arrived in town from abroad; and being, in the evening, at the house of his father, Richard Clarke, on School Street, a mob attempted to get into the door, broke windows, and did other damage; but, though a pistol was fired from the second story vigilant and influential friends of the patriot cause promptly appeared, checked the outrage, and persuaded the mob to disperse. No person was seriously injured.

The town-meeting held the next day was brief, but to the point. Hancock was the moderator. A committee was appointed to wait on the consignees, and to say to them, that it was the desire of the town that they would give the final answer to the request whether they would resign their appointment; which elicited the following letter: —

BOSTON, Nov. 18, 1773.

SIR, — In answer to the message we have this day received from the town, we beg leave to say that we have not yet received any orders from the East-India Company respecting the expected teas; but we are now further acquainted, that our friends in England have entered into general engagements in our behalf, merely of a commercial nature, which puts it out of our power to comply with the request of the town.

We are, sir, your most humble servants,

RICHARD CLARKE AND SONS.
BENJAMIN FANEUIL, JUN., for SELF and
JOSHUA WINSLOW, ESQ.
ELISHA HUTCHINSON, for my
BROTHER and SELF.

This answer was voted to be unsatisfactory, and this last town-meeting on the tea question now dissolved. Its calmness and dignity were ominous. "This sudden dissolution," Hutchinson says, "struck more terror into the consignees than the most minatory resolves.

On the next day (Nov. 19), the consignees, in a petition, asked leave " to resign themselves, and property committed to their care, to His Excellency and their Honors, as guardians and protectors of the people;" and that measures might be devised "for the landing and securing the teas until the petitioners could safely dispose of them, or could receive directions from their constituents." This elicited discussion in the press, and debates in the council. It was urged against the scheme, that it was no part of the legitimate functions of this body to become the trustees and storekeepers of certain factors for the East-India Company: they might as well become the trustees and storekeepers of all individuals. "The council," Hutchinson says, "desired me, upon one pretence or another, to adjourn the consideration of the petition of the consignees until the 29th."

The consignees now endeavored to secure the landing of the tea that was expected; while the popular leaders were resolute that the tea should never be sold in Boston, though they were ready to agree to a temporary storage of it until the consignees could have time to consult their principals, provided it was subject "to the inspection of a committee of gentlemen."[1] The committee of correspondence now invited the committees of Dorchester, Roxbury, Brookline, and Cambridge to meet in conference, at the selectmen's chamber, in Faneuil Hall. Having ing unanimously voted to use their joint influence to

---

[1] The chairman of the Board of Selectmen, John Scollay, says, Dec. 23, 1773, "Had the consignees, on the town's first application to them, offered to have stored the tea, subject to the inspection of a committee of gentlemen, till they could write their principals, and until that time [agreed that] no duty should be paid, which, no doubt, the commissioners of the customs would have consented to . . . I am persuaded the town would have closed with them." It was the determination, he says, "that the tea should not be landed subject to a duty."

prevent the landing and sale of the expected tea, they authorized (Nov. 22) a joint committee, of which Warren was a member, to address a letter to other towns, representing, that they were reduced to the dilemma either to sit down in quiet under this and every burden that might be put upon them, or to rise up in resistance as became freemen; to impress the absolute necessity of making immediate and effectual opposition to this detestable measure; and soliciting their advice. Charlestown was so zealous in the cause that its committee was added. These committees continued to hold conferences, Hutchinson wrote, "like a little senate." On this day (Nov. 22) the " Gazette " said, "Americans! defeat this last effort of a most pernicious, expiring faction, and you may sit under your own vines and fig-trees, and none shall hereafter dare to make you afraid."

The selectmen, deeply concerned for the peace of the town, — Hancock, the commander of the Cadets, being one, — now had conferences with the consignees, which are related with much particularity in the town-records, but need not be dwelt on "Though we labored," John Scollay, one of the selectmen, says, "night and day in the affair, all our efforts could not produce an agreement between them and the town."[1] The selectmen plainly said to the consignees, that nothing less than sending the tea back to England would satisfy the people. Some of the Tory party also at this time urged an arrangement to this effect; but the consignees would only agree (Nov. 27) that nothing should be done in a clandestine

[1] John Scollay's Letter, Dec. 23, 1773, is admirable. It is in Mass. Hist. Soc. Coll., 4th series, iv. 379.

way; that the vessels should come up to the wharves; and that, when they received the orders that accompanied the teas, they would hand in proposals to the selectmen, to be laid before the town.[1] For better security, they retired to the country; and even Hutchinson now thought of going to the castle, that he might, in personal safety, "more freely give his sense of the criminality of the proceedings."

When the Boston tea commissioners had braved public opinion more than a month after their brethren in Philadelphia had resigned, the intelligence spread — Sunday morning, November twenty-eighth — that a tea ship was in the harbor.[2] It was the "Dartmouth," Captain Hall, owned by a Quaker, Francis Rotch, two persons whose movements for a few days greatly exercised the public mind. The selectmen, in the expectation of receiving the promised proposal of the consignees, held a session of their board at twelve o'clock, another at five o'clock, and continued its session until nine o'clock, when they learned that

[1] Hutchinson says, in his History (iii. 425), "that he advised that the tea ships should be anchored without the castle, and there wait for orders." He also says that the custom in England, in instances of acts deemed unconstitutional, was referred to in the council. One member observed, "that the last riot (at Clarke's house) was not of the most enormous kind; that, in Sir Robert Walpole's time, mobs had been frequent in England. Government there was then forced to give up the excise; . . . the people would not bear the Cider Act; . . . that the disorders among the people here were caused by unconstitutional acts of parliament." The "Annual Register" of 1832 contains a record of the popular action that was required to extort from the ruling classes the Reform Bill. The riots were terrible.

[2] The "Boston Gazette" of Nov. 29 thus announced the arrival of the first cargo of tea in Boston: "Yesterday morning, Captain Hall, in the ship 'Dartmouth,' came to anchor near the castle, in about eight weeks" from London. On board, "it is said, are one hundred and fourteen chests of the so-much-detested East-India Company's tea, the expected arrival of which pernicious article has for some time past put all these northern colonies in a very great ferment."

they could not see the consignees that evening, nor could the intelligence of their locality be obtained. The selectmen, seeing the storm rising, desired to get the expected proposals, in order that a regular town-meeting might be called before any other meeting could take place.[1] The committee of correspondence were also in session this day, and obtained from the owner of the "Dartmouth" a promise not to enter her until Tuesday. They issued a circular letter to the committees of Cambridge, Charlestown, Dorchester, and Roxbury, convening "the little senate" on the next morning. The following characteristic words, in the original draft,[2] are in Warren's handwriting: —

"A part of the tea shipped by the East-India Company is now arrived in this harbor, and we look upon ourselves bound to give you the earliest intimation of it; and we desire that you favor us with your company at Faneuil Hall, at nine o'clock forenoon, there to give us your advice what steps are to be immediately taken in order effectually to prevent the impending evil; and we request you to urge your friends in the town to which you belong to be in readiness to exert themselves in the most resolute manner to assist this town in its efforts for saving this oppressed country."

The journals of Monday[3] announced that the "Dartmouth" had anchored off the Long Wharf; that other

[1] John Scollay's Letter. [2] Bancroft, who has the original manuscript.
[3] This morning the following notification was posted up through this town :—
"Friends! Brethren! Countrymen! — That worst of plagues, the detested tea shipped for this port by the East-India Company is now arrived in this harbor; the hour of destruction, or manly opposition to the machinations of tyranny, stares you in the face; every friend to his country, to himself and posterity, is now called upon to meet at Faneuil Hall, at nine o'clock this day (at which time the bells will ring), to make a united and successful resistance to this last, worst, and most destructive measure of administration.
"BOSTON, Nov. 29, 1773"

So that it yet remains doubtful what will be the consequence of this importation; but, it is said, the gentlemen to whom the tea is consigned are disposed

ships with the poisonous herb might be expected; and, conceding to the consignees a disposition to do all in their power to quiet the public mind, even to ship the tea back to the place it came from, they repeated the assurance that the tea would not be suffered to be landed or to be sold; for it was the "determination of almost all the people, both of town and of country, resolutely to oppose the artful measures of the East-India Company in every possible way." The journals also contained a call for a public meeting, to be held in Faneuil Hall at nine o'clock, — which had been printed in a hand-bill form and posted over the town, — to make united and successful resistance to the last, worst, and most destructive measure of the British Administration. By the side of this call, there was an inspiring voice from the country in the proceedings of a noble town-meeting held in Cambridge. How the hearts of the patriots must have throbbed, and their purpose must have been strengthened, by fearless and high-toned resolves, pronouncing Boston to be struggling for the liberties of the country; announcing that the men of Cambridge could no longer remain idle spectators, and pledging themselves to be ready, at the shortest notice, to join the men of Boston and of other towns in any measure that might be thought proper to deliver them and their posterity from slavery! The brave Colonel Gardner lived here, was one of the

to do every thing in their power to quiet the minds of the people relative thereto, and are willing that baneful article should be re-shipped to the place from whence it came. Be that as it may, however, we are assured it will not be permitted to be landed or sold here; it being the determination of almost all the people, both of town and country, resolutely to oppose this artful measure of the India Company in every possible way.— *Massachusetts Gazette (Tory), Nov. 29, and Boston Gazette (Whig).*

foremost of the patriots, and redeemed this pledge when he poured out his blood by Warren's side at Bunker Hill.

At nine o'clock, on the ringing of the bells, a great concourse gathered in and around Faneuil Hall; for again the yeoman left his field, the mechanic his shop, and the merchant his counting-room, to turn politicians and act for the country.[1] "The form of a town-meeting," Hutchinson says, "was assumed, the selectmen of Boston, town-clerk, &c., taking their usual places; but, the inhabitants of any other towns being admitted, it could not assume the name of a legal meeting of any town." The selectmen were John Scollay, John Hancock, Timothy Newell, Thomas Marshall, Samuel Austin, Oliver Wendell, and John Pitts, — in most cases Scollay's name appearing first in signatures to official papers, — who were serving their country well, and whose names are household words; and the ever-faithful William Cooper was the town-clerk. The meeting chose for the moderator, Jonathan Williams, who hitherto had not been prominent, but was a citizen of character and wealth. The meeting voted, that, "as the town of Boston, in a full legal meeting, had resolved to do the utmost in its power to prevent the landing of the tea, this body were absolutely determined that the tea which had arrived should be returned to the place whence it came, at all hazards." The meeting then, better to accommodate the people, adjourned to the Old South Meeting-house, where it is said "five or six thousand of respectable inhabitants met, — men of the best characters and of the first fortunes."[2]

[1] See page 69.   [2] Scollay's Letter.

Governor Hutchinson came into town from Milton early in the morning. He says, "Although this meeting or assembly consisted principally of the lower ranks of the people, and even journeymen tradesmen were brought to increase the number, and the rabble were not excluded, yet there were divers gentlemen of good fortune among them." The consignees were within two miles of Castle William, having in their possession an order from the governor for their admission to that place of refuge. "They," Hutchinson says, "apprehended they should be seized, and, may be, tarred and feathered and carted, — an American torture, — in order to compel them to a compliance:" groundless apprehensions, certainly; for neither revenge, nor a spirit of hostility to rights of property or persons, formed a part of the programme of the popular leaders.

The meeting at the Old South deliberated long on the question. Crown officials name, as leading characters in the debates, Samuel Adams, Warren, Hancock, Young, and Molineux. "Adams was never in greater glory," Hutchinson says. It needs the words uttered on this occasion by earnest men, whose souls were in their work, to do them justice. A few of the speakers talked in a style that was violent and inflammatory; others were calm, and advised moderation, and, by all means, to abstain from violence; but the men who appeared to have the confidence and esteem of the people were unanimous that the tea should be sent back to London.[1] A patriot from Rhode Island says he was so unexpectedly entertained and instructed by the regular and sensible conduct of the

---

[1] Williamson's Examination.

meeting, that he should have thought himself rather in the British senate than in the promiscuous assembly of a people of a remote colony, had he not been convinced by the genuine integrity and manly hardihood of its rhetoricians, that they were not tainted by venality nor debauched by luxury.[1] The speeches that elicited this tribute perished with the hour. The meeting resolved, that no duty on the tea should be paid in Boston; and, to give the consignees time to make the expected proposals, adjourned till three o'clock. On learning of the first vote passed in Faneuil Hall, the consignees withdrew to Castle William.[2]

It is remarked, that Whigs and Tories united in the action of this meeting;[3] which indicates, that the candid among the friends of the ministry were desirous to wash their hands of any sanction of this scheme of absolute power. Both these parties were also represented in the council, which happened, by adjournment, to be in session at the Town House, not three hundred yards' distance from the excited concourse who had gathered in and around the Old South. Governor Hutchinson was present.[4] On the Tory side were Judges Danforth, Leonard, and Russell, who had many years been members; Isaac Royall, for thirty years of the house or the council; and John Erving, one of the most eminent of American merchants. On the Whig side were James Bowdoin, the future governor; James Pitts, of inflexible public virtue; Samuel Dexter, an 'able man, and a

---

[1] Boston Gazette, Dec. 20, 1773.   [2] Hutchinson, Dec. 2, 1773.
[3] Scollay's Letter, Dec. 23, 1773: "These meetings consisted of all sorts, both Whig and Tory."   [4] Letter, Dec. 2.

benefactor of learning; Artemas Ward, the future general; and John Winthrop, a professor in Harvard College, of great fame in the philosophic world, and of large political service. These ten members, who, by their private worth and public virtue, were worthy representatives of their political friends, discussed the terms of an elaborate and statesman-like report on the petition of the consignees, which had been made at the previous session. It traced the progress of events candidly and truthfully, and ascribed the prevailing excitement to unconstitutional taxation. I have space to state only one of its points, — that touching on the issue of the hour. The consignees asked for measures to secure the landing of the teas. The report averred that the duty on the tea must be either paid or secured on its being landed; and, were the Board to direct or advise any measure for landing it, they would of course advise to a measure for procuring the payment of the duty. The vote on the acceptance of this report was unanimous. The council would only advise the governor to renew his orders to the sheriffs and justices to preserve the public peace.[1] Hutchinson pointed "to the rabble that were together," and urged the council to join him in some measure to break up the unlawful assembly.[2] He says, members thought the consignees ought to decline to execute their trust. When he asked, " whether the council would give him no advice upon the disorders then prevailing," the answer was, " that

[1] The full report of the proceedings of the council on the petition of the consignees was printed in the journals of Dec. 27, 1773.

[2] Whilst the rabble were together in one place, I was in another not far distant, with His Majesty's council, urging them to join with me in some measure to break up this unlawful assembly, to no purpose. — *Letter, Dec.* 1, 1773.

the advice already given was intended to meet the case." The action of the Board was calculated to confirm the resolution of the people. While it shrank from encouraging a spirit of hostility to personal rights, it did justice "to the high sense of liberty derived from the manners and constitution of the mother-country," entertained "by the town and the province."

The governor this afternoon requested the justices of the town to meet, and use their endeavors to suppress any riots the people might engage in. The meeting, at its adjournment in the Old South, on motion of Samuel Adams, voted that the tea in Captain Hall's ship must go back in the same bottom; it informed the owner of the vessel that the entry of the tea, and the captain that the landing of it, would be at their peril; it appointed a watch of twenty-five men for the security of vessel and cargo, with Edward Proctor for the captain that night; and it voted that the summons of the justices by the governor was a reflection on the people. Near the close of the day, Hancock stated that the tea consignees did not receive their letters from London until the previous evening, and that they were so dispersed that they could not have a meeting early enough to make their proposals, and were desirous of further time; when the meeting, out of great tenderness to them, adjourned to the next morning.

The meeting on Tuesday was viewed with the deepest interest by the Crown officials and by the people. The public utterances of the previous day were reported to the governor, who says that nothing could have been more inflammatory, — one of the speakers said that the only way to get rid of the tea was to throw it overboard,— but Hutchinson looked upon the men of fortune who were present and acted, as a bond of security for the safety of the tea. "I can scarcely think," he wrote, "they will prosecute their mad resolves." But he saw that the tea ship, now under the surveillance of a watch, was virtually in hands outside the law, and judged that the constituted authorities, in this case, were powerless.[1] He said, that, if the meeting went to the length it threatened to go, he should be obliged to retire to the castle, as otherwise he could not make any exertion of strength in support of the king's authority.[2] He decided that he could not let the meeting go on longer in silence, though what he could say or do might not check the course of those whom he termed "usurpers."[3] He felt some apprehension as to the firmness of the consignees. There was great pressure now made on them by their friends, to persuade them to resign their trust. "The friends of old Mr. Clarke," he says, "pressed his sons and other consignees to a full compliance. . . . I hope the gentlemen will continue firm, and should have not the least doubt of it, if it had not been for the solicitations of the friends of Mr. Clarke."[4] And thus Hutchinson, by repressing every idea of concession, aided, even more than the council, the progress of events that tended to the result of independence.

The adjourned meeting came to order at nine o'clock in the morning. The consignees, in a letter addressed to John Scollay, one of the selectmen,

---

[1] History, iii. 431.   [2] Letter, Dec. 1, 1773.
[3] History, iii. 431.   [4] Letter, Dec. 1, 1773.

made their long-expected proposals to the meeting. Expressing sorrow that they could not return satisfactory answers to the two messages of the town, they said that it was utterly out of their power to send the teas back, but were ready to store them until they could have time to write to their constituents, and receive their further orders respecting them. This letter irritated the meeting, and it would take no action on it. Sheriff Greenleaf now came in with a proclamation in his hands, from the governor, which he begged leave of the moderator to read. Objection was made; but Samuel Adams spoke in favor of granting the request, when the meeting consented to hear it. The governor charged the meeting of the preceding day with "openly violating, defying, and setting at naught the good and wholesome laws of the province under which they lived;" and, as great numbers were again assembled for like purposes, the governor, as His Majesty's representative, bore testimony against this violation of the laws. "I warn," he said, "exhort, and require you, and each of you, thus unlawfully assembled, forthwith to disperse, and to surcease all further unlawful proceedings, at your utmost peril." Immediately there was a long and very general hiss, and then a vote that the meeting would not disperse. Mr. Copley, the son-in-law of Mr. Clarke, inquired whether the meeting would hear the Messrs. Clarke, whether their persons would be safe to come from and return to the place where they were, and whether the meeting would grant Mr. Copley two hours to consult with them. The answers were in the affirmative, and the meeting adjourned until two o'clock.

The report of the proceedings at the adjourned meeting fills two columns of the journals; but the action that bears on the progress of events may be briefly stated. Rotch the owner, and Hall the captain, of the "Dartmouth," and the owners of two other vessels expected with teas, were sent for; and all promised that the teas should not be landed but should go back in the same ships. Mr. Copley, in an apology for the time he had taken, said that he had to go to the castle, where the consignees informed him, that, as they resolved to adhere to their proposals, it would be inexpedient for them to appear in the meeting; adding to their former proposal, that the tea would be submitted to the inspection of a committee. This was now voted to be unsatisfactory. Resolves were passed to the effect, that all who imported teas were enemies to the country; that the teas should be returned to the place whence they came; and the meeting voted to send these resolves to the other colonies and to England. The committee of correspondence were charged to make provision for the continuance of the watch; and they, if occasion required, were directed to alarm the country by ringing the bells in the day, and by tolling them in the night; the brethren present from the country were thanked " for their countenance and union," and desired to afford their assistance on the notice being given; and it was voted, "That it is the determination of this body to carry these votes and resolutions into existence, at the risk of their lives and property." Francis Bernard, in his narrative laid before the privy council, in 1773, says, "The persons who principally proposed the questions on which the above resolutions and proceedings were founded, were Mr. Adams, Mr. Molineux, Dr. Young, and Dr. Warren; and they used many arguments to induce the people to concur in these resolutions." The meeting dissolved.

This was another of the remarkable popular demonstrations of this period. The comment on its proceedings does not differ materially on the points of order or spirit, whether by Whig or Tory. Hutchinson says, "A more determined spirit was conspicuous in this body than in any of the former assemblies of the people. It was composed of the lowest as well, and probably in as great proportion, as of the superior ranks and orders; and all had an equal voice. No eccentric or irregular motions, however, were suffered to take place. All seemed to have been the plan of a few, it may be of a single person."[1] Samuel Adams says, "The business of the meeting was conducted with decency, unanimity, and spirit."[2] A Rhode-Island patriot says, "The people determined the tea should not be landed; the determination was deliberate, was judicious; the sacrifice of their rights, of the union of all the colonies, would have been the effect, had they conducted with less resolution."[3]

The committee of correspondence, Bernard says, "met after the dissolution of this meeting, called in committees from other towns to join with them, up a military watch or guard to prevent the landing of the tea, who were armed with muskets bayonets, and, every half hour during the night, regularly passed the word, 'All is well,' like sen-

---

[1] Hutchinson's History, iii. 433.   [2] Letter, Dec. 31, 1773.
[3] Boston Gazette, Dec. 20, 1773.

tinels in a garrison."[1] This committee, besides sending relations of these events to all the towns,[2] with their eye on the union idea that one colony should not take an important step without consulting the other colonies, wrote (Dec. 5) to Rhode Island and New Hampshire, and (Dec. 6) to New York and Philadelphia, explaining their course at this critical conjuncture; and they acted in the faith — their words — that "harmony and concurrence in action, uniformly and firmly maintained, must finally conduct them to the end of their wishes, namely, a full enjoyment of constitutional liberty." There came now from other colonies cheering assurances, that the Boston action had been watched with the deepest interest, and hailed with the liveliest satisfaction. When, for instance, the resolutions of the first town-meeting on the tea reached Philadelphia, the peal of its bells gave expression to the general joy; and this inspiring detail was now read by the Bostonians.[3] Yet the Philadelphia patriots doubted whether the Boston action would come up to the manifesto; and, in letters expressing this doubt, they warmly urged firmness: for, they said, if Boston were to fall back in any degree, it would bring on it reproach, scorn, and irretrievable loss of confidence; but, by carrying its resolves into execution, it would convince the world that it could act with virtue and resolution. A letter, heralded as the voice of Philadelphia, read: "Our tea

---

[1] Bernard's MS.   [2] Bancroft, vi. 478.

[3] These relations appeared in the Boston journals prior to the destruction of the tea. A letter from Philadelphia, dated Dec. 11, and printed in the "Boston Gazette," Dec. 20, says, "Your resolutions of the 29th ult. were publicly read at our Coffee House, last Thursday, to a large company of our first merchants, who gave three cheers by way of approbation."

consignees have all resigned, and you need not fear: the tea will not be landed here nor at New York. All that we fear is, that you will shrink at Boston. May God give you virtue enough to save the liberties of your country!"[1]

The true patriots abroad who thus earnestly counselled the men of Boston could not know the thorough action of its popular leaders. The committee of correspondence, it is said in the press, took every step which prudence and caution could suggest to execute the purpose of the town. It happened that the next tea ship, commanded by Captain Coffin, arrived (Dec. 7), the "Gazette" said, " not only with the plague (tea) on board, but the small-pox;" which occasioned immediate action by the selectmen as a Board of Health. The orders they gave to prevent a clandestine landing of the tea in her were of the most peremptory character.[2] A third tea vessel arrived, under Captain Bruce; and soon the two were directed to be anchored by the side of the "Dartmouth," off Griffin's Wharf, more recently called Liverpool Wharf, on Purchase Street. One guard answered for the three vessels. This force, it is related, was from twenty-four to thirty-four strong, and served nineteen days and twenty-three hours.

[1] Boston Gazette, Dec. 13, 1773.

[2] The selectmen (Dec. 8), in an order to the keeper of the hospital at Rainsford Island, the quarantine-ground, say, " Our directions are, that you take the whole of the tea from between decks upon the deck of the 'Briggandine.' If the weather be fair, let it lay on the deck the whole day, to be aired, and at night see it put between decks again; and you, with the true men you are ordered to take down with you, are to remain on board during the time the tea is on deck, and on no account to absent yourselves, and by no means suffer one chest of tea to be landed or taken away by any one. If any attempt should be made, you are immediately to dispatch a messenger to inform the selectmen thereof."

The determined opposition to the landing of the teas led to apprehensions that the officials might use the naval force to effect their purpose: there was talk, in such case, of making resistance; and the community was now greatly excited. "Where," Hutchinson said, "the present disorder will end, I cannot make a probable conjecture: the town is as furious as in the time of the Stamp Act." — "The flame," Abigail Adams, wife of John Adams, wrote (Dec. 5), "is kindled; and, like lightning, it catches from soul to soul. Although the mind is shocked at the thought of shedding human blood, more especially the blood of our countrymen, and a civil war is of all wars the most dreadful, such is the spirit that prevails, that, if once they are made desperate, many, very many of our heroes will spend their lives with the speech of Cato in their mouths. My heart beats at every whistle I hear, and I dare not express half my fears." The actors in these scenes were accustomed to meet in the home in which this American matron presided, and Warren was the beloved family physician. One of her sons, John Quincy Adams, then in his seventh year, broke one of his fingers about that time, and Warren was called in to treat it. Years after this lad had been the chief magistrate of the nation, he related to me the details of the accident; and, with interesting revolutionary reminiscences, he mingled glowing tributes to his patriot-mother and the venerated martyr of Bunker Hill.

The legal status of the tea ships now became an element in this case. A vessel, twenty days after her arrival in port, was liable to seizure for the non-payment of duties on articles imported in her; nor, on landing only a part of a cargo, could she be legally cleared in Boston or entered in England. This, in a few days, would be the case of the "Dartmouth." There was now business detail, not necessary to dwell on, between the consignees, the owner, and the master; and the governor officially advised Admiral Montague of the case, who ordered the ships of war "Active" and the "King Fisher" to guard the passages to the sea, and to permit no unauthorized vessels to pass; so that Hutchinson said it was not possible for the "Dartmouth" to get out of the harbor. He said (Dec. 7) that "the patriots found themselves in a web of inextricable difficulties." Every movement was reported to the committee of correspondence. The owner of the "Dartmouth," Rotch, was summoned (Dec. 11) before the committee, Samuel Adams chairman, and was asked why he had not kept his pledge to send his vessel and tea back to London; and he plead that it was out of his power to do this. He was advised to apply for a clearance and a pass, Adams saying, "The ship must go: the people of Boston and the neighboring towns absolutely require and expect it."

Two days later (Dec. 13), the journals arraigned the owner of the "Dartmouth" because he had not applied to the officers of the customs for a clearance, and declared that the obstinacy of the tea commissioners rendered them infinitely more obnoxious to the public than the stamp-masters were. They contained resolves, passed in the country towns, in support of Boston on this question, which indeed, before this, continued to appear from time to time. Thus Dorchester (printed Dec. 6), in legal town-meeting, gave the assurance, "that, should this country be so unhappy as to see a day of trial for the recovery of its rights, by a last and solemn appeal to Him who gave them, they should not be behind the bravest of our patriotic brethren." Marblehead (the resolves were printed on the 13th of December) declared that the proceedings of the brave citizens of Boston and of other towns, in opposition to the landing of the tea, were rational, generous, and just; that they were highly honored for their noble firmness in support of American liberty; and that the men of that town were ready with their lives to assist their brethren in opposing all measures tending to enslave the country. The proceedings may be weary reading to-day; but they were then of the deepest interest and of the gravest import, and show the life of the time.[1] On this day, the committees of the five

[1] The "Gazette" of Dec. 13 contains little besides advertisements, and matter about the tea question. Under the date of Philadelphia, Dec. 1, is an account of the sailing of a tea ship from London for that port, and the assurance that "she will meet with such a reception that will convince the world that we are neither to be frightened or cajoled out of our liberty by nabobs, ministers, and ministerial hirelings." Under the date of New York, Dec. 6, is an account of the declination of the tea consignees of that city to receive the teas. Under the date of Salem, Dec. 7, the following: "By what we can learn from private intelligence as well as the public proceedings of a number of principal towns contiguous to the capital, the people, if opposed in their proceedings with respect to the tea, are determined upon hazarding a brush; therefore those who are willing to bear a part in it, in preserving the rights of this country, would do well to get suitably prepared." The proceedings of Marblehead appear in full.

The following is under the editorial head: "The East-India tea commissioners still remain immured at Castle William. Their obstinacy has rendered them infinitely more obnoxious to their countrymen than even the stamp-masters were. If Mr. Rotch, the owner of Captain Hall's ship, does not intend she shall depart directly with the tea she brought, he ought explicitly to declare it, that the people may know what to depend upon and how to conduct themselves. It does not appear that she is yet in readiness, or that he has even made a demand at the Custom House for a clearance. The minds of the public are greatly irritated at his delay hitherto to take this necessary step towards complying with their peremptory requisition."

neighboring towns already named, had an important session in Faneuil Hall. Its doings cannot be related. Of this session of the "little senate," and of other sessions at this time, it is written: "No business transacted matter of record." There can hardly be a doubt that the following hand-bill, which, on the next day, was posted over the town, emanated from this source: "Friends! Brethren! Countrymen! — The perfidious arts of your restless enemies to render ineffectual the late resolutions of the body of the people, demand your assembling at the Old South Meeting-house, precisely at ten o'clock this day, at which time the bells will ring."

The meeting on Tuesday (Dec. 14) is said to have been larger than the previous meetings. People from the neighboring towns came in to attend it. A citizen of Weston, Samuel Phillips Savage, was selected for the moderator. Its business may be briefly related. The master of the third tea ship, Bruce, promised to ask for a clearance for London when all his goods were landed except the tea. Rotch, the owner of the "Dartmouth," was directed to appear, and to apply forthwith to the collector for a clearance for her; and Benjamin Kent, Samuel Adams, and eight others, were appointed to accompany him. On their return, Rotch reported that the collector desired to consult with the comptroller, and promised an answer on the following morning. The meeting then adjourned until Thursday. On this day (14th), the committee of correspondence was in session in the morning and evening, and completed their preparations; but there is no record of their doings.

On Wednesday (Dec. 15), the committee appointed

by the meeting accompanied Rotch to the Custom House, to ask a clearance of the collector, Harrison; the comptroller, Hallowell, being present. The owner said that he was required and compelled at his peril by the meeting to make the demand for a clearance of his vessel for London, with the tea on board; and one of the committee stated that they were present only as witnesses. The collector answered, that, as articles subject to duty were on board, and the revenue was not paid, he could not, consistently with his duty, give a clearance until the ship was discharged of those articles. The vessel could not have gone to sea; for on this day Hutchinson wrote, "It is notorious that the ship cannot pass the castle without a permit from the governor, for which a fee had been granted by a province law in force more than seventy years." He said that he would willingly call the council together; but he reasoned, "To cause them to be convened, and to obtain no other advice from them than they gave before, would tend to strengthen and confirm the people in their extravagances." As he mused on the drifting of the current, he wrote, in a private letter to Lord Dartmouth, "Before the peace, I thought nothing so much to be desired as the cession of Canada. I am now convinced, that, if it had remained to the French, none of this spirit of opposition to the mother-country would have yet appeared; and I think the effects of it worse than all we had to fear from the French or Indians." Such was the mental mood of the representative of George III., on whose decision, the next day, hung such vast issues.

Thursday, the sixteenth of December, was by far the most momentous in the annals of Boston.[1] The

[1] Bancroft, vi. 484.

eyes of the patriots of the other colonies were upon it; or, more precisely, the committees of correspondence, the representatives of a national party, were looking with anxiety, perhaps with lurking doubt, to see how the branch of the party in Boston would act in the crisis. To say nothing of letters received by its committee which the public did not see, there appeared in the journals of this morning, matter which could not fail to influence public opinion, — renewed assurances that not a chest of tea would be allowed to be landed in New York or Philadelphia, — evidences that the same spirit animated the patriots of South Carolina: and it was the injunction from abroad, repeated in line upon line, both by the interior towns of the province and from the remote colonies, for the town to be firm and resolute. To meet these expectations required an uncommon work. Thus far the popular leaders had found moral force, — public opinion embodied in petition, remonstrance, and resolves, — adequate to every exigency; and, notwithstanding occasional disturbances of the peace, which were always deplored, the patriots had been as true to the idea of order as they had been faithful to the cause of liberty. Two months' efforts, however, only procured, as to the consignees, a repetition of the original rough and peremptory answer, "No resignation;"[1] and, as to the teas, a flat refusal to return them. It was plain that action which would meet the demand of the patriots, united as they never were before,[2] involved a departure from the line of law, and hence a revolutionary deed.

It was necessary also that the action should be

---

[1] Letter of Samuel Cooper, Dec. 17, 1773.   [2] *Ib.*

immediate. The twenty days allowed to one of the ships, the "Dartmouth," for a clearance, were out this day; after which, as the popular leaders had grounds for believing, the revenue officials would take possession of her, and land the teas under cover of a naval force; and opposition to this would inaugurate a work of blood. Though it might have been clear that the hour for civil war had not come, yet it was evident that public duty required an effectual resistance to the landing of the teas, even though this might require their destruction; and though their destruction might prove the passage of an American Rubicon. The patriots would gladly have avoided the stern work before them, if they could have done it with honor. But submission and a violation of their pledges were not to be thought of for a moment; and it was resolved to follow the only course that would meet the case thoroughly. The considerations seem to be of a weighty character. The closer the train of events is scanned the more fully will it appear that the patriots did not proceed blindly in the work they were upon; but, as if they had a forecast of the consequences that were to flow from their action, they conducted in what went before it in such manner, that, conscious that their hands were void of offence, they might after it not only be pronounced free from the imputation involved in doing a deed of sedition, but be judged worthy of the precious verdict rendered to those who faithfully serve their country.

The day was rainy; no hand-bills are named as having been posted in the streets, and no rally-words are seen in the journals; but the feeling was general that something unusual was about to occur; for the inhabitants of the town mostly suspended business and flocked to the Old South; and the people came in for twenty miles around. "Nearly seven thousand persons," it is said, "gentlemen, merchants, yeomen, and others, respectable for their rank and abilities and venerable for their age and character, constituted the assembly." It was remarked there was a greater meeting of the Body than ever, and its spirit surprised all those who viewed the scene.

The committee chosen to accompany Rotch to the collector reported in detail the manner in which the application for a clearance had been denied. Rotch, by order, came in, and was told that he was expected to make his protest at the Custom House, apply to the governor for his pass to go by the castle, and proceed on this day with his vessel on his voyage for London; when he replied that it was impracticable to comply with this requirement. He was told that the twenty days in which he promised the Body his vessel should sail expired this day; and, being asked whether he would now direct the "Dartmouth" to sail, replied that he would not. The meeting, after directing Rotch to use all possible dispatch in making his protest and procuring his pass, adjourned until three o'clock.

The afternoon proceedings may be as briefly related, though the report occupies over a column of the journals. Information was given that several towns had agreed not to use tea; when it was voted that its use was improper and pernicious; and that it would be well for all the towns to appoint committees of inspection, "to prevent this detested tea" from coming among them. It was moved, "whether it be the sense and determination of this body to abide by their former resolutions with respect to the not suffering the tea to be landed." Samuel Adams, Thomas Young, and Josiah Quincy, jun., now made speeches. I have met with only an extract of the address of the last-named patriot, who was passionately devoted to the liberty of his country. The hectic flush on his cheek and his failing strength, indicated, too certainly, his early death. He said: —

"It is not, Mr. Moderator, the spirit that vapors within these walls that must stand us in stead. The exertions of this day will call forth events which will make a very different spirit necessary for our salvation. Whoever supposes that shouts and hosannas will terminate the trials of the day entertains a childish fancy. We must be grossly ignorant of the importance and value of the prize for which we contend; we must be equally ignorant of the power of those who have combined against us; we must be blind to that malice, inveteracy, and insatiable revenge, which actuate our enemies, public and private, abroad and in our bosom, to hope that we shall end this controversy without the sharpest, the sharpest conflicts, — to flatter ourselves that popular resolves, popular harangues, popular acclamations, and popular vapor will vanquish our foes. Let us consider the issue. Let us look to the end. Let us weigh and consider before we advance to those measures which must bring on the most trying and terrific struggle this country ever saw."

In reply to this plea for moderation, it was said, "Now that the hand is at the plough, there must be no looking back." At half past four, the vote was passed, *nemine contradicente*, that the tea should not be landed. Many desired that the meeting might be dissolved, and motions to this effect were made; but it is related, "Some gentlemen of the country informing the Body that their several towns were so very anxious to have full information as to this matter, that they were quite desirous the meeting should be continued until six o'clock, especially as Mr. Rotch had been met on his way to Milton for a pass;" and the motions for a dissolution were overruled.

The interest now centred on Thomas Hutchinson, the royal governor, who was at his country-seat at Milton. It is not named, that he had with him, at an unusual place to be in on a winter's day, any of his truest friends or wisest official advisers, to plead, as they did nearly four years before in the case of the removal of the troops, that he ought to bow to public opinion. He yielded then to a demand mostly local; but now it was virtually the united voice of America which urged that the technical forms of law ought to be made to bend to a wise expediency. He acted on his own responsibility in this case. His course does not show one sign of vacillation from first to last, but, throughout, bears the marks of clear, cold, passionless inflexibility. It was with him a foregone conclusion to refuse the pass. He had peremptorily said that, when the "Dartmouth" had been regularly cleared, he would give a pass for her to go to sea, but not before; and he resolved to adhere to his word. When the persevering Rotch once more appeared, to ask for a pass, Hutchinson did little else than ply questions touching the intention of the people respecting the teas. Rotch told him that they had no other intention than to force the teas back to England, but that there might be some who desired that the vessel might go down the harbor, and be brought to by a shot from the castle; so that it might be said that the people had done every thing in their power to send the tea back. Hutchinson caught at this straw of the patriots of easy virtue with the instinct of a drowning man. He tendered to Rotch a letter, addressed to Admiral Montague, commending ship and goods to his protection, if Rotch would agree to have his ship haul out into the stream; but he replied that none were willing to assist him in doing this, and the attempt would only subject him to the resentment of the people. Hutchinson revolved anew the idea of the destruction of the tea; but, he says, "nobody suspected this until an attempt should be made to land the tea." He sternly repeated his former refusal to grant a pass. He said, "To have granted a pass to a vessel which I knew had not been cleared at the Custom House, would have been a direct countenancing and encouraging the violation of the acts of trade." With this answer passed his last opportunity for concession. Seldom in human affairs have greater issues hung on so narrow a point. Seldom has a decision been more fatal to reputation. It is the judgment of a candid British historian, that concession was unwisely denied.[1]

Rotch, about sunset, left Milton, and went directly to the Old South, now dimly lighted with candles, and crowded with patriots anxious to hear from the governor. It was nearly six o'clock, and quite dark, when Rotch re-appeared in the assembly, and related the result of his visit to the governor. The people gave vehement huzzas; and the cry arose, "A mob! a mob!" The call to order rose above all other cries, and it was heeded. One of the patriots, Dr.

[1] Lord Mahon, vi. 2, says that concession was unwisely declined by the governor.

Young, now said that Rotch was a good man, who had done all in his power to gratify the people; and charged them to do no hurt to his person or property. The final question was calmly put to him, "Whether he would send his vessel back with the tea in her, under the present circumstances?" This was his answer: "He could not possibly comply, as he apprehended a compliance would prove his ruin." He also admitted, that, if called upon by the proper persons, he should attempt to land the tea for his own security. Samuel Adams then gave the word, "This meeting can do nothing more to save the country." At this signal, a number of resolute men appeared at the door of the church, sounded a warwhoop, which was answered from the galleries, when they passed on. Silence was immediately commanded, a peaceable demeanor was enjoined, and the meeting preserved its order to its close. The great purpose of all its pleadings and proceedings had been to devise means to preserve the tea without its being saleable; but, no one being able to suggest any plan for effecting this object, the meeting, with great cheering, was dissolved.

The band who sounded the warwhoop had their faces disguised, wore blankets and other Indian costume, and carried hatchets. They were called Mohawks. The numbers have been variously estimated, being stated at from thirty to sixty.[1] John Adams says, "Depend upon it, they were no ordinary Mohawks;"[2] but he does not give the names

[1] Bancroft, vi. 486, names "forty or fifty." In the "Memoir of Hewes" are the names of fifty-eight. One Charlestown man, who is not named, was of the party. Dr. Young and Paul Revere are on the list, though not Warren.

[2] John Adams's Works, ii. 334.

of any of the party; and it is doubtful whether more than few of them have ever been authentically identified. They came from a room in the rear of Edes and Gill's printing-office, on Queen, now Court, Street, at the corner of Brattle Street. As they passed by the Old South, numbers naturally joined them; and the throng went directly to Griffin's Wharf, where the three ships lay that contained the teas. They had been vigilantly guarded from the hour of their anchorage in the harbor. At nine o'clock of the night on which the "Dartmouth" arrived, and even as she lay under the stern of the admiral's sixty-four gun ship, a guard of twenty-five men went on board; and thus sharply had the three vessels been watched, day and night, to prevent the teas in them being landed.[1] Bernard says, "Mr. Hancock, the governor's captain of the Cadet Company, was one of the guard on board the ships."[2] The body of the people who had composed the great meeting repaired to the wharf, and stood in silence around the guard.

The party, "whooping like Indians," the writer of the "Dartmouth's" journal says, "came on board the ship; and, after warning myself and the custom-house officer to get out of the way, they unlaid the hatches and went down the hold, where were eighty whole and thirty-four half chests of tea, which they hoisted upon deck, and cut the chests to pieces, and hove the tea

[1] In the "Memoir of Hewes" are citations from "the original of the journal of the "Dartmouth."
[2] Bernard's MS. Huchinson, Dec. 14, says of the watch, "I sent for the colonel of the regiment, and acquainted him he ought to suffer none of his men to appear in arms but by authority derived from me. He consulted with the other field officers, and made return that it was not in their power to restrain the men from appearing on this occasion."

all overboard, where it was damaged and lost." I have not met with any thing so particular as to the other ships. Notwithstanding the whoop, mentioned to have been given when the party went on board, they proved themselves quiet, orderly, and systematic workers; the parties in the ships doing faithfully the part assigned to them. In about three hours, they broke open three hundred and forty-two chests of tea, and cast their contents into the water. There was no interference with them; no person was harmed; no other property was permitted to be injured; and no tea was allowed to be purloined. There is much anecdote illustrative of these facts; but I have not space to relate it. "The whole was done with very little tumult," Hutchinson says. "All things were conducted with great order, decency, and with perfect submission to government," wrote John Adams.[1] "We do console ourselves that we have acted constitutionally," is the remark of John Scollay.[2] The inquirer will seek in vain in this deed for the tiger-like growl of an infuriated mob. It was action performed out of a sense of duty. The town was never more still of a Saturday night than it was at ten o'clock of that memorable evening.[3] The men from the country carried great news to their villages.[4]

Joy as for a great deliverance now instinctively thrilled the American heart. "You cannot imagine," Samuel Adams wrote "the height of joy that sparkles in the eyes and animates the countenances as well as the hearts of all we meet on this occasion."[5] — "This," John Adams says, "is the most

[1] Letter, Dec. 17, 1773.   [2] Letter, Dec. 23, 1773.   [3] John Adams.
[4] Bancroft, vi. 486.   [5] Letter, Dec. 31, 1773.

magnificent movement of all. There is a dignity, a majesty, a sublimity, in this last effort of the patriots that I greatly admire. . . . This destruction of the tea is so bold, so daring, so fixed, intrepid, and inflexible, and it must have so important consequences [1] and so lasting, that I cannot but consider it an epocha in history."[2] — "We are in a perfect jubilee," wrote a New-York Whig, who happened to be in Boston, saying that the proceedings were "lenient and regular to the last:" — "The spirit of the people throughout the country is to be described by no terms in my power. Their conduct last night surprised the admiral and English gentlemen, who observed that these were not a disorderly rabble (as they have been represented), but men of sense, coolness, and intrepidity. I am obliged to conclude abruptly, wishing my beloved countrymen in New York may be as resolute and successful as the brave Bostonians, who, in spite of opposition and calumny, are an honor to mankind."[3]

The people of the other colonies expressed like joy on the reception of the news of the destruction of the

---

[1] Verses in the "New-Hampshire Gazette," Sept. 12, 1776, commence: —

"What discontents, what dire events,
From trifling things procced?
A little Tea, thrown in the sea,
Has thousands caused to bleed."

Robert Burns has the following, in a song to the tune of "Gillicrankie":—

"When Guilford good our Pilot stood,
An' did our hellim thraw, man,
Ae night, at tea, began a plea,
Within America, man:
Then up they gat the maskin-pat,*
And in the sea did jaw,† man;
An' did no less, in full congress,
Than quite refuse our law, man."

[2] Adams's Works, ii. 323.   [3] Evening Post, Jan. 3, 1774.

* Teapot.   † Jerk.

tea. In New York, "when the inhabitants received the intelligence, they were in high spirits; vast numbers of the people collected" and "highly extolled the Bostonians:"[1] in Philadelphia, the news was received "with the ringing of bells and every sign of joy and universal approbation;" a great public meeting voted "the most perfect approbation, with universal claps and huzzas;" and all "rejoiced that the virtue of Boston appeared firm and triumphant."[2] North Carolina gave the inspiring assurance, that the act was the only remedy left to save the colonies from destined slavery; and that the actors, besides the satisfaction arising from a conscientious discharge of duty due to posterity, had the approbation of the whole continent.

This generous judgment is in the spirit of fraternity out of which grew the American Union. Facts show that there was the same spirit in all the thirteen colonies, — that any of the East-India Company's ships would have been met in the same determined manner. Circumstances devolved on the patriots of Massachusetts the duty of meeting the first tea importation. They were presented with a bitter cup, which they would have refused, could they have done it honorably. A community of easy political virtue, by choosing the policy of non-action, would have left the teas in the hands of the crown-officials. Then the patriots might have received praise from the class who charged them with sedition and rebellion, and doomed them to all the degrees of punishment. But these right-minded men felt that non-action was neglect of duty; and they grandly rose up to the mark of a

[1] Boston Gazette, Jan. 3, 1774.   [2] *Ib.*, Jan. 24, 1774.

rare opportunity. A prompt home-criticism reads, "The people have been mild and considerate; they have been temperate and patient. When their mildness was called timidity, and their consideration want of courage, they did not cease to reason and entreat. When their temperance was treated with insult, and their patience with contempt, they felt the injury, though they stayed their vengeance. When the situation of public affairs called them to resolve upon their danger and duty, they were unanimous and determined; and when the exigency of the times increased, and resolutions alone were vain, they proceeded to action with order and discretion, and executed the only remaining duty without unnecessary outrage and intemperate revenge."[1]

[1] Boston Gazette, Dec. 20, 1773, in an article signed "Marchmont Nedham," written by Josiah Quincy, jun. John Adams (Works, ii. 324) vindicated the destruction of the tea, contending that it was absolutely necessary. His words are: The patriots "could not send it back. The governor, admiral, collector, and comptroller would not suffer it. It was in their power to have sent it, but in no other.... To let it be landed would be giving up the principle of taxation by parliamentary authority, against which the continent had struggled for ten years."

A curious pamphlet of the time is entitled, "The Wonder of Wonders," &c., purporting to be an account of the appearance of an angel, devil, and ghost, to a gentleman of the town of Boston, on the nights of the 14th, 15th, and 16th of October, 1773, as he related the affair to one of his neighbors, on the morning of the last visitation. It was designed as a warning to all those who, to aggrandize themselves, entail wretchedness on millions of their fellow-creatures. It has four plates: 1. Devil. 2. An angel, with sword in one hand, and a pair of scales in the other. 3. Beelzebub, holding in his right hand a folio book, and in his left a halter. 4. A ghost, having on a white gown, his hair much dishevelled This pamphlet has a strain of remark, quite sensible, on the destruction of the tea, which concludes, "Therefore, when every legal method made use of for returning that pernicious and destitute commodity had proved abortive, a number of Indians from Natick and elsewhere came in the night and demolished it."

Hutchinson (Jan. 2, 1774) took the following commercial view of the destruction of the tea: "Our liberty men had lost their reputation with Philadelphia and New York, having been importers of teas from England for three or four years past, notwithstanding the engagements they had entered into to the con-

It is praise enough to say of Warren, that he is seen constantly by the side of Samuel Adams through the whole of these interesting occurrences. His name is found on the petitions for town-meetings, and on nearly all the committees of the public assemblies. He was presented to the privy council as one of the prominent actors in these proceedings, and was held up by his political opponents at home as one

trary. As soon as the news came of the intended exportation of teas of the East-India Company, which must of course put an end to all trade in teas by private merchants, proposals were made both to Philadelphia and New York for a new union, and they were readily accepted; for, although no teas had been imported from England at either of those places, yet an immense profit had been made by the importation from Holland, which would entirely cease if the teas from the East-India Company should be admitted. This was the consideration which engaged all the merchants."

A Tory pamphlet, 1775, entitled "A Few Remarks," on the Continental and Provincial Congress of 1774, ascribes "the great misery" of the time to the opposition to the tea duty, and thus characterizes the destruction of the tea: "An action of such a gross, immoral nature as cannot be justified upon the principles of equity or policy; an action which laid the foundation for the miseries and calamities we are now groaning under; an action of such a malignant, atrocious nature as must expose the wicked perpetrators of it, without sincere repentance, to the vengeance of that being who is a God of order, not of confusion; and who will punish all thieves as well as liars in the lake which burn with fire and brimstone."

Another pamphlet, entitled "A Friendly Address to all Reasonable Americans," &c., 1774, contains comments on the destruction of the tea. The following shows its tone: "Now the crime of the Bostonians was a compound of the grossest injury and insult. It was an act of the highest insolence towards Government, such as mildness itself cannot overlook or forgive. The injustice of the deed was also most atrocious, as it was the destruction of property to a vast amount, when it was known that the nation was obliged in honor to protect it. At the same time, it was very notorious that the intention of the perpetrators was by this example to lead and excite others, when the expected opportunity should present, to the same wanton excess of riot and licentiousness."

The quarrel with America was stated in the following way, in a London Rhyme copied into "Moore's Diary," under the date of Nov. 10, 1775: —

> "Rudely forced to drink tea, Massachusetts in anger
> Spills the tea on John Bull, — John falls on to bang her,
> Massachusetts enrag'd, calls her neighbors to aid,
> And gives Master John a severe bastinade'
> Now, good men of the law' pray who is in fault,
> The one who begins, or resists the assault?'"

of the Mohawks. He was not one to shrink from any post of duty; and it is not more improbable that he was one of the band who threw the tea overboard, than that his friend, John Hancock, should have been one of the guard who protected the actors.

Warren, in the progress of events, was soon called into wider fields of action; and other records, with the luminous annals of Boston, bear to posterity similar "testimonials of his accomplishments as a statesman, and his integrity and services as a patriot."[1]

[1] Perez Morton's Eulogy.

CHAPTER X.

THE BOSTON PORT ACT AND THE AMERICAN UNION.

WARREN'S LETTERS. — EFFECT OF THE DESTRUCTION OF THE TEA. — THE BOSTON PORT ACT: ITS RECEPTION IN BOSTON; IN THE COLONIES. — THE DEMAND FOR A CONGRESS. — THE PROGRESS OF UNION.

DECEMBER, 1773, TO JUNE, 1774.

"I EVER scorned disguise: I think I have done my duty,"[1] Warren wrote, after valuable service in the uprising of the great day of Lexington and Concord; and these words may indicate the frankness and fidelity with which he counselled and acted with the popular leaders through the period of sullen discontent which began on the passage of the Townshend Revenue Bill, and ended on the destruction of the tea.[2] The direct sequence of this event was severe penal legislation, which was the proximate cause of the Revolutionary War. Warren's spirit rose with the rising storm. His letters, both private and official, written without a thought of effect, delineate unconsciously much individual character which imprints itself on the reader's mind. These unstudied utterances, rich in thought and feeling, reveal his inner life and the secret of his personal influence. They

---

[1] Warren to General Gage, Cambridge, April 20, 1775.

[2] Dr. Belknap says that there succeeded from 1767 a period of sullen discontent, which came to an end on the 16th of December, 1773, in the bold act of destroying the tea in Boston harbor. This brought on the war.

show devotion to principle, love of liberty with fidelity to order, and large sympathetic power. They are far more. They are gushings of the warm lifeblood of the time, — sibylline leaves, on which are inscribed glowing characters, to be read and to enkindle evermore.

The official letters are so numerous as to preclude the printing of more than a selection. One of the private letters of this period was addressed to Arthur Lee, who was in London, and is dated five days after the tea was destroyed. In this letter, Warren expresses the opinion, that, unless there was a change in the policy of the Administration, Americans would be as indifferent to the interest of the mother-country as to that of any other European nation.

Joseph Warren to Arthur Lee.

BOSTON, Dec. 21st, 1773.

SIR, — My respected friend, Mr. Adams, informs me of the honor he has done me by mentioning my name to you in his letters. I can by no means lose so fair an opportunity of opening a correspondence with one to whom America is under such great obligations. Be assured, sir, we are not insensible to your merits. The clear manner in which you have treated the dispute between Great Britain and this country has, we doubt not, enlightened many in the parent State as well as in this country. But nothing seems able to penetrate the Egyptian darkness which is so palpable in the court atmosphere. We have long waited for something wise and good in the public counsels of the nation; at least we hoped that chance would lead to some measures, which, if not so designed, might eventually have produced some agreeable effects. But hitherto the unpropitious star which rules unhappy Britain has disappointed our wishes; every step taken by the Administration has increased the distance between her and the colonies; and I fear, that, unless a speedy alteration is made in the system of American policy, a few years will render us as indifferent to the interests of the mother-country as to that of any other State in Europe. However, as it is my firm opinion that a connection upon constitutional principles may be kept up between the two countries, at least for centuries to come, advantageous and honorable to both, I always respect the man who endeavors to heal the wound, by pointing out proper remedies, and to prevent the repetition of the stroke, by fixing a stigma on the instrument by which it was inflicted. This country is inhabited by a people loyal to their king, and faithful to themselves; none will more cheerfully venture their lives and fortunes for the honor and defence of the prince who reigns in their hearts, and none will with more resolution oppose the tyrant who dares to invade their rights. From this short but true character of this people, it is easy to see in what manner a wise king or a sagacious minister would treat them. But ———!

Mr. Adams will give you a full account of the tea shipped by the East-India Company for this place. It now is in the power of that company to make the use of Dutch tea as unpopular in this country as they can desire. They may easily, by a proper application to an all-powerful ministry, lay the colonies under such obligations as would be greatly to the company's advantage. But it is certain the whole navy of Britain will not prevent the introduction of Dutch tea; nor will her armies prevail with us to use the English tea, while the act imposing a duty on that article remains unrepealed. I congratulate you on the honor conferred on your brother by the city of London: in distinguishing merit, they honor themselves.

This will be presented to you by Dr. Williamson, who has labored abundantly in the glorious cause in which we are engaged. I hope soon to be convinced, that the freedom I have taken in writing to you is not disagreeable.

I am, sir, with great esteem, your most obedient humble servant,

JOSEPH WARREN.[1]

---

[1] I copy this letter from the "Life of Arthur Lee," ii. 262, the original not being among the Lee papers in Harvard-College Library.

The following is in the "Boston Gazette" of Dec. 20, 1773:—

"The brethren of the Honorable Society of Free and Ancient Accepted Masons are hereby notified, that the Most Worshipful Joseph Warren, Esq., Grand Master of the continent of America, intends to celebrate the Feast of St. John the Evangelist, on Monday, the 27th December inst., at Freemasons' Hall, Boston, where the brethren are requested to attend the festival.

"By order of the Most Worshipful Grand Master,

"WM. HOSKINS, *G. Sec.*

"N.B. — Tickets may be had of Messrs. Nathaniel Coffin, jun.; William Molineux, jun.; and Mr. Daniel Bell. The tables will be furnished at two o'clock."

The records of the Boston Committee of Correspondence contain evidences of Warren's labor in the patriot cause. Whenever there appears an enumeration of the members present, his name is among them. He was placed (Dec. 25, 1772) on a permanent working committee — one to draft replies to the letters that were received from the towns; the members being Samuel Adams, Joseph Warren, Nathaniel Appleton, Joseph Greenleaf, and Thomas Young. He was often put on special committees. He was, for instance, on a committee (Feb. 25, 1773) to prepare a petition to the legislature on the subject of the salaries of the judges, and the chairman of the committee to present it. He was directed to prepare (Sept. 7, 1773) a circular letter, to be sent out to the several towns in the province, and also one to be sent to the colonies. He was chairman (Nov. 9, 1773) of a committee of three, to circulate the proceedings of the town; and (Dec. 8) of another committee, to "collect and state in the public newspapers" certain things respecting the East-India Company's tea. He was directed (Dec. 17), at a meeting when Speaker Cushing and Samuel Quincy were called in, to frame a declaration relative to the tea, and to draw up a narrative of the recent proceedings. He was (Dec. 30) on a committee "to invite a correspondence with New York and Philadelphia;" and was the chairman (Jan. 8, 1774) of a committee to draft a reply to letters received from Newport and Portsmouth, both of which drafts are copied into the records. I select the reply to Newport: —

BOSTON, Jan. 24, 1774.

GENTLEMEN, — We can never enough adore that Almighty Disposer of events who has [as] it were by general inspiration, awakened a whole continent to a sense of their danger, and afforded them the needed wisdom and fortitude to lay hold on the means of their redemption from the most debasing and insupportable slavery.

The ample declaration of the resolution of our brethren at Newport, whose example, we flatter ourselves, will persuade the colonies, assures us of the advice and assistance of that respectable people, when the aid of either shall be required.

A frequent and full communication of our sentiments upon every occasion you judge requisite will much gratify us. By such communication throughout the colonies, the honest party will become initiated in the necessary means of recovering and securing their greatly infringed rights.

The present dispute inflames millions. Even in the infant colony of West Florida, we find the flame of patriotism kindled, and making progress. It behooves us, brethren, to be steady and determined; to possess ourselves with a thorough understanding of every article of our invaluable rights; and to embrace the opportunity, which cannot be far distant, of having them established on a firm foundation. Unanimity and harmony, in such a momentous undertaking, will, with God's blessing, ensure its success.

The Province of New Hampshire seems thoroughly in earnest to second their brethren in every laudable measure for the recovery and security of their liberty; and even the distressed Canadians hope for relief from our exertions.

Happy shall we be, if, in so noble, so righteous a struggle, we finally prevail; glorious, should we even miscarry.

We are, gentlemen, your most humble servants,

WILLIAM COOPER, *Clerk*.

This letter is one of the many utterances which show the common faith in a righteous cause; and the hope of its triumph was based on the union there seemed to be growing in support of it from "the infant colony of West Florida" to "the distressed Canadians." The thought, wrought into verse, appeared at the head of a spirited communication in the "Boston Gazette:" —

"From Florida, where heat intensely reigns,
To where we sought the Gaul on icy plains,

> One mortal flame through every breast may spread,
> By insult prompted, and by freedom led:
> The two-edged sword may supersede the pen,
> And every son of Adam say 'Amen.'"

The writer, as he contemplated the time when the sword might supersede the pen, said, in this appeal, "There is no time to be lost. A congress or a meeting of the States is indispensable. Let the Gordian knot be tied, and whatsoever the people shall do shall prosper."[1] The reliance was not in the feeble arm of a single colony, but in a people united into a common nationality.

The view taken of the effect of the destruction of the tea, by the two great exponents of their several parties, Hutchinson and Adams, was essentially the same. Hutchinson said that it had created a new union among the patriots.[2] Samuel Adams wrote, "The ministry could not have devised a more effectual measure to unite the colonies. Our committee have on this occasion opened a correspondence with the other New-England colonies, besides New York and Philadelphia. Old jealousies are removed, and perfect harmony subsists between them."[3] The act was looked upon as necessary to the union of the colonies; or, more exactly, to unite "the honest party", or the national party. In fine, the destruction of the tea was one of those events, rare in the life of nations, which, occurring in a peculiar state of public opinion, serve to wrest public affairs from the control of men, however wise or great, and cast them into the irresisible current of ideas. If, in America, it so awakened a whole continent to such a sense of

---

[1] Boston Gazette, Dec. 27, 1773. [2] Letter, January, 1774.
[3] Letter to James Warren, Dec. 28, 1773.

danger, that there seemed to be a general inspiration, created by the Almighty Disposer of events, in England it roused and angered the intensest of nationalities. Even those classed the friends of America pronounced the act to be rebellion. Singularly enough, the only statesman in power, who characterized the deed accurately, was Lord Dartmouth, who termed it a "commotion.

As the destruction of the tea was a blow aimed at the policy of the Administration, and not at the national sovereignty, the patriots expected to see their friends vindicate it in England. It was long held, even by Samuel Adams, that, as the principle, which, developed, would entail arbitrary power in America, would undermine public liberty in England, the liberal party there would persist in their efforts until there was a change of measures. This view is often expressed in the journals. The broadside, issued in New York, relating to the destruction of the tea, for instance, closed with the following verse: —

> "The making Boston harbor into tea,
> And those who made, and helped to make it,
> The toast of all Americans will be;
> Nor one true Briton will refuse to take it."[1]

On the reception of the same intelligence in Philadelphia, "A New Song" appeared in the newspapers, describing the event, one verse of which was: —

> "Squash into the deep descended,
> Cursèd weed of China's coast:
> Thus at once our fears were ended;
> British right shall ne'er be lost."[2]

---

[1] Handbill in New-York Hist. Soc. Collections.
[2] Dunlap's Penn. Packet, Jan. 3, 1774.

Candid Tories, even after the destruction of the tea, conceded that the people were as loyal subjects as any in the British dominions. Isaac Royall was one of this class. He had long been in political life, lived in princely style at Medford, a town about five miles from Boston, where, as a man of the world, he dispensed a generous hospitality. He had an uncommouly wide intercourse with men of all parties, and seems to have understood the aims of his countrymen. He wrote (Jan. 18, 1774) to Lord Dartmouth as follows: "I have been of His Majesty's Council and House of Representatives here thirty years without intermission, the last twenty of which has been at the council board. I firmly believe this people to be as truly loyal to His Majesty, as cordially affected to the illustrious House of Hanover, and as ardently desirous that there may never be wanting one of that august family to sway the British sceptre until time shall be no more, as any of his subjects in all his extended dominions. Please to observe, sir, however, that I don't pretend to justify any disturbances which have [been], although they are not more nor greater perhaps than often occur in large and free governments."[1] This may be set against the whole of the diatribes of the lower tier of Tory scribblers. Samuel Adams now said of the patriots, "They wish for nothing more than a permanent union with her (the mother-country) upon the condition of equal liberty. This is all they have been contending for; and nothing short of this will or ought to satisfy them:" and, months later, in October, Washington said that he did not know a man in the colonies who desired independence.

[1] MSS. Mass. Hist. Society.

The charge, however, continued to be kept up, that the patriots intended to deny British sovereignty; that the destruction of the tea was a proof of it; and that an army was necessary to retain the colonies in subjection. The period of five months following this act — December to May — was one of deep and even painful interest. In all mouths were the questions, What measures will the ministry take? Will they destroy the trade of Boston? Will they arrest the popular leaders? Will they annul the charter of Massachusetts? Will they resort to military rule?[1] As solutions of these questions were awaited, time passed heavily on. John Adams wrote (April 9), "Still! silent as midnight! The first vessels may bring us tidings which will erect the crests of the Tories again, and depress the spirits of the Whigs;" and such was the calmness, that he said, "There is not spirit enough on either side to bring the question to a complete decision."[2] The calmness was the "boding" quiet in which those who feel themselves the objects of inevitable calamity await the result in anxious silence, uncertain when or where the work of ruin is to begin, or by what means it is to be avoided.[3]

The Tory threat of introducing an army, or of arresting the popular leaders, did not stop the work of organization by the Whigs. The journals said that the committees never had so much business on their hands; and the committee of correspondence was uncommonly active. A town-meeting was held in the spring to provide for the annual commemoration of the massacre Samuel Adams was the

---

[1] John Adams's Works, ii. 324.   [2] *Ib.* ix. 337
[3] Reed's Life of Joseph Reed, i. 58.

moderator; Warren, as the chairman of the usual committee, took the lead in all the proceedings; and John Hancock delivered the oration before a great assembly of the citizens. The orator predicted fresh aggressions on American freedom, pointed to union as the path of security, and urged the people to be ready to take the field when danger called. He said, "The committee of correspondence have done much to unite the inhabitants of the whole continent for the security of the common interests;" but urged that the posture of affairs demanded a general congress, to lay a firm foundation for the common safety, and the security of their rights and liberties. "Surely," the orator said, "our hearts flutter no more at the sound of war than did those of the immortal band of Persia;" and in "the most animating confidence that the noble struggle for liberty would terminate gloriously for America," he thanked God for an illustrious roll of patriots (naming only Samuel Adams), "whom nothing could divert from a steady pursuit of the interests of their country," who "were at once its ornaments and safeguard," and "whose revered names, in all succeeding times, would grace the annals of their country." The orator exceeded the anticipations of his friends; and his oration was pronounced "an elegant, pathetic, and spirited performance."[1]

Soon after the 5th of March, William Goddard, the printer of the "Maryland Journal," arrived in town, with letters from the patriots of Philadelphia and New York, warmly commending "the establishment of a post-office on constitutional principles," or inde-

[1] John Adams's Works, ii. 332.

pendent of parliament; and (March 15) he had a conference with the committee of correspondence on the subject. The project was promptly indorsed by the members. Warren was appointed chairman of the sub-committee to mature the action, and reported an elaborate letter in favor of it. "When we consider," this letter says, "the importance of a post, by which not only private letters of friendship and commerce, but public intelligence, is conveyed from colony to colony, it seems proper and necessary that such a one should be established as shall be under the direction of the colonies."[1] Samuel Adams wrote (March 21), — "The colonies must unite to carry through such a project; and, when the end is effected, it will be a pretty grand acquisition." Mr. Goddard was delighted with the heartiness with which the patriots entered into this measure, and wrote (March 23) of them to Mr. Lamb, of New York, "For my part, I have not terms to convey to you the sentiments I entertain of their magnanimity, wisdom, patriotism, and urbanity. The Southern colonists, particularly New York, have great credit here for the part they have taken in this business; and the people are willing to give them the glory of originating one of the greatest plans that, as they say, was ever engaged in since the settlement of our country."[2] The journals contain much matter relative to the progress of what is termed this "grand design." In announcing the intelligence that the British ministry had dismissed Franklin from the office of postmaster-general, the "Gazette" (April 25, 1774) said, "Remarkable

---

[1] MSS. of Journals of Committee of Correspondence.
[2] Lamb Papers in the archives of the New-York Hist Society.

coincidence between the measures of the Americans and the measures of the British Administration. While the ministry are dismissing the postmaster-general from his place, the Americans are dismissing the office for ever. The designs of Providence and the policy of Britain, from the beginning, have co-operated to accelerate that amazing velocity with which the ball of empire rolls to this western world!"

The reports from the mother-country, in March, showed that the event, — the destruction of the tea — which had given an impetus to American union was stirring profoundly the English mind. Still all was uncertainty as to the measures which might be adopted. The transactions at Liberty Tree, Samuel Adams wrote (March 31), "were treated with scorn and ridicule; but, when they heard of the resolves of the body of the people at the Old-South Meeting-house, the place from whence the orders issued for the removal of the troops in 1770, they put on grave countenances." He remarked that no mention was made of America in the king's speech. "I never," are the words of the patriot, "suffer my mind to be ever much disturbed with prospects. Sufficient for the day is the evil thereof. It is our duty, at all hazards, to preserve the public liberty. Righteous Heaven will graciously smile on every manly and rational attempt to secure that best of all the gifts to man from the ravishing hand of lawless and brutal force." It continued to be said by the Tories, that an army would speedily be sent to Boston. Three weeks later, when the news was more alarming, Adams wrote (April 21) to John Dickinson, "May God prepare this people for the event, by inspiring them with wisdom and fortitude! They stand in need of all the countenance that their sister-colonies can afford them, with whom to cultivate and strengthen a strict union was a great object in view."

The solemn tone of this letter indicates the serious nature of the intelligence that was now appearing in the journals relative to England. The accounts printed there of the proceedings in Boston, culminating in the destruction of the tea, roused a proud nationality into so terrific an energy as to sweep before it, hurricane like, men and parties; and a small band, of whom the sturdy John Cartwright, a Cato of those days, was an exponent, seemed to have been the sole inheritors of the political ideas of a Locke and a Milton, of an Eliot and a Hampden. The product of this anger was a system of penal measures, designed for a people, who, it was charged, were not only animated by the spirit, but red with the deed, of rebellion.

The long interval of suspense in America terminated, when, on the 2d of May, the Boston journals printed the king's speech transmitting to parliament the papers relating to the transactions of the town in relation to the tea, and announced that Lord North had moved the Boston Port Bill. In subsequent issues they abounded with citations from the British press, which embodied the counts in which the town was arraigned at the bar of public opinion in England. The arrogant philippic was as severe, and about as just, on the illustrious and venerable Franklin, as it was on the glorious town; for he was characterized as the emblem of iniquity in gray hairs. It was the sum of the great news, that the ministry, or the nation, were resolved to enforce their doctrine of the right of the British Parliament to legislate, in all cases whatsoever, by the sword.

Another arrival brought the Port Act, which received the royal signature on the 31st of March, and was printed in the Boston journals on the 10th of May. It provided for a discontinuance of the landing or shipping of all merchandise at Boston or within its harbor. It was authoritatively announced that an army was on its way to Boston; and that British ships of war, by blockading the town for a fortnight, could starve its people into submission. Heretofore obnoxious acts of parliament had borne on all the colonies: but this act was the beginning of a coercive policy on one colony; and it was based on the theory, that jealousies between the colonies, antagonist interests, and different modes of social life, formed an insurmountable barrier to any such union as would rise to the dignity of national power; and that Massachusetts, being left to struggle alone, would be crushed.

The committee of correspondence now voted to invite a conference of the eight neighboring towns, to deliberate on the critical state of public affairs; and Warren was directed to prepare the invitation, which he immediately reported. He was also directed to draft a letter, to be sent to Philadelphia. The invitation to the eight towns was in the following terms, which is copied from the original in Warren's handwriting: —

BOSTON, May 11, 1774.

GENTLEMEN, — We have this day received information, that a Bill has passed the two houses of the British Parliament for blocking up the harbor of Boston until the tea, lately destroyed at one of the wharves in this town, be paid for. We know that you must feel the indignity as sensibly as we do; therefore request that you would meet us in Faneuil Hall, at three o'clock in the afternoon of Thursday next, that we may together consult what is proper to be done in this critical state of our public affairs.

We are, gentlemen, with much esteem, your friends and fellow-countrymen. Signed by direction and in behalf of the committee of correspondence for Boston, WILLIAM COOPER, *Sec.*

When Warren penned this circular, however it may have been with a few leading spirits, the surface of the public mind outside of Massachusetts was calm. "The other provinces," Dr. Ramsay remarks, "were but remotely affected by the fate of Massachusetts. They were happy, and had no cause, on their own account, to oppose the government of Great Britain;"[1] and it did not accord with the selfish maxim that hitherto had governed States, for a people, under such circumstances, to run the risk of incurring the resentment of the mother-country, by taking the part of a proscribed neighbor.[2] So undemonstrative were the other provinces, that John Adams thought, that, as it had been for ten years past, things would go on for more years than he would live, oscillating like a pendulum, between a redress of American grievances and absolute parliamentary authority. "Our children," he said, "may see revolutions, and be concerned and active in affecting them, of which we can form no conception."[3] It is well nigh impossible to exaggerate the interest with which the people of Boston and Massachusetts now watched political movements in the other colonies.

In the afternoon of the 12th of May, the delegates

---

[1] Ramsay's American Revolution, i. 113.   [2] *Ib.*
[3] Letter, April 9, 1774, in Works, ix. 337.

from Dorchester, Roxbury, Brookline, Newton, Cambridge, Charlestown, Lynn, and Lexington, assembled at the selectmen's room, at Faneuil Hall. "The lowly men who now met there were, most of them, accustomed to feed their own cattle; to fold their own sheep; to guide their own plough; all trained to public life in the little democracies of their towns: some of them captains in the militia, and officers of the church according to the discipline of Congregationalists; nearly all of them communicants, under a public covenant with God. They grew in greatness as their sphere enlarged."[1] Among them were patriots who sat in the council-halls or stood on the battle-fields of the subsequent nine years' struggle, who were in the convention that formed the Federal Constitution, and who occupied high places in the new national government. Modern art could have photographed in this scene the inner life of this trial-hour, — its hopes and its fears, its calm faith, its fearful passion, and its high resolve.

Samuel Adams was chosen to preside over this conference. He was fifty-two years of age. He had labored with so single an eye for his country, that he was crowned with the laurel. In him principle was kindled into power by a steady enthusiasm; virtue was made strong by an ever-present religion; and over all presided an imperial mental dignity. In word and work he had been a truly great man, noble in impulse, immovable in purpose, wise in counsel, fertile in resources.[2] So signally had the progress of

---

[1] Bancroft, vii. 35.

[2] Jefferson (Works, i. 21) says, "I can say that he was truly a great man, wise in counsel, fertile in resources, immovable in his purposes." John Adams's opinion of this "great character" is given in his works, especially vol. x. 364.

events vindicated the accuracy of his judgment, that patriots, who thought at times that he went too far, now conceded that he had been in the right, and were paying to him the tribute to ability of coming round to a pioneer opinion. He was a prophet who had honor in his own country; for the press of his native town, reflecting public opinion, said that America, for his integrity, fortitude, and perseverance in her cause, had erected to him a statue in her heart.[1] Fame had sounded his name abroad; for it was said of him in England by his friends, that many considered him the first politician in the world;[2] and by his enemies that he was the would-be Cromwell of America.[3] Each revelation of his great pioneer work supplies fresh evidence of the justice of this contemporary eulogy; and thus time, like the refiner's fire, brings out new lustre in the halo that encircles this venerable name.

The utterances of the patriot were now like an oracle. "There is no crime," are his words, "alleged in the act as committed by the town of Boston;[4] but we have been tried, condemned, and are to be punished by the shutting-up of the harbor until we shall disgrace ourselves by servilely yielding up, in effect, the just and righteous claims of America.[5] It is the expectation of our enemies, and some of our friends

---

[1] Boston Gazette, March, 1775.

[2] Quincy's Letter, Dec. 7, 1774; in Life, 258.

[3] London pamphlet, Independence the Object of Congress. "It is necessary the public should be made acquainted with a very conspicuous character, no less a man than Mr. Samuel Adams, the would-be Cromwell of America." A Tory writer, in Draper's "Gazette," Jan. 11, 1776, says Samuel Adams had "an oily tongue;" and that, "by artful wiles and smooth demeanor, he talked the people out of their understandings."

[4] Letter to James Warren, May 14, 1774.   [5] Ib.

are afraid, that this town singly will not be able to support the cause under so severe a trial. Did not the very being of every seaport town, and, indeed, of every colony, considered as a free people, depend upon it, I would not even then entertain a thought so dishonorable of them as that they could leave us to struggle alone.[1] The people generally abhor the thought of paying for the tea,—the condition on which we are to be restored to the favor of Great Britain.[2] The heroes who first trod on Plymouth shore fed on clams and muscles, and were contented. The country which they explored and defended with their richest blood, and which they transmitted as an inheritance to their posterity, affords us a superabundance of provision. Will it not be an eternal disgrace to this generation if it should now be surrendered?[3] The people are in council; their opposition grows into a system; they are united; they are resolute; and it requires but a small portion of the gift of discernment for any one to foresee that Providence will erect a mighty empire in America."[4]

There is no report of the speeches that were made at this conference. The Boston delegates reminded their brethren from the country, that the trade of Boston might be recovered by paying for the tea that was destroyed; but the delegates from the other towns held it unworthy even to notice the offer, and promised, on their part, to "join their suffering brethren in every measure for relief." The business of the conference was embodied in a report, drafted by a subcommittee, on which were Warren, Colonel Gardner

---

[1] Letter to James Warren, May 14, 1774.   [2] Letter, May, 1774.
[3] Letter, May 14.   [4] Letter, May, 1774.

of Cambridge, and others, which pronounced the Port Act contrary to natural right and the usages of international law. The conference also adopted a circular letter, to be sent to the committees of the other colonies, proposing a general cessation of trade with Great Britain. "This act," the circular says of the Port Act, "fills the inhabitants with indignation. The more thinking part of those who have hitherto been in favor of the measures of the British Government, look upon it as not to have been expected even from a barbarous State. This attack, though made immediately upon us, is doubtless designed for every other colony who will not surrender their sacred rights and liberties into the hands of an infamous ministry. Now, therefore, is the time when all should he united in opposition to this violation of the liberties of all."

The committee of correspondence, on this day (May 12), requested the selectmen to call a town-meeting, "to consider the important and interesting news lately received from England;" when a warrant was immediately issued for one to be held at Faneuil Hall. A great concourse gathered, hundreds who could not get in standing around the hall as the proceedings went on. Samuel Adams was the moderator; Dr. Cooper offered prayer; and his brother, the town-clerk, read the Port Act. The journals say that its nature and tendency, as well as its design, were explained. Dr. Young says, "The infamous act was read and descanted upon with a freedom and energy becoming the orators of ancient Rome; and no one hesitated to declare it, in every principle, repugnant to law, religion, and common sense."[1] Several judicious and manly proposals, the journals say, "were made to meet the emergency, which were discussed with a candor, moderation, and firmness of mind becoming a people resolved to preserve their liberty." They were referred to a committee to propose measures for the relief of the citizens, of which Warren was a member, to report at an adjournment. This was the origin of a new committee, called the donation committee, on which, as will be seen, Warren was a zealous worker. The meeting voted to recommend to the other colonies to come into a joint resolution to stop all trade, importation and exportation, with Great Britain and the West Indies till the Port Act was repealed; and this was urged as a measure that "would prove the salvation of North America and her liberties." The vote was ordered to be transmitted by the moderator to all the other colonies. After appointing a committee to confer with Marblehead, the meeting adjourned. It was said that it was large and respectable;[2] that many who had been hitherto cool in the common cause distinguished themselves in their zeal for its support;[3] that its unanimity was as perfect as human society can admit of.[4] The "Gazette," in reporting the proceedings, said, "It appears that the drift of the Administration and their good friends in England is to break the union of the American colonies; and that devoted Boston shall feel the unparalleled tokens of their displeasure. But let us not be dismayed. Let us persevere to the end, and resolve to yield our lives and fortunes before we will submit to

[1] Letter, May 13. Life of John Lamb, '84.
[2] Journals.
[3] Dr. Young's Letter.
[4] Boston journals.

the iron yoke of tyranny! And let the sacred truth be hallowed in the mind of every American, 'By uniting, we stand; by dividing, we fall!'"

While the steady, vigorous, sensible, and persevering Paul Revere,[1] as "an express," was bearing this union message to the Southern colonies, General Gage, with an appointment as governor to supersede Hutchinson, was at Castle William, where he arrived on the day of the meeting. His instructions directed him to arrest, for transportation and trial, Samuel Adams, Hancock, Warren, and other popular leaders.[2] His commission was extraordinary. It made him captain-general and governor-in-chief of His Majesty's Province of Massachusetts Bay, while he retained his authority as commander-in-chief of the British forces in North America; and it was announced that an army would soon follow him. His object was to procure submission of the town and the colony to the constituted authorities; to execute rigorously the Port Act, and arrest the ringleaders of the people in the proceedings in Boston of November and December.

General Gage was not unpopular. His prior intercourse with the Bostonians had been agreeable, and his urbane manners and social turn won him personal friends; but he did not comprehend the men and things around him, and was fitted neither to overawe nor to conciliate. His earliest civil movements indicated weakness, and his military operations showed incapacity. But public affairs were now at the mercy of events: personal character was of little account in comparison with the policy which it had been resolved

---

[1] Young's Letter, May 13.   [2] Bancroft, vii. 38.

to carry out; and it may be safely said, that no wisdom in a subordinate official could have stayed the march of revolution.

Four days after the town-meeting, General Gage landed (May 17) at Long Wharf, and was received with unusual marks of respect. The military, consisting of a troop of guards, a regiment of militia, a company of artillery, and the Cadets, under Lieutenant-colonel Coffin, paraded in King Street; and, although it rained, there was a great concourse of people. The governor was received by the council and civil officers, under a salute from the ships and batteries, and was escorted to the Town House by the Cadets; receiving, as he passed the military array in King Street, the salutes of the officers. His commission was read in the council-chamber and the usual oaths administered, when three volleys were fired by the military, and three cheers given by the people; and then followed an elegant dinner in Faneuil Hall. It had been reported, that, if the new governor were permitted to land, he would be treated with indignity; and the popular leaders, by this parade, hoped to remove any unfavorable impressions which that report might have made as to the character and disposition of the inhabitants.[1]

Governor Gage proposed several toasts at the dinner in Faneuil Hall, which were well received; but, on naming Hutchinson, there was a general hiss. As governor, he made some show of authority on the destruction of the tea, which he looked upon as unhappy, and termed "the boldest stroke which had yet been struck in America."[2] On the next day, he

---

[1] S. A. Wells's MSS.   [2] Hutchinson's History, iii. 439.

went from Milton into town, and summoned a meeting of the council, but could not get a quorum; when, there being much excitement, by the advice of friends he took lodgings at the castle, on the pretence of visiting his sons.[1] Three days later, he returned to town, and met the council at Cambridge, when, after much division of opinion, it was concluded to direct the attorney-general to lay the matter before the grand-jury.[2] From this time the governor endeavored to avoid political controversy with the popular leaders, preferring to await intelligence from England as to the disposition of the ministry. He met the general court as usual in January, but did not refer to the proceedings on the tea in his message. The salary of the judges was the local question of the session, which elicited a world of tedious ancient lore from the lawyers; but the general issue, which the king pushed to extremities, became paramount in interest and importance. On the reception of the Port Act, the governor was charged with advising this measure; but he averred that he was not called upon for an opinion, and, if he had been, that he could never have brought himself to have advised one so severe and distressing.[3] On the morning after receiving the news of his removal, he again changed his residence to the castle, where he[4] held consultations with General Gage, received complimentary addresses from his political and personal friends, and soon (June 1) sailed for London.

On the day after the commission of General Gage

---

[1] Hutchinson's History, iii. 438.   [2] *Ib.*, 439.
[3] Letter to Colonel Williams, May 14, 1774.
[4] Hutchinson's History, iii. 459.

was proclaimed (May 18), the Port-act meeting reassembled in Faneuil Hall, with Samuel Adams as the moderator. The committee on ways and means, to relieve those who might suffer from want of work, asked further time to prepare their report, and recommended to their fellow-citizens patience, fortitude, and a firm trust in God.[1] After passing resolves relative to the importance of the trade of Boston, the meeting adjourned until the 30th. There was now much discussion, in conversation and by the press, on a proposition to indemnify the East-India Company for the tea that had been destroyed; and the subject was debated in this meeting. A letter, written on the evening of this day, says, "We have many among us who are for compromising matters, and put forward a proposition to pay for the tea. George Irving has declared this day, that, if it should be promoted, he is ready to put down two thousand pounds sterling towards it, and will take it on himself to wait on Governor Gage, and know what his demands on us are; which circumstance John Amory mentioned at the town-meeting this day, which was in general rejected, though he urged the matter much."[2]

"The town of Boston," Samuel Adams wrote on the same day, "now suffers the stroke of ministerial vengeance in the common cause of America; and I hope in God they will sustain the shock with dignity. They do not conceive that their safety consists in a servile compliance of this barbarous act." Others of less faith and insight, who saw the cloud blackening and lowering, but could not see the light behind it, wrote in a different strain. "Imagine to yourself,"

---

[1] Boston Evening Post, May 23.   [2] Letter of John Andrews, May 18.

a letter on the same day runs, "the horror painted on the faces of a string of slaves, condemned by the Inquisition to perpetual drudgery at the oar. Such is the dejection imprinted on every countenance we meet in this once happy but now totally ruined town"[1] Party spirit also was now rising. The same observer wrote, "Such is the cursed zeal that now prevails, — animosities run[ning] higher than ever, each party charging the other as bringing ruin on their country, — that, unless some expediency is adopted to get the port open by paying for the tea (which seems to be the only one), I am afraid we shall experience the worst of evils, — a civil war, — which God avert."[2] The military force, known to be near, emboldened the Tories, who laid the evils to the committee of correspondence; the distress exasperated the Whigs to such a degree that the popular leaders found it hard to restrain them. Their feeling is expressed by a London letter in the journals: "This accursed tea is the very match that is appointed to set fire to a train of gunpowder that has been long, though secretly, laid by our ministry and your governor, — joint agents in that most infernal business of destroying the liberties of three millions of British subjects."[3]

Meantime the Port Act was doing faithfully the work of uniting the colonies; for the expression of indignation and of sympathy was wide and spontaneous. The law was received in New York directly from England, and the people felt the wrong done to Boston as a wound to themselves.[4] It was circu-

[1] Letter of John Andrews, May 18.
[2] *Ib.*, June 12.
[3] Boston Gazette, May 16.
[4] Bancroft, vii. 40.

lated with great zeal and rapidity. In some places it was printed on mourning-paper, and in others it was burned in the presence of great collections of the people. The public opinion is embodied in the responses that were made on receiving the appeal of Boston of the 13th of May. On the 30th, — when the Port-act meeting was continued by adjournment to the 17th of June, — the Boston journals contain in full the information gathered by Paul Revere, who had just returned; and it was said, "Nothing can exceed the indignation with which our brethren in Rhode Island, Connecticut, and Philadelphia, have received this proof of ministerial madness." The development of fraternity seemed to the Whigs amazing. The Tories continued sceptical and blind. Hutchinson sailed for England, in the belief that the people were so divided among themselves "that a union of the colonies was utterly impracticable."[1] Governor Gage was no wiser; for he informed Lord Dartmouth (March 31), that, if the other colonies intended to go any farther in behalf of Boston than giving good words, it was not known here.

On the 1st of June, the Port Act went into effect, when the ships of war were moored around the town in a manner effectually to blockade the port. "Our enemies," Samuel Adams wrote, "are already holding up to the tradesmen their grim picture of misery, to induce them to yield to tyranny. I hope they will not prevail upon them; but this is to be feared, unless their brethren in the other colonies will agree upon measures of speedy support and relief." There was another danger, — that of premature conflict. "I

---

[1] Life of Josiah Quincy, 231.

hope," he added, "by refraining from every act of violence, we shall avoid the snare that is laid for us by the posting of regiments so near us. Violence and submission would at this time be equally fatal."[1] This day was observed in Virginia as one of fasting and prayer, and in Philadelphia by expressions of mourning. "The Port Act," Bancroft says, "had been received on the 10th of May; and, in three weeks, the continent, as one great commonwealth, made the cause of Boston its own."[2]

The committee of correspondence, when they had reason to expect personally far more than words of detraction, and when a naval and military force were gathering in the town, went on calmly in their great work; and its journal presents Warren as one of the foremost members. He was placed (May 20)[3] on a committee to draft the merchants' agreement; was (May 27) on a committee to draw up an address to counteract the addresses that were presented to Hutchinson; was the chairman (June 2) of a committee to draft a solemn League and Covenant, and of a committee (June 6) — Thomas Young and Joseph Greenleaf being the others — to draft letters to send to the committees of New York, Philadelphia, Connecticut, and Rhode Island.[4] The paper termed the League and Covenant, reported to the committee on the 5th of June, contained a pledge to suspend all

---

[1] Samuel Adams to Stephen Hopkins, May 30, 1774.

[2] Bancroft, vii. 55.

[3] The "Boston Gazette" of May 23, 1774, says, "By letters from London, we learn that, at a late meeting in London of the Society for Supporting the Bill of Rights, Mr. Samuel Adams, the Hon. John Adams, Esq., and Dr. Joseph Warren, all of this town, were unanimously elected members of that society; and that the proper certificates of their admission were ordered to be sent to the new members."

[4] Journals of the Committee.

commercial intercourse with Great Britain, and not to purchase or consume any merchandise imported from that country after the first day of August. It was proposed to publish the names of those who refused to sign this agreement. This League and Covenant, having been adopted by the committee, was sent to all the towns, accompanied with a spirited circular, urging the people to enter into it, "as the last and only method of preserving the land from slavery without drenching it in blood."

An article in the "Evening Post" (6th), characterized by Warren's vehement spirit, urged the adoption of the League and Covenant and the necessity of a congress. "If the colonies," it says, "blind to their own true interest, shall madly prefer the present hour to true happiness, and will not fully join us in what we have a right to ask, and they are bound by every consideration in nature to grant, let us then give up; for, though I am for dying rather than betray the rights of America, yet I am not for sacrificing the town for nothing! And, mind it, O ye colonies!—be it remembered by future generations,— that the event of this struggle insures happiness and freedom or miserable slavery to this continent. Act, then, like men. Appoint a general congress from the several colonies. Unite as a firm band of brothers, and ward off the evil intended, or expect the derision of schoolboys and the execrations of posterity." A communication in the same paper also says, "Before we make many important moves, we want to have the grand congress or states-general, chosen by the whole continent, meet and form the union and the plans for operation."[1]

[1] Boston Evening Post, June 6, 1774.

The patriots now entered upon a week which promised to be marked by an uncommon interest in matters pertaining to the town and to the province. The general court, "by the king's particular commands," was in session at Salem; and the governor had signified that it would be held there "until His Majesty should have signified his royal will and pleasure for holding it again at Boston." The army, for which the Tories had been impatient, began to arrive, when the people, it was said, would speak and act openly. The local question was now industriously agitated of compensation for the tea,[1] and there was

---

[1] Some of the most unflinching patriots, having reconciliation in view, at first were in favor of indemnifying the East-India Company for the destruction of the tea. The Pennsylvania patriots (Bancroft, vii. 97) advised this course. Dr. Franklin — and the country had no truer patriot — sent the following letter, dated Feb. 2, 1774, to the representatives of the town of Boston. This is copied from the papers of Samuel Adams: —

"GENTLEMEN, — I received the honor of your letter, dated Dec. 21, containing a distinct account of the proceedings at Boston relative to the tea imported there, and of the circumstances which occasioned its destruction. I communicated the same to Lord Dartmouth, with some other advices of the same import. It is yet unknown what measures will be taken here on this occasion; but the clamor against the proceedings is high and general. I am truly concerned, as I believe all considerate men are with you, that there should seem to be any necessity for carrying matters to such extremity, as, in a dispute about public rights, to destroy private property. This (notwithstanding the blame justly due to those who obstructed the return of the tea) it is impossible to justify with people so prejudiced in favor of the power of parliament to tax America as most are in this country. As the India Company, however, are not our adversaries, and the offensive measure of sending their teas did not take its rise with them, but was an expedient of the ministry to serve them, and yet avoid a repeal of the old Act, I cannot but wish and hope, that, before any compulsive measures are thought of here, our general court will have shown a disposition to repair the damage, and return compensation to the Company. This all our friends here wish with me; and that, if war is finally to be made upon us, which some threaten, an act of violent injustice on our part, unrectified, may not give a colorable pretence for it. A speedy reparation will immediately set us right in the opinion of all Europe. And though the mischief was the act of persons unknown, yet, as probably they cannot be found or brought to answer for it, there seems to be some reasonable claim on the society at large in which it hap-

the great measure of inaugurating a congress: the Tories were as zealous for the former as the Whigs were for the latter.

A meeting of the tradesmen was held on the 15th of June, in which the question of paying for the tea was sharply discussed. Some of the patriots stood at the door of the hall in which the meeting was held, and opposed such a step. "Some smart things," Dr. Young writes, "were said *pro* and *con* on the subject; but it clearly appeared the general sense to submit to all extremities before a shadow of concession was extorted from them" Still the Tories were strong enough to ward off decisive action and to postpone the subject; and this fact gave Warren no little uneasiness. As distrustful of his ability as he was anxious for the cause, he wrote, that afternoon, the following letter to Samuel Adams, urging him to be present at the adjournment of the Port-act meeting, on Friday the 17th, when a warm engagement was expected with the Tories.

---

pened. Making voluntarily such reparation can be no dishonor to us, or prejudice to our claim of rights, since parliament here has frequently considered in the same light similar cases; and, only a few years since, when a valuable saw-mill, which had been erected at a great expense, was violently destroyed by a number of persons, supposed to be sawyers, but unknown, a grant was made out of the public treasury of two thousand pounds to the owner, as a compensation. I hope in thus freely, and perhaps too forwardly, expressing my sentiments and wishes, I shall not give offence to any. I am sure I mean well; being ever, with sincere affection to my native country, and great respect to the assembly and yourselves,

"Gentlemen, your most obedient and most humble servant,
B. FRANKLIN.

"Hon. THOMAS CUSHING,
SAMUEL ADAMS,
JOHN HANCOCK,
WILLIAM PHILLIPS, } Esquires."

THE PORT ACT AND THE UNION. 317

Joseph Warren to Samuel Adams.

BOSTON, June 15, 1774.

SIR, — This afternoon was a meeting of a considerable number of the tradesmen of this town; but, after some altercations, they dissolved themselves without coming to any resolutions, for which I am very sorry, as we had some expectations from the meeting. We are industrious to save our country, but not more so than others are to destroy it. The party who are for paying for the tea, and by that making a way for every compliance, are too formidable. However, we have endeavored to convince friends of the impolicy of giving way in any single article, as the arguments for a total submission will certainly gain strength by our having sacrificed such a sum as they demand for the payment of the tea. I think your attendance can by no means be dispensed with next Friday. I believe we shall have a warm engagement. The committee had a letter laid before them this evening, from Baltimore, which more comports with my sentiments of public affairs than any yet received from the southward. That letter, with several others to you, will be forwarded in the morning. Vigilance, activity, and patience are necessary at this time: but the mistress we court is LIBERTY; and it is better to die than not to obtain her. If the *timidity* of some and the *treachery* of others in this town does not ruin us, I think we shall be saved. I fear New York will not assist us with a very good grace; but she may perhaps be ashamed to desert us: at least, if her MERCHANTS offer to sell us, her MECHANICS will forbid the auction. You will undoubtedly do all in your power to effect the relief of this town, and to expedite a general congress; but we must not suffer the town of Boston to render themselves contemptible, either by their want of fortitude, honesty, or foresight, in the eyes of this and the other colonies.

I beg you will not fail to bring with you all such papers and letters as may serve our righteous cause at our meeting Friday.

I am, dear sir, with great respect, yr. H. sev[t].,

J. WARREN.

Mr. S. ADAMS, at Salem.

P.S. — I think religion and policy require that a day be set apart for publicly addressing the King of kings.[1]

---

[1] This letter is copied from the original, in Mr. Bancroft's possession.

The word from Baltimore, which was this evening so inspiring to Warren, was a generous outpour of patriotic spirit: "Could we," the Baltimore Whigs wrote to Boston, "remain a moment indifferent to your sufferings, the result of your noble and virtuous struggles, in defence of American liberties, we should unworthily share in those blessings which (under God) we owe in greatest measure to your perseverance and zeal in support of our common rights, that they have not ere now been wrested from us by the rapacious hand of power. Permit us, therefore, as brethren and fellow-citizens embarked in one common interest, most effectually to sympathize with you, now suffering and persecuted in the cause of our country; and to assure you of our readiness to concur in every reasonable measure that can be devised for obtaining the most effectual and speedy relief to our distressed friends." After relating the progress of measures towards a congress, and the proposition to proceed by petition and remonstrance, the letter says, "We cannot see the least ground for expecting relief by it. The contempt with which a similar petition was treated in '65, and many others since that period, convince us that policy and reason of State, instead of justice and equity, are to prescribe the rule of our future conduct; and that something more sensible than supplications will best serve our purpose."[1] The following reply is copied from the original in Warren's handwriting: —

BOSTON, June 16, 1774.

GENTLEMEN, — We last evening received your generous and affectionate letter, 3d instant, enclosing your noble and spirited resolves.

[1] Samuel Adams's Papers.

Nothing gives us a more animating confidence of the happy event of our present struggle for the liberties of America, or offers us greater support under the distress we now feel, than the assurances we receive from our brethren of their readiness to join with us in every salutary measure for preserving the rights of the colonies, and of their tender sympathy for us under our sufferings. We rejoice to find the respectable county of Baltimore so fully alarmed at the public danger, and so prudent and resolute in their measure to secure the blessings of freedom to their country. Our general assembly is now sitting at Salem, about twenty miles from this town; we expect that members for a general congress will speedily be elected by them; we hope by the next post to send you a full account of their proceedings. Post just going off, we can only add, that we are, gentlemen, with the most unfeigned respect and esteem.

P.S. — We think your caution of inclosing your letter to a friend is extremely just at this crisis of our affairs, and we shall follow your example.

To Mr. SAMUEL PURVIANCE, jun., in Baltimore,
    to be communicated to the Committee of Correspondence there.

It would be interesting to follow Warren through the next day, the 17th of June, and to give his talk in private, and his public speech; but the personal notices of him are too scanty to frame such a piece of genuine biography. On this day, the Port-act town-meeting was to meet, by adjournment, in Faneuil Hall, — the first town-meeting in the presence of British troops since the March meetings in 1770; and it may be inferred, that his morning hours were not without apprehension on account of being obliged to meet an engagement with the Tories, under peculiar circumstances, without that tower of strength to lean upon, Samuel Adams. Nor could it have been without anxiety for the work which he knew was before his friend in the general court at Salem; but it is history, that, as the evening shades came on, his heart was bounding with joy.

The public mind was greatly excited: Faneuil Hall could not contain the numbers who gathered; and hundreds who gave their countenance to the meeting remained outside. It was necessary to choose a moderator *pro tem.*, on account of the absence of Samuel Adams; and James Bowdoin was first chosen, who, it was ascertained, was not at home, and then John Rowe, who happened to be engaged. The "Hon. John Adams, Esq.," was then chosen, who accepted.[1] He had long avoided politics; had been rather a counsellor than an actor,[2] and he had not always approved of the popular action.[3] This was his first appearance in a Boston town-meeting as a leader; indeed, it was his entrance upon a quarter of a century's uninterrupted political life, during which it was his felicity to act as chief magistrate over the people whose liberties he was now laboring to maintain. The patriot was often introspective, and sets down many frank revelations of the inner man. He felt more spirits and activity since the reception of the Port-act news than he had had for years.[4] He had also more faith. He saw that the town of Boston must suffer martyrdom; but it was his consolation that it was in "the cause of truth, of virtue, of liberty, and of humanity:" it would "have a glorious resurrection to greater wealth, splendor, and power than ever."[5]

It was a principal object of the meeting to receive and act upon an expected report from the committee of ways and means to provide employment for the

---

[1] Town Records.
[2] Life of John Adams, Works, i. 42.
[3] *Ib.*, 146.
[4] Letter, May 12, 1774.
[5] *Ib.*, 3.

poor. The Boston records say, that "Dr. Warren acquainted the town that they (the committee) thought best to defer making a report till they had heard from the other governments; whereupon they were directed to sit again."[1] It was stated that there had been much talk out of doors, as well as writing in the papers, concerning payment for the tea; and the request was made, that, in case any gentleman had any thing to offer on the subject, he would speak freely, in order that a matter of so much importance might be fairly discussed in the presence of the body of the people. Among others, Thomas Boylston, a wealthy merchant and a public benefactor, spoke on this question; but he had not gone far before the people became impatient, and tried to stop him. The moderator interposed to check the confusion, and expressed his mortification that a citizen of Mr. Boylston's age, sense, and experience of life, was not listened to with the respect to which he was entitled. Instead, the moderator said he witnessed what he could describe best in the words of Milton, —

> "I did but prompt the age to quit their clogs,
> By the known rules of ancient liberty,
> When straight a barbarous noise environs me
> Of owls and cuckoos, asses, apes, and dogs;" —

uttering the last line with uncommon emphasis, and with gestures pointing to the part of the hall from which the noise came. Though the rebuke restored order, Mr. Boylston declined to go on.[2] Young, a zealous patriot, the next day, wrote, "In vain were the Æschinæ called upon to expose propositions fit only to be whispered in the conclave of the addressers

---

[1] Young's Letter, June 19, 1774. [2] John Adams's Works, i. 146.

composed of a few men."[1] The meeting adjourned until the afternoon.

At three o'clock, the committee of correspondence laid before the town, probably through Warren, the answers that had been received to their appeal. It is not necessary to present an abstract of them: some acceded to the proposition to stop trade, others preferred to await the decision of a congress which was proposed by Providence and New York, and all urged the necessity of making united effort. The town passed an admirable resolution, enjoining the committee of correspondence to write to all the other colonies, and acquaint them that the town was deliberating on the steps to be taken on the present exigency, and were awaiting with anxiety the result of a continental congress, whose meeting they impatiently desired, in whose wisdom they could confide, and in whose determination they should cheerfully acquiesce.[2] This meeting was again adjourned. It proved to be uncommonly satisfactory to the patriots. The journals say that it was as full and respectable as ever was known, and was never exceeded in firmness and unanimity; that its speeches on the state of affairs would do honor to any assembly; that not one, though called upon, had any thing to say in favor of paying for the tea; and that all were for withstanding the utmost efforts of tyranny, rather than make free surrender of the rights of America.

While the patriots, guided by Warren, were thus successful in the town-meeting, their brethren in Salem, under the lead of Samuel Adams, were adopting an important measure in the general court, a

[1] Letter of Thomas Young, June 19, 1774.   [2] Boston Town Records.

glance at the proceedings of which seems to be required to show the progress of events. For months, indeed for years, the call had been frequent in the colonies for a union after the manner of the United Provinces, and for a congress as the necessary step towards it. Such a body was formally proposed by a town-meeting in Providence, and the committees of correspondence of Philadelphia, New York, and Connecticut, and the assembly of Virginia; and the New York committee requested the patriots of Massachusetts to appoint the time and place.[1] It was resolved to do this to-day in the general court. Samuel Adams, having reason to fear executive interference, locked the door of the hall in which the House of Representatives were assembled, and proposed the resolves which provided for a congress, to be convened on the first

[1] The citations I have made from the journals show how constantly a congress had been called for. A town-meeting in Providence, R.I., on the 17th of May, instructed the deputies from that town to propose a congress in the assembly at the next session. On the 21st of May, the committee of correspondence of Philadelphia, in a letter sent by Paul Revere to the Boston committee, proposed a congress. On the 23d of May, the New-York committee of correspondence, in a letter addressed to the Boston committee, made the same proposition. The House of Burgesses of Virginia, after their dissolution by the Earl of Dunmore, in consequence of their resolutions of sympathy with Boston, and at the celebrated meeting at the Apollo Tavern, on the 27th of May, recommended the committee of correspondence to communicate with their several corresponding committees on the expediency of calling a general congress, which resolves were printed at length in the "Boston Gazette" of June 13. No time or place was named. On the 3d of June, the Connecticut committee of correspondence, in a letter addressed to the Boston committee, made suggestions as to the time and place; and, on the 4th, sent a copy of this letter to the New-York committee. On receiving this letter, the New-York committee, on the 10th of June, sent to the Connecticut committee their letter of the 23d of May, proposing a congress; and stated, that, on the 7th of June, they had written to the Boston committee, requesting them "to appoint the time and place for holding the congress," where they would be ready to meet the deputies of the other colonies. Hence the specification by Massachusetts of the time and place. The Rhode-Island assembly adopted a series of resolutions, recommending a congress, and selected delegates, on the 15th of June.

of September, at Philadelphia. While these resolves were under consideration, Secretary Flucker appeared at the door, and, on being denied admission, sent in a messenger to inform the House that he had a message from the governor. The messenger was informed that the House had ordered the door to be kept locked. The Secretary, standing on the stairs leading to the hall, read to a large number of people a proclamation by Governor Gage, dissolving the general court. The House, however, went on, and completed its business. The resolves were adopted. James Bowdoin, Samuel Adams, John Adams, and Thomas Cushing, were selected as the delegates of Massachusetts. Bowdoin subsequently declining, Robert Treat Paine was selected in his place; and a tax was laid to defray their expenses. The House also recommended contributions to be made for the relief of Boston and the neighboring town of Charlestown, which were the most affected by the Port Act.[1]

---

[1] A whole page of the "Boston Gazette" of June 13 was filled with matter showing the sympathy of the colonies with Boston, nearly all from Virginia and Maryland. One of the resolutions of Queen Anne's County, Maryland, May 30, is, "That they look upon the cause of Boston, in its consequences, to be the common cause of America."

Before this date, measures had been taken to relieve those who might suffer from the Port Act. On the 3d of June, the Connecticut committee of correspondence informed the Boston committee of correspondence that both houses of the assembly had passed resolutions to contribute to their relief. Contributions soon began to flow into Boston.

One of the pamphlets of the day is entitled, "The First Book of the American Chronicles of the Times." The first verse runs, "And behold! when the tidings came to the great city that is afar off, the city that is in the land of Britain, how the men of Boston, even the Bostonites, had arose, a great multitude, and destroyed the tea, the abominable merchandise of the East, and cast into the midst of the sea," — "the king waxed wroth." After a description of the passage of the Port Act, are the following verses relating to the patriotic charity: —

The Boston representatives could not know that British authority was at an end in Massachusetts, or that the moderator of that day's town-meeting, in a few years, would be the chief magistrate of an independent nation; but, as they returned from Salem that afternoon,[1] they could feel, that, in a spirit of fidelity to duty, they had taken the leading steps to promote a union which were expected by their countrymen. In the evening, Adams, Cushing, Quincy, Warren, Young, and other popular leaders, assembled at Warren's residence, forming "a very important and agreeable company;"[2] and as they communed with each other, one home, at least, in the distressed town, was lighted as with the glory of the after-time. Their hearts were gladdened by the high spirit evinced in the town-meeting, by the zeal of the yeomanry in signing the League and Covenant, and by the general refusal to pay for the tea; for "neither in the general assembly of the province nor in the grand meeting of the capital was there a single symptom of inclination to comply with the demand, though enforced by a distressing blockade."[3] Then the evidences were increasing of the outpour of generous sympathy which the naked injustice of the Port Act occasioned. Besides the voice from Baltimore,

"24. And it came to pass that the New-Yorkites, the Philadelphites, the Marylandites, the Virginites, the Carolinites, took pity on their brethren the Bostonites; for there was like to be a famine in the land.

"25. And they got ready their camels and their asses, their mules and their oxen, and laded them with their meat, their fine wheaten flour, their rice, their corn, their beeves and their sheep, and their figs and their raisins, and their wine and their oil, and their tobacco abundantly, and six thousand shekels of silver, and threescore talents of gold, and sent them by the hands of the Levites to their brethren, and there was joy in the land."

[1] Thomas Young's Letter, June 19, 1774.   [2] *Ib.*   [3] *Ib.*

already cited[1] and the cheering intelligence in the journals, there was read a letter from New York, which was pronounced to be " as encouraging as any thing they had from any part of the continent.[2] There was now a genuine communion of feeling, — a noble surrender of the American mind to the grand emotion of fraternity; and well might the popular leaders feel a glow of inspiration. One of the exulting band wrote, " Our rejoicing was full from an interchange of interesting advices from all quarters."[3] A cluster of morning-stars of a new constellation were rejoicing in the blossoming of American nationality.

[1] See page 318.
[2] Young's Letter.   [3] *Ib.*

CHAPTER XI.

THE REGULATING ACT AND THE SUFFOLK RESOLVES.

THE REGULATING ACT. — HUTCHINSON AND THE KING. — THE RECEPTION OF THE ACT IN THE COLONIES. — THE RESISTANCE TO IT. — THE SUFFOLK RESOLVES. — THEIR EFFECT ON PUBLIC OPINION.

1774. JUNE TO SEPTEMBER.

WARREN'S words became more and more the mirror of the passions of his countrymen.[1] The important service which he rendered in promoting the passage of the famous Suffolk Resolves brought his name prominently before the general congress. These resolves were occasioned by the passage of two additional penal acts by parliament; one regulating the Government of Massachusetts, and the other altering the mode of administering justice. They were signed on the 20th of May. They were designed to carry into effect the principle, that parliament had the right to legislate for the colonies in all cases whatsoever.

As George III. was about to enter upon the work of enforcing these despotic acts, Hutchinson arrived (July 1) in London, when he was immediately sent for by Lord Dartmouth; and, without even being obliged to change his dress, the ex-governor was ushered into the royal closet, where he had a confer-

[1] Bancroft, vii. 173.

ence with the king of nearly two hours on American affairs, of which Hutchinson has left a circumstantial relation. The conversation commenced in the following way: —

King. — How do you do, Mr. Hutchinson, after your voyage?

Hutchinson. — Much reduced, sir, by sea-sickness, and unfit upon that account, as well as my New-England dress, to appear before Your Majesty. [Lord Dartmouth observed, "Mr. Hutchinson apologized to me for his dress; but I thought it very well, as he has just come ashore;" to which the king assented.]

King. — How did you leave your Government? and how did the people receive the news of the late measures of parliament?

Hutchinson. — When I left Boston, we had no news of any act of parliament except the one for shutting up the port, which was extremely alarming to the people. [Lord Dartmouth said, "Mr. Hutchinson came from Boston the day that act was to take place, the first of June. I hear the people of Virginia have refused to comply with the request to shut up their ports from the people of Boston; and Mr. Hutchinson seems to be of opinion, that no colony will comply with that request."]

King. — Do you believe, Mr. Hutchinson, that the account from Virginia is true?

Hutchinson. — I have no other reason to doubt it except that the authority for it seems to be only a newspaper; and it is very common for articles to be inserted in newspapers without any foundation. I have no doubt, that, when the people of Rhode Island received the like request, they gave this answer, — that, if Boston would stop all the vessels which they then had in port, which they were hurrying away before the act commenced, the people of Rhode Island would then consider of the proposal. [The king smiled.]

Lord Dartmouth. — Mr. Hutchinson, may it please Your Majesty, has shown me a newspaper, with an address from a great number of merchants, another from the Episcopal clergy, another from the lawyers, all expressing their sense of his conduct in the most favorable terms. [Lord Dartmouth thereupon took the paper out of his pocket, and showed it.]

King. — I do not see how it could be otherwise. I am sure his conduct has been universally approved of here by people of all parties.

Hutchinson. — I am very happy in Your Majesty's favorable opinion of my Administration.

King. — I am entirely satisfied with it. I am well acquainted with the difficulties you have encountered, and with the abuse and injury offered you.

The conversation for some time turned on the publication of Hutchinson's private letters, and then went on as follows: —

King. — In such abuse, Mr. Hutchinson, as you have met with, I suppose there must have been personal malevolence as well as party rage.

Hutchinson. — It has been my good fortune, sir, to escape any charge against me in my private character. The attacks have been upon my public conduct, and for such things as my duty to Your Majesty required me to do, and which you have been pleased to approve of. I don't know that any of my enemies have complained of a personal injury.

King. — I see they threatened to pitch and feather you.

Hutchinson. — Tar and feather, may it please Your Majesty; but I don't remember that I was ever threatened with it.

Lord Dartmouth. — Oh, yes! when Malcolm was tarred and feathered, the committee for tarring and feathering blamed the people for doing it, that being a punishment reserved for a higher person; and we suppose you were intended.

Hutchinson. — I remember something of that sort, which was only to make diversion, there being no such committee, or none known by that name.

King. — What guard had you, Mr. Hutchinson?

Hutchinson. — I depended, sir, on the protection of Heaven. I had no other guard. I was not conscious of having done any thing of which they could justly complain, or make a pretence for offering violence to my person. I was not sure, but I hoped they only meant to intimidate. By discovering that I was afraid, I should encourage them to go on. By taking measures for my security, I should expose myself to calumny, and be censured as designing to render them odious for what they never intended to do. I was, therefore, obliged to appear to disregard all the menaces in the newspapers, and also private intimations from my friends, who frequently advised me to take care of myself.

The king was particular in inquiries relative to several of the popular leaders.

King. — Pray, what does Hancock do now? How will the late affair affect him?

Hutchinson. — I don't know to what particular affair Your Majesty refers.

King. — Oh! a late affair in the city, — his bills being refused. [Turning to Lord Dartmouth], Who is that in the city, my lord? [Lord Dartmouth not recollecting.]

Hutchinson. — I have heard, sir, that Mr. Haley, a merchant in the city, is Mr. Hancock's principal correspondent.

King. — Ay, that's the name.

Hutchinson. — I heard, may it please Your Majesty, before I came from New England, that some small sums were returned, but none of consequence.

King. — Oh, no! I mean within this month, — large sums.

Lord Dartmouth. — I have heard such rumors, but don't know the certainty.

Hutchinson. — Mr. Hancock, sir, had a very large fortune left him by his uncle; and I believe his political engagements have taken off his attention from his private affairs. He was sensible, not long ago, of the damage it was to him, and told me he was determined to quit all public business; but soon altered his mind.

King. — Then there's Mr. Cushing. I remember his name a long time. Is not he a great man of the party?

Hutchinson. — He has been many years speaker; but a speaker, sir, is not always the person of the greatest influence. A Mr. Adams is rather considered as the opposer of Government, and a sort of Wilkes in New England.

King. — What gave him his importance?

Hutchinson. — A great pretended zeal for liberty and a most inflexible natural temper. He was the first that publicly asserted the independency of the colonies upon the kingdom, or the supreme authority of it.[1]

---

[1] I am indebted to George Bancroft for the use of the "Extracts from the Journal of Thomas Hutchinson, Governor of Massachusetts." This manuscript

The king made particular inquiries in relation to the productions of the country. On the same day, he wrote to Lord North of the colonies, "I have seen Mr. Hutchinson, late governor of Massachusetts, and am now well convinced they will soon submit. He owns the Boston Port Bill has been the only wise and effectual method."[1]

The modern revelations of the temper of the king are remarkable and important. It is history, that his unintelligent, iron will was bending his minister, Lord North, to the task of fixing the old-world policy of centralization on a people who had for their root individual liberty, civil and religious, tempered by respect for law. These sweeping acts cut down, trunk and branch, the old and dearly cherished rights of Massachusetts, invading even those palladiums, — the town-meeting, and trial by jury; and the rough drafts of them, Gordon says, on their being received at Boston, "were instantly circulated through the continent, and filled up whatever was before wanting of violence and indignation in most of the colonies. Even those who were moderate, or seemed wavering, now became resolute and resentful. Nothing was to be heard of but meetings and resolutions"[2] Each colony felt that its own right of framing its internal government was in danger. "If," Lord Mahon says, "one charter might be cancelled, so might all: if the rights of any one colony might hang suspended on the votes of an exasperated majority in

has the following: "Copied from the original by Mr. Rives. — EDWARD EVERETT. London, Feb. 1, 1843."

[1] Lord Mahon's "History of England," Appendix to vol. ii., has extracts from the letters of George III. to Lord North.

[2] Gordon's History, i. 377.

England, could any other deem itself secure?"[1] The king was soon to learn, in the words of Dr. Ramsay, "that, to force on the inhabitants a form of government to which they were totally averse was not within the fancied omnipotence of parliament."[2]

Warren shared the feelings of his countrymen at this hour; and, on the reception of the bills, before they were passed into laws, early in June, by the committee of correspondence, they excited the indignation of the members. Samuel Adams had long seen, that Great Britain, by oppressive measures, was hastening the day of independence. "Our people," he wrote to Charles Thompson, as he dwelt on the desire to unite all "in one indissoluble bond," "think they should pursue the line of the constitution as far as they can; and, if they are driven from it, they can then with propriety and justice appeal to God and the world." And as he counselled prudence, moderation, and fortitude, he grandly wrote, "I would wish to have all the impartial and reasonable world on our side. I would wish to have the humanity of the English nation engaged in our cause; and that the friends of the constitution might see and be convinced, that nothing is more foreign from our hearts than a spirit of rebellion. Would to God they all, even our enemies, knew the warm attachment we have for Great Britain, notwithstanding we have been contending these ten years with them for our rights!"

To the deep feeling awakened by the Boston Port Act, the new acts added the stimulus of common interests; and, on the 20th of June, the "Boston

---

[1] History of England, vi. 8.   [2] Ramsay, i. 132.

Gazette" said, "The present aspect of affairs is highly favorable to the liberties of America. The whole continent seems inspired by one soul, and that soul a rigorous and determined one." A week later, there was another great town-meeting in Faneuil Hall, the adjournment of the Port-act meeting of the 17th, when Samuel Adams was in the chair. So large were the numbers, that the meeting adjourned to the Old South Meeting-house, where, as William Cooper, the town-clerk, was reading the letters that had passed between the committees of correspondence, one of the Tories moved that the Boston committee be censured and annihilated. Samuel Adams left the chair, and Thomas Cushing took the place of moderator. Those in favor of the motion were patiently heard; and, when it was dark, and they said they had more to offer, the meeting was adjourned to the next day. Samuel Adams spoke during this long debate. A vast majority rejected the motion; and the town passed a vote urging the committee "to persevere with their usual activity and firmness, and continue steadfast in the way of well-doing." A protest was made by a hundred and twenty-nine citizens, against the doings of the committee of correspondence, the solemn League and Covenant, and the proceedings of the town in indorsing the work of the committee. On the next day (June 29), Governor Gage, in a proclamation, "strictly enjoined and commanded" all magistrates to arrest all who signed the League and Covenant, or who asked others to sign it.

The month of July was full of excitement. On the first, Admiral Graves arrived in the "Preston:" other regiments also arrived; and it was supposed that there would be arrests of the popular leaders. It is recorded in the journals of the committee of correspondence, that, on the 5th a report being prevalent that some gentlemen were to be apprehended, it was unanimously voted, "We will attend to the committee of correspondence as usual, unless prevented by brutal force." On the 26th, a donation committee was finally organized, to receive and distribute the contributions that were flowing in from the colonies to relieve the poor of Boston; and Warren was appointed a member. On this day, a committee of safety was chosen, which consisted of James Bowdoin, Samuel Adams, John Adams, John Hancock, William Phillips, Joseph Warren, and Josiah Quincy. A committee, in the name of Boston, appealed to those dear companions in the cause of God and their country, their friends and brethren of the province, to whom they looked for that advice, example, and wisdom, that would give strength to their understanding, vigor to their action, and, with the blessing of God, save them from destruction.

General Gage, on the 6th of August, received officially the two acts relative to Massachusetts; one altering the charter, and the other relating to the administration of justice, which the patriots called the Regulating Act and the Murder Act: also commissions for thirty-six counsellors, who, instead of being chosen in the old way of election, were appointed by the king, and were termed mandamus counsellors. The instructions of Lord Dartmouth, on the 2d of June, were long, minute, and determined; averring that whatever violence might be attempted should be resisted with firmness, — for the dignity, power, and the very existence of the empire were in issue; and declaring, that, should ideas of independence take root, the union between the col onies and kingdom would cease, and destruction must follow disunion. The act went into operation imme diately; and various functionaries under it promptly prepared to exercise authority, — the counsellors, twenty-five of whom accepted, to have sessions, the sheriffs to summon jurors, and the judges to hold courts.

More than ever before were eyes now fixed on the patriots of Boston and Massachusetts, when the hitherto invincible British power commanded the submission of a free people — in the words of the protest of the minority of the lords against the acts — to a Governor and Council intrusted with powers which the British Constitution had not trusted His Majesty and Privy Council; so that lives and property were subject to absolute power. The issue concerned territory wider than Massachusetts; for it was now to be determined, whether the old world, or, more precisely, the Tory party of England, was to shape the institutions of the new world, or whether America should, as of right, frame her own law. The interest felt by the people of the other colonies in the result was intense; not so much because they were moved by oppression actually felt, as by a conviction, on the part of the majorities who sided with the Whig or national party, that a foundation was laid, and a precedent about to be established, for future oppressions.[1] Their views were expressed through their organs, the committees of correspondence, in

[1] Ramsay's History, i. 113.

letters addressed to the Boston committee. "We view," a letter from Cape Fear, North Carolina, says, "the attack made by the minister upon the colony of Massachusetts Bay to be intended to pave the way to a general subversion of the constitutional rights of North America"[1] A letter from South Carolina, accompanying a sloop load of rice, says, "Your situation at this time is truly hazardous and trying; but you will not fail for want of support, because all British America are your friends. For God's sake, be firm and discreet at this time!" Christopher Gadsden, of Charleston, wrote[2] to Samuel Adams, — in a letter not printed,—"We will not think so basely of you as to imagine you will pay for an ounce of the tea;" and, before he could get a reply, he thus renewed the injunction: "We depend on your firmness, and that you will not pay for an ounce of the damned tea."[3] The committee of the town of Brooklyn, Connecticut, accompanied its contributions with a letter (Aug. 11), in which they said to Boston, "You are held up as a spectacle to the whole world. All Christendom is longing to see the event of the American contest. And do, most noble citizens, play your part manfully, of which we make no doubt. Your names are either to be held in eternal veneration or execration. If you stand out, your names cannot be too much applauded by all Europe and all future generations." An able Tory address, circulated first in the Pennsylvania assembly, and widely copied, said of the growing Whig organization, in staring capitals, "It is the beginning of republicanism," which, it was declared, was setting up anarchy above order.

[1] Letter, July 28, 1774. [2] June 2, 1774. [3] June 28, 1774.

The word that came in from the country towns of Massachusetts was not less decisive. Among the letters were two from patriots who fought in the Bunker-hill Battle. Colonel William Prescott, who commanded in this action, said to Boston, in the name of the men of Pepperell, " Be not dismayed nor disheartened in this day of great trial. We heartily sympathize with you, and are always ready to do all in our power for your support, comfort, and relief, knowing that Providence has placed you where you must stand the first shock. We consider we are all embarked in one bottom, and must sink or swim together " Colonel Thomas Gardner, of Cambridge, who fell by Warren's side, nobly wrote to the Boston Committee: —

Thomas Gardner to Boston Committee of Correspondence.

CAMBRIDGE, Aug. 12, 1774.

FRIENDS AND BRETHREN, — The time is come that every one that has a tongue and an arm is called upon by their country to stand forth in its behalf; and I consider the call of my country as the call of God, and desire to be all obedience to such a call. In obedience thereunto, would administer some consolation unto you, by informing you of the glorious union of the good people of this province, both in sentiment and action. I am informed from good authority, that the committee of correspondence for the several towns in the county of Worcester, have assembled, are in high spirits, and perfectly united. The committee for Cambridge and Charlestown are to have a conference to-morrow; and I trust the whole county of Middlesex will soon be assembled by delegates from the respective towns in said county. I have the greatest reason to believe, that the people will choose to fall gloriously in the cause of their country than meanly to submit to slavery. I am your friend and brother,

THOMAS GARDNER.

In this crisis-hour, when the people were expected to prevent the execution of the Regulating Act,

Samuel Adams left Boston[1] (Aug. 10) to attend the meeting of the general congress, and Warren became the central figure in the political movements of Massachusetts. His impetuous fearlessness, Bancroft says of him, as he was now acting, was tempered by self-possession, gentleness, and good sense; and he "had reluctantly become convinced, that all connection with the British parliament must be broken off."

[1] Wednesday morning, the Hon. Thomas Cushing, Esq , Mr. Samuel Adams, John Adams, and Robert Treat Paine, Esqrs., — the delegates appointed by the Honorable Commons House of Assembly for this province to attend the general congress, to be holden at Philadelphia some time next month, — set out from hence, attended by a number of gentlemen, who accompanied them to Watertown, where they were met by many others, who provided an elegant entertainment for them. After dinner they proceeded on their journey, intending to reach Southborough that evening.

Some days before the departure of the committee for the congress, Mr. Bowdoin sent them a letter, acquainting them that he had had hopes of proceeding with them to the congress; but Mrs. Bowdoin's ill state of health, occasioned by a long-continued slow fever, necessitated him to lay aside all thoughts of it. — *Boston Gazette, Aug.* 15, 1754.

John Andrews, in a letter, dated Boston, Aug. 6, 1774, gives the following relation of Samuel Adams: "The ultimate wish and desire of the high-government party is to get Samuel Adams out of the way, when they think they may accomplish every one of their aims. But, however some may despise him, he has certainly very many friends: for, not long since, some persons (their names unknown) sent and asked his permission to build him a new barn, the old one being decayed, which was executed in a few days; a second sent to ask him to repair his house, which was thoroughly effected soon; a third sent to beg the favor of him to call at a tailor's shop, and be measured for a pair of clothes, and choose his cloth, which were finished, and sent home for his acceptance; a fourth presented him with a new wig; a fifth, with a new hat; a sixth, with six pair of the best silk hose; a seventh, with six pair of fine thread ditto; an eighth with six pairs of shoes; and a ninth modestly inquired of him, whether his finances were not rather low than otherwise. He replied, it was true that was the case; but he was very indifferent about those matters so that his poor abilities were of any service to the public: upon which the gentleman obliged him to accept of a purse containing about fifteen or twenty joannes. I mention this to show you how much he is esteemed here. They value him for his good sense, great abilities, amazing fortitude, noble resolution, and undaunted courage; being firm and unmoved at all the various reports that were propagated in regard to his being taken up and sent home, notwithstanding he had repeated letters from his friends, both in England as well as here, to keep out of the way."

It was necessary that the revolutionary work at hand, though it should be thorough, as in the case of the destruction of the tea, should be systematic.

On the day on which this letter is dated, at a meeting of the committee of correspondence and selectmen of Boston, Warren was named at the head of the delegation, to meet in a county convention that was to be held at Stoughton, of which he gives some account in the following letter: —

Joseph Warren to Samuel Adams.

Boston, Aug. 15, 1774.

DEAR SIR, — Our public affairs have not changed their appearance since your departure. The people are in high spirits, and have the greatest confidence in the wisdom and spirit of the congress, whose decisions they seem determined to abide by. Mr. Gage sent, the day before yesterday, for the selectmen, and informed them, that he had received an act of parliament prohibiting their calling town-meetings without a license from him. They told him, that they should obey the laws of the land; and that they had had two adjournments of their meeting, and knew of no occasion to call another. He replied, that " he would endeavor to put the act in execution; and, if any ill consequences followed, they only were blamable. As to their adjournment, he must consider of it; for by such means they might keep their meeting alive these ten years." Upon this, they left him. On Friday, agreeable to a request from the other towns in this county, the selectmen and committee of correspondence met, and chose five members to attend the county congress at Stoughton to-morrow: Joseph Warren, William Phillips, Esq., Mr. Oliver Wendell, Dr. Benjamin Church, Mr. John Pitts. Mr. Phillips has refused. We shall elect a member to fill his place.

General Lee leaves us to-day. Enclosed you have a hint which I think very important; but it ought to come from a member for some other colony: nay, if it was done wholly by the other members of the congress, I should like it better, as it will perhaps be injurious to you to come into such resolutions. With respect to some who are sworn in as members, the poor fellows hang their heads already. Some spirited resolutions of the congress will drive them to despair. The gentlemen from the Royal Governments may possibly think, that, although our council is appointed by mandamus, we are, nevertheless, upon as good a foundation, in that respect, as themselves. But they will consider, that it is not simply the appointment of the council by the king that we complain of; it is the breach thereby made in our charter: and, if we suffer this, none of our charter-rights are worth naming; the charters of all the colonies are no more than blank paper. The same power that can take away our right of electing councillors by our representatives can take away from the other colonies the right of choosing even representatives; and the bill for regulating the Government of Canada shows plainly that it would be very pleasing to the ministry to deprive the Americans totally of the right of representation; and, indeed, by the Acts of the British parliament, and by the instructions given to governors, they are already deprived of all the advantages derived from representation. A fair state of this matter, done by the masterly hand of some of our worthy friends at the congress, would open the eyes of many. I am sure the congress will be able to convince the world, that the present American representation is a shadow, and not a substance; and I am certain, that, unless it is put upon a better footing, the people themselves will, in a few years, readily consent to throw off the useless burthen. But I am perhaps too much like the declaimer who delivered a lecture upon the art of war to the illustrious general Hannibal.

Mrs. Adams and your family are well. The doctor and she set out for the Eastern country to-day. Mrs. Cushing and family are in good health. Mr. Adams's friends in town are well, as I heard his lady was last Saturday. Please to present my very respectful regards to your three brethren, and believe me to be your fast friend and H. serv[t.]

Jos. Warren.

P.S. — While writing, Mr. Pitts comes in, and informs me that Dr. Williamson has written to his friend in Philadelphia; assuring him that the ministry have lately written instructions to General Gage not to take one step against the Americans, if the opposition to ministerial measures should be general.

The celebrated Colonel Putnam is now in my house, having arrived, since I subscribed this letter, with a generous donation of sheep.[1]

---

[1] I copy this letter from the original, in the hands of Mr. Bancroft.

Warren's guest, Colonel Putnam, remained in town several days. "The old hero, Putnam," Dr. Young writes, "arrived in town on Monday, bringing with him one hundred and thirty sheep from the little parish of Brooklyn. He cannot get away, he is so much caressed, both by the officers and citizens. He has had a long combat with Major Small, in the political way, much to the disadvantage of the latter. He looks fresh and hearty, and, on an emergency, would be as likely to do good business as ever."[1] The patriot received due notice in the newspapers, which said, he was so well known through North America, that no words were necessary to inform the public further than that his generosity led him to Boston, to cherish his oppressed brethren, and support them by every means in his power.

The provisions of the Regulating Act forbade town-meetings, except by the permission of the governor; but the most of the towns of Suffolk met, and chose delegates — in all sixty — to attend a convention, held on the 16th, at Stoughton, at Colonel Doty's tavern. It was called "a county congress." Some of the towns had not had the requisite notice: it was found that "the committees of many towns were not specially authorized to negotiate the affairs of a county congress;" and, to enable all towns and districts to choose delegates, and thus "to show contempt for the act of parliament touching town-meetings," the convention, after adopting the form of a call,[2] and choosing a committee to send it to the towns, adjourned to the 6th of September, in the town of

---
[1] Letter, Aug. 19, 1774.
[2] The call is in Proceedings of Mass. Hist. Soc., 1858–60, 291.

Dedham. One of the Boston delegates says, "We were perfectly unanimous and firm in the common cause. Colonel Thayer particularly said, we must all appear undisguised upon one side or the other. Good Mr. Dunbar gave us the most extraordinary liberty-prayer that ever I heard. He appeared to have the most divine, if not prophetical, enthusiasm in favor of our rights, and stood with us till eight o'clock at night. We rode all together in the berlin, with four horses and two servants, and returned at eleven o'clock at night in good health."[1] On the day of this convention, the judges of the inferior court of Great Barrington were forced by the people to pledge their honor that they would do no business.[2]

Warren's time was now greatly occupied with public affairs. Among his students was Dr. William Eustis, subsequently member of congress, governor of Massachusetts, and secretary of war. He was now about twenty-one. His amiable character, fine address, and culture, won the strong attachment of Warren. The young student is found by the side of his instructor in trying scenes. He now sent the following note, in a neat handwriting, to Samuel Adams: —

BOSTON, Aug. 18, 1774.

I am [ ] inform you that Dr. Warren would do *himself* the pleasure to write you; but opportunity will not permit it. He sends you the enclosed, and wishes you much prosperity.

Sir, your very humble servant, W. EUSTIS.[3]

Mr. ADAMS.

This was an exciting week, and the committee of correspondence was often in session. "Letters and

---

[1] Benjamin Kent to Samuel Adams, Aug. 20, 1774.
[2] Bancroft, vii. 103. [3] Samuel Adams's manuscript papers.

resolves," Young writes on the 19th, "come in to us from all quarters, and still on the rising tenor. Thirteen were received last Tuesday evening, and many are come to hand since. We meet every day or two as usual, and proceed with great harmony." Warren now wrote to Samuel Adams, that the county meeting, already appointed, would have important consequences: —

Joseph Warren to Samuel Adams.

BOSTON 21 Aug. [1774].

MY DEAR SIR, — I received yours from Hartford, and enclose you the vote of the House, passed the 17th of June. I shall take care to follow your advice respecting the county meeting, which, depend upon it, will have very important consequences. The spirits of our friends rise every day; and we seem animated by the proofs, which every hour appear, of the villainous designs of our enemies, which justify us in all we have done to oppose them hitherto, and in all that we can do in future. A non-importation and non-exportation to Britain, Ireland, and the West Indies, is now the most moderate measure talked: it is my opinion, that nothing less will prevent bloodshed two months longer. The non-importation and non-exportation to Britain and Ireland ought to take place immediately, — to the West Indies not until December next; because, should the non-exportation to the West Indies take place immediately, thousands of innocent people must inevitably perish: whereas, if it takes place at some distance, they, and the proprietors of the islands, may use their influence to ward off the blow; and, if they fail in that, they may come to the continent, where they will be treated with humanity. [By] stopping the exportation of flaxseed to Ireland, and giving them immediate notice, they may obtain a repeal of the Act soon enough to get their supply before sowing-time. This stoppage of exportation of flaxseed will not fall heavy upon any one in this country, as scarcely any farmer raises more than four, six, or eight bushels; but it will throw a million of people in Ireland out of bread. There are about one hundred thousand acres of land sowed in Ireland with flaxseed every year; and it is computed, that, with dressing and spinning, weaving, bleaching, &c., ten persons are employed by every acre; and the ministry will not find it easy to maintain so many persons in idleness, especially as the national revenue, if computed (as the best writers have computed) at eight millions sterling, will be one-eighth part lost by the loss of their trade with America and the West Indies. In my next, I will endeavor to make some calculations of the interest which the British nation have in the West Indies and Ireland; also how many Irish peers and peers of Great Britain: and, if I can (though I hardly know how to go about it), will give some pretty near guess at the number of members in the House of Commons, whose chief fortunes lie in Ireland and the West Indies. I enclose you all the papers, as far as they are printed. I think nothing material is omitted. The extract of a letter from London, dated June first, is from Mr. Sheriff Lee. The lord said to be virulent against America, in the cabinet, is Dartmouth, in the letter. The lord said to be brought over to American justice is Temple. The letter was written to the Hon. Mr. Cushing.

I have now a matter of private concern to mention to you, by the desire of Mr. Pitts. Our friend, Mr. William Turner, has, as you know, been persecuted for his political sentiments, and ruined in his business. The dancing and fencing master, named Pike, in Charleston, South Carolina, is about leaving the school, and has invited Mr. Turner to take his place. I am myself, and I know you are, always deeply interested for the prosperity of persons of merit, who have suffered for espousing the cause of their country. If you can, by giving Mr. Turner his true character, interest the gentlemen with you in his favor, you will do a benevolent action, and oblige Mr. Pitts, Mr. Turner, and myself. If they could be induced to write to their friends, and know what encouragement he might expect, it might save him the expense of a journey which he can ill afford to take.

I am, dear sir, your most obedient servant,   J. W.

P.S. — Please to make my respectful compliments to your three fellow-laborers. As far as I have been able to get information, their families and friends are in health. Let them know that I consider every thing I write to one of you is written to all. Great expectations are formed of the spirited resolves which the congress will pass relative to our traitors by mandamus.

There was delay in organizing a body to receive the donations that were sent to Boston. The town, at the meeting on the 17th of June, authorized the overseers of the poor, as they were "a body politic by law," in concert with the committee of the ways and means of employing the poor, to receive and dis tribute the donations made to the town. Accord ingly, the earliest replies to the committee are signed by order of this board. On the 19th of July, this body desired to be discharged from further service in relation to this subject; and, on the 26th of July, the committee on donations was finally organized. It was a body distinct from the committee of correspondence, and its duties were urgent and arduous. One of them was to reply to the letters that were sent with the contributions; and Warren wrote some of these replies. One of them was the following, addressed to Stonington, Connecticut: —

Joseph Warren to the Stonington Committee.

BOSTON, Aug. 24, 1774.

GENTLEMEN, — Your elegant and benevolent favor of the 1st instant yielded us that support and consolation amid our distresses, which the generous sympathy of assured friends can never fail to inspire. 'Tis the part of this people to frown on danger, face to face; to stand the focus of rage and malevolence of the inexorable enemies of American freedom. Permit us to glory in the dangerous distinction; and be assured, that, while actuated by the spirit and confident of the aid of such noble auxiliaries, we are compelled to support the conflict. When liberty is the prize, who would shun the warfare? Who would stoop to waste a coward thought on life? We esteem no sacrifice too great, no conflict too severe, to redeem our inestimable rights and privileges. 'Tis for you, brethren, for ourselves, for our united posterity, we hazard all; and permit us humbly to hope, that such a measure of vigilance, fortitude, and perseverance will still be afforded us, that, by patiently suffering and nobly daring, we may eventually secure that more precious than Hesperian fruit, the golden apples of freedom. We eye the hand of Heaven in the rapid and wonderful union of the colonies; and that generous and universal emulation to prevent the sufferings of the people of this place gives a prelibation of the cup of deliverance. May unerring Wisdom dictate the measures to be recommended by the congress! May a smiling God conduct this people through the thorny paths of difficulty, and finally gladden our hearts with success!

We are, gentlemen, your friends in the cause of liberty,

JOSEPH WARREN, *Chairman.*

To the Committee of Correspondence at Stonington.

"This letter," Hollister says, "that rises like a heavenly vision into the regions where such poets as Milton hymn their prophetic songs, is still in the keeping of the town-clerk of Stonington. It does, indeed, 'stir the heart like the sound of a trumpet,' and is worthy to be carved for an epitaph upon a monument of granite, that should for ever rest upon the ashes of Warren."[1]

On the same day, Warren replied to the town of Preston, in the letter of which was the remark, that their people, on the reception of the second and third unrighteous Acts of Parliament, were anxiously looking "for some important event" to take place; that, while it was becoming to be watchful, there "was great reason to fear that nothing short of another kind of resistance would regain and secure their privileges;" and that it had given them fresh alarm to hear that arms were not suffered to be carried out of town. The reply indicates the difficulty the patriots of Boston encountered in avoiding both submission and violence.

Joseph Warren to the Preston Committee.

BOSTON, Aug. 24, 1774.

GENTLEMEN, — We received by Captain Belcher your letter of the 20th, and the sum of money you were kind enough to send for the sup-

[1] This letter is printed by Hollister in his History of Connecticut, ii. 157.

port of our poor. It gives us pleasure amidst our sufferings to find our brethren determined to assist and support us while we are struggling for American freedom. Our enemies, we know, will use every artifice that hell can suggest and human power can execute to enslave us; but we are determined not to submit. We choose to effect our salvation from bondage by policy, rather than by arms; considering that the blood of freemen who fight for their country is of more value than the blood of a soldiery who fight for pay. We doubt not but a virtuous continental adherence to [the] non-importation, non-exportation, and non-consumption agreement, will produce such changes in Britain as will compel them to give us every thing we wish. But if *this* should fail, and we should be obliged to seek redress in the way you have hinted, we flatter ourselves that we shall act like *men*, and merit the approbation of all America. The conduct of our adversaries is to us astonishing. Policy is no more their guide than justice. They have shut their eyes against daylight; and, if they lead the British nation into the pit they have digged for us, the blame must be laid to their own door. The motions of our governor are like those of other machines: they move as they are directed. He is clad in the garb of ministerial instructions, and has declared his determination implicitly to obey them. We shall always receive with gratitude your advice and assistance, not doubting that the end of our warfare will be freedom to America.

We are, with sincerity, gentlemen, your very humble servants,

J. WARREN,
Per order of the Committee of Donations.

P.S. — The arms have been several times detained in going out of town, but never finally stopped. Even if a private gentleman carries one out of town with him for diversion, he is not permitted to bring it back again.

To the Gentlemen the Committee of the Town of Preston.[1]

Warren now took the lead in an important movement, designed to systematize the opposition to the

---

[1] I copy this letter from 4th series of Coll. Mass. Hist. Society, iv. 54. In this volume will be found a large number of the letters addressed to the Donation Committee, and the replies to them; the correspondence and notes filling 278 pages, printed from two letter-books now in the archives of the Society. Nearly all these letters remained in manuscript until they appeared, in 1858, in this volume. The letters addressed to the town of Boston constitute a noble monument of the generous and fraternal spirit that made the American Union.

execution of the Regulating Act, which was spontaneous throughout the province. Before this time, the people of the other colonies not merely counselled, but enjoined on, the citizens of Massachusetts to defeat this law. There was a county convention[1] held at Worcester, on the 9th of August, which, without other action than passing resolves, had adjourned to the last Tuesday of the month. It is worthy of remark, that these resolves, which were ordered to be circulated by handbills, aver that the people bore true allegiance to the king, while they make this declaration· "We have within ourselves the exclusive right of originating each and every law respecting ourselves, and ought to be on an equal footing with His Majesty's subjects in England."

[1] At this time, Governor Gage had a military force at Salem, in which town he was required by law to convene the council and legislature; and he now attempted to break up a town-meeting, which was called on the 20th of August, for the choice of delegates to a county convention. He issued the following proclamation:

"Province of the Massachusetts Bay. By the Governor. A Proclamation.

"Whereas certain handbills have been posted in sundry places in the town of Salem, calling upon the merchants, freeholders, and other inhabitants of said town, to meet at the Town-house Chamber, on Wednesday next, at nine o'clock in the morning, to consider of and determine upon measures for opposing the execution of divers late Acts of Parliament;—

"And whereas, by a late Act of Parliament, all town-meetings called without the consent of the governor (except the annual meetings in the months of March and May) are illegal;—

"I do hereby strictly prohibit all persons from attending the aforesaid or any other meeting not warned by law, as they will be chargeable with all the ill consequences that may follow thereon, and answer the same at their utmost peril.

"Given at Salem, the 23d day of August, 1774. THOS. GAGE.

"By His Excellency's command,
    THOS. FLUCKER, *Sec.*
        "God save the king."

The inhabitants met, sent a committee to wait on Governor Gage to argue the law, who sent a detachment of soldiers to disperse the meeting. Meantime the people quickly chose the delegates, and adjourned. The baffled governor arrested the officials who called the meeting.—*Siege of Boston*, 13.

The committee of the town of Worcester now requested a conference with the committee of Boston, to agree on a general plan in relation to resisting the Regulating Act. On the invitation of the Boston committee, there was a convention of the delegates of the four counties of Suffolk, Essex, Middlesex, and Worcester, at Faneuil Hall, on the 26th of August. One of the Essex delegates was Elbridge Gerry, who, by similarity of taste, disposition, principles, and aims, was in close friendship with Warren. This was the most general political consultation held since the remarkable convention of 1768. Warren was chosen the chairman. The meeting voted that the officials under the new act were unconstitutional officers, and chose a committee to report the measures that might be expedient. Their report, on the next day, was read repeatedly, and accepted paragraph by paragraph. It provided for a thorough defeat of the Regulating Act. It recommended the important step of a Provincial Congress, in order to mature " an effectual plan for counteracting the systems of despotism;" and that, previous to the congress, courts held under the act ought to be properly opposed. In a resolve, they said that all who attempted to execute this act ought to be held in the highest detestation; and that individuals who maintained "the rights of the province and continent" in resisting it ought to be defended by the whole province, if necessary. The convention recommended the choice, as soon as may be, of delegates to the proposed congress. These resolves were not intended for the public, but were an agreement for perilous political action. This was not a declaration of independence, nor was even the thing intended. Whatever might have been the consequences, it was a blow levelled at the measures of the Administration rather than at the sovereignty of the British Empire.

On this day, Warren, in behalf of the committee of donations, replied to a letter of the committee of Norwich, Connecticut, who, in sending on a contribution of sheep, say in their letter, that they should be glad to know of the true state of affairs " per return of the gentlemen who drive the sheep." In replying, Warren drew a lifelike sketch of affairs in the town and province, and announced the plan, agreed upon that day, to avoid an action with the soldiery until it should be necessary.

Joseph Warren to the Committee of Norwich.

BOSTON, Aug. 27, 1774.

GENTLEMEN, — Your letter, with the two hundred and ninety-one sheep, were received safely, and met with a very hearty welcome. We have good reason to think that our oppressors see their mistake, and that they will ere long be convinced that Americans are not to be fritted or wheedled out of their rights. The arm of a tyrant is never supported by justice, and therefore must fall. Mr. Gage is executing the late Acts of Parliament, in their several branches, to the best of his ability. He is furnished with a council who will be careful (as their existence depends on the will of his master) to study his inclination, and to act every thing in conformity to his pleasure. We don't expect *justice* from them, and have no hopes that they will be guided by the laws of equity or the dictates of conscience. Certainly, men who will serve such an Administration as the present, and suffer themselves to be promoted at the expense of the charter of their country, must be destitute of every idea of right, and ready instruments to introduce abject slavery. Mr. Gage may issue his precepts, and his council may sanctify them; his juries may give verdicts, and an unconstitutional and venal bench may pass judgments: but what will this avail, unless the *people* will acquiesce in them? If the *people* think them unconstitutional, of what importance are their determinations? *Salus populi suprema lex esto* is a precious old maxim. The ministry have forgot it; but the people are determined to remember it.

We consider a suspension of trade through the continent with Great Britain, Ireland, and the West Indies, as the grand machine that will deliver us. If this should fail, we must then have recourse to the last resort. As yet, we have been preserved from action with the soldiery; and we shall endeavor to avoid it, until we see that it is necessary, and settled plan is fixed on for that purpose. The late Acts of Parliament are such gross infringements on us, that our consciences forbid us to submit to them. We think it is better to put up with some inconvenience, and pursue with patience the plan of commercial opposition, as it will be more for the honor and interest of the continent, as well as more consistent with the principles of humanity and religion.

Mr. Gage finds himself very unequal to the task that is set him, and is at a loss for measures. He sees, and is astonished at, the spirit of the people. He forbids their town-meetings, and they meet in counties. If he prevents county meetings, we must call provincial meetings; and, if he forbid these, we trust that our worthy brethren on the continent, and especially of the town of Norwich, in Connecticut, will lend us their helping arms in time of danger, and will be no less conspicuous for their fortitude than they now are for their generosity.

We have nothing important to inform you of besides what you see in the public papers. Should any thing worthy your notice take place, we shall gladly communicate it to you.

We are, gentlemen, your grateful friends and humble servants,

JOSEPH WARREN,
Per order the Committee of Donations.

To the Gentlemen the Committee of the Town of Norwich.[1]

The following hastily written note shows how energetically Warren was "helping forward the political machines in all parts of the province:" —

Joseph Warren to Samuel Adams.

BOSTON, Aug. 29, 1774.

DEAR SIR, — I have enclosed all the late public papers worthy your notice, and shall, by the next opportunity, give you all the public

[1] This letter is printed in Mass. Hist. Soc. Collections, 4th series, iv. 46.

intelligence in my power. Haste now prevents it, as I am constantly busied in helping forward the political machines in all parts of this province. Friend Quincy is going to London. I wish he may have such letters from you and the other gentlemen of the congress as may make him immediately noticed by persons of distinction there. Messrs. Paine of Worcester, Oliver of Salem, Winslow of Roxbury, and Pepperell of Roxbury, have resigned their seats at the Board. Nothing will satisfy the people here but a resolve of the congress never to commence any commercial intercourse with Britain whilst one person who has accepted a commission, or acted under the authority of the late Acts of Parliament, is [in] any office of power or trust in America. This, say they (and justly), is the only measure that can save us from being perpetually plagued with villains who will traduce their country to advance themselves to places of trust and gain. Mr. Webster, the bearer hereof, a merchant of Philadelphia, is a man of very extensive political knowledge, especially respecting commerce. I wish you to see him and converse with him.

I shall write you particulars by the next opportunity, and am your most humble servant and constant friend,   JOS. WARREN.[1]

The determination to avoid a collision with the British soldiery was put to a severe test by the endeavors of both parties to secure what they could of the scanty stock of arms and ammunition in the province. The powder belonging to towns and the province was kept in the Powder House, in Charlestown, in the portion which is now Somerville. The towns had withdrawn their portion. Very early on the morning of the 1st of September, a detachment of soldiers went from Boston in boats, landed at Temple's farm, passed over to Quarry Hill to the Powder House, and carried the powder and some cannon to Castle William. This was the occasion of the famous "Powder Alarm," which was sounded not merely through Middlesex county, but through the

[1] This letter is printed from the original in the possession of Mr. Bancroft.

province and into other colonies, causing a great commotion. There was a large gathering before evening; and, the next morning, the people, with arms in their hands, assembled in Cambridge. The ever-vigilant committees, early in the morning, sent several messengers into Boston asking the aid of the committee of correspondence. Warren, on being informed that his presence was needed to prevent an immediate outbreak, at six o'clock, notified such of the committee as he could, crossed over the ferry to Charlestown, met several of its committee of correspondence, and by eight o'clock was in the midst of the excited multitude in Cambridge. Counsellor Danforth was addressing about four thousand people, and resigning his commission. Warren now used his influence efficiently to prevent a collision with the troops, spent the day with this company of freemen, and was witness of their patience, temperance, and fortitude, as they compelled obnoxious officials to obey the popular will. The governor wisely remained inactive. In Warren's judgment, had the troops marched out of Boston against this body of men, not a man would have returned. On this day, he addressed a letter in reply to the committee of the town of East Haddam, which, in contributing "its mite for the relief of the poor," said, "As you are the first that are attacked as the head of all America, and so more immediately suffering, yet all the members, in a greater or lesser degree, are suffering with you."

Reply to East Haddam.

BOSTON, Sept. 1, 1774.

GENTLEMEN, — The town of East Haddam, in their letter of the 24th August, discover such a cordial sympathy for our distress, and give such a pleasing proof of their resolution to assist us, as makes us more than ever determined to support our sufferings with a philosophic fortitude. Boston is the stage on which our tyrants choose to act at present; but how soon they will choose to figure in some spot where they have a greater probability of success, time only will discover. We hope, however, to convince them, that not only Boston, but all America, is designed by Heaven for an asylum for oppressed and injured virtue, rather than to be a theatre of sport for usurping despots. The late Acts of Parliament are cruel and oppressive to the last degree. That for blockading our harbor is perhaps without a parallel; but we are, nevertheless, of opinion that they have operated for our advantage. Our enemies imagined, that, by exhibiting to our view some signal instances of their immediate power to distress us, we should be intimidated; that we should submit to kiss the rod, and beg them to accept of our obedience. They now see that we are neither to be persuaded nor frighted from that standard which we are most sacredly bound to protect. They have done their utmost, and it is ineffectual. In policy, we flatter ourselves they have not exceeded us. Arms are as yet untried. There was a time when some *good* men among us were insensible of their danger, and seemed to prefer obscurity to action; but the late manœuvres of tyranny have roused them from their lethargy, and they now pant for the field in which the fate of our country is to be decided.

Nothing has so damped the spirits of those who aspire to be our masters, as the accounts we are daily receiving of the glorious spirit that inspires the different parts of the continent. Some have believed, or have pretended to believe, that, if the faction in Boston was quelled, the provinces would acquiesce in whatever changes Administration were pleased to make in the charter and constitution of the Massachusetts Bay. But now they see that a firm bond is formed in America, which the most powerful monarch on earth will not easily break.

You will be pleased to accept our most hearty wishes for a continuance of your friendship; and gratitude and justice oblige us to tell you, that the Colony of Connecticut have behaved to us like brothers, and signalized themselves in the cause of American liberty in such a manner as will redound to their honor so long as the sun and moon endure.

The generous benefaction from the town of East Haddam, so modestly mentioned in your letter, excites those emotions which the grateful hearts of their brethren here can better conceive than express.

We are, gentlemen, with sincerity, your much obliged servants,

JOSEPH WARREN,
Per order of the Committee of Donations.
To Mr. DANIEL BRAINERD and others of the Committee of East Haddam.[1]

Warren now wrote to Samuel Adams, that he never saw a more glorious prospect than there then was, and that the generous spirit of their ancestors seemed to have revived beyond the most sanguine expectations. Though it seemed to him that the cord which bound the province to the king was by his act cut asunder, yet he was aware that the subject of a change in the Government should be handled very gently and cautiously, lest the Massachusetts patriots should be thought, for the advantage of their colony only, to aim at more than the other colonies were willing to contend for with Britain. Thus was the idea of union ever present with the popular leaders. It will be seen, that, though the first of the two following letters is without date, both were of the 4th of September: —

Joseph Warren to Samuel Adams.

DEAR SIR, — Our friends, Drs. Church and Young (whose letters I have seen), write so fully to you by this conveyance, that it will be needless for me to take up your time in giving a minute account of what has passed since my last. I can only assure you, that I never saw a more glorious prospect than the present. The generous spirit of our ancestors seems to have revived beyond our most sanguine expectations. I promised you, in my last, some account of the mighty

[1] This letter is printed in 4th series of Mass. Hist. Soc. Collections, iv. 58.

expedition against the Arsenal at Cambridge; but, as you will have a particular detail of that campaign in the public papers, you will not wish me to take up your time. Friday morning, about six o'clock, I received a message from Charlestown, informing me that some boys and negroes had called at Mr. Sewall's house at Cambridge; and, by the imprudent discharge of a pistol by a person in the house, they were provoked to break the windows, but very soon left the house without doing further damage. The informant besides assured me, that the county of Middlesex were highly incensed against Mr. Brattle and some others, and advised that some person from Boston should go up to Cambridge. This message was scarcely finished when a billet was brought, requesting me to take some step in order to prevent the people from coming to immediate acts of violence, as incredible numbers were in arms, and lined the roads from Sudbury to Cambridge. I summoned the committee of correspondence; but, as care had been taken to caution every man who passed the ferry from alarming Boston, I judged it best not to inform the person who warned the committee of the business they were to meet upon. They, therefore, made no great haste to get together. After waiting some time, I took as many of the members as came in my way to Charlestown, fearing that something amiss might take place. I saw the gentlemen at Charlestown, who begged us to move forward to Cambridge. On our way, we met the Lieutenant-governor Oliver. He said he was going to the general, to desire him not to march his troops out of Boston. We thought his precaution good, and proceeded to Cambridge. We there saw a fine body of respectable freemen, with whom we spent the day, and were witnesses of their patience, temperance, and fortitude, a particular account of which you have per this conveyance. The accounts from the western counties are such as must give the most exalted idea of the resolution and intrepidity of the inhabitants. The people from Hampshire County crowded the county of Worcester with armed men; and both counties received the accounts of the quiet dispersion of the people of Middlesex with apparent regret, grudging them the glory of having done something important for their country without their assistance. Had the troops marched only five miles out of Boston, I doubt whether a man would have been saved of their whole number. But enough of this. We find it difficult here to regulate the little matters in which we are engaged. You move in a larger orbit. However, I hope your superior abilities will not fail of carrying you safely through.

You will, I am sure, consider the very great difference that there is between this and the other colonies. Their commerce glides in its usual channels. Their charters have not yet been torn to pieces by the harpies of power. They retain their usual forms of trials by juries, in courts duly constituted. What is left for us? If we acquiesce but for an hour, the shackles will be fixed for ever. If we should allow the county courts to sit one term upon the new establishment, what confusion, what dissensions, must take place! Our friends — I mean particularly you, Mr. Cushing, Mr. Adams, and Mr. Paine — are capable of representing to your brethren the impossibility of our continuing long in a state of inactivity. Our all is at stake. We must give up our rights, and boast no more of freedom, or we must oppose immediately. Our enemies press so close that we cannot rest upon our arms. If this province is saved, it must be by adopting measures immediately efficacious. I have mentioned, in my letters to you, the most mild plan that can be adopted; viz., non-importation and non-exportation to Britain, Ireland, and the West Indies. I mentioned some of my reasons for believing that our liberties might thereby be secured; but it may not be amiss to try how far some further steps for securing our rights might (if absolutely necessary) be approved by our brethren on the continent. I firmly believe, that the utmost caution and prudence is necessary to gain the consent of the province to wait a few months longer for their deliverance, as they think the cord by which they were bound to the King of Britain has been, by his act, cut in sunder. They say they have a right to determine for themselves under what government they will live hereafter. But I shall now only subscribe myself your friend and humble servant,

JOSEPH WARREN.

Dr. Adams informs me that your lady and family are in health, and present their love and duty to you.

Joseph Warren to Samuel Adams.

BOSTON, Sept. 4, 1774.

DEAR SIR, — Since closing my letter of this day, which, I believe was without date, I have received some little agreeable intelligences which I cannot fail to communicate. The Solemn League and Covenant was signed by the people of the towns in the neighborhood of Falmouth, Casco Bay. The traders and people of Falmouth ridiculed the scheme, and refused signing it. The 31st day of August, the ship-carpenters who were building vessels for the Falmouth merchants demanded their dues, and refused to work longer. The employers remonstrated, told them their vessels would rot on the stocks, and said they could not dismiss them. The tradesmen, of all kinds, were resolute. They who had contracted to furnish the merchants with lumber likewise declared they could have nothing to do with them. On Monday, the merchants of Falmouth had a meeting; and, by Wednesday night, the whole town signed the agreement. Last Thursday evening, three fire-clubs met in this town: one club voted out of their society Messrs. J. G——, H. L——, and C——, and another voted out Mr. A——; a third voted out Mr. S——, all addressers. Indeed, the contention is who shall most distinguish themselves at this grand crisis. I wish much to be in England at this time; but the sacrifice of my particular interest at this time, by such a step, would be greater than I can afford to make. I fear Messrs. Oliver, lieutenant-governor, and Colonel Leonard are both going there immediately; and I hope they will not be suffered to tell their tale uncontradicted. The resumption of the old charter of this colony is much talked of; but I think should be handled very gently and cautiously whenever brought upon the tapis, lest a jealousy should arise in the minds of any concerning it, and lest we should be thought of as aiming at more than the colonies are willing to contend for with Britain for the advantage of this colony only. But I know you can remind our friends of Mr. Pitt's remark, that three millions of slaves would be fit engines to enslave the British Empire; and you will not have occasion to tell a judicious American, that one colony of freemen will be a noble bulwark for the rights of all America. Connecticut and Rhode Island are instances that must immediately occur. May God bless you and my other friends with you! (*mutatis mutandis.*) What I write to you I write to all. Pray furnish me with the fullest intelligence as soon as possible.

I am, dear sir, your friend and humble servant, J. WARREN.[1]

The Regulating Act was now resisted with great energy. The temper of the people was manifested in various ways in the country and in the town. At Newbury Bridge, the citizens stationed an old man with a drum, who, when he saw a prominent Tory

---

[1] These letters are from the originals in the possession of Mr. Bancroft.

about to enter, paraded with his drum, and went through the streets, crying as he beat the drum, "A Tory has come to town."[1] In Bridgewater, as the mandamus counsellor stood up in meeting, and read as usual the psalm, the congregation refused to sing.[2] In Boston, opposite Joy's Buildings, which are near the Town House, there were shops occupied by a chaisemaker, a tailor, a barber, a shoemaker, and two others, in each of which there was a bell; and, when a mandamus counsellor or a high Tory went by, one gave the signal by ringing his bell, and the ringing was kept up through all the shops until the obnoxious passer-by was out of sight.[3] So great was the rage against all charged with introducing arbitrary power, that the fatal *à la lanterne* policy was suggested. "Some really think," Young wrote, "an example or two will be made in a very short time. I cannot say I would be uneasy to hear it was done."[4]

Gage, in the conviction that the time for conciliation, moderation, and reasoning was over,[5] ordered cannon to be carried from the Common to the Neck, or main entrance to the town. This commencement of a fortification added fuel to the general flame, and created great alarm. "We are," Paul Revere says, "in spirits, though in a garrison; the spirit of liberty was never higher than at present; our new-fangled counsellors are resigning their places every day; our justices of the courts, who now hold their commission during the pleasure of His Majesty or the governor, cannot get a jury that will act with them. In short, the Tories are giving way everywhere in our

---

[1] Letter of John Andrews.   [2] Newspaper.   [3] John Andrews's Letter.
[4] Letter of Dr. Young.   [5] Gage's Letter, Sept. 2, 1774.

province."[1] On the same day, Dr. Young wrote to Samuel Adams, " The temper of your countrymen is in the condition your every wish, your every sigh, for years past, panted to find it. Thoroughly aroused and unanimously in earnest, something very important must inevitably come of it " He promised that the action of Suffolk should not come short of that of other counties.

On the next day (Sept. 5), when the general congress met, James Bowdoin wrote that six regiments were in town, and that it was said that two or three more were coming from Canada, and two from Ireland. The journals stated, that the force which was encamped on Fort Hill distinguished itself in the famous battle of Minden. There was war-preparation also going on on the side of the patriots; and the newspapers describe the parades of the volunteer corps, as they practised the military art: so that a journal said, "The spirit of the people was never known to be so great since the settlement of the colonies as it is at this time. People in the country for hundreds of miles are prepared and determined to die or be free."

While the public mind was excited, the Suffolk convention, on the 6th of September, re-assembled at the house of Mr. Richard Woodward, in Dedham; every town being represented. The delegates chose Richard Palmer president, and William Thompson clerk. After choosing a large committee to mature the business, with Warren for their chairman, the

---

[1] Letter, Sept. 4, 1774, to John Lamb, in the archives of the New-York Historical Society. I am indebted to the librarian, George H. Moore, Esq., for every facility in consulting the manuscripts in this prosperous institution.

convention adjourned, to meet again at Milton, where, on the 9th of September, Warren reported to the convention the paper known in history as the Suffolk resolves, which he drafted. It is said that they were read several times, and unanimously adopted, paragraph by paragraph. The first resolution cheerfully acknowledges George III. as justly entitled to the allegiance of the British realm: succeeding resolutions arraign the recent Acts of Parliament as violative of the laws of nature, the British Constitution, and the charter of the province; and provide for a forcible resistance to them as the attempts of a wicked Administration to enslave America. The action recommended is the boldest and most thorough of the time. The resolves declare the intention to act merely on the defensive, "so long as such conduct may be vindicated by reason and the principles of self-preservation, but no longer." They pledge submission to such measures as "the wisdom and integrity of the Continental Congress" might recommend for the restoration of their rights, and for the renewal of "the union between Great Britain and the colonies, so earnestly wished for by all good men." They fixed the day for the assembling of a Provincial Congress. One of the resolutions embodied that adherence to social order as the basis of political action, which, for the past six years, had characterized the course of the wise popular leaders. This resolve heartily recommends all persons to abstain from routs, riots, or licentious attacks upon the property of any persons whatsoever, as being subversive of all order and government;" but urges the patriots, by a steady and manly opposition, "to convince these enemies, that, in a contest so important, in a cause so solemn, their conduct should be such as to merit the approbation of the wise, and the admiration of the brave and free of every age and of every country."[1]

The convention, early in its session, appointed a large and most respectable committee, with Warren for chairman, to remonstrate with Governor Gage against the new fortification, and the insults which his soldiers had offered the citizens. The committee waited on him, when the chairman presented to him an address, representing that the works might be used to aggravate the miseries of the distressed town, by interrupting the supplies of provisions; expressing an inability to determine whence could originate the governor's policy towards a loyal and orderly community; declared that, though the people were resolved, by divine assistance, never to submit to the new Acts, yet they had no inclination to war on the troops; representing that the existing ferment resulted from seizing the powder in the Arsenal at Charlestown, and withholding the powder in Boston from its proprietors, and, more particularly, from the fortifying the sole avenue by land into Boston. "Nothing," the committee said, in conclusion, "short of restoring the town to its former state, and the cessation from insult, could put the inhabitants in that tranquillity in which every free subject ought to live." To this the governor verbally expressed himself as follows: "Good God! gentlemen, make yourselves easy, and I will be so. You have done all in your

---

[1] These resolves fill one side of the newspapers. They embody, even in the high-wrought language in which they are expressed, the spirit of the time, and show Warren's turn of mind. I copy the whole in the Appendix: hence the brief abstract in the text.

power to convince the world and me that you will not submit to the Acts, and I'll make representation home accordingly, for which I will embrace the earliest opportunity."[1] He subsequently gave a written reply to the address of the committee, in which he said, that it was not possible for him to interrupt the intercourse between town and country; he urged the general good behavior of the army to balance the individual cases of insult; he asked for the occasion of such numbers going through the country armed, and for the private removal of the guns from the Charlestown battery; and concluded by remarking, "that he found the refusal to submit to the late Acts of Parliament to be general, and that he should lay the fact before His Majesty.'

After considering this reply, the committee were of opinion, that the answer could not be satisfactory to the country. "And farther," the journals say, probably in Warren's language, "that His Excelleney, in his reply, had been pleased to propose several questions, which, if unanswered by the committee, would leave on the minds of persons not fully acquainted with the state of the facts, some very disagreeable impressions concerning the conduct and behavior of this county and province;" and they unanimously agreed, on the same day, to present to the governor another address, which was longer than the first. It says that the governor was too well acquainted with the human heart, not to be sensible that it is natural for people to be soured by oppression and jealous for their personal security, when their exertions for the preservation of their personal

[1] John Andrews's Letter.

rights were construed into treason and rebellion. It recapitulated facts relative to the new fortification, the army, and the distressed condition of the town; and pointed to the late hostile acts of the governor as a sufficient justification for their proceedings for self-defence, for which he seemed at a loss to account. It earnestly solicited the governor to desist from action that had a tendency to create alarm, and particularly from fortifying the entrance to the town of Boston. It averred and asked the governor so to represent to His Majesty, "that no wish of independency, no adverse sentiments or designs towards His Majesty, or his troops now here, actuate his good subjects in this colony; but that their sole intention is to preserve pure and inviolate those rights to which, as men and English-Americans, they are justly entitled, and which have been guaranteed to them by His Majesty's royal predecessors." Warren signed this address as chairman. The sequel is related in the journals, which contain both addresses over Warren's name. As he was in the habit of supplying matter to the press, it is probable that the following interesting relation is from his pen: —

"The address was delivered to Mr. Secretary Plucker, by the chairman, with a desire that he would, as soon as was convenient, present it to the governor, and request His Excellency to appoint a time for receiving it in form. The secretary informed the chairman, the ensuing day, that he had seen the governor, and had given him the copy of the address, but that he declined receiving it in form. The chairman mentioned to him the importance of the business, declaring his belief that the troops were not in any danger; and that no person has, so far as he has been informed, taken any steps which indicated any hostile intention, until the seizing and carrying off the powder from the magazine in the county of Middlesex; and that, if any ill consequences should arise that should affect the interest of Great Britain, the most candid and judicious, both in Europe and America, would consider the author of the ferment now raised in the minds of these people as accountable for whatever consequences might follow from it. He therefore desired the secretary once more to make application to His Excellency, and to state the affair to him in that serious manner which the case seemed to require. The secretary accordingly made a second application to the governor; but received for answer, that he had given all the satisfaction in his power, and he could not see that any further argumentation upon the subject would be to any good purpose. Upon this, the committee were again convened; and it was unanimously resolved that they had executed the commission intrusted to them by the county to the utmost of their ability. And, after voting, that the reply to His Excellency's answer should be inserted in the public papers as soon as possible, they adjourned without day.

"It is observable that every vote passed by the delegates of the county, and by the committee appointed to wait on the governor, was unanimous."

The resolves of the convention of Suffolk were adopted by men who were terribly in earnest. They said that "the power but not the justice, the vengeance but not the wisdom, of Great Britain," were acting with unrelenting severity; and the liberal world is agreed on this judgment. They said that it was an indispensable duty which they owed to God, their country, themselves, and posterity, by all lawful ways and means in their power to maintain, defend, and preserve those civil and religious rights and liberties for which many of their fathers fought, bled, and died, and to hand them down entire to future generations." These liberties may be said to have been embodied in one word, — republicanism; and when the titled world regarded this element with obloquy, the patriots, as a party, clung to it as the all of their political life.

Warren sent these resolves, with a letter dated the 11th of September, to the Massachusetts delegates in congress in Philadelphia; and Paul Revere was the messenger, who carried also the addresses delivered to Governor Gage. These papers, as they were listened to in congress on the 18th, elicited great applause. "The esteem," John Adams says, "the affection, the admiration for the people of Boston and the Massachusetts which were expressed, and the fixed determination that they should be supported, were enough to melt a heart of stone. I saw the tears gush into the eyes of the old, grave, pacific Quakers of Pennsylvania."[1] The sympathy which the members expressed for their suffering countrymen was in character with the constituency, who, by their flow of contributions, were making Boston the granary of America. In a resolve, which was unanimously passed, the congress denounced the late Acts, "most thoroughly approved the wisdom and fortitude with which opposition to these ministerial measures had hitherto been conducted; earnestly recommended to their brethren a perseverance in the same firm and temperate conduct" that was indicated in the Suffolk resolves; and expressed the hope that the effect of the united efforts of North America in behalf of Massachusetts "would carry such conviction to the British nation of the unwise, unjust, and ruinous policy of the present Administration as quickly to introduce better men and wiser measures." Another resolve recommended a continuation of contributions from all the colonies to alleviate the distresses of their brethren of Boston. "These resolves," Samuel Adams wrote to Dr.

---

[1] John Adams's Letter, Sept. 18, 1774.

Channey, "give a faint idea of the spirit of congress. I think I may assure you, that America will make a point of supporting Boston to the utmost."[1]

It is always difficult to harmonize the views of earnest men; and it is not strange, that, when unity of action was vital, the patriots of other colonies should have feared that the Massachusetts patriots might break the line of opposition by advancing too hastily before the rest,[2] or that the Boston popular leaders should have been anxious to hear from congress. The great news of the indorsement by the colonies of the Suffolk resolves was brought by Paul Revere, and was printed in the journals of the 26th, in the form of brief letters, addressed to Warren by Peyton Randolph, the president, Thomas Cushing, one of the Massachusetts delegates, and a copy of the resolutions passed by congress, attested by Charles Thomson. It was, with the exception of the rule adopted in that body in voting, the first account of what had been done in their secret session. "It was," a letter says, "the only thing which the members of congress were at liberty to mention to the people out of doors here. The congress will support Boston and the Massachusetts, or perish with them; but they wish that blood may be spared if possible, and all ruptures with the troops avoided."[3] The patriots were now in high spirits.

Governor Gage was surprised and astonished to see the union of the colonies. Like his predecessor, he watched and reported signs of its formation; and he confessed that the movements were beyond all con-

---

[1] Letter, Sept. 18, 1774. [2] See Clymer's Letter in Quincy's Life, 172.
[3] Letter in newspapers, Sept. 26, 1774.

ception. He now informed Lord Dartmouth of the approval by congress of the Suffolk resolves. The comments by the Tories on these resolves were voluminous and uncommonly severe. They said it was a mystery which filled their minds with surprise and astonishment, that the gentlemen of congress were disposed to enter into a league, offensive and defensive, with the New-England and other Presbyterian republicans; but the fact was notorious to the world: it could neither be denied nor palliated; for they hastily and eagerly published (and it was the first thing they did publish) their cordial approbation of the Suffolk resolves for erecting an independent government in New England. They said that a rebellion was evidently commenced in New England, in the county of Suffolk, without room for retreating. They pronounced the resolves "nothing short of a declaration of independency." They said that the men who had occasioned the political troubles in Massachusetts, having become desperate themselves, had no other card to play but to involve the whole country in their rebellion. They wrote that they had persuaded themselves "that congress would open the door for a settlement, by advising Boston to pay for the tea. But, alas! how have we been disappointed! As soon as they (congress) received by express an authentic copy of the Suffolk resolves, they broke through all these rules of secrecy, and at once gave such a blast from the trumpet of sedition as made one half of America shudder."[1]

[1] The citations are from Tory pamphlets of the time, entitled, "What Think Ye of the Congress now?" and "A Few Remarks upon some of the Votes and Resolutions of the Continental Congress." The last pamphlet, "printed for the purchasers," which was called "The Grey Maggot," asserted that the only

In due time, there appeared in the newspapers quotations from the British press of similar tenor. It was the union that gave joy to the heart of the Whig, and supplied venom to the pen of the Tory. "The friends of America," an editorial in a Boston journal says, " have the satisfaction to learn, that the resolve of the late Continental Congress, respecting the votes of the county of Suffolk, published in the late English papers, have not only surprised but quite confounded the ministry, as by it they perceive the union of the colonies to be complete, and that their present menaces only mark their despair."

apology which could be made for the conduct of the Continental Congress in adopting the Suffolk resolves was, that they came into this vote immediately after drinking thirty-two bumpers of Madeira. It was replied, in the "Pennsylvania Journal," that the Suffolk resolves were acted upon in the forenoon.

CHAPTER XII.

MASSACHUSETTS AND THE GENERAL CONGRESS.

THE STATE OF THE PROVINCE. — THE QUESTION OF LOCAL GOVERNMENT. — LETTERS OF WARREN AND ADAMS. — A PROVINCIAL CONGRESS. — COMMITTEE OF SAFETY. — PREPARATION FOR WAR.

SEPTEMBER, 1774, TO JANUARY, 1775.

WARREN, soon after the adoption of the Suffolk resolves, was required by the progress of events to take a prominent part in the organization and administration of a provisional government for the colony. His agency in the process by which Massachusetts passed from allegiance to the British Crown to become a part of an American nationality, renders this portion of his life not only of deep interest, but of much importance.

The province of the Massachusetts Bay included the territory which is now the State of Maine, and comprised an area of about thirty-nine thousand square miles. It was divided into fourteen counties, and over two hundred towns.[1] The population was not far from three hundred and fifty thousand. There

---

[1] The "London Chronicle" of the 27th of August, 1774, has the following description of Massachusetts. It is not quite accurate. The population is stated at too low a figure. The council was elected by the old council and the House : —

"The province of Massachusetts is divided into fourteen counties, and is generally thought to contain nearly 250,000 inhabitants.

"The council is composed of twenty-eight members, chosen by the House of Representatives.

were thirteen Episcopal churches and about four hundred Congregational societies. It will be, perhaps, a sufficient introduction to the letters of Warren of this period to remark, that there was a traditionary love for "the old charter," under which the colony

"The House of Representatives consists of about 128 or 129 deputies, sent from the different towns. Of these, Boston sends four members.

"There are five judges in the superior court of judicature for the province. Besides that court, every county has an inferior court, composed of four judges.

"There are about four hundred religious assemblies in the colony, mostly Independents; the rest are four or five Presbyterian meetings, with some assemblies of Baptists and Quakers. In all the colony there are only thirteen English churches.

"They have a college, founded in 1638, at Cambridge, four miles from Boston, in which there are three professorships, — Divinity, Mathematics, and Philosophy and Oriental Languages. This college has very lately made a number of the Independent clergy doctors in divinity. The same thing was attempted in 1692, under the authority of an Act of their general court; but that Act was disallowed by the king in council. At that time, the Rev. Mr. Mather, president of the college, was the only person honored by a diploma.

"The militia consists of between thirty and forty regiments, very badly disciplined.

"There are three custom-houses in the province, — at Boston, Salem, and Falmouth. All the other seaport towns are branches of these three ports.

"In this province are no less than five hundred justices of the peace.

"As to the capital, which is Boston, it is ruled by seven men, chosen yearly, called selectmen. In the town is a militia regiment of twelve companies, a troop of horse, a company of cadets, a company and train of artillery, all militia.

'The climate is indifferent. It is intolerably hot in summer, and intolerably cold in winter; during four or five months in winter, the ice, from one to two feet thick, covers the streets of Boston. The inhabitants do not exceed 13,000. In 1768, there died of white people 369, of black 48; total, 414. Now, admitting that only one person out of thirty-one dies yearly, we shall not find the inhabitants exceed the above-mentioned number. Consumptions make great havoc amongst them.

"The harbor is a very large and a very good one, and they carry on a very extensive trade wherever they can sell their commodities, which consist principally of fish, oil, lumber, rum of their own distilling, pot and pearl ashes, shipping of all sorts, &c., &c., &c. In 1768, 629 vessels were cleared out from Boston, and the same year 566 entered. Of the vessels cleared out, 43 were for London, 22 for other parts of the island, 4 for Ireland; in all, for Great Britain and Ireland, 69. For different parts of Europe, 22; for the West Indies, 138; for the colonies on the American continent, 400. Of the vessels entered inward, 67 were from Great Britain and Ireland, 16 from different parts of Europe, 150 from the West Indies, and 333 from the continental colonies."

had enjoyed popular liberty in large measure, and which was so thoroughly democratic that the men of the Tory school said that there was not an ingredient of royalty in it. Under it the people elected their governor, and managed their exclusively local concerns. Since the reign of William and Mary, the new charter had been the Government, or the "Constitution," as it was called, which, with the English Constitution, was regarded as guaranteeing the fundamentals of free institutions, — representation, the right of the majority to rule, trial by jury, the habeas corpus, the town-meeting, freedom of the press, the immunities embodied in Magna Charta and the Bill of Rights, — in a word, civil and religious liberty. The people needed but to recur to "Blackstone's Commentaries" to learn a line of precedents that "maintained the superiority of the laws above the king;"[1] and it was an American idea, that parliament could not go, in legislation, beyond the limits fixed by the constitution. It was said by the colonists, "that the authority of parliament, in its proper extent, is justly supreme; and the same ought to be said of the general assembly of the colonies:" and it was held as fundamental, that "the making of laws for internal police was essential to liberty." In the "Broken Hints," which Joseph Hawley gave to John Adams when on his way to congress, the Regulating Act is characterized as calculated to "introduce perfect despotism," — as "evil against right, — utterly intolerable to every man who has any idea or feeling of right or liberty."[2] A

---

[1] Blackstone's Commentaries, concluding chapter.
[2] The "Broken Hints" was printed in "Niles's Principles of the Revolution."

wanton violation of municipal charters is pronounced the great and leading justification of the event which drove King James from the throne.[1] Hawley, in dwelling on the Regulating Act, said, "We must fight." When John Adams read this to Patrick Henry, the great Virginian solemnly exclaimed, "I am of that man's mind."

The state of affairs in Massachusetts at this time is described in the following letter: —

"As to public affairs here, I shall only say that things seem to be running into confusion; and that all the ministerial measures that have been of late pursued here look as if they were designed to drive the people, if possible, into something which they might call rebellion. The late Act for better regulating the civil government of this province has operated just as I expected it would. It has, in effect, dissolved the Government. The people will never acknowledge the new counsellors. Several of them refused to take their places. The people in different parts of the country have obliged some others to resign; so that there are none now but what are in Boston. A stop is also put to the holding the courts of justice upon the new plan. Thus we have neither legislative nor executive powers left in the province. There are but two possible ways to restore order and good government here: one is, by repealing the Acts which have been the sole occasion of these commotions; and this, I firmly believe, would quickly end them. The other, by laying the country waste by fire and sword, and extirpating the present inhabitants, leaving none to be governed, if that can be called restoring government. Any hostile measures short of this will never answer the end. They will not alter the sentiments of the people, whose spirit universally is now risen to a degree not easily to be conceived. Which part of the alternative the Ministry will adopt, God knows. The people expect, and are determined to abide, even the horrors of a civil war rather than give up their just rights."[2]

This temperately written account of the condition of the province will not agree either with the contem-

---

[1] Hallam's Constitutional History, ii. 146-147.
[2] Letter, dated Boston, Sept. 13, 1774, in London Chronicle, Nov. 18, 1774.

porary exaggerated relations of the Tories or of the Whigs. The former describe the province as being in anarchy, and the latter as in a state of nature, but as still and peaceable as it was when Government was in full vigor.[1] The people were far from being in a state of nature: for a body of local law was as much respected as ever, and the police of the towns had full authority to arrest violators of the peace; and there were many disturbances, and invasions of personal rights, which the popular leaders deplored, and endeavored to redress. In general, the affairs of society went on as before. Individuals enjoyed security, even though they differed from the public sentiment, if they accommodated themselves so far to the times as to restrain their temper and observe a neutrality.[2] In repelling the charge of being rebels and hypocrites, and claiming to be true to the king, the Whigs asked, "Can it be said of any other part of all the British dominions, what is known to be true of New England, that, in all the four provinces so called, there never was known so much as one single native Jacobite? And could we catch the Pretender, or any other usurper here, we would soon give a good account of him at the Court of Great Britain."[3] The patriots did not intend to deal blows upon the Royal Oak;[4] but they meant, at every hazard, to keep their native soil clear for the roots of the tree of liberty.

There were now among the Whigs a party ripe for

---

[1] Gordon's History, i. 427. [2] Ib., 428. [3] Letter, Sept. 10, 1774.
[4] In Walker's "Tracts on Independency," printed in 1648, there is a curious plate, representing the temper of the times under the figure of a Royal Oak, with a motley crowd about it hewing it down, one of the mottoes of which is, "Let's kill him, and sell his inheritance."

extreme measures, who impatiently waited for the action of the other colonies, — the same element that was seen in the town-meetings six years before, — who were for declaring Massachusetts to be separated by the king from the empire, raising the Pine-tree Flag, and fixing on the terms on which they would continue to be of the old nationality, offering them for the king to accept or reject, as he might think fit. In a word, they would leave the general congress nothing to do but to prosecute the work which they might inaugurate.[1] Another class kept steadily in view the necessity of a unity of the colonies as the requisite element for success. "Our salvation," Joseph Hawley now said, "depends upon an established persevering union of the colonies." — "All possible devices and endeavors must be used to establish, improve, brighten, and maintain such union."[2] This class were not willing that Massachusetts should go any further than there was reason to believe she would be supported by the other colonies.

Warren's letters show in a striking manner his appreciation of this consideration. His words are, "Nothing can be more important than this." On the day after he sent the Suffolk resolves to the Massachusetts delegates, he wrote to them the following weighty letter, stating the public feeling, and anxiously asking how far congress would support Massachusetts.

Joseph Warren to Samuel Adams.

BOSTON, September 12, 1774.

GENTLEMEN, — I wrote yesterday by Mr. Revere, and requested your advice concerning our public affairs; but I wrote in so much haste that I believe I was not explicit enough.

---

[1] Gordon, i. 429.   [2] "Broken Hints."

Many among us, and almost all in the western counties, are for taking up the old form of government, according to the first charter. It is exceedingly disagreeable to them to think of being obliged to contend with their rulers, and quarrel for their rights every year or two. They think this must always be the case in a government of so heterogeneous a kind as that under which they have lived. They say, too, that no security can be given them that they shall enjoy their estates without molestation, even if the late charter should be again restored in all its parts, since the possession of their lands may be rendered precarious by any alterations in the charter which the parliament shall think fit to make.

Other persons, more especially in the eastern counties, think that it will be trifling to resume the old charter. They say that the connection between the king and the people is dissolved by his breaking the compact made between them; and they have now a right to take what form of government they please, and make such proposals of a certain limited subjection to the king, as they shall judge convenient, which he may accept or reject, as he pleases.

I know you are deeply engaged; but nothing can be more important than this subject, and I beg you would give me immediate advice; and pray do not fail to inform how far the other colonies will be likely to favor us, and what conduct is necessary to insure at least their approbation. Our general assembly is called to meet on the fifth day of October. The county of Essex, in their county convention, have resolved to instruct the representatives of their several towns, when met agreeably to the precept at Salem, to resolve themselves (if it can be obtained in the House) into a provincial convention. I would gladly know whether it is probable that we can have any service from you at that time; and, *inter nos*, let me know whether it will be agreeable to elect Mr. —— and Mr. Adams.

I subscribe myself your known friend.

The following letters, in reply to this letter, are so important, that I print them entire. One of them seems to be incomplete. It will be seen that the one without date was written on the 24th of September: —

Samuel Adams to Joseph Warren.

PHILADELPHIA, September, 1774.

MY DEAR SIR, — Your letter of the 12th instant, directed to Mr. Cushing and others, came duly to hand. The subject of it is of the greatest importance. It is difficult, at this distance, to form a judgment, with any degree of accuracy, of what is best to be done. The eastern and western counties appear to differ in sentiment with regard to the two measures mentioned in your letter. This difference of sentiment might produce opposition, in case either part should be taken. You know the vast importance of union. That union is most likely to be obtained by a consultation of deputies from the several towns, either in a House of Representatives or a Provincial Congress. But the question still remains, which measure to adopt. It is probable the people would be most united, as they would think it safest, to abide by the present form of government, — I mean according to the charter. The governor has been appointed by the Crown, according to the charter; but he has placed himself at the head of a different constitution. If the only constitutional council, chosen last May, have honesty and courage enough to meet with the representatives chosen by the people by virtue of the last writ, and jointly proceed to the public business, would it not bring the governor to such an explicit conduct as either to restore the general assembly, or give the two Houses a fair occasion to declare the chair vacant? In which case the council would hold it till another governor should be appointed. This would immediately reduce the government prescribed in the charter; and the people would be united in what they would easily see to be a constitutional opposition to tyranny. You know there is a charm in the word "constitutional."[1]

Samuel Adams to Joseph Warren.

PHILADELPHIA, September 25, 1774.

MY DEAR SIR, — I wrote you yesterday by the post. A frequent communication at this critical conjuncture is necessary. As the all-important American cause so much depends upon each colony's acting agreeably to the sentiments of the whole, it must be useful to you to know the sentiments which are entertained here of the temper and conduct of our province. Heretofore we have been accounted by many,

[1] This letter is printed from the Samuel-Adams Papers. It has no signature.

intemperate and rash; but now we are universally applauded as cool and judicious, as well as spirited and brave. This is the character we sustain in congress. There is, however, a certain degree of jealousy in the minds of some, that we aim at a total independency, not only of the mother-country, but of the colonies too; and that, as we are a hardy and brave people, we shall in time overrun them all. However groundless this jealousy may be, it ought to be attended to, and is of weight in your deliberations on the subject of your last letter. I spent yesterday afternoon and evening with Mr. Dickinson. He is a true Bostonian. It is his opinion, that, if Boston can safely remain on the defensive, the liberties of America, which that town has so nobly contended for, will be secured. The congress have, in their resolve of the 17th instant, given their sanction to the resolutions of the county of Suffolk, one of which is to act merely upon the defensive, so long as such conduct may be justified by reason and the principles of self-preservation, but *no longer.* They have great dependence upon your tried patience and fortitude. They suppose you mean to defend your civil constitution. They strongly recommend perseverance in a firm and temperate conduct, and give you a full pledge of their united efforts in your behalf. They have not yet come to final resolutions. It becomes them to be deliberate. I have been assured, in private conversation with individuals, that, if you should be driven to the necessity of acting in the defence of your lives or liberty, you would be justified by their constituents, and openly supported by all the means in their power; but whether they will ever be prevailed upon to think it necessary for you to set up another form of government, I very much question, for the reason I have before suggested. It is of the greatest importance, that the American opposition should be united, and that it should be conducted so as to concur with the opposition of our friends in England. Adieu, SAMUEL ADAMS.[1]

Before these letters could have been received by Warren, he was chosen, at a meeting of the freeholders at Faneuil Hall, one of the delegates to the proposed Provincial Congress. The Boston delegation consisted of the four representatives, Cushing, Samuel Adams, Hancock, and William Phillips, with

---

[1] This letter is printed from the papers of Samuel Adams.

Warren, Benjamin Church, and Nathaniel Appleton. The instructions which the town gave to the delegates, not improbably prepared by Warren, are so brief and important that I copy them. It will be seen that they come fully up to, while they do not go beyond, the resolution of the general congress, passed on the 17th.

"GENTLEMEN, — As we have chosen you to represent us in the great and general court, to be holden at Salem on Wednesday the 5th day of October next ensuing, we do hereby instruct you, that, in all your doings as members of the House of Representatives, you adhere firmly to the charter of this province, granted by their majesties King William and Queen Mary, and that you do no act which can possibly be construed into an acknowledgment of the validity of the Act of the British Parliament for altering the Government of the Massachusetts Bay; more especially, that you acknowledge the honorable board of counsellors, elected by the general court, at their session in May last, as the only rightful and constitutional council of this province. And we have reason to believe, that a conscientious discharge of your duty will produce your dissolution as a House of Representatives. We do hereby empower and instruct you to join with the members who may be sent from this and the other towns in the province, and to meet with them at a time agreed on in a general Provincial Congress, to act upon such matters as may come before you in such a manner as shall appear to you most conducive to the true interest of this town and province, and most likely to preserve the liberties of all America."

The following card from Warren was printed in the "Boston Gazette" of the 26th of September. It is one of a class of facts which show the absence, in the great movement of the American Revolution, of the theological element, which in the old world had played so great a part in the wars and dealings of the nations: —

SEPTEMBER 24, 1774.

MESSIEURS PRINTERS, — As I have been informed that the conduct of some few persons of the Episcopal denomination, in maintaining principles inconsistent with the rights and liberties of mankind, has given offence to some of the jealous friends of this country, I think myself obliged to publish the following extract of a letter, dated Sept. 9, 1774, which I received from my worthy and patriotic friend, Mr. Samuel Adams, a member of the congress now sitting in Philadelphia, by which it appears, that, however injudicious some individuals may have been, the gentlemen of the Established Church of England are men of the most just and liberal sentiments, and are high in the esteem of the most sensible and resolute defenders of the rights of the people of this continent.

And I earnestly request my countrymen to avoid every thing which our enemies may make use of to prejudice our Episcopal brethren against us, by representing us as disposed to disturb them in the free exercise of their religious privileges, to which we know they have the most undoubted claim, and which, from a real regard to the honor and interest of my country and the rights of mankind, I hope they will enjoy unmolested as long as the name of America is known in the world. J. WARREN.

After settling the mode of voting, which is by giving each colony an equal voice, it was agreed to open the business with prayer. As many of our *warmest friends are members of the Church of England,* I thought it prudent, as well on that as on some other accounts, to move that the service should be performed by a clergyman of that denomination. Accordingly, the lessons of the day and prayer were read by the Rev. Mr. Duché, who afterwards made a most excellent extemporary prayer, by which he discovered himself to be a gentleman of sense and piety, and a warm advocate for the religious and civil rights of America.

The journals of the committee of correspondence attest the continuous labors of Warren in its business. "We meet daily," Church, a member writes. "Daily occurrences demand our attention. An armed truce is the sole tenure by which the inhabitants of Boston possess life, liberty, or property." And John

Pitts, another member, wrote to Samuel Adams, "In your absence, there have been, as usual, the improvement of the ready pens of a Warren and Church, the criticism of a Greenleaf, the vigilance and industry of a Molineux, and the united wisdom of those who commonly compose the committee." The following letter shows the state of things at the time of the assembling of the Provincial Congress: —

Joseph Warren to Samuel Adams.

BOSTON, September 29, 1774.

DEAR SIR, — My last letter of the 26th instant you will doubtless have received by the post before this reached you. Since then, there have been arrivals from England, by which we learn that the ministry are still inflexible and obstinate. The consequence then is, that, if America sees better days, it must be the result of her own conduct. The fortifications on Boston Neck are carried on without intermission. The troops are availing themselves of every opportunity to make themselves more formidable, and render the people less able to oppose them. They keep a constant search for every thing which will be serviceable in battle; and whenever they espy any instruments which may serve or disserve them, — whether they are the property of individuals or the public is immaterial, — they are seized, and carried into the camp or on board the ships of war. Mr. Joseph Scott, of this town, has sold them a number of shells, cow horns, chain shot, &c., to the amount of £500 sterling; and yesterday, about noon, they were carried on board one of the ships. The people are enraged against Mr. Scott, and he keeps incog. About two hundred carpenters were employed the last week in providing barracks for the troops. This week the works are entirely forsaken, — a few hands, indeed, are raised from the regiments, but by no means enough to carry on the buildings with expedition.

The employment was profitable to the tradesmen, and drew cash from the king to circulate in this impoverished town; but, in consequence of the proceedings of the committee, they desisted, and discovered a great aversion to do any thing displeasing [to] their brethren in the country, or that could possibly be injurious to the cause of American freedom.

The treatment which the inhabitants receive from the soldiery makes us think that they regard us as enemies rather than as fellow subjects.

Some of our warm advocates can hardly brook the many private insults we receive; and, were it not that your august body had cautioned us against any engagement with them, I fear bloodshed would have ensued before this.

When they carried the machines from Mr. Scott's, it made us "tremblingly alive all o'er;" and it is as much as our grave, serious people can effect to keep people from action at some particular times. The determination of the congress is waited with much impatience: that, we expect, will be decisive.

In your letter from England were enclosed two pamphlets; but as I knew you had one of them at Philadelphia, some time ago, and that Dr. Winthrop had sent you the other, I did not think it worth while to burden the carrier with them.

Mr. Samuel Phillips, jun., of Andover, was this day carrying about a dozen fire-arms over Charlestown ferry. The sloop-of-war lying in the river dispatched a boat, and seized them. A load of straw, said to be the property of Major Goldthwait, was this day bringing to town for the use of the soldiers; but the high sons of Roxbury gave it to the flames.

Your worthy family are all well, and would have you informed that they think of you, though they are not with you.

Josiah Quincy, Esq., sailed for London last Monday.

People were so rapacious for the intelligence brought from the congress by Mr. Revere, that I thought myself bound to publish an extract from your letter; and, although it was done without your permission, I know you will forgive it.

Please let Mr. Cushing know, that I should not have published his letter but at the earnest request of a number of our most valuable friends.

These publications, I think, you would approve, if you were sensible of the animation they give to our dejected friends.

The inconnection and want of form in this hasty production pleads for its excuse, that Mr. Revere waits for it.

I am, dear sir, with the utmost sincerity, your friend and humble servant, JOSEPH WARREN.[1]

MR. ADAMS.

---

[1] This letter is printed from the original in the possession of Mr. Bancroft. Only the last paragraph, commencing "I am," &c., and the signature, are in Warren's handwriting.

The action of the committee of correspondence, referred to in this letter, related to work in building barracks for the army. The committees of thirteen towns met in Faneuil Hall, agreed upon a systematic plan in relation to a refusal of supplies, and declared all to be inveterate enemies to their country who furnished any materials whatever that would enable the troops to distress the inhabitants. The journals also contain a particular account of an interview which Warren now had with Governor Gage, in relation to the new fortification, and the purchase of stores. General Gage, in his official letters, dwelt on the difficulties he encountered in consequence of the action relative to labor and supplies.

The governor now had to meet the more serious movement of a Provincial Congress. He issued a precept, on the 1st of September, for a return of representatives to the general court, to be convened on the 5th of October, at Salem; but, he says, when he saw the resolves passed by some of the counties, and "the instructions given by the town of Boston and some other towns to their representatives," he issued a proclamation, on the 28th of September, declaring a general court inexpedient, discharging all persons elected from giving their attendance, and announcing his intention not to be present at the time and place he had named. Agreeably to the plan agreed upon, ninety of the representatives elect met, on the 5th of October, at Salem. After waiting a day for the appearance of the constitutional governor, they resolved themselves into a Provincial Congress, elected John Hancock their chairman and Benjamin Lincoln their secrètary, passed a series of resolves, and adjourned to meet at Concord. The action of the governor, as it was neither a dissolution nor a prorogation of the legislature, was declared by the patriots to be without the warrant of law.

The Provincial Congress assembled, on the 11th of October, at Concord. Many towns that did not choose representatives elected delegates to this congress. There were two hundred and eighty-eight[1] members, — all but twenty present, — who were sent by two hundred and twelve towns.[2] John Hancock was elected their president, and Benjamin Lincoln their secretary. The congress met first in the Court House, but adjourned to the Meeting-house.

Many of the delegates had taken part in the county conventions, and subsequently were distinguished in civil or military life. There were returned from the towns in Suffolk county, besides Cushing, Samuel Adams, Hancock, and Warren, William Heath and Benjamin Lincoln, generals throughout the Revolutionary war: from Essex were John Pickering, Azor Orne, Jonathan Greenleaf, and Elbridge Gerry, who were distinguished in political life: from Middlesex were Nathaniel Gorham, a prominent member of the convention that formed the Federal Constitution; William Prescott, and Thomas Gardner, colonels in the Bunker-hill battle; Richard Devens, an active member of the committee of safety; James Barrett, the commander of the militia at Concord on the 19th of April; James Prescott, subsequently a judge, and Henry Gardner, soon to be the treasurer: Hampshire returned Seth Pomeroy, a veteran of Louisburg fame; and Joseph Hawley, a patriot of decidedly the largest

[1] Shattuck's History of Concord.   [2] Journals of the Provincial Congress.

influence in the western part of the province: Plymouth sent James Warren, a pioneer patriot, who became president of the Provincial Congress; Bristol, Robert Treat Paine, the poet and jurist; and York sent James Sullivan, the scholar, statesman, and future governor: from Worcester came Artemas Ward, the first commander of the colonial army; and Moses Gill and Timothy Bigelow, distinguished in political life. The memories of many other delegates are cherished for their character and intelligent public service. The congress was a fine representation of the great interests of the province as well as of its patriotism.

The proceedings of this body show that Warren shared largely in its confidence and in its labors. His letters indicate that he felt the responsibility of the hour, and meant to act with caution. He and his associates from Boston had before them a difficult *rôle:* for they found themselves "by far the most moderate men"[1] of the congress, the members in general being in favor of forming a new government; and it was a duty not to fall in with what was popular, but to do what was right. The shallow declaimers of the day were rash; but the thinkers said, "These are great and profound questions. We are grieved to find ourselves reduced to the necessity of entering into the discussion of them."[2]

The last letter of Warren shows his feeling on the vital question of "taking up" a new local government, or of proceeding, without outside advice or authority, as a separate, independent, sovereign State.

---

[1] Letter of John Pitts, Oct. 16, 1774.
[2] Address of Middlesex-county Convention.

The resolve of congress of the 17th of September was a recommendation to defend, in a firm and temperate way, the civil constitution; and, in doing this, to use so much of the law as remained. This also was the advice of Samuel Adams. And John Adams, after he had learned with certainty the views of the members, wrote, "The proposal of some among you of re-assuming the old charter is not approved here at all. The proposal of setting up a new form of government of our own is less approved still." He wrote of the future in the following warning tone: —

"They [the members] will not, at this session, vote to raise men or money or arms or ammunition. Their opinions are fixed against hostilities and ruptures, except they should become absolutely necessary; and this necessity they do not yet see. They dread the thoughts of an action because it would make a wound which would never be healed; it would fix and establish a rancor which would descend to the latest generations; it would render all hopes of a reconciliation with Great Britain desperate; it would light up the flames of war, perhaps through the whole continent, which might rage for twenty years, and end in the subduction of America as likely as her liberties."[1]

Such language must have increased the anxiety of the popular leaders in the Provincial Congress. A close inspection of its proceedings shows, that little of a positive character was done for ten days, or until after it met at Cambridge. It was evidently awaiting the final action of "The Grand American Congress," as the Philadelphia body was termed. It was now said, that "the whole attention and conversation were wrapped up in the congress."[1] An intelligent Boston patriot, John Pitts, in a letter to Samuel Adams, relative to the views of the members of the Provincial

[1] Letter to William Tudor, Oct. 7, 1774.   [2] Newspaper.

Congress on the question of "a subordinate government," said, "Without doubt they would be cautious to take the sense of your body, from whose wisdom we hope for relief."[1] In fact, it had long been an understanding, reached through the organization of committees of correspondence, that the patriots of one colony should take no important step without the concurrence of the patriots of the other colonies. In this spirit, the proceedings relative to the tea had been carried on. In this spirit, the people had refused to obey the officials acting under the Regulating Act. In this spirit, the wise popular leaders meant to proceed in the formation of a new Government. Man had not attained to perfection in Massachusetts: there were mobs, personal insults, and silly gasconade; and the violent talked as though they were ready, at the head of a town or a county or a colony, to brave the British Empire. This was the effervescence of the hour. It was the material which for years supplied what truth there was in the wanton misrepresentations of the patriots by the Tories, who said that this was the patriot cause. To the statesmen of that day, in all the colonies, who, amidst the unavoidable confusion in upholding this cause, held on to social order and national unity, is the world indebted for the American Revolution.

Warren, in the letter just printed, said that the determination of congress was awaited with much impatience, and that would be decisive; and that people were rapacious for intelligence from it. It is said, in the newspapers, that "the congress continued in private, solemn deliberation; and, as the members

[1] Letter, Oct. 16.

were under some honorary ties of secrecy, nothing had transpired of their proceedings." Ten days later, nothing had transpired from this body; but it was reported, that Paul Revere, who went as "an express from Boston to the delegates," was waiting in Philadelphia for the result of the determinations of congress. A week later, on the 20th of October, the "Massachusetts Gazette" contained this announcement: "A gentleman last evening favored us with the following resolves, just come to hand from Philadelphia." They were five in number, the first having been passed on the 8th of October: —

"*Resolved*, That this congress approve of the opposition made by the inhabitants of the Massachusetts Bay to the execution of the late Acts of Parliament; and, if the same shall be attempted to be carried into execution by force, in such case all America ought to support them in their opposition."

The four other resolves were designed to meet the condition of affairs in the province. One recommended, that the people continue "peaceably and firmly in the line they are now conducting themselves, — on the defensive;" another substantially advised a suspension of action relative to instituting a new Government, until the effect was known of an application for a repeal of the Act by which their charter rights were infringed. Samuel Adams now wrote to Dr. Young: —

"I think our countrymen discover the spirit of Rome or Sparta. I admire in them that patience, which, you have often heard me say, is characteristic of the patriot.... *Inter arma silent leges.* I have written to our friends to provide themselves, without delay, with arms and ammunition, get well instructed in the military art, embody themselves, and prepare a complete set of rules, that they may be ready in case they are called to defend themselves against the violent attacks of despotism. Surely the laws of self-preservation will warrant it in this time of danger and doubtful expectation."[1]

On the afternoon of the day of the publication of these resolves, the Provincial Congress appointed a committee to consider what it was necessary to do for the defence and safety of the province. I need not present in detail the proceedings on this report, or the doings of the congress. The debates for several days were long and earnest; but there is no report of the speeches. The deliberations resulted in the adoption, on the 26th, of a series of resolves, which provided for the creation of a "committee of public safety," as a sort of directory to take care of the commonwealth, which may be summed up as an authority to organize the militia, and to provide military stores when they should take the field. The resolves also provided for officers to command this force. On the next day, the congress elected, by ballot, nine of its members to compose the committee; choosing first three from Boston, and then nine from the country. They elected Hancock, Warren, and Church from the town; Richard Devens of Charlestown, Benjamin White of Brookline, Joseph Palmer of Braintree, Norton Quincy (who declined), Abraham Watson of Cambridge, Azor Orne of Marblehead. Subsequently, John Pigeon of Newton, William Heath of Roxbury, and Jabez Fisher of Wrentham, were added. The congress next elected "five commissaries," who were called a committee of supplies,— David Cheever, Moses Gill, Jeremiah Lee, Benjamin Lincoln, and Benjamin Hall. Three general officers

[1] Letter, dated October, 1774, in Samuel Adams's Papers.

were then chosen,—Jedediah Preble, Artemas Ward, and Seth Pomeroy. On the 28th, Congress passed a resolve, inviting "the constitutional members of His Majesty's council of this colony by the royal charter, chosen last May," to meet with the congress at their adjournment; and, on the 29th, appointed Henry Gardner receiver-general, to receive the usual revenue for the use of the province at the hands of the constables, collectors, and other persons. The congress appointed a day of public thanksgiving, "in particular from a consideration of the union which so remarkably prevailed, not only in the province, but throughout the continent, at this alarming crisis." The congress, on the 29th, adjourned until the 23d of November. It declined to take action on the formation of a new Government, and adhered strictly to the recommendations of the Continental Congress. Warren's name occurs on committees from the commencement to the close of the session.

He now began a great service as a member of the committee of public safety, the executive of the colony. It met on the 2d of November, at Cambridge, and organized by the choice of John Hancock as chairman; but he did not attend the next session, and Warren's name stands on its journal at the head of the list of members present at this meeting.

The committee voted to purchase provisions for an army; and, at the second meeting, on the 8th, they voted to procure all the arms and ammunition which they could of the neighboring provinces. On the evening of the next day, Cushing and the two Adamses came into the town from congress, where the people testified their joy at their safe arrival by ringing the bells, some of them till midnight. Hancock did not attend the next meeting of the committee of safety, on the 15th, when it was voted to have seven large pieces of cannon carried out of Boston.

Warren, in behalf of the committee of donations, now replied to a letter from the committee of Middletown, Connecticut, which enumerated things that "roused their attention and zeal," and induced them "to unite with their brethren throughout the continent." They said the claim of parliament was enforced by "the grossest violation of royal faith, in tearing up by the roots the ancient charter" of Massachusetts, and "by all the evils of Pandora's box let loose in the new form of Government imposed" upon the people. The reply to this spirited letter is as follows: —

Reply to Middletown.

BOSTON, November 17, 1774.

GENTLEMEN, — Your kind letter of the 17th of October came safe to hand. When we reflect on the great importance of the controversy in which we are engaged; when we consider that America will be free and happy or servilely wretched, according as we conduct ourselves, — we tremble. But that we are contending for our rights, — that the continent supports us, — makes us confident and determined. The plan which has been so long concerted, to deprive America of her rights, seems now to be executing, and that the ministry have chosen the town of Boston as their first victim.

That we are sequestered from all America, for a criterion by which they shall determine how far the idea of despotic government is compatible with the sentiments of free-born Americans, gives us no concern, because the spirit which is discovered in Middletown has diffused itself through the continent. Many have been the devices, subtle have been the schemes, and low the artifices, made use of to sow dissension and division: but the virtue of our country has risen superior to them all; and we see a band now formed which will encourage our friends and confound our enemies. The Ministry have hitherto kept the people of

Great Britain ignorant of the true state of America. They have by bribes and falsehoods deceived the nation. Truth and justice were never so effectually enveloped in the thick clouds of calumny and detraction. The mercenary writers they have employed to misrepresent, vilify, and abuse the Bostonians, afford us a striking instance of the base methods they pursue to ruin us. We have, however, the best grounds to think that the tide is turning in our favor. The eyes of the people of Britain begin to be opened. "The coolness, temper, and firmness of the Americans' proceedings, the unanimity of all the colonies in the same sentiments of their rights, and of the injustice offered to Boston, and the patience with which those injuries are at present borne, without the least appearance of submission, have a good deal surprised and disappointed our enemies; and the tone of public conversation, which has been so violently against us, begins evidently to turn." This is the language of as good a friend as America has in England, and whose authority we can rely on. And, if. this most desirable change had taken place before the proceedings of the American Congress were known in England, what may we expect upon their being known? Had not the present ministry discovered such rancor and such malice in their proceedings in respect to America, we should expect every thing to our wishes. But we have had such full demonstration of their diabolical designs against us, that we can look for nothing from them but what our own virtue and spirit can extort.

The regular, firm, and spirited conduct of the continent, if they should even fail of success, will eternally redound to their honor; and, should they meet that success which their cause merits, they must be the happiest people on whom the sun shines. The propriety and zeal with which the town of Middletown have treated the indignity which is offered to their country, seems to be a renewing that glorious ardor which warmed the breasts of their progenitors. It is a disposition which has heretofore been attended with prosperity. The support which they have formerly so liberally afforded the town of Boston in their sufferings demands our warmest gratitude. This recent instance of their good wishes for our success, and the readiness and forwardness which they discover to do every thing in their power for maintaining and preserving the rights of their country, and for supporting and feeding any who are immediate sufferers by the vengeance of their enemies, cannot fail to excite gratitude from every friend to the rights of mankind, and from the town of Boston in particular. We are not insensible, although there is a probability that our grievances will be redressed, that every thing yet depends on our own virtue and resolution; great patience, vigilance, and public spirit are still necessary. The point has been so long and so strenuously contended for, that our enemies never will give it up till they are compelled by the last and most unavoidable necessity. Our cause is so just, and we are so sensible how necessary it is to defend it, that we have no doubt, but, with the blessing of heaven upon us, and upon the many good friends engaged for us, we shall be able to hold on and hold out until oppression, injustice, and tyranny shall be superseded by freedom, justice, and good government. And we cannot but flatter ourselves, that, while we are contending for justice for ourselves, we shall be instrumental in calling back that virtue which of late years has fled from the councils of our parent country.

We are, gentlemen, your friends and obliged humble servants
JOSEPH WARREN,
Per order of the Committee of Donations.

P.S. — We have just now, by Captain Sheppard, from London, received His Majesty's proclamation for dissolving the late Parliament of Great Britain, whose conduct respecting America will be remembered with horror through all succeeding generations.

To the Committee of Correspondence for the Town of Middletown.[1]

Warren, four days after penning this magnetic utterance, sent a remarkable letter to Josiah Quincy, jun., who was in London. He was a kindred spirit, and closed his "Observations on the Port Bill" in the following strain: "America hath in store her Bruti and Cassii, her Hampdens and Sydneys, — patriots and heroes, who will form a band of brothers, — men who will have memories and feelings, courage and swords, — courage that shall inflame their ardent bosoms till their hands cleave to their swords, and their swords to their enemies' hearts."[2] His biographer, in printing Warren's letter, remarks, that it "is

---

[1] This letter is printed in fourth series of Mass. Hist. Soc. Collections, iv. 117.
[2] These words form the conclusion of Quincy's "Observations on the Port Bill."

peculiarly interesting, because few similar records of his mind remain, and as it evidences that the life he sacrificed on Bunker Hill was offered, not under the excitement of the moment, but with a fixed and deliberate purpose. No language can be more decisive of the spirit which predominated in his bosom: 'It is the united voice of America to preserve their freedom, or lose their lives in defence of it.'"[1] The passages I have put in italics are placed by Bancroft at the beginning of one of the chapters of his History:[2] —

To Josiah Quincy, jun.

BOSTON, November 21, 1774.

DEAR SIR, — As nothing interesting which I am at liberty to communicate has taken place since your departure from home, except such matters as you could not fail of being informed of by the public papers, I have deferred writing to you, knowing that, upon your first arrival in London, you would be greatly engaged in forming your connections with the friends of this country, to whom you have been recommended. Our friends who have been at the Continental Congress are in high spirits on account of the union which prevails throughout the colonies. *It is the united voice of America to preserve their freedom, or lose their lives in defence of it. Their resolutions are not the effect of inconsiderate rashness, but the sound result of sober inquiry and deliberation. I am convinced, that the true spirit of liberty was never so universally diffused through all ranks and orders of people, in any country on the face of the earth, as it now is through all North America.* The Provincial Congress met at Concord at the time appointed. About two hundred and sixty members were present. You would have thought yourself in an assembly of Spartans or ancient Romans, had you been a witness to the ardor which inspired those who spoke upon the important business they were transacting. An injunction of secrecy prevents my giving any particulars of their transactions, except such as by their express order were published in the papers; but, in general, you may be assured that they approved themselves the true representatives of a wise and brave people, deter-

[1] Life of Josiah Quincy, jun., 181. [2] Vol. vii. chap. 16.

mined at all events to be free. I know I might be indulged in giving you an account of our transactions, were I sure this would get safe to you; but I dare not, as the times are, risk so important intelligence.

Next Wednesday, the 23d instant, we shall meet again according to adjournment. All that I can safely communicate to you shall be speedily transmitted. I am of opinion, that the dissolution of the British Parliament, which we were acquainted with last week, together with some favorable letters received from England, will induce us to bear the inconvenience of living without government until we have some farther intelligence of what may be expected from England. It will require, however, a very masterly policy to keep the province, for any considerable time longer, in its present state. The town of Boston is by far the most moderate part of the province: they are silent and inflexible. They hope for relief; but they have found from experience that they can bear to suffer more than their oppressors or themselves thought possible. They feel the injuries they receive; they are the frequent subject of conversation: but they take an honest pride in being singled out by a tyrannical Administration as the most determined enemies to arbitrary power. They know that their merits, not their crimes, have made them the objects of ministerial vengeance. We endeavor to live as peaceably as possible with the soldiery; but disputes and quarrels often arise between the troops and the inhabitants.

General Gage has made very few new manœuvres since you left us. He has indeed rendered the intrenchments, at the entrance of the town, as formidable as he possibly could. I have frequently been sent to him on committees, and have several times had private conversations with him. I have thought him a man of honest, upright principles, and one desirous of accommodating the difference between Great Britain and her colonies in a just and honorable way. He did not appear to be desirous of continuing the quarrel in order to make himself necessary, which is too often the case with persons employed in public affairs; but a copy of a letter *via* Philadelphia, said to be written from him to Lord North, gives a very different cast to his character. His answer to the Provincial Congress, which was certainly ill judged, I suppose was the work of some of that malicious group of harpies, whose disappointments make them desirous to urge the governor to drive every thing to extremes; but, in this letter (if it be genuine), he seems to court the office of a destroyer of the liberties, and murderer of the people, of this province. But you have doubtless read the paper, and thought with indignation on its contents.

I wish to know of you how affairs stand in Great Britain, and what was the principal motive of the dissolution of parliament. *If the late Acts of Parliament are not to be repealed, the wisest step for both countries is fairly to separate, and not spend their blood and treasure in destroying each other.* It is barely possible that Britain may depopulate North America; but I trust in God she can never conquer the inhabitants: and, if the cruel experiment is made, I am sure, whatever fortunes may attend America, that Britain will curse the wretch, who, to stop the mouths of his ravenous pack of dependants, bartered away the wealth and glory of her empire.

I have not time to say more at present than to assure you, that from this time you may expect to hear from me, news or no news, by every vessel; and that my earnest wish is, that your abilities and integrity may be of eminent service to your country.

I am, dear sir, your most obedient servant, JOSEPH WARREN.

General Gage's letters now show, that he realized the import of the political unity which had been reached by the patriots. On informing Lord Dartmouth, on the 15th, that he had issued a proclamation declaring the Provincial Congress an unlawful body, and tending to riot and rebellion, he said that it had been encouraged to go to the lengths it had gone by the general union, and the readiness of the New-England provinces to appear in arms; and that the proceedings of the Continental Congress astonished and terrified all considerate men.

A few days after Gage had issued his proclamation, and when, according to his representation, "all considerate men" were in terror, the Provincial Congress, on the 23d of November, renewed its session. It invited John Adams and Robert Treat Paine to attend the meetings; the other delegates to the General Congress, Cushing and Samuel Adams, being members. It is not necessary to relate here in detail the proceedings of this body. The political centre was now "the grand American Congress;" and the chief committee of the session was the one appointed to consider its doings. Joseph Hawley was the chairman; and the other members were Samuel Dexter, Joseph Warren, Jeremiah Lee, James Warren, Elbridge Gerry, and Benjamin Church. Their report was a grateful indorsement of the proceedings of the General Congress, and an adoption of the "Association," and recommending the people to observe it. This body continued the preparatory work of defence, but went no farther. On the last day of the session (Dec. 10), a report which had been made on the question of "assuming civil government," was taken up, considered, and ordered to lie on the table. This congress issued an address to the inhabitants, briefly explaining and urging the measures that had been adopted. It presented the general intelligence from England, together with the increase of the army and navy, as exciting the strongest jealousy, that the system of colony administration, destructive to American liberty, was to be pursued, and to be attempted with force to be carried into execution. In a tone alike solemn and elevated, it is said, "You are placed by Providence in the post of honor because it is the post of danger; and, while struggling for the noblest objects, — the liberties of your country, the happiness of posterity, and the rights of human nature, — the eyes, not only of North America and the whole British Empire, but of all Europe, are upon you." It is added, "Let us be, therefore, altogether solicitous, that no disorderly behavior, nothing unbecoming our characters as Americans, as citizens, as Christians, be justly chargeable to us."

Warren was now serving in the committee of correspondence, which continued its vigilant watch of passing events. The following note is copied from the original in his handwriting, dated two days after the adjournment of congress: —

BOSTON, December 12, 1774.

GENTLEMEN, — We think it our duty to inform you, that one of the transports sailed from this port yesterday, in the afternoon, with several hundred soldiers on board. There are various conjectures concerning her destination; but it is generally believed she is designed for Newport, and that the troops are to take possession of the fortress there. The vigilance of our enemies is well known. They doubt not the bravery of our countrymen; but, if they can get our fortresses, our arms, and ammunition into their custody, they will despise all our attempts to shake off their fetters. We are convinced, that you will do what prudence directs upon this important occasion, and are, with great esteem, your friends and humble servants.

Several town-meetings were held in December, in Boston, on political affairs. Warren was placed on the inspection committee, created to carry into effect the "Association" of the Continental Congress; on a committee to prepare a vote of thanks to the colonies for the contributions made for the poor of the town, and on another to frame an answer to General Gage. On the 30th of December, he was chosen a delegate to the second Provincial Congress. In the records of the committee of safety, he is named on a committee to inspect the commissary stores in Boston.

Warren was now engaged in the various duties — town, provincial, and national — by which the patriots, as a party, were carrying on their work. Though there was, strictly speaking, neither local nor general government, yet the majority of the people, in most of the colonies, was so decisively arrayed in support of the measures of the patriots, that the recommendations, both local and general, were obeyed as rigidly as though they had the authority of law.

The Tory party was now uncommonly active in Boston and elsewhere. Its organs denounced the patriots as hypocrites, independents, republicans, sowers of sedition, and rebels. It had long been said in Boston by adherents of this party, that the local charter, or constitution, was based on principles "much too democratic, and subversive of all peace, good order and government," and ought to be annihilated. It was said in the British House of Commons, by Lord George Germaine, that "there could not be a better thing than to do away with town-meetings;" and he would bring "the Constitution of America as similar to the Constitution of England as possible." He said that Massachusetts was governed by "a tumultuous and riotous rabble;" and "he would not have men of a mercantile cast every day collecting themselves together, and debating about political matters:" for they "ought to follow their mercantile employment, and not trouble themselves with politics and government, which they do not understand."[1] A divine said from his pulpit in Charleston, South Carolina, "that mechanics and country clowns had no right to dispute about politics, or what king, lords, and commons had done or might do."[2] These cita-

---

[1] Parliamentary History, xvii. 1195.

[2] The following is copied from a newspaper of October, 1774: —

"A reverend divine in Charlestown, South Carolina, has been lately dismissed from his congregation for his audacity in standing up in his pulpit, and impudently saying, that mechanics and country clowns had no right to dispute about politics, or what king, lords, and commons had done or might do. All such divines should be taught to know, that mechanics and country clowns (infamously so called) are the real and absolute masters of king, lords, commons,

tions show the spirit of the party which now ruled England, which had sympathizers in the colonies and claimed the right of legislating "in all cases whatsoever" for America; and the Regulating Act was the assertion of this right.

But the united colonies demanded a repeal of this Act, as well as of other Acts conceived in a similar spirit. Warren wrote, that, if this were not done, "the wisest step for both countries was to separate, and not to spend their blood and treasure in destroying each other;"[1] and Franklin said to the ministry, that the colonies "must risk life and every thing" rather than submit to the claim of altering the local laws and charters at will."[2] The united voice of America urged, and even commanded, the people of Massachusetts to resist to the bitter end the new law. It was the vote of congress of the 8th of October, pledging the faith of the colonies to Massachusetts, that hardened George III. to listen to no terms.[3]

The tone of the Whigs, on the adjournment of the Continental Congress, was exultant in the extreme. The union step of instituting committees of correspondence had grown into the national measure of the "Association" for non-importation, non-exportation, and non-consumption. It is not necessary to discuss the question, whether these were sound or wise measures to carry out on the eve of a war. It

---

and priests, though (with shame be it spoken) they too often suffer their servants to get upon their backs, and ride them most barbarously."

[1] Letter, Nov. 21, 1774.

[2] Franklin said this to an agent of the ministry in December, 1774. Hints, &c., Sparks's Franklin, v. 22. One of the conditions of reconstruction was, "All powers of internal legislation in the colonies to be disclaimed by parliament." [3] Bancroft, vii. 145.

was great statesmanship to attain the result of united counsels. It was soon related in the journals, that "committees were appointed in almost every seaport from Georgia to New Hampshire, to observe that the Continental Association be complied with in every article therein recommended." At this time, the congress aimed neither at independence nor at civil war; but for redress of grievances, and a restoration of harmony with the mother-country.

The point fairly reached was that of a party supporting a real American union. The feeling of the hour was nowhere more earnestly expressed than in the utterances from South Carolina. "Be comforted, ye oppressed Bostonians! and exult, ye northern votaries of liberty! that the sacred rays of freedom, which used to beam from you on us, are now reverberated with double efficacy back upon yourselves, from your weaker sister Carolina, who stands foremost in her resolution to sacrifice her all in your defence." Again: "Many thanks to the worthy congress re-echoes from the generous breasts of grateful thousands. . . . Oh glorious day! Oh happy union! From Nova Scotia to Georgia, one mighty mind inspires the whole. When I consider the unanimity, the firmness, the wisdom of our late representatives, I feel a joy unutterable, and an exultation never felt before"[1] It would be easy to fill pages with similar citations from the newspapers of other colonies. The following is extracted from a glowing communication in the "Pennsylvania Packet:" — "The American congress derives all its power, wisdom, and action, not

---

[1] "South-Carolina Gazette:" an article copied into the "Essex Gazette," Dec. 27, 1774.

from scrawled parchment signed by kings, but from the people. A freeman, in honoring and obeying the congress, honors and obeys himself. . . . I almost wish to hear the triumphs of the jubilee of the year 1874; to see the medals, pictures, fragments of writings, &c., that shall be displayed to revive the memory of the proceedings of congress in the year 1774. If any adventitious circumstances shall give precedency on that day, it shall be to inherit the blood, or even to possess the name, of a member of that glorious assembly."[1]

This language marks the hour of an outburst of genuine Americanism, when a great party were inspired with the purpose of freeing their country, by a change of Administration, from the control of a party who claimed the right, not merely to mould their forms of government, but to monopolize the fruits of their labor. "For what purpose," Lord Carmarthen asked, in the debate on the Regulating Act, "were they (the colonists) suffered to go to that country, unless the profits of their labor should return to their masters here"?[2] Union meant resistance to this arrogance and mastership. It meant more, — it meant action in behalf of rights common to humanity. The great utterances of congress are pervaded by the spirit of universal liberty. The words of the representative patriots of that time, whether they came from a Christopher Gadsden of South Carolina, an Alexander Hamilton of New York, a John Dickenson of Pennsylvania, or a Samuel Adams of Massa-

---

[1] This extract, taken from a communication originally printed in the "Pennsylvania Packet," and copied into the "Essex Gazette," Dec. 20, 1774.

[2] Parliamentary History, xvii. 1208.

chusetts, were broad and decisive. All are summed up in the words of Washington, who was soon to be the representative of his country. He pronounced the issue to involve "the most essential and valuable rights of mankind."[1] The hour had its symbol. On the first American flag was inscribed the motto, "Liberty and Union."[2]

In this spirit Warren and the other popular leaders were conducting affairs in Massachusetts. Neither this province, Washington now said, nor any other province, desired, "separately or collectively, to set up for independence;" but, he added, "none of them will ever submit to the loss of those rights and privileges without which life, liberty, and property were insecure."[3] In this spirit of self-preservation, and by the advice of a body whose voice was as the voice of American law, the local popular leaders went on during the winter with the work of military preparation. Meantime the donations flowed into Boston; and the letters which accompanied them continued to be "on the rising tenor." One of them, from Durham, New Hampshire, addressed to the Boston committee, was printed. "What you receive," the Durham committee say, "comes not from the opulent, but mostly from the industrious yeo-

[1] Letter, Oct. 9, 1774.

[2] At Taunton, in October, 1774, a "Union flag" was raised on the top of a liberty pole, "with the words LIBERTY AND UNION thereon." At Shutesbury, the inhabitants erected a pole with a flag of liberty. In January, 1775, the sleds containing wood for the inhabitants of Boston bore a "Union flag."

William Molineux died on the 22d of October, after an illness of three days, at the age of fifty-eight. He is characterized in an obituary notice "as a noted merchant." His time was applied to the public service with unremitted ardor. He is called the friend of mankind. There is an obituary notice of him in the "Boston Gazette" of October 24, 1774.

[3] Letter, Oct. 9, 1774.

manry in this parish. We have but few persons of affluence; but they cheerfully contributed. . . . This is considered by us not as a gift, or an act of charity, but of justice to those who are bravely standing in the gap between us and slavery, defending the common interest of the whole continent. . We can with truth assure you, gentlemen, that, in this quarter, we are engaged, to a man, in your defence, and in defence of the common cause. We are ready to communicate of our substance largely, as your necessities require; and, with our estates, to give our lives, and mingle our blood with yours, in the common sacrifice to liberty."[1]

Throughout the province, ordinary pursuits gave way to the duty which engrossed all minds and stirred all hearts; for the great business of the hour was organization, in compliance with the recommendations of the Continental and the Provincial Congresses. The inhabitants, in their several towns, now signed agreements to meet for military drill, elected officers, and entered into pledges to obey, at a minute's warning, a summons to take the field. These bands of citizen-soldiers, on parade days, repaired to the churches, where the village pastor prayed for strength from on High; and the village Hampdens uttered the exhortation to fight to the last, if need be, for the ancient liberties.[2]

[1] This letter was printed in the journals in December.

[2] We hear from Cohasset (the only free port in the county of Suffolk), that, on the 17th of last month, the military company in that place appeared in the field, lodged their arms, and marched to the meeting-house. Their officers then voluntarily resigned their commissions; a moderator and clerk were chosen; after which, the Rev. Mr. Browne, by desire of the moderator, made a prayer, and delivered an animated speech on the exigencies of the times. They then sang the former part of the 44th Psalm, and proceeded to the choice of officers,

The national spirit of the time is embodied in the following song, which is ascribed to Warren,[1] and was printed this year in the newspapers: —

A SONG ON LIBERTY.
To the tune of the " British Grenadier."

That seat of science, Athens, and earth's proud mistress, Rome,
Where now are all their glories? We scarce can find their tomb.
Then guard your rights, Americans, nor stoop to lawless sway;
Oppose, oppose, oppose, oppose for North America.

Proud Albion bowed to Cæsar, and numerous hosts before,
To Picts, to Danes, to Normans, and many masters more;
But we can boast Americans have never fallen a prey ·
Huzza! huzza! huzza! huzza for free America!

We led fair Freedom hither, and lo! the desert smiled;
A paradise of pleasure now opened in the wild:
Your harvest, bold Americans, no power shall snatch away;
Preserve, preserve, preserve your rights in free America.

Torn from a world of tyrants, beneath this western sky
We formed a new dominion, a land of liberty:
The world shall own we're freemen here, and such will ever be.
Huzza! huzza! huzza! huzza for love and liberty!

God bless this maiden climate, and through her vast domain
May hosts of heroes cluster that scorn to wear a chain,
And blast the venal sycophants who dare our rights betray:
Assert yourselves, yourselves, yourselves for brave America.

Lift up your hearts, my heroes, and swear, with proud disdain,
The wretch that would ensnare you shall spread his net in vain:
Should Europe empty all her force, we'd meet them in array,
And shout huzza! huzza! huzza! huzza for brave America!

The land where Freedom reigns shall still be masters of the main,
In giving laws and freedom to subject France and Spain;
And all the isles o'er ocean spread shall tremble and obey
The prince who rules by Freedom's laws in North America.[2]

when the three worthy gentlemen who had lately borne commissions were unanimously chosen to be their *leaders*. They cheerfully accepted the trust, fully sensible that all authority under God is derived constitutionally from the people. — *Mass. Gazette, Dec.* 16, 1774.

[1] Duyckinck's Cyclopedia, i. 443.

[2] I copy this song from the "Massachusetts Spy" of May 26, 1774. It differs in arrangement, and materially in sentiment, from the copy in Duyckinck's "Cyclopedia of American Literature," vol. i. 443. It is said here of Warren, " His 'Free America,' written not long before his lamented death, shows that he possessed facility as a versifier."

CHAPTER XIII.

WARREN'S SECOND ORATION.

WARREN AND THE COMMITTEES. — THE STRUGGLE IN EUROPE. — THE POSITION OF MASSACHUSETTS. — FRANKLIN AND THE MINISTRY. — MILITARY PREPARATIONS. — THE SECOND PROVINCIAL CONGRESS. THE COMMITTEE OF SAFETY. — PUBLIC OPINION. — WARREN'S SECOND ORATION.

1775. JANUARY TO MARCH.

"I AM convinced that our existence as a free people absolutely depends on acting with spirit and vigor. The ministry are even yet doubtful whether we are in earnest when we declare our intention to preserve our liberty."[1] These words were written by Warren, and he was interpreting them by efficient action. The journals of the committee of public safety show clearly enough the nature of some of his service. One of the January votes was, "that Dr. Warren be desired to wait on Colonel Robinson," in relation to securing certain brass cannon and seven-inch mortars; and they ordered supplies of arms and ammunition to be deposited at Concord and Worcester.[2]

The inspection committee, on which Warren was placed by the town, grew directly out of the action of the Continental Congress. It is stated in the Boston journals of the 5th of January, "that all the southern provinces have heartily adopted the reso-

[1] Letter, Feb. 10, 1775. [2] Journals of the Committee of Safety.

lutions of the late respectable Continental Congress, and are taking proper steps to carry them into full execution;" and, a few days later (Jan. 9), it is reported that the assemblies of Rhode Island, Connecticut, Pennsylvania, and Maryland had met, and taken steps to carry the whole of these measures into execution. It is added, "In the other colonies, where the assemblies have not yet met, they are all with vigor and unanimity exerting themselves in the same important and glorious cause; so that, it is thought, there never was framed a set of human laws that were more strictly and religiously observed than these will be." When petitioners of Marshfield applied to General Gage for leave to hold a meeting "according to the Act of Parliament," Samuel Adams wrote in a letter, "They will be dealt with according to the law of the Continental Congress, the laws of which are more observed throughout this continent than any man's laws whatever." It was one of the duties of the inspection committees and the committees of correspondence to see that the non-importation agreement was strictly observed; and the newspapers contain many advertisements of cargoes of vessels to be sold by auction, under the direction of these committees, and "agreeably to the American Congress Association." In some instances, freight in vessels that had violated this agreement was thrown overboard, which was the case with an invoice of salt, coal, and tiles that arrived at Charleston, South Carolina; the committee being present.

The progress of events in America, made known through the press, was attracting more and more the attention of the political world. The British minister at the Court of Vienna, Sir John Murray Keith, wrote, "There is not a man of sense in Europe who does not think, that the question now in agitation between Great Britain and her colonies is one of the most important, as well as most singular, that has been canvassed for many centuries."[1] The Americans, who had to meet this question, uttered the same sentiment in private letters, in official papers, and through the press. Well might a looker-on, far away from the din of the struggle, pronounce the question "most singular;" for the authoritative voices of the two American centres of action — the Continental Congress, and the Provincial Congress of Massachusetts — were not only disclaiming a desire of independence, but were professing affectionate fealty to the king. The men who spoke for Massachusetts were solemnly pronouncing the controversy to be a calamity, and were ordering that prayers be offered to Almighty God, "that his blessing might rest upon all the British Empire, upon George III., their rightful king, and upon all the royal family, that they might all be great and lasting blessings to the world."[2]

It ought ever to be borne in mind, that, from the beginning of the controversy, the people of Massachusetts made no demands on the sovereignty for an extension of popular power. The following candid, temperate, and just summary of their past action and position was printed in the "Philadelphia Journal" of the 1st of January, 1775: "The people of Massachusetts have hitherto acted purely on the defensive:

---

[1] Keith's Memoirs, ii. 35; Letter, Jan. 21, 1775.

[2] Vote of the Provincial Congress, Feb. 16, 1775, recommending a day of fasting and prayer.

they have only opposed those new regulations which were instantly to have been executed, and would have annihilated all our rights. For this absolutely necessary and manly step, they have received the approbation of the Continental Congress, one of the most respectable assemblies in the world. They aim at no independency, nor any thing new, but barely the preservation of their old rights."

Since the passage of the Act authorizing the East-India Company to export tea to America, the issue had been on the original question of taxation; but the ministry, alarmed at the union of the colonies, declared now to Franklin, through friendly agents, that they would concede the point of taxation, — would repeal the Tea Act and the Boston Port Act; but that the two Acts relating to Massachusetts — the Regulating Act and the Act concerning the administration of justice — must remain as permanent amendments to the local constitution, and as a standing example of the power of parliament. When the momentous issue was narrowed down to the preservation of old customs and rights, the reply of the great American was prompt and decided, and spoke the united voice of the party who constituted the majority of his countrymen: "While parliament claims the right of altering American constitutions at pleasure, there can be no agreement; for we are rendered unsafe in every privilege."[1] Subsequently, Franklin sent, through Lord Howe to Lord North, the following as his last words· "The Massachusetts must suffer all the hazards and mischiefs of war rather than admit the alteration of their charter and laws by

[1] Bancroft, vii. 224.

parliament. They that can give up essential liberty to obtain a little temporary safety deserve neither liberty nor safety."[1]

The journals reported from time to time the concentration of military and naval force at Boston, and said that, when the whole of the army should arrive, it would consist of about sixty-four hundred men. On the 18th of January, General Gage wrote to Lord Dartmouth, " The eyes of all are turned upon Great Britain; and it is the opinion of most people, that, if a respectable force is seen in the field, the most obnoxious of the leaders seized, and a pardon proclaimed for all others, Government will come off victorious, and with less opposition than was expected a few months ago." A letter was now on the way from Lord Dartmouth to the general, containing directions, as " the first essential step to be taken towards re-establishing Government," to arrest and imprison the principal actors and abettors in the Provincial Congress. On the 21st of January, a gentleman in Boston, in writing to his friend in London, said that the Continental Congress " had drawn a line by the banks of the ocean;" had " claimed their own exclusive jurisdiction in all interior concerns and in all cases of taxation;" had " left to Great Britain the exclusive sovereignty of the ocean, and over their trade ;" and had placed both upon constitutional principles; and that " it was in vain, it was delirium, it was frenzy, to think of dragooning three millions of English people out of their liberties."[2] He added,

[1] Bancroft, vii. 242.

[2] From the southern papers we learn, that, agreeably to the recommendation of the Grand Council of America, the several colonies as far as Georgia were continuing their collections for the poor sufferers by the execrable Port Bill.

There is a spirit prevailing here such as I never saw before. I remember the conquest of Louisburg, in 1745; I remember the spirit here when the Duke D'Anville's squadron was upon this coast, when forty thousand men marched down to Boston, and were mustered and numbered upon the Common, complete in arms, from this province only in three weeks; but I remember nothing like what I have seen these six months past." Neither the king, his ministers, nor the Tory majority in parliament, could be convinced "by the blaze of genius and the burst of thought"[1] of Camden, Chatham, and Burke, that there was any thing more serious than "the acts of a rude rabble, without plan, without concert, and without conduct."[2] The first lord of the admiralty declared "the Americans were neither disciplined nor capable of discipline."

The task of restraining the rash among the patriots was becoming harder every day. The leaders on both sides now expected the commencement of war. In the judgment of Lord Dartmouth, if the arrest of the members of the Provincial Congress should occasion hostilities, it were better that the conflict should begin on such grounds than in a riper state of the rebellion. Samuel Adams, on the 29th of January, wrote, "We appear to be in a state of hostility; the general, with —— regiments, with a very few adherents, on one side, and all the rest of the inhabitants

---

What can better manifest the union of the colonies, and their firm affection for and sympathy with each other, than these donations, or place in a more striking point of light the inhumanity of that parliament which has made such large and distant charities absolutely necessary to prevent thousands of the inhabitants from starving? — *Essex Gazette, Jan.* 15, 1775.

[1] Josiah Quincy, in Gordon's History, i. 446.   [2] Dartmouth's words.

of the province, backed by all the colonies, on the other. . . . They (the people) are resolved not to be the aggressors in an open quarrel with the troops; but, animated with an unquenchable love of liberty, they will support their righteous claim to it to the utmost extremity.'

On the 1st of February, the second Provincial Congress assembled at Cambridge, of which Warren was a member and a prominent actor. It was composed largely of the members of the preceding congress. Warren's name appears in connection with most of the proceedings. On the 9th, the congress re-appointed a committee of safety in a resolve which reads, "That the Hon. John Hancock, Esq., Dr. Joseph Warren, Dr. Benjamin Church, jun., Mr. Richard Devens, Captain Benjamin White, Colonel Joseph Palmer, Mr. Abraham Watson, Colonel Azor Orne, Mr. John Pigeon, Colonel William Heath, and Mr. Jabez Fisher, be, and hereby are, appointed a committee of safety, to continue until the farther order of this or some other congress or House of Representatives of this province." It was made their duty to observe the movements of all who should attempt to carry into execution the Regulating Act, or the Act relating to the administration of justice; and five of them, one to be an inhabitant of Boston, were authorized, in case they should judge such an attempt was to be made, "to alarm, muster, and cause to be assembled with the utmost expedition," so much of the militia of the province as they should judge to be necessary to oppose such attempts. Another resolve authorized "Hon. Jedediah Preble, Esq., Hon. Artemas Ward, Esq., Colonel Seth Pomeroy, Colonel

John Thomas, and Colonel William Heath" to be general officers, who, as such, for the purpose of resisting all attempts to execute the two Acts, should command the said militia "so long as it should be retained by the committee of safety, and no longer." One of the committee of supplies, Mr. Hall, had declined; and Elbridge Gerry was chosen in his place.

Warren, on the day these resolves were passed, was in Boston.[1] On the next day, while a committee

[1] A letter, dated Boston, Feb. 6, 1775, says that the Tories, "sensible what effects a continental union must produce," were straining every nerve to counteract the measures of a general congress. The following handbill was distributed this day through the town, — which shows the Tory side at this juncture: —

"Friends, countrymen, and citizens, — Have you read and weighed His Majesty's speech? the address of the lords and commons of Great Britain? I fear we have got into the wrong box; therefore let us not any longer be led by frenzy, but seize upon and deliver up to justice (at once) those who have seduced us from our duty and happiness, or, depend upon it, they will leave us in the lurch! Nay, I am assured some of them (who had property) have already mortgaged all their substance for fear of confiscation: but that shall not save their their necks; for I am one (of forty misled people) who will watch their motion, and not suffer them to escape the punishment due to the disturbers of our repose. Remember the fate of Wat Tyler, and think how vain it is for Jack, Sam, or Will to war against Great Britain, now she is in earnest! It is greatly inferior to the giants waging war against Olympus! These had strength; but what have we? Our leaders are desperate bankrupts! Our country is without money, stores, or necessaries of war, — without one place of refuge or defence! If we were called together, we should be a confused herd, without any disposition to obedience, without a general of ability to direct and guide us; and our numbers would be our destruction! Never did a people rebel with so little reason; therefore our conduct cannot be justified before God! Never did so weak a people dare to contend with so powerful a State; therefore it cannot be justified by prudence. It is all the consequence of the arts of crafty knaves over weak minds and wild enthusiasts, who, if we continue to follow, will lead us to inevitable ruin. Rouse, rouse, ye Massachusetians, while it be yet time! Ask pardon of God, submit to our king and parliament, whom we have wickedly and grievously offended. Eyes had we, but we saw not; neither have we heard with our ears. Let not our posterity curse us for having wantonly lost the estates that should have been theirs, or for entailing misery upon them, by implicitly adhering to the promises of a few desperadoes. Let us seize our seducers, make peace with our mother-country, and save ourselves and children. Amen.

"A YEOMAN OF SUFFOLK COUNTY.

"BOSTON, Sabbath Eve, Feb. 5, 1775."

of the congress were observing "the motion of the troops," said to be on their way to Cambridge, Warren sent the following letter to Samuel Adams, in which he evinced the spirit which impelled him to share with his countrymen the fortune of the day of Bunker Hill: —

Joseph Warren to Samuel Adams.

BOSTON, Feb. 10 1775.

DEAR SIR, — We were this morning alarmed with a report, that a party of soldiers was sent to Cambridge, with design to disperse the congress. Many here believed it was in consequence of what was yesterday published by their order. I confess I paid so much regard to it as to be sorry I was not with my friends; and, although my affairs would not allow of it, I went down to the Ferry in a chaise with Dr. Church, both determined to share with our brethren in any dangers that they might be engaged in: but we there heard, that the party had quietly passed the bridge, on their way to Roxbury; up[on] which we returned home. I have spent an hour this morning with Deacon Phillips, and am convinced that our existence as a free people absolutely depends in acting with spirit and vigor. The ministry are even yet doubtful whether we are in earnest when we declare our resolution to preserve our *liberty*; and the common people there are made to believe we are a nation of noisy cowards. The ministry are supported in their plan of enslaving us by assurances that we have not courage enough to fight for our freedom. Even they who wish us well dare not openly declare for us, lest we should meanly desert ourselves, and leave them alone to contend with Administration, who they know will be, politically speaking, omnipotent, if America should submit to them. Deacon Phillips, Dr. Church, and myself are all fully of opinion, that it would be a very proper step, should the congress order a schooner to be sent home with an accurate state of facts, as it is certain that letters to and from our friends in England are intercepted, and every method taken to prevent the people of Great Britain from gaining a knowledge of the true state of this country. I intended to have consulted you, had I been at Cambridge to-day, on the propriety of a motion for that purpose, but must defer it until to-morrow. One thing, however, I have upon my mind, which I think ought to be immediately attended to. The resolution of the congress, published yesterday, greatly affects one Wheston, who has hitherto been thought firm in our cause, but is now making carriages for the army. He assisted in getting the four field-pieces to Colonel Robinson's, at Dorchester, where they are now. He says the discovery of this " will make him ; " and he threatens to make the discovery. Perhaps resentment and the hope of gain may together prevail with him to act the traitor. Dr. Church and I are clear, that it ought not to be one minute in his power to point out the general the place in which they are kept; but that they ought to be removed without [delay]. Pray do not omit to obtain proper orders concerning them. I am, sir, in great haste,

Your very humble servant, Jos. WARREN.[1]

Please to present my affectionate regards to Colonel Hancock and other worthy friends.

Warren sat in congress on the next day; for he is named with Hawley, Hancock, and others, on a committee to report a resolve, expressing "the determination of this people coolly and resolutely to support their rights at all hazards." At the next meeting, he was placed on a committee of three, to consider what it was expedient to do for the encouragement of the manufacture of saltpetre; and, on the last day of the session, was on a committee to report a resolve to create a committee to correspond with the neighboring governments; and then, with Hancock, Cushing, Gerry, Samuel Adams, and Heath, he was elected by ballot on this committee, to whom were added, by hand-vote, Devens, Palmer, and Gill. A conference was held, through a committee, with a delegation present from Connecticut. Having appointed the sixteenth of March as a day of fasting and prayer, the congress adjourned until the twenty-third of March.

[1] This letter is copied from the original, in Warren's handwriting, in the possession of Mr. Bancroft.

The letter of Warren shows how deeply he was interested in the proceedings of this body; and the committees on which he was placed indicate the large confidence which the members felt in him.

This congress issued an address "To the inhabitants of the Massachusetts Bay." On this being reported, it was "read and considered in paragraphs," and then ordered to be recommitted for amendments, when Dr. Church and Dr. Warren were added to the committee. The report made by the committee was accepted. It was printed in a pamphlet containing an abstract of the proceedings of the former Provincial Congress. Its tone is unusually solemn. It renewed the recommendation to carry into execution the plan projected by the wisdom of the whole continent, as collected in the general congress. It deprecated "a rupture with the mother-State;" yet it urged every preparation for necessary defence. It recommended the people to have proper magazines duly prepared, and strictly to adhere to the resolutions of the several congresses, on the principle that "subjects generally pay obedience to the laws of the land;" urging this weighty consideration: "We can conceive of no greater punishment for the breach of human laws than the misery that must inevitably follow your disregarding the plans that have, by your authority, with that of the whole continent, been projected." The closing words are, " Your conduct hitherto, under the severest trials, has been worthy of you as men and Christians. . . . The whole continent of America has this day cause to rejoice in your firmness. We trust you will still continue steadfast; and, having regard to the dignity of your characters as freemen, and those generous sentiments resulting from your natural and political connections, you will never submit your necks to the galling yoke of despotism prepared for you; but, with a proper sense of your dependence on God, nobly defend those rights which Heaven gave, and no man ought to take from us." It will be observed, that the inhabitants of Massachusetts are appealed to as though they were in "natural and political connections" with a common country, and not as though they were, or aspired to be, a separate, independent, and sovereign nation.

On the day after the adjournment of the Provincial Congress, Governor Gage informed Lord Dartmouth of its proceedings, remarking, "If this Provincial Congress is not to be deemed a rebellious meeting, surely some of their resolves are rebellious, though they affect not to order, but only to recommend measures to the people." Three days later, he again wrote Lord Dartmouth of this body, and evinced considerable anxiety in relation to an assumption of Government and the Connecticut delegation: "I have tried to get intelligence if they had presumed to usurp the Government entirely, and choose a governor, and am informed that the measure was talked of, but could not be carried. Some people from Connecticut, termed a committee, and amongst them the governor's son, came to the congress; which caused much speculation, and of course many reports. Some say their business was to offer an aid of men... I can only yet discover that it was a visit of curiosity." Not unlikely the information relative to an assumption of Government was communicated by Church; for it was now said that there was a traitor in the congress.

Four days after Warren had acted so conspicuous a part in the Provincial Congress, he addressed the following calm and important letter to Arthur Lee: —

BOSTON, Feb. 20, 1775.

DEAR SIR, — My friend, Mr. Adams, favored me with the sight of your last letter. I am sincerely glad of your return to England, as I think your assistance was never more wanted there than at present. It is truly astonishing that Administration should have a doubt of the resolution of the Americans to make the last appeal rather than submit to wear the yoke prepared for their necks. We have waited with a degree of patience which is seldom to be met with: but I will venture to assert, that there has not been any great alloy of cowardice; though both friends and enemies seem to suspect us of want of courage. I trust the event, which I confess I think is near at hand, will confound our enemies, and rejoice those who wish well to us. It is time for Britain to take some serious steps towards a reconciliation with her colonies. The people here are weary of watching the measures of those who are endeavoring to enslave them: they say they have been spending their time for ten years in counteracting the plans of their adversaries. They, many of them, begin to think that the difference between [them] will never be amicably settled; but that they shall always be subject to new affronts from the caprice of every British minister. They even sometimes speak of an open rupture with Great Britain, as a state preferable to the present uncertain condition of affairs. And although it is true that the people have yet a very warm affection for the British nation, yet it sensibly decays. They are loyal subjects to the king; but they conceive that they do not swerve from their allegiance by opposing any measures taken by any man or set of men to deprive them of their liberties. They conceive that they are the king's enemies who would destroy the Constitution; for the king is annihilated when the Constitution is destroyed.

It is not yet too late to accommodate the dispute amicably. But I am of opinion, that, if once General Gage should lead his troops into the country, with design to enforce the late Acts of Parliament, Great Britain may take her leave, at least of the New-England colonies, and, if I mistake not, of all America. If there is any wisdom in the nation, God grant it may be speedily called forth! Every day, every hour, widens the breach. A Richmond, a Chatham, a Shelburne, a

Camden, with their noble associates, may yet repair it; and it is a work which none but the greatest of men can conduct. May you be successful and happy in your labors for the public safety!

I am, sir, with great respect, your very humble servant,

Dr. LEE. JOS. WARREN.[1]

This valuable letter contains an off-hand analyzation of the aspect of a great movement. During the next four days, the committee of safety held meetings in Charlestown, and Warren was present. The business transacted was important. The unusual record is made in the journal of the proceedings on the 21st, that the votes were passed unanimously. Thus: "Voted, unanimously, by the committee of safety, that the committee of supplies purchase all kinds of warlike stores sufficient for an army of fifteen thousand men." On the next day, the business consisted of the details of preparation, one of them being a provision for the re-assembling of congress on the arrival of the "re-enforcements coming to General Gage." On the 23d, the committee met at forty-five minutes after seven in the morning; and, besides other matters, it was agreed, that a letter should be prepared, and be ready for transmission to the commanding officers of the militia and minute-men, directing them, on receipt of it, to assemble "one-fourth part of the militia;" and that this should be printed, and that certain couriers should deliver the letters. The committee of supplies were ordered to buy "twenty hogsheads of rum, and send them to Concord." On the 24th, provision was made for the road

---

[1] I copy this letter from the original, in Warren's handwriting, in the archives of Harvard-College Library. I am indebted to the courteous librarian, John L. Sibley, Esq., for every facility in the use of books and papers of this institution.

each courier should take when he carried the letters to the militia to take the field. The committee now adjourned to meet on the 7th of March, at the house of Captain Steadman, of Cambridge. Warren, during the proceedings of these four days, was placed on several special committees. One vote desired him to apply to the company in Boston formerly under Major Paddock, to learn "how many of them might be depended on, officers and men, to form an artillery company, when the constitutional army of the province should take the field."

The Provincial Congress had provided for certain "rules and regulations for the officers and men of the constitutional army which might be raised in the province" (Feb. 10). The committee of safety had fixed this army at fifteen thousand men; but they were to be only conditionally summoned into the field. Among the manuscripts of this committee is a remarkable letter, addressed, on the 22d of February, by that admirable patriot Joseph Hawley to Thomas Cushing, enjoining upon him (Cushing), as he loved his country, to use his utmost influence with the committee of safety, that the militia be not mustered, and that hostilities be not commenced, until Massachusetts "had the express categorical decision of the continent, that the time is absolutely come that hostilities ought to begin, and that they would support us in continuing them." All the assurance or security of such effectual and continued aid as would be absolutely necessary, Hawley said, "was contained in a resolution of about six lines, and they consisting of terms and expressions not the most definite or of certain or precise meaning. The words used in the resolution to state the case wherein hostilities are to be commenced, are, in my opinion, by far too loose; to wit, 'when the Acts shall be attempted to be carried into execution by force,' as well as the words made use of to secure the aid of the colonies; to wit, 'All America ought to support them in such opposition;' not that they will actually support them, but a mere declaration that it would be reasonable and just that such support should be afforded. Is this a treaty, offensive and defensive, of sufficient precision to make us secure of the effectual aid of the other colonies in a war with Great Britain?"[1] There was no bolder spirit or more sterling character than Joseph Hawley; but he shrunk from the step of war without an assurance of the full sanction of the American Union. At this time, Josiah Quincy, jun., was about embarking at London for home; and he was commissioned by the friends of the cause abroad to enjoin on the people of Massachusetts " by no means to take any steps of great consequence, unless on a sudden emergency, without the advice of the Continental Congress."[2]

Military events of an irritating nature rendered the preservation of the peace difficult, and the occurrence of "a sudden emergency" imminent. Such were the dismissal of Hancock from the command of the Cadets, the seizure of arms and ammunition, and the employment of the military to sustain civil action. To counteract the "American Association," which had been adopted by the Continental Congress, the Tory party inaugurated a "Loyal Association,"

---

[1] Letter of Joseph Hawley to Thomas Cushing, Feb. 22, 1775.
[2] Gordon, i. 467.

the signers of which pledged themselves to oppose the proceedings of committees and congresses as the acts of unconstitutional assemblies. On the application of a portion of the people of Marshfield, who had signed this Tory pledge, General Gage stationed a small force in this town, which, being under good discipline, did not disturb the inhabitants, were not molested, and remained until the 19th of April. This forbearance was ascribed by the Tories to the cowardice of the minute-men. In continuance of the policy of disarming the patriots Colonel Leslie, on Sunday the 26th of February, was sent from Boston with a body of troops to seize certain military stores deposited at Salem; but the spirited conduct of the inhabitants defeated the object of this expedition, and the detachment thought itself fortunate, in view of the minute-men who spontaneously gathered, in getting safely back to Boston. Even this show of hostility did not provoke the committee of safety to give the order for a general muster of the troops into the field. The militia and minute-men continued to meet for drill in the towns all over the province; and, in many cases, the expenses were met by appropriations from the town-treasury.

This was the state of things when the king, not harboring a thought of concession, "left the choice of war or peace" to depend on the submission of Massachusetts to the Regulating Act.[1] As the sword was hanging by a thread, the words sent to its patriots, along with the donations which had now continued in an uninterrupted flow for nine months, grew more and more tender. The committee of Fal-

[1] Bancroft, vii. 174.

mouth (now Portland), which, like Charlestown, was soon to become a holocaust for American liberty, said of its contribution, " It is for suffering brethren, who are standing in the gap between us and slavery. ... We are but few in number, and of small ability; and, as we earn our bread by the sweat of our brow, shall ever hold in utter detestation both men and measures that would rob us of the fruits of our toil; and are ready with our labor, with our lives, and with our estates, to stand or fall in the common cause of liberty. And, if we fall, we shall die like men and like Christians, and enjoy the glorious privileges of the sons of God." The reply of the committee on donations was scarcely less touching: " Your letter, though short, is very refreshing. Though the lines are few, the matter is very comprehensive. What could you have said more ? The committee are greatly obliged, and not a little strengthened. You will please accept their sincere thanks for that cordial affection expressed in your letter, and manifested in a way the most convincing. May the Lord bless you and reward you a thousand fold!"[1] This interchange of sentiment shows the silken cords that were intwining communities into the sacred relations of country, by cementing a union, not defined on parchment, but fragrant with the blossoming of fraternal sympathy.

The press mirrored each fresh detail in the march of events towards American nationality. It now contained instalments of foreign intelligence, showing England's fierce temper; reports of the regiments

---

[1] These letters will be found printed in the Collections of the Massachusetts Historical Society, 4th series, vol. iv.

sent to Boston; the parades of Alarm Lists through the colony; the choice of military officers in every county of Delaware, Maryland, and Virginia; the resolves of Fairfax County, adopted at a meeting when "Colonel George Washington was in the chair,"[1] taxing every tithable person for the purchase of arms; the expedition of Leslie at Salem; "the alarm that flew like lightning;" the last number of "Novanglus," proving the destruction of the tea "just, proper, and right," avowing that committees of correspondence "were intended by Providence for great events," and declaring that Britain could restore harmony by desisting from taxing the colonies, and "interfering with their internal concerns." These details indicate the sentiment, which, suggested by the common sense and heart, passed from mouth to mouth, in the home, in the street, in the club, in the caucus, in the public meeting, formed public opinion, and was a type of the political momentum of modern times.

The American mind at the time interpreted rightly the importance of the movement. Two utterances showing this, are recorded side by side in the journals,—the memorable Charge of Judge William Henry Drayton, enjoining a maintenance of the laws and the rights of the constitution at the hazard of life and fortune; and the "Novanglus"[2] of John Adams, claiming for the basis of the patriots the principles that all men were by nature equal; that kings are but the ministers of the people, holding delegated power;

[1] Essex Gazette, March 7, 1775.
[2] The "Essex Gazette" of Feb. 21, 1775, contains the second number of "Novanglus," and the Charge, pronounced "remarkable," of William Henry Drayton, delivered to the several grand juries in South Carolina.

and that the people, whenever power was used to oppress them, had a right to resume it and place it in other hands. Rising above the provincial and the theological, the narrow and the transient, the patriot urged, that these "were the principles of Aristotle and Plato, of Livy and Cicero, of Sidney, Harrington, and Locke, — the principles of nature and eternal reason." As the actors in these scenes mused on the development of these principles, they reproduced as applicable, an old prophecy of the future glory of America: —

> "But (if I fail not in my augury,
> And who can better judge events than I?)
> Long-rolling years shall late bring on the times
> When with your gold-debauched and ripened crimes
> Europe (the world's most noble part) shall fall,
> Upon her banished gods and virtue call
> In vain; while foreign and domestic war
> At once shall her distracted bosom tear
> Forlorn and to be pitied even by you.
> Meanwhile your rising glory you shall view:
> Wit, learning, virtue, discipline of war,
> Shall for protection to your world repair
> And fix a long illustrious empire there.
> Your native gold (I would not have it so,
> But fear the event) in time will follow too:
> Late Destiny shall high exalt your reign,
> Whose pomp no crowds of slaves, a needless train,
> Nor gold (the rabble's idol) shall support,
> Like Montezume's or Guanapaci's court;
> But such true grandeur as old Rome maintained
> Where fortune was a slave, and virtue reigned."[1]

The patriots now designed to commemorate the Boston massacre. This was usually done in the

[1] This was printed in the "Essex Gazette" of Feb. 21, 1775, where it is said to be copied from the close of Abraham Cowley's fifth "Book of Plants," p. 130, translated into English, and published in London, 1689. It is the edition of 1711.

In the "Massachusetts Spy" of the 10th of March, 1774, is a "Song for the Fifth of March," which was written for this paper. It contains a prediction

town-meeting; but it was one of the objects of the Regulating Act to suppress meetings for such a purpose. The main theme of the discourse on the occasion was the danger, to a free people, of standing armies in time of peace; but this theme would have to be treated in the presence of the British army. Then the Tory party of the town was numerous and exultant. "We have," Samuel Adams wrote on the 4th, "almost all the Tories of note in the province in this town, to which they have fled for the general's protection. They affect the style of Rabshakeh; but the language of the people is, 'In the name of the Lord, we will tread down our enemies.'" It was given out that it would be at the price of the life to any man to speak of the massacre, and that the military were determined that reflection on the king or the royal family should not be allowed to pass with impunity. The duty which, when parties were irritated and exasperated to the verge of civil war, most men would not at least seek, it was characteristic of Warren's heroic nature to covet. At his own suggestion, he was appointed the orator. He sought the duty in no selfish spirit, but to enable him, as the

of the triumphs of "The American Ensign." There are phrases in this song similar to what may be found in Warren's letters. I copy the three closing verses, — the allusion is to Hancock, who was the orator: —

> "Blest Freedom's the prize, thither bend all your eyes;
> Stern valor each visage inflames:
> These lands they have won, and still claim as their own;
> And no tyrant shall ravish their claims.
>
> A ray of bright glory now beams from afar,
> Blest dawn of an empire to rise;
> The American ensign now sparkles a star,
> Which shall shortly flame wide through the skies.
>
> Strong knit is the band which unites the blest land,
> No demon the union can sever:
> Here's a glass to fair Freedom! come, give us your hand!
> May the ORATOR flourish for ever!"

organ of the community, to bear open testimony, that "the Americans would make the last appeal rather than submit to the yoke that was prepared for their necks; that their unexampled patience had no alloy of cowardice."[1] The popular leaders, in so critical a conjuncture, were naturally desirous to be sure of their man. "To-morrow," Samuel Adams wrote, "an oration is to be delivered by Dr. Warren. It was thought best to have an experienced officer in the political field on this occasion, as we may possibly be attacked in our trenches." The patriots looked forward to the day with deep interest, and not without apprehension.

The anniversary coming on Sunday, the commemoration took place on Monday. It is said that many people came in to the town from the country to take part in it, and there was "a prodigious concourse." This indicates that the streets were thronged as they are on a modern Fourth of July. In the morning, the citizens, "legally warned by an adjournment of the Port-bill meeting," assembled in Faneuil Hall, with Samuel Adams for the moderator, and transacted the usual business relative to the selection of the orator. It was reported, that the committee of the Old South Meeting-house were willing it should be used on the occasion; and the town adjourned to meet at half past eleven o'clock in the church.

The Old South was crowded. In the pulpit, which was draped in black, were the popular leaders, who, from year to year, had been selected by the people to be the exponents of their cause. Those named as being present, besides Samuel Adams and William

[1] Bancroft, vii. 256.

Cooper, the town-clerk, were Church, Hancock, and the selectmen. The moderator, observing several British officers standing in the aisles, requested the occupants of the front pews to vacate them, and courteously invited the strangers to occupy these seats; when about forty officers, dressed in their uniforms, filled these pews, or sat upon the pulpit stairs.

The audience consisted mainly of the actors in the public meetings of preceding years,— the men who had opposed the Revenue Acts, had protested against military rule, had summoned the convention of 1768, had demanded the removal of the troops, had organized committees of correspondence, had destroyed the tea, and had resisted the Regulating Act. They now felt that they were parts of an organization known as the "Grand American Union." As yet, this party did not desire independence; but one of their number — probably Warren — said, on this morning, in the press, that, if the ministry would not hearken to the wise and just proposals of the Continental Congress, it could be demonstrated by a million of reasons that the people must look forward to the last grand step for defence; that "the Americans would be compelled by the great law of nature to strike a decisive blow; and, following the example of the once oppressed United Provinces, publish a manifesto to the world, showing the necessity of dissolving their connection with a nation whose ministers were aiming at their ruin."[1] Warren's personal friends were determined to protect him from insult.

The audience manifested some impatience at a little

[1] Boston Evening Post, March 6, 1775.

delay in the appearance of the orator. He was prepared to meet violence, and rode in a chaise to a building opposite the Old South, there put on a robe, and, to avoid pressing through the crowd, went to the rear of the building, and, by a ladder, entered it through the window back of the pulpit. Classic and loving pens have drawn the traits of this type of American manhood: "Amiable, accomplished, prudent, energetic, eloquent, brave, he united the graces of a manly beauty to a lion heart, a sound mind, a safe judgment, and a firmness of purpose which nothing could shake.[1] He possessed a clear understanding, a strong mind, a disposition humane and generous, with manners easy, affable, and engaging, but zealous, active, and sanguine in the cause of his oppressed country.[2] He was a powerful orator, because he was a true man, and struggled for man's highest rights;[3] a patriot, in whom the flush of youth and the grace and dignity of manhood were combined, stood armed in the sanctuary of God to animate and encourage the sons of liberty, and to hurl defiance at their oppressors."[4] The tender words of eulogy uttered on the next commemoration of this day, after his spirit had passed from earth, and as "his loved idea and numberless virtues" were recalled, indicate the sympathy that existed between the speaker and the audience. "We mourn thine exit, illustrious shade, with undissembled grief; we venerate thine exalted character: we will erect a monument to thy memory in each of our

[1] Edward Everett's Speech, May 28, 1833.
[2] Mercy Warren: "History of the American Revolution," i. 221. She was a sister of James Otis, and knew Warren personally.
[3] Magoon's Orators of the Revolution, 159.
[4] Knapp's Biographical Sketches, 114.

grateful hearts, and to the latest ages will teach our tender infants to lisp the name of Warren with veneration and applause."[1]

The silence was oppressive as the orator advanced to the pulpit, and began in a firm tone of voice:[2] "My ever-honored fellow-citizens! It is not without the most humiliating conviction of my want of ability that I now appear before you; but the sense I have of the obligation I am under to obey the calls of my country at all times, together with an animated recollection of your indulgence, exhibited upon so many occasions, has induced me once more, undeserving as I am, to throw myself upon that candor which looks with kindness on the feeblest efforts of an honest mind." After an exordium imbued with the sterling virtue of sincerity, the orator proceeded to the conclusion with great energy and pathos, receiving the warm applause of friends, and occasional tokens of dissent from portions of his audience.

The orator, at the beginning, stated the following proposition: "That personal freedom is the natural right of every man, and that property, or an exclusive right to dispose of what he has honestly acquired by his own labor, necessarily arises therefrom, are truths which common sense has placed beyond the reach of contradiction; and no man or body of men can, without being guilty of flagrant injustice, claim a right to dispose of the persons or acquisitions of any other man or body of men, unless it can be proved that such a right had arisen from some compact between the parties in which it has been explicitly and freely granted."

[1] Peter Thacher's Oration, 1776.   [2] Knapp's Sketches.

The orator, in a retrospective survey of the settlement of the country "by the illustrious emigrants," delineated their labors and perils in these western regions, in rescuing them from their rudest state, and defending them from the savage; regarding man in this state, and even anarchy itself, as "infinitely less dangerous" than arbitrary power. Then this widely extended continent was let alone, and grew; Britain saw her commerce extend, and her wealth increase; the colonist found himself free, and thought himself secure; both countries, flourishing, happy, and united in affection, thought not of distinct or separate interests. The colonist gloried in the British fame. "He dwelt under his own vine and under his own fig-tree, and had none to make him afraid. He knew, indeed, that, by purchasing the manufactures of Great Britain, he contributed to its greatness; he knew that all the wealth that his labor produced centred in Great Britain: but that, far from exciting his envy, filled him with the highest pleasure; that thought supported him in all his toils. When the business of the day was passed, he solaced himself with the contemplation, or perhaps entertained his listening family with the recital, of some great, some glorious transaction which shines conspicuous in the history of Britain; or perhaps his elevated fancy led him to foretell, with a kind of enthusiastic confidence, the glory, power, and duration of an empire which should extend from one end of the earth to the other: he saw, or thought he saw, the British nation risen to a pitch of grandeur which cast a veil over the Roman glory, and, ravished with the præview, boasted a race of British kings whose names should echo through those realms where Cyrus, Alexander, and the Cæsars were unknown, — princes for whom millions of grateful subjects, redeemed from slavery and Pagan ignorance, should, with thankful tongues, offer up their prayers and praises to that transcendently great and beneficent Being by whom kings reign, and princes decree justice."

The orator then traced the rise and progress of the aggressions on the natural right of the colonists to enjoy personal freedom and representative government, "until this wicked policy had shaken the empire to its centre." Yet it was still persisted in, regardless of the voice of reason, deaf to the prayers and supplications, and unaffected by the flowing tears, of suffering millions; and, as a consequence, "the hearts of Britons and Americans, which had lately felt the generous glow of mutual confidence and love, now burn with jealousy and rage." The Briton looked on the American with an envious eye; and the American beheld the Briton as the ruffian, ready " first to take his property, and next, what is dearer to every virtuous man, the liberty of his country."

The orator then passed to the scenes arising out of the resolution of the British Administration to sustain this aggressive policy by force, which reason scorned to countenance, and placemen were unable to execute. He dwelt on the features of that night of unequalled horror, when the troops fired on the people, the sad remembrance of which took full possession of his soul. One of the victims was so mangled by the bayonet, that his brains fell upon the pavement; and to this the orator referred when he said, " Come, widowed mourner, here satiate thy grief:

behold thy murdered husband gasping on the ground; and, to complete the pompous show of wretchedness, bring in each hand thy infant children to bewail their father's fate. Take heed, ye orphan babes, lest, while your streaming eyes are fixed upon the ghastly corpse, your feet slide on the stones bespattered with your father's brains. Enough! This tragedy need not be heightened by an infant weltering in the blood of him that gave it birth. Nature, reluctant, shrinks already from the view, and the chilled blood rolls slowly backward to its fountain. We wildly stare about, and with amazement ask, Who spread this ruin round us? What wretch has dared deface the image of his God? Has haughty France or cruel Spain sent forth her myrmidons? Has the grim savage rushed again from the far distant wilderness? Or does some fiend, fierce from the depth of hell, with all the rancorous malice which the apostate damned can feel, twang her destructive bow, and hurl her deadly arrows at our breast? No: none of these; — but, how astonishing! it is the hand of Britain that inflicts the wound. The arms of George, our rightful king, have been employed to shed that blood which freely would have flown at his command when justice, or the honor of his crown, had called his subjects to the field." The cry that arose for revenge was referred to, and the departure of the troops as the close of this drama.

The orator then spoke of the existing exigency, when a gracious prince had been persuaded " to erect the hostile banner against a people ever affectionate and loyal to him, and his illustrious predecessors of the house of Hanover," and to enforce obedience to

Acts of Parliament destructive to liberty. Though armed men again filled the streets, the people were not intimidated, but resolved that liberty must be preserved. It was a Roman maxim, never to despair of the commonwealth. It may prove salutary now. "Short-sighted mortals see not the numerous links of small and great events which form the chain on which the fate of kings and nations is suspended." Ease has often made a people effeminate: hardship and danger have called forth virtues that commanded the applause of an admiring world. "Our country loudly calls you to be circumspect, vigilant, active, and brave. Perhaps (all-gracious Heaven avert it!) perhaps the power of Britain, a nation great in war, by some malignant influence, may be employed to enslave you. But let not even this discourage you. Her arms, 'tis true, have filled the world with terror; her troops have reaped the laurels of the field; her fleets have rode triumphant on the sea; and when or where did you, my countrymen, depart inglorious from the field of fight? You, too, can show the trophies of your forefathers' victories and your own; can name the fortresses and battles you have won; and many of you count the honorable scars of wounds received whilst fighting for your king and country. Where justice is the standard, heaven is the warrior's shield; but conscious guilt unnerves the arm that lifts the sword against the innocent."

The orator, in conclusion, said that the attempt of parliament to raise a revenue from America, and the denial of the right to do it, "had excited an almost universal inquiry into the rights of mankind in general," and created such a liberality of sentiment and jealousy of power as would, better than an adamantine wall, secure the people against the approach of despotism. The Boston Port Act had created those sympathetic ties that must for ever endear the people to each other, and "form those indissoluble bonds of friendship and affection on which the preservation of our rights so evidently depend; the mutilation of the charter has made every other colony jealous for its own; for this, if once submitted to by us, would set afloat the property and Government of every British settlement on the continent." The following are the closing paragraphs:—

"Our country is in danger, but not to be despaired of. Our enemies are numerous and powerful; but we have many friends, determined to be free, and heaven and earth will aid the resolution. On you depend the fortunes of America. You are to decide the important question on which rest the happiness and liberty of millions yet unborn. Act worthy of yourselves. The faltering tongue of hoary age calls on you to support your country. The lisping infant raises its suppliant hands, imploring defence against the monster, slavery. Your fathers look from their celestial seats with smiling approbation on their sons who boldly stand forth in the cause of virtue, but sternly frown upon the inhuman miscreant, who, to secure the loaves and fishes to himself, would breed a serpent to destroy his children.

"But, pardon me, my fellow-citizens, I know you want not zeal or fortitude. You will maintain your rights, or perish in the generous struggle. However difficult the combat, you will never decline it when freedom is the prize. An independence on Great Britain is not our aim. No: our wish is, that Britain and the colonies may, like the oak and ivy, grow and increase in strength together. But, whilst the infatuated plan of making one part of the empire slaves to the other is persisted in, the interest and safety of Britain as well as the colonies require that the wise measures recommended by the honorable, the Continental Congress be steadily pursued, whereby the unnatural contest between a parent honored and a child beloved may probably be brought to such an issue as that the peace and happiness of both may be established upon a lasting basis. But, if these pacific measures are ineffectual, and it appears that the only way to safety is through fields of blood, I know you will not turn your faces from our foes, but will undauntedly press forward until tyranny is trodden under foot, and you have fixed your adored goddess, Liberty, fast by a Brunswick's side, on the American throne.

"You, then, who nobly have espoused your country's cause; who generously have sacrificed wealth and ease; who have despised the pomp and show of tinselled greatness; refused the summons to the festive board; been deaf to the alluring calls of luxury and mirth; who have forsaken the downy pillow to keep your vigils by the midnight lamp for the salvation of your invaded country, that you may break the fowler's snare and disappoint the vulture of his prey, you then will reach this harvest of renown which you so justly have deserved. Your country shall pay her grateful tribute of applause. Even the children of your most inveterate enemies, ashamed to tell from whom they sprang, while they in secret curse their stupid, cruel parents, shall join the general voice of gratitude to those who broke the fetters which their fathers forged.

"Having redeemed your country, and secured the blessing to future generations, who, fired by your example, shall emulate your virtues, and learn from you the heavenly art of making millions happy, with heartfelt joy, with transports all your own, you cry, 'The glorious work is done!' Then drop the mantle to some young Elisha, and take your seats with kindred spirits in your native skies."[1]

---

[1] This oration was printed in the "Boston Gazette" of March 17, 1775. It was also printed in a pamphlet with the following titlepage: "An Oration delivered March sixth, 1775, at the request of the inhabitants of the town of Boston: to commemorate the bloody tragedy of the Fifth of March, 1770. By Dr. Joseph Warren.

Tantæ molis erat, Romanam condere gentem. — *Virgil's Æn.*
Qui, metuens vivit, liber mini non erit unquam. — *Hor. Epis.*

Boston: Printed by Edes and Gill, in Queen Street, and by Joseph Greenleaf in Union Street, near the Market, M.DCC.LXXV."

An edition was printed, probably in 1775, in a pamphlet in New York by John Anderson, at Beekman's Slip. The titlepage has no date.

It has several times since been reprinted. A volume of the orations commemorative of the Fifth-of-March tragedy, was printed in Boston, by Peter Edes, with a preface dated January, 1785. These orations, with Perez Morton's "Eulogy," were printed by William T. Clapp, Boston, the second edition of which is dated 1807.

The speeches in which prominent actors in Grecian and Roman story develop their policy or promote their objects, not words actually spoken, but what the relator thought were fitting to have been spoken, are regarded as valuable delineations of the temper of those times. But here are the words of an earnest and representative man, uttered on the eve of a great war, and in the presence of the military power whom he was soon to meet in the field. For the sake of the cause, —

"He dared to speak what some scarce dared to think."

His speech, imbued with the spirit of a high chivalry and faith, resounds with the clash of arms.[1]

Though it is said that some of the officers groaned as the enthusiastic audience applauded, yet they were generally quiet to the close of the oration. One of them, seated on the pulpit stairs, in the course of the delivery, held up one of his hands with several pistol bullets on the open palm, when the orator, observing the action, gracefully dropped a white handkerchief on them.[2] After the delivery, when it was moved that the thanks of the town be presented to the orator for the oration " on the commemoration of the horrid massacre," some of the officers struck their canes on the floor, others hissed, others exclaimed, "Oh fie, fie!"[3] which was understood as a cry of fire, and

[1] Magoon's Orators of the American Revolution, 167.
[2] Everett's Life of Warren, 182.
[3] Several accounts of this disturbance have been printed. The following is from manuscript in J. Greene's "Almanack," loaned to me by Dr. S. A. Green : —
"March 6. Oration delivered at the Old South Meeting-house, by Dr. Joseph Warren. After which a number of the army, in particular Captain B.' Chapman, of the Eighteenth, and ———, of the Royal Irish, put on their hats when the town was upon business, nominating persons, holding up their hands

there was a scene of panic. The patriots were prepared for any exigency. The Northenders, who idolized Warren, did not mean to be trifled with. "The assembly," Samuel Adams says, "was irritated to the greatest degree, and confusion ensued. They (the officers), however, did not gain their end, which was apparently to break up the meeting; for order was soon restored, and we proceeded regularly and finished the business.[1] I am persuaded, that, were it

in the negative after a full vote, and, when the motion was making for the next oration, raising their voices, striking their canes on the floor, and by other indecent and insolent conduct, as far as in their power, endeavored to affront the town, and, if possible, make a disturbance."

[1] The following is the official record connected with this oration

"At a meeting of the freeholders and other inhabitants of the town of Boston, legally warned, at Faneuil Hall, March 6, 1775, by adjournment of the Port-bill meeting, Mr. Samuel Adams, moderator, —

"The committee, appointed by the town, the 5th of March last, to apply to a proper gentleman to deliver an oration on the 5th of March instant, to perpetuate the memory of the horrid massacre perpetrated on the evening of the Fifth of March, 1770, by a party of soldiers under the order and eye of Captain Thomas Preston, of the Twenty-ninth Regiment, reported:

"That, having met together for the purpose mentioned in the town's vote, they had made choice of Joseph Warren, Esq., to deliver an oration on the 6th of March instant, who had accordingly accepted of such service.

"The foregoing report having been made by Mr. Samuel Adams, chairman of the committee, the question was put, whether the same shall be accepted. Passed in the affirmative.

"Upon a motion made, the town took into consideration what time would be best for the oration to be pronounced, as also the place that would be most suitable for the purpose, whereupon —

"*Voted*, That the oration be delivered at half-past eleven o'clock, at the Old South Meeting-house, the hall not being capacious enough to contain the inbahitants that may attend on this occasion; the committee of that society having, upon application, consented that said meeting-house should be made use of for this service.

"*Voted*, That the Hon. John Hancock, Esq., Mr. Samuel Austin, and Mr. William Cooper, be a committee to wait upon Joseph Warren, Esq., and acquaint him that it is the desire of the town that the oration may be delivered at the Old South Meeting-house, at half-past eleven o'clock this forenoon.

"Upon a motion, *Voted*, That this meeting be now adjourned to the Old South Meeting-house, to meet there at half-past eleven o'clock.

"The town met, according to adjournment, at the Old South Meeting-house, at half-past eleven o'clock.

not for the danger of precipitating a crisis, not a man of them would have been spared. It was provoking enough to the whole corps, that, while there were so many troops stationed here, with the design of suppressing town-meetings, there should yet be one for the purpose of delivering an oration to commemorate a massacre perpetrated by soldiers, and to show the danger of standing armies."

"The scene was sublime," Samuel L. Knapp says. "There was in this appeal to Britain — in this description of suffering, dying, and horror — a calm and high-

---

" The committee appointed to wait on Joseph Warren, Esq., to acquaint him with the vote of the town respecting the time and place of the delivery of the oration, —

" Reported that said gentleman was ready to comply with the orders of the town, made known to him by their committee.

" Upon a motion made, *Voted*, That there be a collection made in this meeting for Mr. Christopher Monk, a young man now languishing under a wound he received in his lungs, by a shot from Preston's butchering party of soldiers, on the 5th of March, 1770.

" An oration to commemorate the horrid massacre of the 5th of March, 1770, and to impress on the minds of the citizens the ruinous tendency of standing armies being placed in free and populous cities, &c., was delivered by Joseph Warren, Esq., to a large and crowded audience, and received by them with great applause.

" Upon a motion made and seconded, *Voted*, That the thanks of the town be, and hereby are, given to Joseph Warren, Esq., for the elegant and spirited oration, delivered by him, at their request, in commemoration of the horrid massacre, perpetrated on the evening of the 5th of March, 1770, by a party of soldiers of the Twenty-ninth Regiment, under Captain Thomas Preston. Also, —

" *Voted*, That Mr. Samuel Adams, the Hon. John Hancock, Esq., Benjamin Church, Esq., Mr. John Pitts, John Scollay, Esq., Colonel Thomas Marshall, and Mr. Samuel Austin, be, and hereby are, appointed a committee to wait on Joseph Warren, Esq.; and, in the name of the town, to require of him a copy of said oration for the press."

Warren returned the following answer: —

" GENTLEMEN, — The same motives which influenced me yesterday to appear before my fellow-citizens, induce me to deliver this copy to you.

" I am, with the sincerest respect, your most obedient servant,
                                             " JOSEPH WARREN.
" MARCH 7, 1775."

souled defiance which must have chilled the blood of every sensible foe. Such another hour has seldom happened in the history of man, and is not surpassed in the records of nations. The thunders of Demosthenes rolled at a distance from Philip and his host; and Tully poured the fiercest torrent of invective when Cataline was at a distance, and his dagger no longer to be feared; but Warren's speech was made to proud oppressors resting on their arms, whose errand it was to overawe, and whose business it was to fight. If the deed of Brutus deserved to be commemorated by history, poetry, painting, and sculpture, should not this instance of patriotism and bravery be held in lasting remembrance? If he —

"That struck the foremost man of all this world," —

was hailed as the first of freemen, what honors are not due to him, who, undismayed, bearded the British lion, to show the world what his country dared to do in the cause of liberty? If the statue of Brutus was placed among those of the gods, who were the preservers of Roman freedom, should not that of Warren fill a lofty niche in the temple reared to perpetuate the remembrance of our birth as a nation?"[1]

[1] Biographical Sketches, 114, 115.

CHAPTER XIV.

ON THE NINETEENTH OF APRIL.

THE COMMITTEE OF SAFETY. — WARREN'S LETTERS. — THE SECOND PROVINCIAL CONGRESS. — MILITARY PREPARATIONS. — WARREN'S VIGILANCE. — COLONEL SMITH'S EXPEDITION. — WARREN LEAVES BOSTON. — HIS SERVICE ON THE NINETEENTH OF APRIL

1775. THE 5TH OF MARCH TO THE 19TH OF APRIL.

WARREN, on the day after the delivery of his oration (March 7), met with the committee of safety in Cambridge, where the deliberations were uncommonly important, — Cushing and Adams being named, for the first time, as having been present. The proceedings related to the proposed army. They were of a similar character at the next meeting of the committee, on the 14th, when a watch was arranged to be kept in Charlestown, Cambridge, and Roxbury, in order that the committees of these towns might be ready "to send couriers forward to the towns where the magazines were placed, when sallies were made from the army by night."

According to Paul Revere, about thirty persons, chiefly mechanics, had agreed to watch the movements of British soldiers and the Tories. These patriots met at the Green Dragon tavern in Union Street. "We were so careful," he says, "that our meetings should be kept secret, that every time we met, every person swore upon the Bible that they would not discover any of our transactions but to Messrs. Hancock, Adams, Drs. Warren, Church, and one or two more. They took turns to watch the soldiers, two by two, by patrolling the streets all night."[1] It was now a common remark, that there was a traitor in the Provincial Congress.

At this time, the ministry were assuring George III. that the union of the colonies could not last; and he said, on the day on which Warren delivered his oration, "I am convinced the line adopted in American affairs will be crowned with success."[2] At this time, Warren, as the organ of the committee of donations, expressed the faith with which the patriots clung to unity as the anchor of their safety, and the interest with which they looked to the decision of Canada.

Joseph Warren to the Committee of Montreal.

BOSTON, March 15, 1775

Messrs. JAMES PRICE and ALEXANDER HAY, at Montreal.

GENTLEMEN, — So handsome a donation as £100. 4s., accompanied by such an animating letter from our brethren at Montreal, cannot fail to excite the warmest gratitude in the breast of every one who wishes prosperity and freedom to his country. The committee to whom your letter comes directed beg leave (as well on their account as in the name and behalf of every virtuous man in the town, more especially of the many thousands who are actually feeling the miseries occasioned by the Boston Port Bill) to offer you their most unfeigned thanks for this convincing proof of your sympathy for the distresses of your fellow-countrymen, and for your firm, disinterested attachment to the rights of your country. It affords singular pleasure to every friend of virtue to find such enlarged and generous sentiments as dictated your letter discovering themselves in places where the utmost diligence and most wicked devices have been made use of to distinguish them. The

[1] Paul Revere's Narrative. [2] Bancroft, vii. 253.

religion lately established in Canada is but too well calculated to banish every idea of freedom, and to familiarize the mind to slavery. But your letter is an agreeable instance how tenacious men are of their rights when they clearly understand them. We wish most heartily that sentiments like yours may be diffused throughout your widely-extended province, to the utter extinction of every imposition, whether civil or religious. Your numbers are great, and it is of course important to us whether you are engaged *for* or *against* us. The decision of the present controversy between Britain and the colonies will give happiness or misery to America for *years*, perhaps for centuries. Unanimity and firmness form the only anchor on which we depend. And we have the strongest assurances that can be given, that the whole continent see with the same eyes, and are actuated by one soul. To war with brethren must be shocking to every brave, every humane mind; but, if brethren and fellow-subjects will suffer themselves to be instruments in the hands of tyrants to *stab our Constitution*, every tender idea must be forgot, and they must be repelled with that heroic spirit which open enemies have experienced.

Our advocates are many, both in Europe and America; but the importance of our prosperity makes it a duty to solicit with earnestness for all the assistance and all the strength which the continent can give.

The inhabitants of Montreal have done worthily. May Heaven reward them! and, while life lasts, the memory of their kindness will never be effaced from the bosoms of the committee of donations.

JOSEPH WARREN, *per order*.[1]

The temper of the public mind was never firmer than it was in the month of March. The donations for the relief of the poor continued to flow into Boston as for a common cause: the letters accompanying them were of the most resolute character; and the evidences multiplied that the colonies would be one and indivisible. The tenor of the reports from the mother-country was thoroughly warlike. It was said, in letters from England, printed in the newspapers, "that the ministry were determined to persevere in

[1] This letter is printed in 4th Mass. Hist. Soc Collections, iv. 237.

the great system of American taxation;" and their reliance was on force. It was the advice in these letters to the Americans, "Prepare for the worst, and persevere in the plan adopted by congress."—"For Heaven's sake, for your own sake, and that of posterity, do not relax your vigilance."[1] There was the natural sequence of general and vigorous preparation for the last resort. It was said in the press, "In contending for liberty, the Constitution should be held in one hand, and the sword in the other. Our union, under Providence, is the rock of our salvation."[2] Such was the lofty spirit in the bosom of the American Republic in the beginning of its grand historic life.

On the 22d of March, the Provincial Congress renewed its session. It immediately ordered a re solve to be printed, which stated the necessity of putting the colony in a complete state of defence, and urged "that any relaxation would be attended with the utmost danger to the liberties of this colony and to all America;" and, for several days, this body was occupied with a consideration of "the rules and regulations for a constitutional army." Still, there was no desire for war; but the door was kept open for reconciliation. On the 1st of April, congress voted, that, if "writs should be issued, in form as the law directs, for calling a general assembly," to be held in May, the towns ought to obey the precepts, instructing the members elect to transact no business with the council appointed by mandamus. Thus was

---

[1] The citations are made from letters printed in the "Essex Gazette" of March 21, 1775.

[2] Editorial in Boston paper, March 27.

evinced the resolution, in matters of civil government, to adhere to the advice of the Continental Congress. But provision was made for the election of a third Provincial Congress, in case such writs were not issued by Governor Gage.

On the 2d of April, a fresh arrival brought the decisive intelligence, that parliament had pledged life and fortune to the king for the subjection of America, that New England was prohibited from the fisheries, and that re-enforcements were on the way to General Gage. On the next day, Warren was placed on a committee to require a full representation from the towns, when the following proclamation appeared in the "Salem Gazette:"—

> IN PROVINCIAL CONGRESS, Concord, April 3, 1775.
>
> Whereas several members of this congress are now absent by leave of the congress, and as the important intelligence received by the last vessels from Great Britain renders it necessary that every member attend his duty, —
>
> *Resolved*, That the absent members be directed forthwith to attend in this place, that so the wisdom of the province may be collected.
>
> By order of the Provincial Congress,
>
> JOHN HANCOCK, *President.*[1]

The soldiers now became more irritating than ever, and even the officers behaved more like a parcel of children than like men. One of the most conspicuous of the officers who disturbed the meeting at the Old South was a captain of the Royal Irish, who fared rather hard; for among those who beset him was a woman, "who threatened to wring his nose."[2] Two days after occurred the well-known case of tarring

---

[1] This proclamation is not printed in the journals of the Provincial Congress.
[2] Andrews's Letter, March 18.

and feathering a citizen of Billerica, by Colonel Nesbitt and party. On the 16th, the day Warren's oration was published, the officers made themselves merry in delivering a mock-oration, of which a letter gives the following account: "A vast number of officers assembled in King Street, when they proceeded to the choice of seven out of their number to represent the selectmen, the latter of whom, with the moderator, went into the coffee-house balcony, where was provided a fellow apparelled in a black gown, with a rusty-gray wig and fox-tail hanging to it, together with bands on, who delivered an oration from the balcony to a crowd of few else besides gaping officers. It contained the most mischievous abuse upon the characters of principal patriots here, wholly made up of the most vile, profane, blackguard language as ever was expressed."[1] This scurrilous speech was printed. There were acts of far more importance occurring every day, in the personal collisions occasioned by the seizures of all kinds of military articles that the patriots endeavored to carry out of the town. Occasionally large detachments of the army were marched into the country. On the 30th of March, the ever-vigilant committee of correspondence summoned "the little Senate" — the committees of the neighboring towns — to meet in their chamber, in Faneuil Hall, at ten o'clock, A.M., on the next day, "to determine on measures of safety;" saying in the summons, "The wisdom of the joint committees has been very conspicuous. The fullest

---

[1] Andrews's Letter, March 18. This collection of interesting letters I consulted in the library of Mr. Bancroft. They are now in the archives of the Massachusetts Historical Society.

exertion of the same wisdom is necessary at this excited time."

While engaged in this varied service, Warren wrote the following letter, which contains one of those salient sentences, which has been much quoted, to show the spirit of the time. Bancroft places the words italicised in his text. The march of Earl Percy, referred to in the letter, occasioned the meeting of the committee of correspondence: —

BOSTON, April 3, 1775.

DEAR SIR, — Your favor of the 21st of December came opportunely to hand, as it enabled me to give the Provincial Congress, now sitting at Concord, a just view of the measures pursued by the tools of the Administration, and effectually to guard them against that state of security into which many have endeavored to lull them. If we ever obtain a redress of grievances from Great Britain, it must be by the influence of those illustrious personages whose virtue now keeps them out of power. The king never will bring them into power until the ignorance and frenzy of the present Administration make the throne on which he sits shake under him. *If America is an humble instrument of the salvation of Britain, it will give us the sincerest joy; but, if Britain must lose her liberty, she must lose it alone. America must and will be free. The contest may be severe; the end will be glorious. We would not boast, but we think, united and prepared as we are, we have no reason to doubt of success, if we should be compelled to the last appeal; but we mean not to make that appeal until we can be justified in doing it in the sight of God and man.* Happy shall we be if the mother-country will allow us the free enjoyment of our rights, and indulge us in the pleasing employment of aggrandizing her.

The members for the Continental Congress are almost all chosen by the several colonies. Indeed, if any colony should neglect to choose members, it would be ruinous to it, as all intercourse would immediately cease between that colony and the whole continent.

The first brigade of the army marched about four miles out of town, three days ago, under the command of a brigadier-general (Earl Percy); but, as they marched without baggage or artillery, they did not occasion so great an alarm as they otherwise would. Nevertheless, great numbers, completely armed, collected in the neighboring towns; and it is the opinion of many, that, had they marched eight or ten miles, and attempted to destroy any magazines or abuse the people, not a man of them would have returned to Boston. The congress immediately took proper measures for restraining any unnecessary effusion of blood; and also passed proper resolves respecting the army, if they should attempt to come out of town with baggage and artillery.

I beg leave to recommend to your notice Mr. Dana, the bearer hereof (a gentleman of the law), a man of sense and probity, a true friend to his country, of a respectable family and fortune.

May Heaven bless you, and reward your labors with success! I am, sir, with great respect, your most obedient humble servant,

JOS. WARREN.[1]

To ARTHUR LEE, ESQ., London.

At this time, Francis Dana, a lawyer and a patriot, sailed for London, and carried letters addressed to Franklin, describing the colony, since the resignation of the mandamus counsellors, to have been "as quiet and peaceable as any colony on the continent," but in a state of most anxious suspense, preparing for the worst. "Much art and pains," Dr. Cooper wrote, "have been employed to dismay us, or provoke us to some rash action; but hitherto the people have behaved with astonishing calmness and resolution. The union and firmness of this and the other colonies have rather grown than diminished; and they seemed prepared for all events." Warren sent by Mr. Dana a copy of his oration to Franklin, with the following letter:—

Joseph Warren to Benjamin Franklin.

BOSTON, April 3, 1775.

SIR, — Although I have not the pleasure either of a personal or epistolary acquaintance with you, I have taken the liberty of sending

[1] This letter is printed in "Life of Arthur Lee," vol. ii. 265.

you by Mr. Dana a pamphlet, which I wish was more deserving of your notice. The abililty and firmness with which you have defended the rights of mankind, and the liberties of this country in particular, have rendered you dear to all America. May you soon see your enemies deprived of the power of injuring you, and your friends in a situation to discover the grateful sense they have of your exertions in the cause of freedom.

I am, sir, with the greatest esteem and respect, your most obedient, humble servant, JOSEPH WARREN.[1]

Dr. FRANKLIN.

The Provincial Congress remained twelve days in session after the peremptory summons of the absent members; and Warren, a part of the time at least, attended the meetings. On the 7th, he was placed on the committee on the state of the province. On the recommendation of this committee, a resolve was passed, providing for delegations to repair forthwith to Connecticut, Rhode Island, and New Hampshire, asking their co-operation and quotas in raising an army for the effectual security of New England and the continent. The same committee prepared for their delegates, instructions which dwelt on the importance " of cementing and continuing that union which had so happily taken place on this continent." Congress sent a circular to the committees of the towns round Boston, earnestly recommending that the militia and minute-men be put in the best posture for defence; but said that plans laid for the general good obliged them to request, that, whatever patience and forbearance it might require for the present, the committees should act on the defensive only until

---

[1] The original of this letter, and the other letters alluded to in the text, are in the archives of the Massachusetts Historical Society, and printed in their proceedings, 1863–64.

the further direction of the congress." They could not advise any measures "that the enemies of the cause might plausibly interpret as a commencement of hostilities." Having fixed on the 11th of May for a day of fasting and prayer, and provided for reassembling on any pressing exigency, congress, on the 15th of April, adjourned.

It was said in the British papers, that, by the 10th of April, an army of thirteen thousand would rendezvous in Boston, and that three major-generals were to be sent over to command it. This report was copied into the Boston journals.[1] According to a statement drawn up by Colonel William Heath, and dated the 20th of March, there were at this time about 2,850 troops at Boston, who were distributed in the following localities: 80 in King Street, 340 on the Neck, 400 at Fort Hill, 1700 on the Common, and 330 at Castle William. The fortifications on the Neck are said to have been skilfully designed and thoroughly executed.[2] Re-enforcements from England and other places were expected soon. There was the feeling among the officers, that the mere presence of the king's troops in the field would produce submission to the Regulating Act, and that there would be no fighting.[3]

In connection with this feeling was the allegation of cowardice. Warren met this charge in the following clear and temperately worded note, printed in his

[1] Essex Gazette, April 11, 1775.
[2] Proceedings of Massachusetts Historical Society, 1858-60, 292, where the report entire may be seen.
[3] Life of Lord Harris, 46, who was an officer. In the Boston papers of April 17, it is said that the Twenty-second, Thirty-fifth, Fortieth, Forty-fourth, Forty-ninth, and Sixty-third Regiments of Foot and the Seventeenth of Dragoons were expected.

oration. It is written in the repose of a heroic spirit, who was deeply moved at the insults that were heaped on his countrymen: —

"The patience with which this people have borne the injuries which have been heaped upon them, and their unwillingness to take any sanguinary measures, has, very injudiciously, been ascribed to cowardice, by persons both here and in Great Britain. I most heartily wish that an opinion so erroneous in itself and so fatal in its consequences might be utterly removed before it is too late; and I think nothing further necessary to convince every intelligent man, that the conduct of this people is owing to the tender regard which they have for their fellow-men, and an utter abhorrence to the shedding of human blood, than a little attention to their general temper and disposition, discovered when they cannot be supposed to be under any apprehension of danger to themselves. I will only mention the universal detestation which they show to every act of cruelty, by whom and upon whomsoever committed, the mild spirit of their laws, the very few crimes to which capital penalties are annexed, and the very great backwardness which both courts and juries discover in condemning persons charged with capital crimes. But, if any should think this observation not to the purpose, I readily appeal to those gentlemen in the army who have been in the camp or in the field with the Americans."

It was now expected that General Gage would order arrests of the popular leaders; it was said that parliament would pass Bills of attainder against the Bostonians; and the aspect of affairs became so serious, that a number of families moved into the country, and carried with them their valuable effects.[1] Samuel Adams and John Hancock were persuaded to retire to the residence of Rev. Jonas Clark, a patriotic clergyman, in Lexington. It is one of the doubtful stories of the time, that the officers formed a scheme to seize Adams, Hancock, and Warren, which an acci-

[1] Newspapers, April 10.

dent frustrated.[1] Warren's friends felt apprehensions for his safety. As one of his students, Dr. Eustis, returned home one evening, he passed a party of officers who appeared to be on the watch; and he advised Warren not to visit his patients that evening. But Warren, putting his pistols in his pocket, replied, "I have a visit to make to Mrs. ——, in Cornhill, this evening, and I will go at once: come with me."[2] It was about this time, when he was moved by the taunts which the officers were uttering, that he said to Eustis, "These fellows say we won't fight: by Heavens, I hope I shall die up to my knees in blood!"[3] One day he was passing the place at the Neck where the gallows stood, and met three officers, one of whom insultingly said, "Go on, Warren: you will soon come to the gallows." Warren turned, walked up to the officers, and calmly asked who it was that uttered these words, but received no reply.[4]

Warren did not attend the meetings of the committee of safety in April. They held their sessions

---

[1] Moore's Diary of the Revolution, i. 157. When George Chalmers was preparing his history of the revolt of the American colonies, he addressed to General Gage a series of questions, some of which refer to this period. One of these related to an alleged design of "the malcontents" to surprise Boston, with a view to "massacre the troops." In one of the replies of Chalmers, he says:—

"On the arrival of two vessels at Marblehead, on the 8th of April, 1775, an unusual hurry and commotion was perceived among the disaffected. It being on a Sunday morning, Dr. Cooper, a notorious rebel, was officiating in his meeting-house, and, on notice given him, pretended sudden sickness, went home, and sent to another clergyman to do his duty in the evening. He, with every other chief of the faction, left Boston before night, and never returned to it. The cause, at the time unknown, was discovered on the 14th of said month, when a vessel arrived with Government despatches, which contained directions to seize the persons of certain notorious rebels. It was too late. They had received timely notice of their danger, and were fled."—4th Series of Mass. Hist. Soc. Collections, vol. iv.

[2] Tudor's Life of Otis, 466.   [3] Ib. See p. 168.

[4] Loring's Hundred Boston Orators, 48.

at Concord. The absence doubtless was for weighty reasons. He had resolved to abandon his profession, and enter the army; and, as the crisis approached, he devoted some time each day to a regular practice of the manual exercise.[1] His letters show that he watched narrowly the motions of the army. As he knew their numbers, knew also the preparations for self-defence that had been matured by the patriots, he was confident, that, in case offensive operations were attempted, the militia would appear in the field in sufficient numbers to defeat them. The organization of a watch, and of couriers to alarm the country, by the committee of safety, have been already stated.

General Gage sent two officers, disguised as farmers, into the interior to ascertain the places where the provincials had gathered stores, sites for encampments, and the state of the country. They, though narrowly watched by the patriots, succeeded in their object; and, besides an interesting narrative showing the spirit of the people, they presented to General Gage a rudely sketched map of the roads as far as Concord and Worcester. It was now (April 4) said in the journals, that a considerable number of army wagons were ready for use, that blacksmiths were employed in making crow's-feet, and the army seemed to be preparing for a march. A week later, it was suggested that Worcester would be the point to which the army would march, with the view to protect the courts under the Regulating Act.[2] A New-York letter, in remarking on the probability that the troops would take the field, said to the Massachusetts patriots, "For Heaven's sake, be watchful and firm, as

[1] Tudor's Otis, 466.   [2] Salem Gazette, April 10.

all, under God, depends on your conduct at this time."[1] The policy of disarming the people had been acted on, though it had not been followed up very energetically. The indications now were, that this policy would be carried out in earnest.

On Friday, the 14th of April, the "Somerset" frigate was moored in Charles River, between Boston and Charlestown;[2] and, on the next day, the Grenadiers and Light Infantry were taken off of duty, on the pretext of learning a new exercise, and the transports were hauled near the sterns of the men-of-war. These movements appeared so suspicious, that, on the following day, Sunday, Warren sent Paul Revere to Lexington[3] with intelligence of these changes, for the guidance of Hancock and Adams. On the next day, preparations were made for a removal of a portion of the stores at Concord.

Little to attract the special attention of the vigilant patriots occurred on Monday, though "they were expecting something serious to be transacted."[4] It happened, that, on the day (15th) on which the movements in Boston attracted attention, Lord Dartmouth wrote to General Gage, that all the cannon, small arms, and military stores that might be either in any magazine, or secreted by the patriots, ought to be seized; and all who, in the opinion of His Majesty's attorney and solicitor-general, had committed acts of treason, ought to be arrested.

On Tuesday evening, the 18th, it was observed that troops were marching towards the bottom of the Common; and a vigilant patriot informed Warren of

[1] Salem Gazette, April 10.   [2] Newspaper.
[3] Revere's Narrative.   [4] *Ib.*

the fact,[1] who immediately sent William Dawes, by way of Roxbury, to Lexington, to inform Hancock and Adams. About ten o'clock, Warren sent an earnest message for Paul Revere, who went to the patriot's house. Revere says, "Warren begged that I would immediately set off for Lexington, to Messrs. Hancock and Adams, and acquaint them of the movement, and that it was thought they were the objects." At half-past ten o'clock that night, Lieutenant-colonel Smith, with about eight hundred Grenadiers and Light Infantry, embarked in long boats, at the foot of the Common, and moved over Charles River, in the direction of Phipps's Farm, or Lechmere's Point, on a secret expedition to destroy the stores collected at Concord, and, it was reported, to seize Hancock and Adams. "General Gage, this evening," Stedman says, "told Lord Percy that he intended to send a detachment to seize the stores at Concord, and to give the command to Colonel Smith, who knew he was to go, but not where. He meant it to be a secret expedition, and begged of Lord Percy to keep it a profound secret. As this nobleman was passing from the general's quarters home to his own, perceiving eight or ten men conversing together on the Common, he made up to them, when one of the men said, "The British troops have marched, but will miss their aim."—"What aim?" said Lord Percy. "Why," the man replied, "the cannon at Concord." Lord Percy immediately returned on his steps, and acquainted General Gage, not without marks of surprise and disapprobation, with what he had just heard. The general said that his confidence

[1] Manuscript.

had been betrayed; for that he had communicated his design to one person only besides his lordship."[1] Gordon says, "When the corps was nearly ready to proceed upon the expedition, Dr. Warren, by a mere accident, had notice of it just in time to send messengers over the Neck and across the Ferry, on to Lexington, before the orders for preventing every person's quitting the town were executed."[2] The lights of the watch-fires, the sounds of the bells, and the signal-guns, proclaimed the faithfulness with which Warren's messengers did their work.

I need not follow Colonel Smith's progress into the country, on this memorable night, until, at half-past four, on the morning of the nineteenth of April, his advance fired on the company of provincials who paraded at Lexington under Captain Parker, and then passed on to Concord, which the detachment reached about seven; nor need I relate the remarkable rapidity with which the agencies which the committee of safety had organized, did the work of alarming the militia, or the prompt response to the summons which occasioned the roads leading to Concord and Lexington to swarm with the minute-men. It is only necessary to relate Warren's connection with the events of this extraordinary day.

A special messenger, early in the morning, brought to Warren the intelligence of the events that occurred in the morning at Lexington. "His soul beat to arms," Dr. Eliot says, "as soon as he learned the intention of the British troops;"[3] and he now called in Mr. Eustis, his student, directed him to take care

---

[1] Stedman's History of the War, i. 119.
[2] Gordon, i. 477.   [3] Eliot's Biographical Dictionary.

of his patients, mounted his horse, and departed for the scene of action.[1] He rode to the Charlestown Ferry. The last person to whom he spoke as he entered the boat was the grandfather of the late John R. Adan, of Boston; and Warren said, as they parted, "Keep up a brave heart! They have begun it, — that either party can do; and we'll end it, — that only one can do."[2] On the way through Charlestown, he met Dr. Welch, a resident, who says, "Eight o'clock in the morning, saw Dr. Joseph Warren just come out of Boston, horseback. I said, 'Well, they are gone out.' — 'Yes,' he said, 'and we will be up with them before night.'" Jacob Rogers, another resident of Charlestown, says, "We were alarmed with various reports concerning the king's troops, which put everybody in confusion. About ten in the morning, I met Dr. Warren, riding hastily out of town, and asked him if the news was true of the men being killed at Lexington. He assured me it was. He rode on." Between nine and ten o'clock, Lord Percy began his march, by the way of Roxbury, to re-enforce Colonel Smith: his column passed through Cambridge; and, according to Dr. Welch, who appears to have accompanied Warren a short time, they were near this force. "Two soldiers," Dr. Welch says, "going to Lexington, tried to steal Watson's horse, at Watson's Corner; the old man, with his cat and hat, pulling one way, and the soldiers the other. Dr. Warren rode up, and helped drive them off. Tried to pass Percy's column; stopped by bayonets. Two British officers rode up to Dr. Warren, in the rear of the British, inquiring 'Where are the troops?'

[1] Thacher's Medical Biography, ii. 238.   [2] Manuscript letter of Mr. Adan

The doctor did not know. They were greatly alarmed. Went home." And Dr. Welch, who returned to Charlestown, relates nothing further that transpired that day until the afternoon.[1]

A meeting of the committee of safety was notified to be held "at Mr. Wetherby's, at the Black Horse, in Menotomy," or West Cambridge; and Watson's Corner was on the route to this place. There is no record of the proceedings of the committee on this day; but the fact is stated that the committee met. General Heath, a member, was present at this meeting, and, on leaving it in the morning, went "by a cross-road" over to Watertown, the British being in possession of the Lexington road.[2] Warren undoubtedly was present at this meeting of the committee. I am unable to locate him for several hours, or until in the afternoon, about the time Lord Percy's column rescued Colonel Smith's party from entire destruction, which was at two o'clock.

The Provincial Congress had clothed the members of the committee of safety with the power, in case of offensive operations, to summon the militia into the field; and they, therefore, were the centre of authority. Warren, in the relations of the day, is spoken of as "the chairman of the committee in Boston." Hancock was the chairman of the whole committee, and Samuel Adams met twice with them. Now, the Provincial Congress, anxious to conform to the recommendations of the Continental Congress, had cautioned the committees of the towns to exercise the utmost forbearance in the great matter of commencing hostilities; and this had been impressed

---

[1] Manuscript statement of Dr. Welch. [2] Heath's Memoirs, 13.

on the towns by the committee of safety. This fact has a bearing on what took place at half-past four, on the morning of this day, at Lexington; and, again, at between nine and ten, at Concord Bridge. It was considered of great consequence to be able to establish the fact that the British fired first; thus to make it clear to the tribunal of the world that they were the immediate aggressors, and to save the colony of Massachusetts from the judgment of having acted inconsiderately. Nothing could have been easier than for the militia, who had assembled in large numbers in Concord, after the firing at Concord Bridge, to have destroyed a British party of about a hundred men, who were at a great distance from the main body; but they were allowed to return over the bridge where the firing took place.

From four o'clock in the morning, couriers were flying in every direction from Lexington; and it is not improbable that the military officers, before twelve o'clock, had the advice of the committee of safety. Adams and Hancock were on the ground, and could have given immediate directions. They were persuaded to retire to what was then known as the second precinct of Woburn, now Burlington, about two miles from Rev. Jonas Clarke's house. I am not able to say whether Adams and Warren met on this memorable day; but they surely were not far apart. "It is a fine day," Adams remarked, as he was walking in the field after the day had dawned. "Very pleasant," answered one of his companions, supposing him to be contemplating the beauties of the sky. "I mean," he replied, "this day is a glorious day for America." So fearless was he of consequences," Dr.

Eliot says, " so intrepid in the midst of danger, so eager to look forward to the lustre of events that would succeed the gloom which then involved the minds of the people."[1]

Warren, about the time Lord Percy met Colonel Smith, rejoined General Heath, as the latter was taking a cross-road leading from Watertown to Lexington, on his way to assume the command of the militia; and the two kept together during the afternoon. There had been no hesitation, on the part of the minute-men, after the British troops, about twelve o'clock, set out on their return from Concord. Before they had left the town, the battle of the day began in earnest, — " an incessant though irregular fire," a British officer writes of the British troops, " which was kept up during the whole of their march back to Lexington, in which they were driven before the Americans like sheep. At that place, they were met by the detachment under Lord Percy, with two pieces of cannon. The two detachments rested on their arms, and received some refreshment. Lord Percy now formed his detachment into a square, in which he enclosed Colonel Smith's party, who were so much exhausted with fatigue, that they were obliged to lie down for rest on the ground, their tongues hanging out of their mouths, like those of dogs after a chase."[2]

Lord Percy had now about eighteen hundred troops under him. On renewing his retreat, he was closely pursued. As he went through West Cambridge, the firing was very sharp. " In this battle," Heath says, " I was several times greatly exposed, in particular at

[1] Eliot's Biographical Dictionary, 10.   [2] Stedman's History, i. 118.

the high grounds, at the upper end of Menotomy (West Cambridge), and also on the plain below the meeting-house; on the latter, Dr. Joseph Warren, — afterwards Major-general Warren, — who kept constantly near me, and then but a few feet distant, a musket-ball from the enemy came so near his head as to strike the pin out of the hair of his earlock. On this plain, Dr. Eliphalet Downer, in single combat with a British soldier, killed him on the spot, by thrusting him nearly through the body with his bayonet."[1]

Authorities agree in stating, that the firing was severe on that portion of West Cambridge known as "the Plain." The reference to Warren's service here, in Bovle's "Eulogy," printed in 1781, shows the impression which his bearing made on his countrymen: —

> "Again the conflict glows with rage severe,
> And fearless ranks in combat mixt appear.
> Victory uncertain! fierce contention reigns,
> And purple rivers drench the slippery plains.
> Column to column, host to host oppose,
> And rush impetuous on their adverse foes,
> When, lo! the hero Warren from afar
> Sought for the battle, and the field of war.
> From rank to rank the daring warrior flies,
> And bids the thunder of the battle rise.
> Sudden arrangements of his troops are made,
> And sudden movements round the Plain displayed.
> Columbia's genius in her polished shield
> Gleams bright, and dreadful o'er the hostile field
> Her ardent troops, enraptured with the sight,
> With shock resistless force the dubious fight.
> Britons, astonished, tremble at the sight,
> And, all confused, precipitate their flight."

The minute-men continued to harass the retreating troops as they left the Plain. After they entered the

---

[1] Proceedings of Mass. Hist. Society, 1858–60, 294.

portion of Charlestown which is now Somerville, and were moving from Prospect Hill, along the road by the bay that makes up from Charles River, their position was again critical; for a force of several hundred militia from Essex County were on or near Winter Hill, and threatened to cut them off. "The militia," Heath says, "continued to hang on the rear of the British, until they reached Bunker Hill, in Charlestown, and it had become so dusk as to render the flashes of the muskets very visible." Bunker Hill is the nearest hill to the main land within the peninsula of Charlestown; and here the British commander formed a line, and, covered by his ships, prepared to make a stand. General Heath was now on a plot of ground known as the Common, just outside of the peninsula; and he says Warren kept near him. Here the order was given for the militia to discontinue the pursuit, and return to Cambridge. General Heath now held the first council of war of the Revolution, at the foot of Prospect Hill.

It is said of Warren by Eliot, "that he was perhaps the most active man in the field;"[1] by Knapp, that "the people were delighted with his cool, collected bravery, and already considered him as a leader whose gallantry they were to admire, and in whose talents they were to confide;"[2] by Morton, that "he appeared in the field under the united characters of the general, the soldier, and the physician; here he was seen animating his countrymen to battle, and fighting by their side; and there he was found administering healing comforts to the wounded;"[3] and by

[1] Eliot's Biographical Dictionary, 473.

Tudor that he would be regarded as "the personal representative of those brave citizens, who, with arms hastily collected, sprang from their peaceable homes to resist aggression, and, on the plains of Lexington and heights of Charlestown, cemented with their blood the foundation of American liberty."[1]

[1] Tudor's Life of Otis, 460. The History of the Siege of Boston contains a full relation of the events of this day.

CHAPTER XV.

SIXTY DAYS OF SERVICE.

THE COMMITTEE OF SAFETY. — THE PROVINCIAL CONGRESS. — ORGANIZATION OF THE ARMY. — LETTERS OF WARREN. — THE THIRD PROVINCIAL CONGRESS. — WARREN ELECTED PRESIDENT. — ELECTED MAJOR-GENERAL.

1775. FROM THE 19TH OF APRIL TO THE 17TH OF JUNE.

WARREN had reason to be proud of the bearing of his countrymen on the nineteenth of April. They made good every confident word which he had uttered on their bravery. The allegation of cowardice would no longer answer, even in England, as an explanation of the forbearance that had been so persistently exercised. All the organizations of the popular party — the local committees, the Provincial and Continental Congresses — had urged the necessity of keeping purely on the defensive; it had been adhered to under the most trying circumstances, even up to the moment of the appearance of the British troops on Lexington Green;[1] but after the fire of their musketry, forbearance was no longer a virtue. The question, Who fired the first gun? was considered to be of great importance. The simple statement which flew through the land, that a British brigade had

---

[1] It is remarkable, that, notwithstanding the exciting and often bitter political controversies during the years preceding the war, not a life was lost in Boston, except the lives occasioned by the firing on the people, in 1770, by the British troops. Much credit is due to the Board of Selectmen in preserving

fired on a provincial company, seemed a vindication of the severe handling which the minute-men gave to the regulars. It was like the sounding of a tocsin. No patriots made the plea, that a portion of the party had madly rushed upon war: but the judgment was as spontaneous as it was righteous, that the firing was the crowning act of a series of aggressions on a loyal and unoffending people; and that the hour had come in which to redeem their pledges of union, by moving to the support of their brethren. The army of citizen-soldiers who hastened to the point of danger, and shut up the British army in Boston, was a magic demonstration of the life and power of American nationality.

Warren was called upon for service when the great

the public peace. The period covered in these pages extends from 1767 to 1775. When arrogance and outrage stirred passion to its depths, these fathers of the town, acting in concert with the other popular leaders, were successful in guiding the expression of indignation through the channels of the law. The successive Boards during this period were as follows: —

1767.	1770.	1773.
Joseph Jackson,	Joshua Henshaw,	John Hancock,
John Ruddock,	Joseph Jackson,	John Scollay,
John Hancock,	John Ruddock,	Timothy Newell,
John Rowe,	John Hancock,	Thomas Marshall,
Joshua Henshaw,	Samuel Pemberton,	Samuel Austin,
Samuel Pemberton,	Henderson Inches,	Oliver Wendell,
Henderson Inches.	Jonathan Mason.	John Pitts.
1768.	1771.	1774.
Joseph Jackson,	Joseph Jackson,	John Scollay,
Samuel Sewall,	John Ruddock,	John Hancock,
John Ruddock,	John Hancock,	Timothy Newell,
John Hancock,	Henderson Inches,	Thomas Marshall,
William Phillips,	Samuel Pemberton,	Samuel Austin,
Timothy Newell,	Jonathan Mason,	Oliver Wendell,
John Rowe.	Ebenezer Storer.	John Pitts.
1769	1772	1775.
Joshua Henshaw,	John Ruddock,	John Scollay,
Joseph Jackson,	John Hancock,	Timothy Newell,
John Hancock,	Samuel Austin,	Thomas Marshall,
Jonathan Mason,	Thomas Marshall,	Samuel Austin,
Samuel Pemberton,	John Scollay,	John Hancock,
Henderson Inches,	Timothy Newell,	John Pitts,
John Ruddock.	Oliver Wendell.	Oliver Wendell

event of the day of Lexington and Concord, like the destruction of the tea, wrested affairs from the control of men, and cast them upon the current of ideas. But I do not feel called upon to trace the effect of the event on the nationality of England, or only incidentally on that of America; but propose, as an act of justice to Warren's memory, to give an idea of his varied labors as he moved on towards the mount of sacrifice.

There is no record of the proceedings of the committee of safety on the 19th of April. They were in session the whole of the day of the 20th, and the night; but only the circulars they issued are recorded. I copy the following letter, addressed to the towns, from the original in Warren's handwriting, which contains much interlineation. It seems to glow with the fire of the battle: —

GENTLEMEN, — The barbarous murders committed on our innocent brethren, on Wednesday the 19th instant, have made it absolutely necessary that we immediately raise an army to defend our wives and our children from the butchering hands of an inhuman soldiery, who, incensed at the obstacles they met with in their bloody progress, and enraged at being repulsed from the field of slaughter, will, without the least doubt, take the first opportunity in their power to ravage this devoted country with fire and sword. We conjure you, therefore, by all that is dear, by all that is sacred, that you give all assistance possible in forming an army. Our all is at stake. Death and devastation are the instant consequences of delay. Every moment is infinitely precious. An hour lost may deluge your country in blood, and entail perpetual slavery upon the few of your posterity who may survive the carnage. We beg and entreat, as you will answer to your country, to your own consciences, and, above all, as you will answer to God himself, that you will hasten and encourage by all possible means the enlistment of men to form the army, and send them forward to headquarters, at Cambridge, with that expedition which the vast importance and instant urgency of the affair demand.[1]

[1] Massachusetts Archives.

On this day of keen anguish, Warren addressed the following letter to General Gage:—

CAMBRIDGE, April 20, 1775.

SIR,—The unhappy situation into which this colony is thrown gives the greatest uneasiness to every man who regards the welfare of the empire, or feels for the distresses of his fellow-men: but even now much may be done to alleviate those misfortunes which cannot be entirely remedied; and I think it of the utmost importance to us, that our conduct be such as that the contending parties may entirely rely upon the honor and integrity of each other for the punctual performance of any agreement that shall be made between them. Your Excellency, I believe, knows very well the part I have taken in public affairs: I ever scorned disguise. I think I have done my duty: some may think otherwise; but be assured, sir, as far as my influence goes, every thing which can reasonably be required of us to do shall be done, and every thing promised shall be religiously performed. I should now be very glad to know from you, sir, how many days you desire may be allowed for such as desire to remove to Boston with their effects, and what time you will allow the people in Boston for their removal. When I have received that information, I will repair to congress, and hasten, as far as I am able, the issuing a proclamation. I beg leave to suggest, that the condition of admitting only thirty wagons at a time into the town appears to me very inconvenient, and will prevent the good effects of a proclamation intended to be issued for encouraging all wagoners to assist in removing the effects from Boston with all possible speed. If Your Excellency will be pleased to take the matter into consideration; and favor me, as soon as may be, with an answer, it will lay me under a great obligation, as it so nearly concerns the welfare of my friends in Boston. I have many things which I wish to say to Your Excellency, and most sincerely wish I had broken through the formalities which I thought due to your rank, and freely have told you all I knew or thought of public affairs; and I must ever confess, whatever may be the event, that you generously gave me such opening, as I now think I ought to have embraced: but the true cause of my not doing it was the knowledge I had of the vileness and treachery of many persons around you, who, I supposed, had gained your entire confidence.

I am, &c., JOSEPH WARREN.

His Excellency GENERAL GAGE.

On the 21st, the committee of safety resolved to enlist out of the Massachusetts forces eight thousand effective men, adopted the forms of the enlisting papers to meet the emergency, and resolved to propose an establishment at an early day after the meeting of congress. The labors of the committee of safety were uncommonly arduous. Dr. Eliot says, "Nothing could be in a more confused state than the army which first assembled at Cambridge. This undisciplined body of men were kept together by a few who deserved well of their country... Dr. Warren was perhaps the man who had the most influence, and in whom the people in the environs of Boston and Cambridge placed their highest confidence. He did wonders in preserving order among the troops."

On the 22d, the Provincial Congress, which had been summoned on the 18th, assembled at Concord, when a letter, addressed by Josiah Quincy, jun., to Samuel Adams, was presented, opened, read, and ordered to be sent to Warren, "to be used at his discretion;" when, in order to be nearer the army, the congress adjourned to meet in the afternoon, at Watertown. On re-assembling here, the congress, after notifying officially the committee of safety of its meeting, adjourned until the next day.

On the 23d, Sunday, congress held an important session. Instead of the usual stillness of the sabbath, there was now the hurry of war. The militia of the neighboring colonies were approaching the scene of action by hasty marches; families, in great distress, were hurrying from the seaport towns into the country; while a large number of the minute-men, so suddenly summoned to the field, were returning to their homes. On this day, Warren read in congress a letter from a Connecticut committee of correspondence well calculated to nerve the desponding and to cheer on the brave· "Every preparation," the letter said, "is making to support your province." — "The ardor of our people is such that they cannot be kept back. The colonels are to forward a part of the best men, and most ready, as fast as possible; the remainder to be ready at a moment's warning." On this day, it was voted to raise an army of 13,600 men, as the quota of Massachusetts in the army of 30,000, which it was resolved ought to be raised. In the afternoon, Hancock, the regular president, being absent, it was voted to choose a president *pro tempore*, when a committee reported that "the vote was full for Dr. Warren." Papers bearing his signature, while acting in this capacity, occur henceforward to the day of his death. He said to-day to Dr. Belknap, "The town must be cleared, and would be soon."[1]

On the 24th, the following commission, which has Warren's autograph, was given to "Captain Ebenezer Winship," and dated, "In committee of safety:" "Sir, you are to enlist a company of rangers, whereof Jonathan Brewer is colonel. You are hereby empowered immediately to enlist a company, to consist of fifty-nine able-bodied and effective men, including sergeants, as soldiers in the Massachusetts service, for the preservation of American liberty, and cause them to muster as soon as possible. — JOS. WARREN, chairman." The signature is in his large handwriting.

On the 25th, the following resolve was passed,

[1] Belknap's Memoirs, 90.

which is in Warren's handwriting: "In committee of safety. Resolved that —— be ordered, with the troops of horse under his command, to proceed forward as an escort to the honorable members of the Continental Congress, on their way to Philadelphia, until they are met by an escort from the colony of Connecticut.—Jos. WARREN, chairman." One of the delegates was Samuel Adams, and the friends parted for the last time.

On the 26th, Warren's intimate friend, Josiah Quincy, jun., died as he reached his native land. His biographer says, "He repeatedly said to the seaman on whose attentions he was chiefly dependent, that he had but one desire and prayer, which was that he might live long enough to have an interview with Samuel Adams or Joseph Warren; that granted, he should die content. This wish of the patriot's heart Heaven, in its inscrutable wisdom, did not grant." On this day, Warren penned the following letter in relation to the New-Hampshire forces, copied from the original, in his handwriting:—

1775, CAMBRIDGE, April 26.

SIR,—Our friends from New Hampshire have shown their readiness to assist us on this day [of] distress: therefore thought it best to give orders for enlisting such as were present in the service of this colony, as many desired something might be done to hold them together until the resolve of your congress is known, when we are ready and desirous they should be discharged from us, and put under such command as you shall direct. Colonel Sargeant has been so kind as to afford his utmost assistance in conducting this matter.

On the 27th, Warren addressed the following letter to Arthur Lee, which shows the views with which he was now acting as the head of the popular cause:—

CAMBRIDGE, April 27, 1775.

MY DEAR SIR, — Our friend Quincy just lived to come on shore to die in his own country. He expired yesterday morning. His virtues rendered him dear, and his abilities useful, to his country. The wicked measures of Administration have at length brought matters to a crisis. I think it probable that the rage of the people, excited by the most clear view of the cursed designs of Administration and the barbarous effusion of the blood of their countrymen, will lead them to attack General Gage, and burn the ships in the harbor. Lord Chatham and our friends must make up the breach immediately or never. If any thing terrible takes place, it will not now do to talk of calling the colonies to account for it, but must be attributed to the true cause, — the unheard-of provocations given to this people. They never will talk of accommodation until the present ministry are entirely removed. You may depend, the colonies will sooner suffer depopulation than come into any measures with them.

The next news from England must be conciliatory, or the connection between us ends, however fatal the consequences may be. Prudence may yet alleviate the misfortunes and calm the convulsions into which the empire is thrown by the madness of the present Administration. May Almighty God direct you. If any thing is proposed that may be for the honor and safety of Great Britain and these colonies, my utmost efforts shall not be wanting.

I am in the utmost haste, surrounded by fifteen or twenty thousand men.   Your most obedient servant,   JOS. WARREN.

P.S. — The narrative sent to Dr. Franklin contains a true state of facts; but it was difficult to make the people willing that any notice should be taken of the matter, by way of narrative, until the army and navy were taken, or driven away.   J. W.[1]

On the 28th, Warren was appointed by the committee of safety to express its sentiments relative to Lord Dartmouth's circular letter to the governors of the colonies. This circular, with other declara-

---

[1] This letter is copied from the original in the archives in Harvard-College Library. It will not agree with the copy in "Life of Arthur Lee," 267. The last sentence of the second paragraph there reads, "If any thing is proposed *which* may be for the honor and safety of Great Britain and these colonies, my utmost efforts shall not be wanting *to effect a reconciliation;*" the four last words being an interpolation.

tions, says that His Majesty was determined to resist every attempt to encourage, in the colonies, ideas of independence. Warren's letter shows that he was of opinion, that the next news from England must be conciliatory, or the connection between the two countries would end. On this day, he was placed on a committee to consider the condition of the inhabitants of Boston; and he was the chairman of a committee appointed by the Provincial Congress to confer with a delegation from New Hampshire. In a letter addressed to the patriots of that colony, congress said, that the conviction was general in Massachusetts and the other colonies, that, by their immediate and most vigorous exertions, there was the greatest prospect of establishing these liberties and saving the country.

On the 29th, the Provincial Congress, and the committee of safety, were in session. I select from the varied business of that day the following report, which has Warren's autograph: —

IN COMMITTEE OF SAFETY, CAMBRIDGE, April 29, 1775.

Agreeably to the order of the Provincial Congress, this committee have inquired into the state and situation of the cannon and ordnance stores, with the provision made for the companies of artillery, and beg leave to report as follows; viz.,

In Cambridge, six three-pounders complete, with ammunition, and one six-pounder.

In Watertown, sixteen pieces of artillery of different sizes. The said six-pounder and sixteen pieces will be taken out of the way, and the first-mentioned six pieces will be used in the proper way of defence.

Captain Forster is appointed to command one of the companies of artillery, and ordered to enlist said company.

Captain William Lee, of Marblehead, [is] sent for to take the command of another; and several other persons [are] sent for to take command for other companies.

JOS. WARREN, *Chairman.*

On the 30th, Sunday, Warren kept mostly with the committee of safety, which met in Cambridge; and he passed an uncommonly anxious and busy day. The Tories in Boston were alarmed at the exodus of the inhabitants, and were desirous to retain them as hostages for the safety of the town. On their remonstrance against the departure of so many, General Gage, on various pretexts, forbade their going out. Warren received a letter on this subject from the selectmen; and the committee on this day were occupied in considering it. Meantime the Provincial Congress, which was also in session at Watertown, directed a letter to be sent in the afternoon to Warren, in which, after expressing the anxiety of the members on account of the distress of the people of Boston, it said this body "sat in almost impatient expectation, by several adjournments, since seven o'clock this morning." The committee of safety reported to Congress, probably through Warren, a resolve providing for a system of permits to facilitate ingress and egress from the town, which was printed with his name attached to it. This subject occasioned the following letter to the selectmen, which I copy from the original in his handwriting, which expresses his feeling for his "ever-dear town of Boston:" —

Joseph Warren to the Selectmen of Boston.

CAMBRIDGE, April 30, 1775.

GENTLEMEN, — Enclosed you have a resolve of congress, which we hope will remove every obstacle to [the] removal of our friends from Boston. The necessity of going from this town to Watertown, in order to lay the proposals of this committee before the Provincial Congress, we hope will suggest to you an apology for any supposed delay. But be assured, that no person now in Boston is more deeply sensible of the distress, nor more desirous of relieving our brethren there, than the members of this committee. Encouragement will be given to-morrow to the wagoners in the country to repair to Boston, to give all possible assistance to our friends in the removal of their effects. I wrote yesterday to General Gage upon the subject, and requested him to take into consideration the expediency of restraining the country from sending in more than thirty wagons at one time; but I have received no answer. If I should receive any, the contents, so far as they respect my ever-dear town of Boston, shall be communicated to you.

I am, gentlemen, with the sincerest respect and warmest affection, your most obedient servant.

Colonel Benedict Arnold had just arrived in the camp from Connecticut, and he proposed to lead an expedition to capture Ticonderoga. Warren was appointed on a committee on this subject, and took great interest in it. I have space, however, for only the following letter, in which he expresses consideration of the rights of a sister colony: —

CAMBRIDGE, April 30, 1775.

It has been proposed to us to take possession of the Fortress of Ticonderoga. We have a just sense of the importance of that fortification, and the usefulness of those fine cannon, mortars, and field-pieces which are there; but we would not, even upon this emergency, infringe upon the rights of our sister colony, New York. But we have desired the gentleman who carries this letter to represent the matter to you, that you may give such orders as are agreeable to you. We are, with the greatest respect, your most obedient servants,

JOSEPH WARREN, *Chairman.*

To ALEXANDER MCDOUGAL.

On the 1st of May, Warren received a reply to his letter of the preceding day, signed by five of the selectmen, who said that General Gage thought he could not officially correspond with Warren, but desired them to reply to his letter. The plan of granting permits was substantially satisfactory; but on various pretexts the people continued to be retained in the town.[1]

On the 2d, the Provincial Congress appointed a committee to wait on Warren, to know whether he could serve them as their president, when he replied by the following note, written on the blank leaf of the letter of the selectmen of Boston: "Doct. Warren presents his respects to the honorable Provincial Congress; informs them that he will obey their order, and attend his duty in congress in the afternoon." He was a good deal disturbed at the action of Connecticut, which had sent an embassy to General Gage; and he addressed the following remarkable letter to the Government of that colony, which I copy from the original in Warren's handwriting: —

CAMBRIDGE, May 2, 1775.

We yesterday had a conference with Dr. Johnson and Colonel Wolcott, who were appointed by your assembly to deliver a letter to, and hold a conference with, General Gage. We feel the warmest gratitude to you for those generous and affectionate sentiments which you entertain towards us. But you will allow us to express our uneasiness on account of one paragraph in your letter, in which a cessation of hostilities is proposed. We fear that our brethren in Connecticut are not even yet convinced of the cruel designs of Administration against America, nor thoroughly sensible of the miseries to which General Gage's army have reduced this wretched colony. We have lost the town, and, we greatly fear, the inhabitants of Boston, as we find the general is perpetually making new conditions, and forming the most unreasonable pretences for retarding their removal from that *garrison*. Our seaports on the eastern coasts are mostly deserted. Our people have been barbarously murdered by an insidious enemy, who, under cover of the night, have marched into the heart of the

[1] The following selectmen signed this letter: John Scollay, Thomas Marshall, Timothy Newell, Samuel Austin, John Pitts.

country, spreading destruction with fire and sword. No business but that of war is either done or thought of in this colony. No agreement or compact with General Gage will in the least alleviate our distress, as no confidence can possibly be placed in any assurances he can give to a people whom he has first deceived in the matter, taking possession of and fortifying the town of Boston, and whom he has suffered his army to attack in the most inhuman and treacherous manner. Our relief now must arise from driving General Gage, with his troops, out of the country, which, by the blessing of God, we are determined to accomplish, or perish in the attempt; as we think an honorable death [far better to meet][1] in the field, whilst fighting for the liberties of all America, [far to be preferable][2] to being butchered in our own houses, or to being reduced to an ignominious slavery. We must entreat, that our sister colony, Connecticut, will afford immediately all possible aid, as at this time delay will be att[ended] with all that fatal train of events which would follow from an absolute desertion of the cause of American liberty. Excuse our earnestness upon this subject, as we know that upon the success of our present ——— depend the lives and liberties of our country and of succeeding generations.

We are, &c.

Warren attended the session of congress in the afternoon; for his name occurs on two committees, — one relating to the inhabitants of Boston, and the other on the subject of making a communication to the Continental Congress.

On the 3d, Warren was appointed by the Provincial Congress one of three persons to procure a copperplate on which to print the colony notes which had been authorized, and to countersign them. On this day, the congress sent to the Continental Congress a brief summary of what the colony had done; and, "with the most respectful submission, whilst acting in support of the cause of America," requested its direction and assistance. It terms the British troops

---

[1] These words are interlined.

[2] There is much blotting in the manuscript at this place.

"the ministerial army." Having stated the steps taken to raise an army, and the application that had been made to Rhode Island, Connecticut, and New Hampshire, congress said that the sudden exigency precluded the possibility of waiting for the direction of the Continental Congress. It expressed the greatest confidence in the wisdom and ability of the continent, and their determination to sustain Massachusetts, so far as it should appear to be necessary for supporting the common cause of the American colonies.

On the 4th, Governor Trumbull wrote a reply to the letter of Warren, which is superscribed, "Hon. Joseph Warren, Esq., chairman of the committee of safety," that dispelled all uneasiness relative to the course of Connecticut. On this day, the committee of safety, in view of the extreme exigency of public affairs, "Resolved, as the opinion of this committee, that the public good of this colony requires, that government in full form ought to be taken up immediately; and that a copy of this resolution be transmitted to the congress now sitting at Watertown." On this day, Warren was appointed chairman of a committee to hold a conference with the embassy from Connecticut, who had come out of Boston after an interview with General Gage; and he was appointed the chairman of a committee, the other members being Gerry and Colonel James Warren, to prepare a letter to the assembly of Connecticut on the subject of its application.

On the 5th, on the complaint that one of General Ward's officers, by insolent behavior, had obstructed the removal of the Bostonians, the Provincial Congress ordered a sharp letter to be sent by one of its members to the general. The first draft of this letter, as reported in Congress, contained the name of the individual, and related to the single case. This was stricken out, and the following inserted, which appear in Warren's handwriting: "Therefore, sir, you are directed to examine into the matter, and give such orders as shall be effectual for the future, strictly to execute, &c. And also that you give directions to your officers carefully to execute the resolves of congress, in all matters in which they are to act, without any levity or indecency of expression or behavior." On this day, congress resolved that General Gage had "utterly disqualified himself to serve this colony as governor, and in every other capacity;" and it issued a precept for a new Provincial Congress.

On the 6th, Warren was appointed by the Provincial Congress the chairman of a committee to consider a letter which had been received from the speaker of the Connecticut assembly. Reports were current in the camp now, that the regulars were about to make an attack somewhere. About six o'clock, P.M., the army paraded, and portions were ordered to lie on their arms all night.

On Sunday, the 7th, the Provincial Congress held three sessions, meeting first at eight o'clock, then at twelve, and at four; and the urgency of the hour is indicated in the resolve it passed, directing the committee on supplies to procure arms and bayonets of any colony on the continent.

On the 8th, Warren, as president of the Provincial Congress in Watertown, signed a letter addressed to "The Hon. Artemas Ward, Esq., general of the

Massachusetts forces," Cambridge, directing him to apprehend certain persons, giving their names, who, on the pretext of searching for fire-arms, were charged with committing robbery; and to hand them over to the committee of safety, in order that, if guilty, they might meet with condign punishment. Warren was this day appointed the chairman of a committee to examine such persons as were recommended for surgeons in the army.

On the 9th, Warren was appointed on a committee "to prepare a spirited application to General Gage respecting his treatment of the inhabitants of Boston;" also on a committee to see what provision could be made to supply enlisted soldiers with effective fire-arms.

On the 10th, the session of the congress was long, and the business that was transacted was important. So direct was the intelligence from Boston, that the regulars would soon take the field, that a committee considered the expediency of removing the cannon and stores at Cambridge farther back into the country. On this day, the committee on remonstrating with Gage, of which Warren was a member, reported a letter, which averred that Congress had endeavored to carry into effect the treaty which he made with the selectmen on the removal of the people, and closed with expressing the hope that His Excellency would no longer permit a treaty with a distressed people to be violated.

On the 11th, the congress held three sessions. At this time, the official papers addressed to Warren, or having his autograph, are numerous. The committee of safety passed the following vote: "That

Mr. William Cooper, jun.,[1] be, and he hereby is, appointed a clerk to Dr. Warren, president of the congress."

[1] William Cooper, senior, the town-clerk, lived to a venerable age. The "Independent Chronicle" of Nov. 29, 1809, has the following notice:

"Last evening departed this life, after a short illness, the venerable William Cooper, Esq., aged eighty-eight years, lamented by his numerous connections and friends and by the citizens of his native town generally. As the first testimony of respect, his death was announced by the tolling of all the bells in the town. His character will hereafter be delineated by some person fully acquainted with its merits: at present, it becomes us only to state, that he has been honored with the suffrages of his fellow-citizens as town-clerk forty-nine years successively; and it is worthy of remark, that, during the whole of that time, he was never absent from his duty at a town-meeting."

The same paper of Dec. 7 has the following communication.

"To record the death of a man eminent for his public and private virtues is a painful duty. The subject of the following lines was truly worthy of the universal admiration and esteem which was manifested towards him. His merits will long be cherished with veneration and respect, and oft will the genuine spirit of patriotism bedew his remembrance with a pearly tear: —

MONODY

ON THE DEATH OF WILLIAM COOPER, ESQ.

Spirits of drooping woe!
Bid the sad numbers flow,
And touch with sympathy the weeping lyre;
Let silent grief pervade the breast,
Each ruder passion sink to rest,
And quench the flame of glowing, fond desire.

Oh for a Shakespeare's or a Milton's pen,
Thy virtues, Cooper! faithful to portray;
Then would I raise a deathless song,
In mournful notes to glide along,
And whilst I struck each trembling string,
Soft Melancholy, wild, should sing,
And musing tell, in sweet and pensive lay,
The bright perfections of the best of men.

Though ne'er ambitious for the "wreath of fame,"
His was the pride of an *unsullied name!*
A feeling soul, with sentiment refined,
A clear perception, and a noble mind ·
In his kind heart did nature sweetly blend
The tender father and the faithful friend;
Whilst on his words persuasion ever hung,
And sage instruction issued from his tongue;
Fair Virtue's mandates he with joy obeyed,
And e'er by Honor were his actions weighed;
In Duty's path his steady course he ran,
True to his God, benevolent to man;

On the 12th, congress was occupied with the vital subject of assuming a civil government for Massachusetts; Warren being in the chair, and this question being the order of the day. After the absent members had been called in, it was moved, "That the sense of the congress be taken on this question; viz., Whether there is now existing in this colony a necessity of taking up and exercising civil government in all its parts." Congress resolved itself into a committee of the whole for the consideration of this question, which placed the president on the floor. It is only said in the journals, that the committee considered the question. It is not said that Warren spoke, so provokingly barren are the official details; but there is the following record: "The president, on a motion made, resumed the chair. The committee then, by the Hon. Joseph Warren, Esq., their chairman, reported that a committee be raised for the purpose of reporting to the congress an application to the Continental Congress, for obtaining their recommendation for this colony to take up and exercise civil government as soon as may be; and that the committee be directed to ground the application on

> Till, verging peaceful to his journey's close,
> He calmly left the scene of human woes;
> His long probation in contentment passed,
> Sunk gently down, and, sighing, breathed his last.
>
> If e'er superior and exalted worth
>   Claimed the sad tribute of a parting tear;
> If virtue yet can homage claim on earth, —
>   Come, shed one drop o'er our loved Cooper's bier.
>
> O' gentle youth,
> Whilst veneration fills thy breast,
> And fond remembrance on his merit dwells,
> Go, imitate his *truth;*
> And, whilst with hope thy throbbing bosom swells,
> Like him be *virtuous*, and like him be *blest*.
>
>   THEODORE.

the necessity of the case." The report was accepted by a large majority, and Warren was appointed the chairman of this committee. Thus, great as the emergency was, the patriots were not prepared to take so important a step as creating a new government, without the sanction of the Continental Congress or of the American Union. On this day, Warren wrote the following note, here copied from the original in his handwriting: —

WATERTOWN, May 12, 1775.
To the Honorable the Committee of Safety.

GENTLEMEN, — Mr. Pigeon is now sick. His business must be attended to. He requests that Mr. Charles Miller, the bearer hereof, may be appointed his assistant, and immediately directed to go upon business. Pray desire the young gentleman you were pleased to appoint to be my clerk to attend here, as I have much writing to do, and want a number of papers copied for the use of the congress.

I am, gentlemen, your most obedient servant, J. WARREN.

On the 14th, Sunday, Warren signed his name as chairman of the committee of safety. The meeting of this body, on this day, was uncommonly important. It resolved, that all the live stock be taken from Noddle's Island, Hog Island, Snake Island, and that part of Chelsea near the sea-coast. Warren sent the following note to Mr. Gill, of the committee of supplies: —

CAMBRIDGE, 14th May, 1775.
Mr. MOSES GILL.

SIR, — The committee of safety are informed that the iron pots provided for the army are immediately under your care, and by your letter are advised that 1,500 were prepared and 500 making. By the account from the commissary, there has been but 800 received. We would inform you, the operations of the army are, on this account, obstructed, and [this] occasions considerable uneasiness. You'll critically examine into this matter, and forthwith order said pots into the camp at Cambridge, in such quantities as to complete the above number. Jos. WARREN, *Chairman.*

P.S. — Should be glad to be informed if the pots are disposed of agreeable to the enclosed vote of 18th of April.

On this day, Warren was communing with Samuel Adams, on the great subject of taking up government, in the following letter: —

CAMBRIDGE, May 14, 1775.

DEAR SIR, — We are here waiting for advice from the Continental Congress respecting our taking up government. We cannot think, after what we have suffered for a number of years, that you will advise us to take up that form established by the last charter, as it contains in it the seeds of despotism, and would, in a few years, bring us again into the same unhappy situation in which we now are. For my part, after the termination of the present struggle, I hope never more to be obliged to enter into a political war. I would, therefore, wish that the Government here might be so happily moulded, that the only road to promotion may be through the affection of the people. This being the case, the interest of the governor and the governed will be the same; and we shall no longer be plagued by a group of unprincipled villains, who have acted as though they thought they had a right to plunder and destroy their countrymen, as soon as they could obtain permission from Great Britain for doing it.

We have some very striking instances of the perfidy of one man, who has been raised by the people to power and trust, in the letters of Hutchinson, many of which I have now in my possession. When he had obtained all the people could bestow, it is probable he would have remained firm in their interest (because it would have been for his advantage to have remained so), had there not been a higher station to which his ambitious mind aspired, which was not in the gift of the people; in order to obtain this, he judged it necessary to sacrifice the people, which he has endeavored to do in the most vile and treacherous manner. I send some extracts from his letters, and intend speedily to have many of them published.

General Gage, I fear, has trepanned the inhabitants of Boston. He has persuaded them to lay down their arms, promising to let them remove with their effects; but he suffers them to come out but very slowly, contriving every day new excuses for delay. It appears to me, that a spirited remonstrance from your congress, and a recommendation forthwith to seize all crown officers on the continent, would be the most effectual method of liberating our friends in Boston. I pray you would first consult our delegates upon this subject, and then, if you think proper, mention it to others. Not a moment of time is to be lost. The distress of that town is not to be expressed by words.

I have hitherto kept a surgeon's place in the army for your son; but I fear it cannot be kept any longer, as the regiment has a number sick, and must have one appointed; and I have no reason to expect your son out at present, as he has tried every way to obtain a pass, but to no purpose, and is, as I am informed, entered upon the list with those whom they are determined to detain. He has attempted to come out under a factitious name, but hitherto without success. However, I hear the people are all treated with much more decency than they used to be; and I doubt not but the spirited measure I have proposed to you, together with what we are doing here, will procure the enlargement of our distressed brethren. We have an army of about seven thousand strong already. If the proposed army of thirty thousand men can be quickly got together, I believe this summer will bring our disputes with Great Britain to a happy issue.

It has been suggested to me, that an application from your congress to the Six Nations, accompanied with some presents, might have a very good effect. It appears to me to be worthy of your attention, as they may be of very great use to us in case of any disturbances in the back settlements. We must now prepare for every thing, as we are certain that nothing but success in our warlike enterprises can possibly save us from destruction. If a number of large battery-cannon, with proper ammunition, could be procured, I believe we should soon settle the business with Mr. Gage; but it was too long before we could be convinced that the madness of our invaders would compel us to make use of such things. If powder could be sent from the other colonies to us, it might be of eminent service now, if it be possible to subdue the army here. I believe we may make our own terms; for we shall have much to offer for the benefit of Great Britain, even after she has lost the power of providing for a set of pimps and traitors amongst us, which is the most she could reasonably have expected, had the ministers succeeded in their plan of enslaving the colonies.

I send you a number of printed papers, which contain our public proceedings. I shall keep this letter open until an opportunity of sending it presents.

MAY 17.

Yesterday Dr. Church was appointed to wait on the Continental Congress with the address from this congress, which renders it unnecessary for me to write so particularly to you as I intended, as you will have from him an exact state of affairs, *viva voce*. I would just observe, that the application made to you respecting the taking the regulation of this army into your hands, by appointing a committee of war, or taking the command of it by appointing a generalissimo, is a matter, I think, must be managed with much delicacy. I am a little suspicious, unless great care is taken, some dissentions may arise in the army, as our soldiers, I find, will not yet be brought to obey any person of whom they do not themselves entertain a high opinion. Subordination is absolutely necessary in an army; but the strings must not be drawn too tight at first. The bands of love and esteem must be principally relied on amongst men who know not of any distinction but what arises from some superior merit. I know your prudence and thorough knowledge of our countrymen, their many virtues and their few faults.

The matter of taking up government, I think, cannot occasion much debate. If the southern colonies have any apprehensions from the northern colonies, they surely must now be for an establishment of civil government here; for, as an army is now necessary, or is taking the field, it is obvious to every one, if they are without control, a military government must certainly take place; and I think I cannot see a question with them to determine which is most to be feared, a military or a civil government.

I am, dear sir, with great esteem, your most obedient servant,

JOS. WARREN.[1]

On the 15th, the congress instructed the committee who were preparing the application to the Continental Congress on the subject of the formation of a local government, to insert in it a clause desiring that body " to take some measures for directing and regulating the American forces." On this day, Warren, in the name of the committee of donations,

---

[1] The original manuscript of this letter is not in Warren's handwriting. The signature is in the large bold hand in which he was accustomd to write.

addressed the following letter to Joseph Reed, of Philadelphia: —

Joseph Warren to Joseph Reed.

CAMBRIDGE, May 15, 1775.

DEAR SIR, — I received your very kind letter, enclosing a bill of exchange of four hundred and twenty dollars, in favor of the distressed poor of Boston, upon Mr. Rotch, which I shall take the first opportunity of sending to him, not doubting but it will be duly honored. The sympathy which you discover to have, both in our sufferings and successes in opposing the enemies to the country, is a fresh proof of that benevolence and public spirit which I ever found in you. I rejoice that our friends in Philadelphia are united, and that all are at last brought to see the barbarous scheme of oppression which Administration has formed. We are all embarked in one bottom: if one colony is enslaved, she will be immediately improved as an engine to subdue the others. This our enemies know, and for this cause they have used every art to divide us one from the other, to encourage every groundless prejudice, which they could hope to separate us. Our arch-traitor, Hutchinson, has labored hard in this service. He seems to have fully adopted old Juno's maxim, —

"Flectere si nequeo superos, Acheronta movebo."

I send you a few extracts from some of his letters, which have fortunately fallen in my hands. I likewise send you a pamphlet containing the regulations for the army. You are kind enough to say, that our friends in Philadelphia will assist with whatever they can, when they know our wants, which fills us with a lively sense of the generosity of your colony. To say the truth, we are in want of almost every thing, but of nothing so much as arms and ammunition; for, although much time has been spent in procuring these articles, yet the people never seemed in earnest about the matter until after the engagement of the 19th ult.: and I verily believe, that the night preceding the barbarous outrages committed by the soldiery at Lexington, Concord, &c., there were not fifty people in the whole colony that ever expected any blood would be shed in the contest between us and Great Britain.

The repeated intelligence I received from the best authority, of the sanguinary, malicious temper of the present Administration, together with a perfect knowledge of the inhumanity and wickedness of the villains at Boston who had the ear of General Gage, compelled me to believe that matters would be urged to the last extremity.

Any assistance, of what kind soever, that can be afforded us by our sister colony, in this all-important struggle for the FREEDOM OF AMERICA,[1] will be received with the warmest gratitude.

I am, dear sir, with much regard and esteem, your most humble servant, JOSEPH WARREN.[2]

On the 16th, Warren, as president of the Provincial Congress, was directed to send by one of the members, Dr. Church, an application to the Continental Congress on the questions of a civil government, and the disposition of the army. The original of this document is in a fair, round handwriting; but its main thought is the same that Warren urged in his private letters. On the question of local government, it said that the colony, though urged by the most pressing necessity, had declined to assume the reins of civil government without the advice and consent of the Continental Congress; and it now asked the favor of the "most explicit advice respecting the taking up and exercising the power of civil government," which was thought to be absolutely necessary for the salvation of the country. It pledged Massachusetts to a ready submission "to such a general plan as it (the Continental Congress) might direct for the colonies;" and promised to make it a duty to establish such a form of local government as should not only most promote the advantage of the colony, "but the union and interest of all America." This admirable and statesman-like paper closed by suggesting that the Continental Congress should take the regulation and general direction of the army.

[1] Underscored in the original by the writer.
[2] This letter is printed in Reed's "Life of Joseph Reed," i. 104.

It is simple justice to say, that this paper dealt with the vast question of local and general government in the national spirit that characterized the whole course of the Massachusetts patriots. On this day, Warren addressed the following letter to Arthur Lee: —

CAMBRIDGE, May 16, 1775.

MY DEAR SIR, — Every thing here continues as at the period of my writing to you a short time ago. Our military operations go on in a very spirited manner. General Gage had a re-enforcement of about six hundred marines the day before yesterday; but this gives very little concern *here*. It is not expected that he will sally out of Boston at present; and, if he does, he will but gratify thousands who impatiently wait to avenge the blood of their murdered countrymen. The attempt he has made to throw the odium of the first commencement of hostilities on the people here has operated very much to his disadvantage, as so many credible people were eye-witnesses of the whole affair, whose testimonies are justly supposed of infinitely greater weight than any thing he has or can bring in support of his assertion. My private opinion is, that he is really deceived in this matter, and is led (by his officers, and some other of the most abandoned villains on earth, who are natives of this country, and who are now shut up with him in Boston) to believe that our people actually begun the firing; but my opinion is only for myself: most people are satisfied, not only that he knows that the regulars began the fire, but also that he gave his orders to the commanding officer to do it. Thus, by attempting to clear the troops from what every one is sure they were guilty of, he has brought on strong suspicion that he himself is guilty of having preconcerted the mischief done by them. Indeed, his very unmanly conduct relative to the people of Boston, in detaining many of them, and contriving new excuses for delaying their removal after they had given up their fire-arms, upon a promise of being suffered to leave town, and carry with them their effects, has much lessened his character and confirmed former suspicions.

The Continental Congress is now sitting. I suppose, before I hear from you again, a new form of government will be established in this colony. Great Britain must now make the best she can of America. The folly of her ministers have brought her into this situation. If she has strength sufficient even to depopulate the colonies, she has not strength sufficient to subjugate them. However, we can yet, without injuring ourselves, offer much to her. The great national advantages derived from the colonies may, I hope, yet be reaped by her from us. The plan for enslaving us, if it had succeeded, would only have put it in the power of Administration to have provided for a number of their worthless dependants, whilst the nation was deprived of the most essential benefits which might have arisen from us by commerce; and the taxes raised in America would, instead of easing the mother-country of her burdens, only would have been employed to bring her into bondage.

I cannot precisely tell you what will become of General Gage: I imagine he will at least be kept closely shut up in Boston; perhaps you will very soon hear something further. One thing, I can assure you, has very great weight with us: we fear, if we push this matter as far as we think we are able, — to the destruction of the troops and ships of war, — we shall expose Great Britain to those invasions from foreign powers which we suppose it will be difficult for her to repel. In fact, you must have a change of men and measures, or be ruined. The truly noble Richmond, Rockingham, Chatham, Shelburne, with other lords, and the virtuous and sensible minority in the House of Commons, must take the lead. The confidence we have in them will go a great way; but I must tell you, that those terms which would readily have been accepted before our countrymen were murdered, and we in consequence thereof compelled to take arms, will not now do.

Every thing in my power to serve the united interest of Great Britain and her colonies shall be done: and I pray that you, your brother, and Mr. Sayre (to whom I beg you would make my most respectful compliments) would write fully, freely, and speedily to me; and let me know, likewise, what our great and good friends in the House of Lords and Commons think expedient and practicable to be done.

God forbid that the nation should be so infatuated as to do any thing further to irritate the colonies! If they should, the colonies will sooner throw themselves into the arms of any other power on earth than ever consent to an accommodation with Great Britain. That patience which I have frequently told you would at last be exhausted is no longer to be expected from us. Danger and war are become pleasing; and injured virtue is now armed to avenge herself.

I am, my dear sir, your most obedient, humble servant,

JOS. WARREN.

P.S. — Please to let Mr. Sayre and Sheriff Lee know that I shall write to them by the first opportunity. This will be handed to you by my good friend Mr. Barrell, who will give you a more particular account of the situation of our public affairs.[1]

On the 17th, Warren drafted a congratulatory letter, in behalf of the Provincial Congress, to the Connecticut colony, on the capture of Ticonderoga, which I copy from the original in his handwriting: —

WATERTOWN, May 17, 1775.

GENTLEMEN, — We have the happiness of presenting our congratulations to you on the reduction of that important Fortress Ticonderoga. We applaud the conduct of both the officers and soldiers; and are of opinion that the advantageous situation of that fortress makes it highly expedient that it should be repaired and properly garrisoned. In the mean time, as we suppose, that, as there is no scruple for keeping all the cannon there, we should be extremely glad if all the battering cannon, especially brass cannon, which can be spared from that place or procured from Crown Point (which we hope is by this time in the hands of our friends), may be forwarded this way with all possible expedition, as we have here to contend with an army furnished with as fine a train of artillery as ever was seen in America; and we are in extreme want of a sufficient number of cannon to fortify those important passes without which we can neither annoy General Gage, if it should become necessary, nor defend ourselves against him. We, therefore, must most earnestly recommend this very important matter to your immediate consideration; and we would suggest it as our opinion, that the appointing Colonel Arnold to take charge of them, and bring them down in all possible haste, may be a means of settling any dispute which may have arisen between him and some other officers, which we are always desirous to avoid, and more especially at a time when our common danger ought to unite us in the strongest bonds of amity and affection.

We are, gentlemen, &c.

On the 18th, Warren was again chosen a member of the committee of safety, his name standing next

---

[1] This letter is copied from the original in Harvard-College Library. The copy in "Life of Arthur Lee," ii. 268-70, is mangled.

to Hancock's. He had this day an unusual duty put upon him, occasioned by the arrest and detention, by an armed party, of Lady Frankland, who had received a permit to go into Boston, as authorized by congress; and one of the party was called to account before this body. On retiring, it was resolved, that the president should gently admonish him, and assure him "that the congress were determined to preserve their dignity and power over the military;" when the offender was called in, and "the president politely admonished him."

On the 19th, congress renewed the powers of the committee of safety in a series of resolves that would occupy several of these pages, confirmed its acts thus far, and put the substantial executive power of the colony into their hands. It gave this body full power to call out the militia, to station the army, and directed the general and other officers to render strict obedience to its orders.

On the 20th, Warren, in the morning, was appointed by congress the head of an important committee to consider how the Massachusetts army could be organized in the most ready and effectual manner; and, in the afternoon, as president, he delivered to General Ward his commission "as general and commander-in-chief of the Massachusetts forces." The oath was administered to him by Hon. Samuel Dexter. It is not mentioned that Warren made an address on this occasion; but he was in the habit of doing it on the delivery of military commissions, as I have already stated. In 1782 John Adams related this incident at a dinner party at the Hague. He says, "Dr. Warren made a harangue in the form of a charge, in the presence of the assembly, to every officer, upon the delivery of his commission; and he never failed to make the officer, as well as all the assembly, shudder upon those occasions. Count Sarsfield appeared struck and affected by this anecdote."

On the 21st, Sunday, the following is the whole of the record of the doings of congress: "Met at four o'clock, P.M., and adjourned to to-morrow morning, eight o'clock." Warren communicated "to Hall's paper," the "Essex Gazette," the following account of what occurred this day: —

"Last Sabbath, about ten o'clock, A.M., an express arrived at General Thomas's quarters, at Roxbury, informing him that four sloops (two of them armed) were sailed from Boston to the south shore of the bay, and that a number of soldiers were landing at Weymouth. General Thomas ordered three companies to march to the support of the inhabitants. When arrived, they found the soldiers had not attempted to land at Weymouth, but had landed on Grape Island, from whence they were carrying off hay on board the sloops. The people of Weymouth assembled on a point of land next to Grape Island. The distance from Weymouth shore to the said island was too great for small arms to do execution; nevertheless, our people frequently fired. The fire was returned from one of the vessels, with swivel-guns; but the shot passed over our heads, and did no mischief. Matters continued in this state for several hours, the soldiers pulling the hay down to the water-side, our people firing at the vessel, and they now and then discharging swivel-guns. The tide had now come in, and several lighters which were aground, were got afloat; upon which our people, who were ardent for battle, got on board, hoisted sail, and bore directly down upon the nearest point of the island. The soldiers and sailors immediately left the barn, and made for their boats, and put off from one end of the island whilst our people landed on the other. The sloops hoisted sail with all possible expedition, whilst our people set fire to the barn, and burnt seventy or eighty tons of hay; then fired several tons which had been pulled down to the water-side, and brought off the cattle. As the vessels passed Horse Neck, a sort of promontory which extends from Germantown, they fired their swivels and small arms at our people pretty briskly, but without effect, though one of the bullets from their small arms, which passed over our people, struck against a stone with such force as to take off a large part of the bullet. Whether any of the enemy were wounded is uncertain, though it it is reported three of them were. It is thought they did not carry off more than one or two tons of hay."[1]

There is an omission in this relation. Bancroft remarks, that "Warren, ever bravest among the brave, ever present where there was danger," was in this affair.

On the 22d, the Provincial Congress sent to Colouel Arnold a letter on the capture of Ticonderoga, similar in sentiment to Warren's letter written to Connecticut on the 17th, and enclosing a copy of it, saying that, as the expedition began in that colony, it ought to take the whole matter under its care and direction "until the advice of the Continental Congress" could be received.

On the 23d, the committee on the organization of

[1] The relation in the text, and the attention that Warren gave to the publication of the letters of Hutchinson in the newspapers, were the close of his connection with the press. His friends, Benjamin Edes and John Gill, of the "Boston Gazette," lived to see the independence of their country. The following notice is in the "Exchange Advertiser" of Sept. 1, 1785: "Died on Friday last, much respected, in the fifty-fourth year of his age, Captain John Gill, for many years a printer in the metropolis." Benjamin Edes lived until 1803. An obituary notice of him, in the "Independent Chronicle" of Dec. 19, says, "On Thursday last, the remains of the aged patriot, Benjamin Edes, were attended to the grave by a numerous and respectable procession of his fellow-citizens.... The services Mr. Edes rendered his country, by his uniform and intrepid conduct during the various conflicts of America against the arbitrary measures of Britain, endeared his memory to all those who estimate the blessings of our independence. In that day he stepped forward as a printer, and devoted his press, free and unshackled, to sound the trumpet in our political Zion, and warn the inhabitants of the danger that threatened them. In the pages of his paper may be found the eloquent language of an Otis, the convincing arguments of S. Adams, the logical reasoning of Warren, the animating fire of Paine, the combined patriots of those days, whose exertions nipped tyranny in the bud, and paved the way to America's glory."

the army, appointed on the 20th, of which Warren was the chairman, reported through "Joseph Hawley per order;" and, among other recommendations, that a lieutenant-general should be appointed by the congress before it should rise.

On the 24th, the Provincial Congress issued an address to their "Friends and fellow-countrymen," urging that they should continue to furnish supplies to support the army, and ought to crown all their exertions by subscribing to a loan of one hundred thousand, lawful money.

On the 25th, Warren had the pleasure of sending to the committee of safety the following note, which I copy from the original in his handwriting: —

WATERTOWN, May 25, 1775.

To the Honorable Committee of Safety.

GENTLEMEN, — Upon my arrival here just this minute, I had the pleasure of being informed, that our worthy friend Colonel Arnold, not having had the sole honor of reducing Ticonderoga and Crown Point, determined upon an expedition against St. John's, in which he happily succeeded. The letters were directed to the committee of safety, but were supposed to be necessary to be laid before the congress. I have not yet seen them; but you will have the particulars from the bearer.

I have also received a letter from the congress of New Hampshire, informing me of a resolve to raise forthwith two thousand men, and more, if it should be necessary. The troops, at least one company, with a train of artillery, from Providence, are in the upper end of Roxbury. To say the truth, I find my health much mended since the morning.

I am, gentlemen, your most obedient servant, J. WARREN.

P.S. — You will be kind enough to communicate the contents of this letter to the general's room, as I love to give pleasure to good men.

On the 26th, Warren addressed the following clear, well-considered, and statesman-like letter to his friend

Samuel Adams, on the all-important question of a civil government and the control of the army: —

Joseph Warren to Samuel Adams.

DEAR SIR, — I see more and more the necessity of establishing a civil government here, and such a government as shall be sufficient to control the military forces, not only of this colony, but also such as shall be sent to us from the other colonies. The continent must strengthen and support with all its weight the civil authority here; otherwise our soldiery will lose the ideas of right and wrong, and will plunder, instead of protecting, the inhabitants. This is but too evident already; and I assure you *inter nos*, that, unless some authority sufficient to restrain the irregularities of this army is established, we shall very soon find ourselves involved in greater difficulties than you can well imagine. The least hint from the most unprincipled fellow, who has perhaps been reproved for some criminal behavior, is quite sufficient to expose the fairest character to insult and abuse among many; and it is with our countrymen as with all other men, when they are in arms, they think the military should be uppermost. I know very well, that, in the course of time, people will see the error of such proceedings; but I am not sure it will be before many disagreeable consequences may take place. The evil may now be easily remedied. I know the temper of our people. They are sensible, brave, and virtuous; and I wish they might ever continue so. Mild and gentle regulations will be sufficient for them; but the penalties annexed to the breach of those rules should be rigorously inflicted. I would have such a government as should give every man the greatest liberty to do what he pleases consistent with restraining him from doing any injury to another, or such a government as would most contribute to the good of the whole, with the least inconvenience to individuals. However, it is difficult to frame a government *de novo* which will stand in need of no amendment. Experience must point out defects. And, if the people should not lose their morals, it will be easy for them to correct the errors in the first formation of government. If they *should* lose *them*, what was not good at first will be soon insupportable. My great wish therefore is, that we may restrain every thing which tends to weaken the principles of right and wrong, more especially with regard to *property*. You may possibly think I am a little angry with my countrymen, or have not so good an opinion of them as I formerly had; but that is not the case. I love,—I *admire* them. The errors they have fallen into are natural and easily accounted for. A sudden alarm brought them together, animated with the noblest spirit. They left their houses, their families, with nothing but the clothes on their backs, without a day's provision, and many without a farthing in their pockets. Their country was in danger; their brethren were slaughtered; their arms alone engrossed their attention. As they passed through the country, the inhabitants gladly opened their hospitable doors, and all things were in common. The enemies of their country alone refused to aid and comfort the hungry soldier. Prudence seemed to dictate that the force made use of to obtain what ought voluntarily to have been given, should be winked at. And it is not easy for men, especially when interest and the gratification of appetite are considered, to know how far they may continue to tread in the path where there are no landmarks to direct them. I hope care will be taken by the Continental Congress to apply an immediate remedy, as the infection is caught by every new corps that arrives.

With regard to the skirmish which happened at Grape Island, you will find a particular account thereof in Hall's paper, which was given him by myself, who was in the action.

Yesterday arrived the three famous generals, Howe, Burgoyne, and Clinton, with twenty of the light-horse: two were lost on the voyage. Pray present my best respects to all friends, particularly our colony members, and, without letting the matter be public, take their opinions upon the former part of this letter. For the honor of my country, I wish the disease may be cured before it is known to exist.

I am, dear sir, your most obedient servant and sincere friend,

JOS. WARREN.

Mr. SAMUEL ADAMS.
CAMBRIDGE, May 26, 1775.

On the 27th, Warren, as the president of congress, sent to the Continental Congress a letter relative to the action of Massachusetts in relation to the capture of Ticonderoga, which contains more elaborately the views he had expressed in his letters to Mr. McDougal of New York, and to Connecticut. "We beg leave," this letter says, "on this occasion most solemnly to assure your honors, that nothing can be more abhorrent to the temper and spirit of this congress and the people of this colony, than any attempt to usurp on the jurisdiction of any of our sister colonies, which, upon the superficial consideration of this step, there may seem to be some appearance of. But we assure ourselves, that such are the candor and generous sentiments of our brethren of the colony of New York, . . . that they will readily overlook this mistake, if it is one, committed in the haste of war. . . . If any of those cannon should arrive within the limits of this colony, we shall hold ourselves accountable for them to your honors, or any succeeding representatives of the continent." So careful were the patriots not to infringe on the local jurisdiction of their brethren, and so true were they to the union. On this day, Warren served under General Putnam in the spirited skirmish on Noddle's Island, when the provincials drove off the live stock. In the "London Chronicle" of this date, appended to an address by the Provincial Congress, "To the inhabitants of Great Britain," Warren's name occurs, for the first time, appended to an official document printed in England.

On the 28th, Warren received a letter from J. Henshaw, who was selected for a mission to Hartford and Crown Point, asking for certain papers and a horse and sulky, which Mr. Gill promised to supply. Henshaw asked Warren's direction in the matter. Many letters of this nature were addressed to Warren, which shows the detail that fell to his lot.

On the 29th, Warren, as president, addressed a letter to the New-Hampshire Congress, urging the importance of maintaining the forts of Ticonderoga and Crown Point. On this day, the second Provincial Congress dissolved.

On the 30th, there was a meeting of the committee of safety, when directions were given to carry to Cambridge the cannon and stores saved from a schooner that had been burned in Chelsea.

The 31st was the day named in the colony charter for the annual election of councillors, and the third Provincial Congress convened in the meeting-house at Watertown. The first entry on its journal states that "Hon. Joseph Warren, Esq.," was unanimously chosen the president. The committee of safety met in this town, and there was held here a convention of congregational ministers. The president of Harvard College, Rev. Samuel Langdon, D.D., preached the election sermon from the text, "And I will restore thy judges as at the first, and thy counsellors as at the beginning: afterwards thou shalt be called the city of righteousness, the faithful city." The discourse began with the following words: "Shall we rejoice, my fathers and brethren, or shall we weep together, on the return of this anniversary?" In Dr. Langdon's view, the controversy threatened "a final separation of the colonies from Great Britain." He announced the vital principle, that "every nation, when able and agreed, has a right to set up over themselves any form of government which to them might appear most conducive to their common welfare;" he uttered the following timely republican injunction: "Let those who cry up the divine right of kings consider, that the only form of government which had a proper claim to a divine establishment was so far from including the idea of a king, that it was a high crime in Israel to be in this respect like other nations;" and he regarded the general agreement "through so many provinces of so large a country," in the adoption of "one mode of self-preservation," of corresponding committees and congresses, as caused by "some supernatural influence on the minds of the main body of the people." There has been a disposition to take a semi-Tory view of the conduct of the people, by giving undue importance to the instances of mob action, and to overlook the remarkable adherence to social order that is seen through ten years of exciting controversy. The words of Dr. Langdon, on this point, are valuable. He said, "Universal tumults, and all the irregularities and violence of mobbish factions, naturally arise when legal authority ceases. But how little of this has appeared in the midst of the late obstructions of civil government! Nothing more than what has often happened in Great Britain and Ireland, in the face of the civil powers in all their strength; nothing more than what is frequently seen in the midst of the perfect regulations of the great city of London." And he bore the following testimony to the general obedience paid, at that time, to the local authorities and the inchoate nationality: "The judgment and advice of the continental assembly of delegates have been as readily obeyed as if they were the authentic acts of a long-established parliament. And in every colony the votes of a congress have had equal effect with the laws of great and general courts." This fact is a part of American history, — a history not made by the few, but by the many, — a history which illustrates at every step the power of an enlightened public opinion.

On the 1st of June, the Provincial Congress ordered letters to be sent to Colonel Arnold, to the assembly of Connecticut, and the Provincial Congress of New Hampshire, on the subject of retaining Ticonderoga and Crown Point.

On the 2d, congress was occupied with the details connected with the organization of the army. Among the papers addressed to Warren as president were memorials relative to the exposed position of the seaport towns; and a large committee was appointed to consider the subject of their protection.

On the 3d, a committee, with Gerry as the chairman, was appointed to hold a conference at Cambridge, with the committee of safety, on the subject of re-enforcing the army, and the general officers were invited to join in it.

On the 4th, Sunday, there were three sessions of the Provincial Congress. Elbridge Gerry, addressed a letter on this day to the Massachusetts delegates, in which he urged strongly the necessity of a local government and " of a regular general." In relation to the latter, Gerry says, " I should heartily rejoice to see this way the beloved Colonel Washington, and do not doubt the New-England generals would acquiesce in showing to our sister colony, Virginia, the respect she has before experienced from the continent in making him generalissimo. This is a matter in which Dr. Warren agrees with me; and we had intended to write you jointly on the affair."[1] Warren, on this day, as "chairman of the committee of safety," united with General Ward, "general of the Massachusetts forces," and Moses

[1] Life of Elbridge Gerry, i. 79.

Gill, "chairman of the committee of supplies," in a strong representation to the Continental Congress of the distresses of the colony, in the assurance, they said, that congress, as the wise guardians of the lives, liberties, and properties of the whole of this extensive continent, would attend to the circumstances of all who, under God, looked up to them for protection and deliverance.

On the 5th, a committee was appointed to examine certain mineral earth that had been submitted to congress, "and, in such inquiry, to consult the Hon. Joseph Warren, Esq., and Professor Sewall."

On the 6th, Warren accompanied General Putnam to Charlestown, in order to effect an exchange of prisoners. Captain Chester and the Wethersfield company formed the escort. Warren and Putnam rode in a phaëton; two of the prisoners, who were officers, were on horseback; a lieutenant was in a chaise; and four wounded marines were in two carts. Warren and Putnam met Major Moncrief and other British officers at the house of Dr. Foster, in Charlestown, where an entertainment was provided. The affair "was conducted with the utmost decency and good humor." On this day, Warren was appointed on a committee to consider the expediency of authorizing armed vessels to cruise on the American coasts, protect its trade, and annoy its enemies. The members were enjoined to observe secrecy.

On the 7th, the business transacted by the Provincial Congress was uncommonly important. Elbridge Gerry, from a committee, reported that it was unnecessary for the colony to augment its forces. A time was assigned for the choice of two major-generals. The president was directed to admonish Mr. Edwards on account of his speech on the committee of safety.

On the 8th, there was an important debate in the Provincial Congress on a report, signed by Gerry as chairman, to the effect that it was unnecessary to increase the force raised for this and other American colonies; when the committees of safety and supplies, and the several committees of the congress, were desired to be present. After debating the subject in the morning and the afternoon in committee of the whole, the report was accepted.

On the 9th, the Provincial Congress adopted a stringent order, directing the committee of safety to certify the claims or pretensions that any gentleman might have to a commission in the service, with a view to reducing the army to order.

On the 10th, the committee of safety presented an elaborate and valuable report, showing the confused state of the army from the date of the 19th of April, in consequence of more enlisting orders having been delivered than were sufficient to enlist the number of men required. "At that time," the committee say, "but few men enlisted; and there was an apprehension that the province was in the utmost danger from the want of men." Hutchinson[1] predicted to Gibbon, that " unless fanaticism got the better of self-preservation, they (the people) must soon disperse, as it

---

[1] Hutchinson was tendered a baronetcy, which he declined. He died in England, on the 3d of June, 1780, suddenly, as he was stepping into his carriage, and was buried at Croyden. He was sixty-nine years of age.

Francis Bernard died June 16, 1779. A brief obituary of him, in the "Gentleman's Magazine," says he was of Nettleham, Lincolnshire.

was the season for sowing their Indian corn, the chief subsistence of New England." This was the time when Warren "did wonders" in keeping the army together.

On the 11th, the Provincial Congress authorized Joseph Hawley to sign an address to the Continental Congress, which strongly reiterated the necessity "of a settled civil polity or government," making reference to the former application of the 16th of May. This address says, "The pressing weight of our distresses has necessitated the sending a special post to obtain your immediate advice upon this subject; and we do most earnestly entreat that you would, as soon as possible, despatch the messenger with such advice." This address repeats the considerations which Warren had urged in official and private letters.

On the 12th, there was a session of the Provincial Congress; but the absorbing topic of the day was the celebrated proclamation of General Gage, declaring "the infatuated multitudes" who were in arms, and their abettors, to be rebels, and offering pardon to all excepting Samuel Adams and John Hancock.

On the 13th, there was a long session of congress. Warren was appointed the chairman of "a committee to consider the subject-matter of a late extraordinary proclamation of General Gage;" and this committee prepared a counter-proclamation, which, though not issued at the time, was printed subsequently in the journals of the Provincial Congress.

On the 14th, the Provincial Congress chose Warren, by ballot, a major-general. The records say a committee was directed "to wait on the Hon. Joseph

Warren, Esq., and inform him that this congress have made choice of him for second major-general of the Massachusetts army, and desire his answer to this congress of his acceptance of this trust." It is stated, that "he was proposed as a physician-general; but, preferring a more active and hazardous employment, he accepted a major-general's commission."[1]

On the 15th, the committee of safety recommended to the council of war, that, as the possession of Bunker Hill appeared of importance to the safety of the colony, it be maintained by a sufficient force being posted there; and, as the situation of Dorchester Hill was unknown to the committee, it recommended to the council of war to take such steps relative to it as "to them should appear to be for the security of the colony." It had been reported for several weeks, that General Gage, when his reenforcements arrived, designed to commence offensive operations; and it was expected in England that his finely appointed army, commanded by generals of experience, would easily disperse the Provincials. So scanty was the supply of powder and of arms, and so great the confusion of the army, there were apprehensions that General Gage might succeed, at least so far as to capture Cambridge; and congress took steps to secure the records and stores. On the 12th of May, this body was formally advised, that, in order to render the country "safe from all sallies of the enemy" in this quarter, it would be necessary to fortify Prospect Hill, the first hill in Charlestown (now in Somerville), nearest to head-quarters; Winter Hill, which is nearest to the peninsula of Charles-

[1] Mass. Hist. Society's Collections, i. 110.

town; and Bunker Hill, just within the peninsula. It is said that Warren was not in favor of occupying so exposed a post as Bunker Hill, which would be in accordance with his usual good judgment. The following incidents are related: On the evening after the affair at Noddle's Island, after General Putnam had warmly urged this measure, but General Ward had enjoined caution, Warren remarked to Putnam, "I admire your spirit, and respect General Ward's prudence. We shall need them both, and one must temper the other." After the march of the army into Charlestown, Ward and Warren, against an occupancy of the heights of this town, said that, "as they had no powder to spare, and no battering cannon, it would be idle to make approaches on to the town." One day, after conversing with Putnam on this subject, Warren rose, and walked two or three times across the room, leaned a few minutes over the back of a chair, in a thoughtful attitude, and said, "Almost thou persuadest me, General Putnam; but I must still think the project a rash one. Nevertheless, if the project be adopted, and the strife becomes hard, you must not be surprised to find me near you in the midst of it"[1] There is nothing unreasonable in these relations, so far as they relate to Warren. In fact, they harmonize with much under his own hand bearing on military operations. His letters show how earnest he was to drive Gage out of Boston; but his pleading for powder, artillery, discipline, and adequate government shows a wise appreciation of the obstacles that were in the path of success. The great

[1] These relations are contained in a memoir prepared by Daniel Putnam, in 1818.

object, however, was self-defence. The commanders of the army received authentic intelligence, that General Gage had fixed on the night of the 18th of June on which to commence offensive operations; and hence the action of the committee of safety. On this day, Warren, as president of the congress, signed letters addressed to Connecticut, New Hampshire, and the Continental Congress. An elaborate report showed the disorganized state of the army, the position of the colonels relative to commissions, and stated that the Massachusetts forces fell considerably short of the 13,600 men which had been ordered to be enlisted.

On the 16th, Warren presided at the session of the Provincial Congress at Watertown. Several colonels and captains were sworn in and commissioned; and the committee on Gage's proclamation, of which Warren was the chairman, reported a spirited rejoinder. The committee of safety met at Cambridge, and the business on its hands must have been uncommonly urgent. It was reported this day in the camp, "that Warren was chosen a major-general, and that Heath was not chosen to any office; but it was supposed that no difficulty would arise from it." The following note, which I copy from the original in his handwriting, superscribed " General Heath, camp at Roxbury, to be delivered immediately," shows that Warren was in Cambridge, and on the most kindly relations with Heath. It is the last word from Joseph Warren under his own hand:—

CAMBRIDGE, June 16.

MY GOOD FRIEND,— Every thing is now going agreeable to our wishes. General Ward has recommended to the congress to take the [ ] we determined upon yesterday. Nothing is wanting but for

every Thing is now go
our Wishes General Ward has
...ded to the Congress to take the
mined upon Yesterday Nothing
but for you to make a Return
Regiment which I wish may
without a Moment's Delay
is an absolute Order of Congress
Brigadiers shall be chosen out of
... I am your most obed.
humble Servant
Jos Warren

you to make a return of your regiment, which I wish may be done without a moment's delay, as there is an absolute order of congress, that the brigadiers shall be chosen out of the colonels.

I am your most obedient, humble servant, JOS. WARREN.[1]

In the evening, he was applied to on public business, and promised that it should be attended to. About nine o'clock, Colonel Prescott, at the head of a detachment of about one thousand men, marched from Cambridge to Charlestown, passed over Bunker Hill, which had been recommended to be held, and threw up a redoubt on the heights near Boston, which have since obtained the name of Breed's Hill. The committee of safety say that this hill was chosen " by mistake." It is stated that Warren passed the night in the transaction of public business.[2]

[1] The original of this note is in the Heath Papers, in the archives of the Massachusetts Historical Society.

[2] Everett's Warren, 158.

CHAPTER XVI.

THE CLOSING SCENE.

WARREN AND THE SEVENTEENTH OF JUNE. — THE COMMITTEE OF SAFETY. — THE CONTINENTAL CONGRESS. — WARREN IN THE BUNKER-HILL BATTLE. — HIS FALL. — THE GENERAL GRIEF. — THE REMAINS. — MONUMENT. — CONCLUSION.

1775. THE SEVENTEENTH OF JUNE.

THE Seventeenth of June was a marked anniversary in Warren's career. Seven years before, on this day, in a town-meeting, he recommended the people to vindicate their rights at the hazard of fortune and life.[1] On the last anniversary, acting still more prominently as a popular leader, his morning hours were full of anxiety, because, for the first time, he had to meet an exigency without the guidance of Samuel Adams; but, in the evening, he was full of joy because of the success of a town-meeting, the choice of delegates to a Continental Congress, and the signs that heralded American Union.[2]

Warren may be said to have lived an age during the twelve months upon which he then entered. There soon happened those exigencies that occur in the progress of great events, in meeting which mediocrity too often fails, but genuine ability rises to the mark of rendering large public service. Warren, growing steadily in self-reliance, discharged the du-

[1] See page 67. [2] See pages 319-326.

ties which fell to his lot in such a manner that his contemporaries said " he filled each of the numerous departments of life that were assigned to him so well, that he seemed born for no other;"[1] and that "his name would live, and fill the world with wonder."[2] His words, as he thus acted, show how his spirit linked itself with the heroic and memorable past of the ages; and yet how simply and tersely[3] he could urge the practical duties of the hour. Though he was an enthusiast for liberty, he appreciated the necessity of joining to it that respect which power only can command. His ideal was liberty without licentiousness. He urged for its full enjoyment the formation of a just government, based on the will, and sustained by the power, of the people, and clothed with adequate authority to cover the rights of person and property with the ægis of law. His last utterances, private and official, plead for such a crowning to the patriot cause. He urged that the Continental Congress should authorize the formation of a local government, and transform, by adoption, the raw militia around him into a national army. On this last morning of his life, he did not know that congress had given its advice to Massachusetts, and appointed a commander-in-chief.

He passed the night of the 16th of June at Watertown, where the Provincial Congress held its sessions; but the journal of the proceedings of this day shows that he was not present at the meeting on the morning of the 17th; for it is recorded of the first item of

---

[1] Eulogy in the Pennsylvania Magazine, June, 1775.
[2] Epitaph in Boston Gazette, June 29, 1775.
[3] See his Letter of the 26th of May.

business, "The report was ordered to lie on the table till the president came into congress."[1] He had declared his intention to share the peril of the day with his countrymen. When an intimate friend, Elbridge Gerry, who had been his room-mate, entreated him not to expose a life so valuable, with something like a presentiment he replied, *Dulce et decorum est pro patria mori.*[2] " It is sweet and becoming to die for the country;" and hence a patriot wrote, "The ardor of dear Doctor Warren could not be restrained by the entreaty of his brethren of the congress."[3]

It may be sufficient as to motive to say, that the same ardor which, for the sake of the cause, had moved him to go where duty was to be performed; which had carried him to Lexington, Grape Island, and Noddle's Island, — prompted his course on this memorable day. But it was also a mark of sound judgment. He had fully resolved that his future service should be in the military line. Confidence by an army in a commander is a vital element of success; and this can be acquired only on the field. Acting, doubtless, with the fixedness of aim which characterized his whole life, he left Watertown early in the morning, with a view of making himself useful, and went to Cambridge.

The committee of safety held its sessions in the Hastings House, on Cambridge Common, in which General Ward had his head-quarters;[4] and Warren

---

[1] Journals of the Provincial Congress, 348.
[2] Life of Elbridge Gerry, i. 84.
[3] Letter of William Williams, June 20, 1775.
[4] This house is still standing. It passed into the hands of Judge Oliver Wendell, and is owned now by the poet, Oliver Wendell Holmes.

met with them. The calls on this body for cannon, horses, powder, re-enforcements, the pressing orders in its journal for the towns to act, and short and hurried notes,[1] attest the thrilling interest of the hour. The intelligence from Colonel Prescott was so decisive, that the British were preparing to move out of Boston and assault his works, that the committee urged General Ward to send forward additional force to Charlestown; and, about eleven o'clock, before General Howe landed in this town, Ward issued orders for more troops to march to the support of Colonel Prescott.

As the armies were making preparations for a battle, letters arrived from Philadelphia, "brought express by Mr. Fessenden,"[2] signed by John Hancock, the president, and Charles Thomson, the secretary, of the Continental Congress. They contained the great news, which was ordered to be kept secret, that the congress had ordered purchases of saltpetre, sulphur, powder, and "five thousand barrels of flour for the use of the continental army," which were to be paid for "out of the continental funds;" and also that it had recommended the people of Massachusetts to form a local government.[3] It was another advance towards nationality. Warren probably opened these letters, and forwarded them to the Provincial Congress. They were read in the afternoon session.[4] Would that Warren could also have known, that a commander-in-chief had been appointed, and that, as he desired, the choice had fallen on Washington![5]

---

[1] The manuscripts are in the Massachusetts archives.
[2] Journals of Provincial Congress, 352.   [3] Ib., 354.   [4] Ib., 352.
[5] The two letters of the Provincial Congress, signed by Warren, were received in the Continental Congress on the 11th of May and the 2d of June; and, after

Between twelve and one o'clock, a horseman rode furiously into Cambridge with the report, that "the regulars had landed at Charlestown,"[1] when the bells were rung, the drums beat to arms, and there were the confusion and hurry incident to an ill-disciplined soldiery; for the camp, "except where Putnam's and Warren's influence had their effects,"[2] was in

long debates, congress, on the 9th of June, came to the following result, which was a full indorsement of the course that was pursued by Massachusetts: —

Resolved, That no obedience being due to the Act of Parliament for altering the charter of the Colony of Massachusetts Bay, nor to a governor or a lieutenant-governor who will not observe the directions of, but endeavor to subvert that charter, the governor and lieutenant-governor of that colony are to be considered as absent, and these offices vacant; and as there is no council there, and the inconveniences arising from the suspension of the powers of government are intolerable, especially at a time when General Gage hath actually levied war, and is carrying on hostilities against His Majesty's peaceable and loyal subjects of that colony, that, in order to conform as near as may be to the spirit and substance of the charter, it be recommended to the Provincial Convention to write letters to the inhabitants of the several places which are entitled to representation in assembly, requesting them to choose such representatives; and that the assembly, when chosen, do elect councillors, which assembly and council should exercise the powers of government until a governor of His Majesty's appointment will consent to govern the colony according to its charter.

This action was not what the popular leaders desired. James Warren wrote (June 21, 1775) to John Adams, "I am well pleased with most of your resolves. I can't, however, say that I admire the form of government presented; but we are all submission, and are sending out our letters for calling an assembly. I hope we shall have as good an opportunity for a good government in some future time." The same patriot wrote to Samuel Adams (June 20, 1775), "We could only have wished you had suffered us to have embraced so good an opportunity to form for ourselves a constitution worthy of freemen."

[1] Captain Chester's Letter, July 22, 1775.

[2] James Warren, June 27, 1775. He succeeded General Warren as president of congress, and wrote, on the 20th of June, 1775, to John Adams as follows: "Had our brave men, posted on ground injudiciously at first taken, had a Lee or a Washington, instead of a general destitute of all military ability and spirit, to command them, it is my opinion the day would have terminated with as much glory to America as the 19th of April. This is our great misfortune, and it is remediless from any other quarter than yours. We dare not supersede him here. It will come well from you, and really merits your attention. That, and a necessary article which makes me tremble to name or think of, is all we want." On the next day, in a letter to Samuel Adams, he urged the necessity of a general; and says that General Ward did not leave his house all day on the 17th.

a confused condition. General Putnam had come from Bunker Hill, and he promptly ordered the remainder of his regiment to Charlestown; but the course of General Ward was regarded as hesitating and inefficient, and elicited severe contemporary comment. He did not leave his house the whole day. It is not necessary, however, to relate the details of the events of the battle-scene that ensued, but only to glance at a few points, in order to show the circumstances under which Warren acted.

It was a very hot summer's day, with a burning sun. Warren was suffering from a nervous headache, and threw himself on a bed; but, after the alarm was given, he rose, and, saying that his headache was gone, started for the scene of action. It is said that one of his students, Dr. Townsend, accompanied him a part of the way on foot, but that, a short distance from the College, Warren was on horseback. He overtook two friends[1] who were walking to the battle-field, and, exchanging with them the usual salutations, he passed along towards Charlestown. He came within range of the British batteries at the low, flat ground which marks the entrance to that portion of the town nearest to Boston, which is a peninsula; and the firing, at the time he passed, between two and three o'clock, must have been severe. He went up Bunker Hill, where another of his students, William Eustis, served on this day as a surgeon. Here Warren had a view of the whole situation. On his left was Mystic River, where there were no floating-batteries. The line of fire from the British began on a point a little inclined to the left,

[1] James Swan and James Winthrop.

where the ships-of-war "Lively" and the "Falcon" lay; and it continued round by Charles River, from Copp's Hill, — the "Somerset," the "Cerberus," the "Glasgow," the "Symmetry" transport, and two floating-batteries, quite to his right. He could see, on the side of Bunker Hill towards Boston, the protection which Captain Knowlton began to construct of the rail-fences, when Colonel Prescott ordered him from the redoubt to oppose the enemy's right wing,[1] and which the New-Hampshire forces, under Colonels Stark and Reed, were extending. Directly in front of the rail-fence, on a small hill at Moulton's Point, he could see the same British regiments which he had beheld so long in Boston, — among them, doubtless, the officers before whom he delivered his Fifth-of-March oration, — now awaiting the order for an assault. A furious cannonade, about this time, was directed upon Roxbury, to occupy the attention of the Provincials in that quarter, while the fire of three ships, three batteries, several field-pieces, and a battery on Copp's Hill, from six different directions, centred on the intrenchments.[2]

Warren went to the rail-fence: here he was on foot. He met General Putnam, who, it is said, offered to receive orders from Warren, who replied, "I am here only as a volunteer. I know nothing of your dispositions; nor will I interfere with them. Tell me where I can be most useful." Putnam directed him to the redoubt, with the remark, "There you will be covered;" when Warren said, "Don't think I came to seek a place of safety, but tell me where the onset will be most furious?" General

[1] Colonel Prescott's Letter, Aug. 25, 1775.   [2] Fenno's Orderly Book.

Putnam again named the redoubt.¹ Warren then went forward to Breed's Hill, and into the redoubt. There was a feeling at this time, in the ranks at this post, so manifest was the peril, that, through the oversight, presumption, or treachery of the officers, the men would be all slain.² They needed encouragement. Warren was enthusiastically received; "all the men huzzaed." He said that he came to encourage a good cause, and that a re-enforcement of two thousand men was on its way to their support.³ Colonel Prescott asked the general if he had any orders to give. Warren replied that he had none, and exercised no command, saying, "The command is yours." This is the relation by General Heath.⁴ Judge Prescott, who heard the fact from his father, the colonel, is more circumstantial in relating the incident. "General Warren," Judge Prescott says, "came to the redoubt, a short time before the action commenced, with a musket in his hand. Colonel Prescott went to him, and proposed that he should take the command; observing that he (Prescott) understood he (Warren) had been appointed a major-general, a day or two before, by the Provincial Congress. General Warren replied, "I shall take no command here. I have not yet received my commission. I came as a volunteer, with my musket, to serve under you, and shall be happy to learn from a soldier of your experience."⁵

Warren undoubtedly served as a volunteer in the

---

¹ This conversation is given by Daniel Putnam from recollection, and is a portion of the 1818 authorities on the Battle of Bunker Hill.

² Peter Brown, who was in the redoubt, to his mother, June 25, 1775.

³ Statement of Joseph Pearce. ⁴ Heath's Memoirs.

⁵ Manuscript by Judge Prescott

battle that began soon after he arrived. It continued, including the two intermissions, about an hour and a half. The town of Charlestown was set on fire in several places by order of the British general, and it was "one great blaze;"[1] the roofs of Boston, and the hills round the country, were covered with spectators; and these features, with the work of the battle, "made the whole a picture and a complication of horror and importance."[2] On such a field, Warren fought a good fight. He was applied to for orders, and gave them.[3] "Regardless of himself, his whole soul seemed to be filled with the greatness of the cause he was engaged in; and, while his friends were dropping away all around him, he gave his orders with a surprising coolness.[4] His character and conduct and presence greatly animated and encouraged his countrymen. His heroic soul elicited a kindred fire from the troops. His lofty spirit gave them confidence.[5] He performed many feats of bravery, and exhibited a coolness and conduct which did honor to the judgment of his country in appointing him a major-general."[6]

The British general was baffled in his flanking design of forcing the rail-fence, and of surrounding the redoubt. His troops met gallantly the line of

---

[1] General Burgoyne's Letter.   [2] Ib.

[3] Captain John Leland, in a petition, April 4, 1776, says, that he "received orders from General Warren." It was stated by American and British contemporaries, that he was the commander. Thus, in a narrative of the battle in "George's Almanac," printed at Cambridge in 1776, it was said that Warren was the commander-in-chief. I heard the statement, made on the ground, of Hon. Horace Maynard, in 1843, who was in the redoubt, who regarded Warren as the commander. A report of his relation was printed in the "Boston Daily Advertiser" of that year.

[4] John Williams Austin, July 7, 1775.   [5] Samuel Adams Wells.

[6] James Warren's Letter, June 2, 1775.

THE CLOSING SCENE. 517

fire poured upon them; but they were twice compelled to fall back. On the third advance, they stormed the redoubt, and the breastwork connected with it, when the ammunition of their defenders had failed. As the regulars, showing "a forest of bayonets," came over one side of the redoubt, the militia fell back to the other side, and there was a brief but fierce hand-to-hand struggle, when the butts of the muskets were used; and Warren was now seen for the last time by Colonel Prescott, who was not among those who ran out of the redoubt, "but stepped long, with his sword up," as he parried the thrusts that were made at his person. So great was the dust arising now from the dry, loose soil, that the outlet was hardly visible. Warren was among the last to go out. Just outside of it, there was much mingling of the British and Provincials, and great confusion, when the firing for a few moments was checked. At this time, Warren endeavored to rally the militia, a contemporary account says, "sword in hand." He was recognized by a British officer, who wrested a musket out of a soldier's hand, and shot him.[1] He fell about sixty yards from the redoubt,[2] being struck by a bullet in the back part of his head, on the right side. Having mechanically clapped his hand to the wound, he dropped down dead.[3] The retreating and the

---

[1] S. A. Wells's Manuscript, ii. 296.   [2] Winslow's Statement.

[3] This account by Gordon (ii. 46) is most likely to be authentic. I have heard several who were in the redoubt, standing on the ground, describe the scene when the British stormed the lines; but their descriptions were confused. Peter Brown, on the 25th of June, 1775, wrote to his mother, "I was in the fort when the enemy came in, and jumped over the walls, and ran half a mile, where balls flew like hailstones, and cannon roared like thunder;" and others made a like swift retreat.

This is the precise time that is fixed for the last portion of certain romantic

pursuing throng passed on by his body. The rail-fence had not been forced, and its brave defenders protected their brethren of the redoubt as they re treated from the peninsula. The victors did not continue their pursuit beyond Bunker Hill.[1]

On the following Sunday morning, Dr. John Warren, who was in Salem on the day previous, went to Cambridge, and received the distressing intelligence

action connected with the British Colonel Small. It is said, that, on the first attack, General Putnam, seeing Colonel Small, struck up the muzzles of the muskets to save the life of his friend; and that, on the retreat, Colonel Small, out of gratitude, endeavored to save Warren's life. This incident makes a prominent feature in Colonel Trumbull's picture of the Battle of Bunker Hill. This relation appeared in print in 1818. On seeing it, Major Alexander Garden, in a letter dated June 2, 1818, says that he met Small in London, when Colonel Trumbull was painting Major Pinckney's portrait. Garden states that Small said, "He (Trumbull) has paid me the compliment of trying to save the life of Warren; but the fact is, that life had fled before I saw his remains."

In the "Eulogium on Warren," printed in 1781, there is a passage in which Warren is represented as addressing words to Captain Chester, who behaved gallantly in the battle: —

> "Ah, fatal ball! Great Warren feels the wound,
> Spouts the black gore! the shade his eyes surround;
> Then instant calls, and thus bespeaks with pain
> The mightiest captain of his warring train, —
> 'Chester, 'tis past' All earthly prospects fly,
> Death smiles! and points me to yon radiant sky.
> My friends, my country, force a tender tear, —
> Rush to my thoughts, and claim my parting care.
> When countries groan by rising woes oppressed,
> Their sons by bold exploits attempt relief.
> Already, long, unaided we've withstood
> Albion's whole force, and bathed the fields with blood.
> No more, my friends, our country asks no more;
> Wisdom forbids to urge the unequal war.
> No longer trust your unavailing might,
> Haste, — lead our troops from the unequal fight!
> Farewell'
> Senates shall hail you with their glad acclaim,
> And nations learn to dread Columbia's name.'
> He could no more!"

[1] Gage was recalled after this battle. He died in England, April 2, 1787. But few words are devoted to him in the "Gentleman's Magazine" of this year, where it is said, that "he commanded at Boston in the beginning of the late unfortunate war."

that his brother was missing. He inquired of almost every person he saw for information of the general. Some said that he was alive and well; others, that he was wounded; and others, that he fell on the field. In this manner several days were passed, each day's information diminishing the probability of his safety.[1] On Monday, the Provincial Congress elected a president "in the room of the "Hon. Joseph Warren, Esq., supposed to be killed in the late battle." Meantime, on Sunday morning, John Winslow, of Boston, subsequently General Winslow, went over the battlefield, and recognized the body of Warren among the dead. His hand was bloody, and was under his head. Dr. Jeffries also is said to have recognized it. He was buried on the field. It was reported in the American camp, that his body was stripped; that it was dug up several times to gratify the curiosity of those who came to see it; and that his coat was sold by a soldier in Boston.[1]

There are several other relations, American and British, of the death of Warren. I select a few of them. Amos Foster says, "I saw General Warren. His clothes were bloody when he cried out to us, 'I am a dead man: fight on, my brave fellows, for the salvation of your country.'" Samuel Lawrence says, "I saw General Warren shot. I saw him when the ball struck him, and from that time until he expired." The following are British accounts: "The celebrated Dr. Warren, who commanded in the Provincial trenches at Charlestown, while he was bravely defending himself against several opposing regulars, was killed in a cowardly manner by an officer's ser-

[1] Belknap's Memoirs, 93.

vant; but the fellow was instantly cut to pieces. Six letters were found in the doctor's pocket, written from some gentlemen in Boston, who were immediately taken into custody."[1] — "At this time, Warren, their (the Provincials') commander, fell: he was a physician, little more than thirty years of age; he died in his best clothes; everybody remembered his fine, silk-fringed waistcoat."[2] — "The unhappy leader in the fatal action of Charlestown (who from ambition only had raised himself from a bare-legged milk-boy to a major-general of the army), although the fatal ball gave him not a moment for reflection, yet had said in his lifetime, that he was determined to mount over the heads of his co-adjutors, and get to the last round of the ladder, or die in the attempt. Unhappy man! His fate arrested him in his career, and he can now tell whether pride and ambition are pillars strong enough to support the tottering fabric of rebellion."[3]

Warren's death cast a gloom over the land. "Whether friend or foe, the generous, the elegant, and the humane, — all, all mingled the sympathetic tear."[4] The general grief attests the hold which he had on the affection of his countrymen. I select a few independent contemporary expressions. "Here fell our worthy and much-lamented friend, Dr. Warren, with as much glory as Wolfe on the Plains of Abraham, at once admired and lamented, in such a manner as to make it difficult to determine whether regret or envy predominates.[5] The loss of Dr. War-

---

[1] British Letter, July 5, 1775.   [2] Letter in Howe's Miscellanies.
[3] Boston News Letter, Jan., 11, 1776.   [4] Christopher Gore, June 24, 1783.
[5] James Warren, June 20, 1775.

THE CLOSING SCENE. 521

ren is irreparable: his death is generally and greatly lamented; but —

Dulce et decorum est pro patria mori.

This is a day of heroes. The fall of one will inspire the surviving glorious band to emulate his virtues, and revenge his death on the foes of liberty and our country.[1] We have yet about sixty or seventy killed or missing; but — among these is — what shall I say? how shall I write the name of our worthy friend, the great and good Dr. Warren.[2] The tears of multitudes pay tribute to his memory.[3] Not all the havoc and devastation they (the British) have made has wounded me like the death of Warren. We want him in the senate; we want him in his profession; we want him in the field. We mourn for the citizen, the senator, the physician, and the warrior.[4] When he fell, liberty wept. He closed a life of glory in a glorious death; and heaven never received the spirit of a purer patriot."[5] "The death"—Samuel Adams wrote to his wife — "of our truly amiable and worthy friend, Dr. Warren, is greatly afflicting. The language of friendship is, how shall we resign him! But it is our duty to submit to the dispensations of Heaven, 'whose ways are ever gracious, ever just.' He fell in the glorious struggle for public liberty."[6] And Arthur Lee, while abroad, in anticipating the meeting of friends, wrote, "Would to God we could number Warren among them, and that it had been permitted him to see the beauties of that fabric which he labored

---

[1] William Tudor, June 25, 1775. [2] J. Palmer, June 19, 1775.
[3] Abigail Adams, June 18, 1775. [4] Abigail Adams, July 5, 1775.
[5] S. A. Wells's MS. [6] Samuel Adams, June 27, 1775.

with so much zeal and ability to rear! *His saltem accumulem donis, et fungar inani munere.*[1]

In just nine months after the Battle of Bunker Hill, the victors were compelled to yield the possession of it to Washington. Four days later, on the 21st of March, 1776, Dr. John Warren went over the field on which his brother slept in a soldier's grave. "The hill," he wrote, "commands the most affecting view I ever saw. . The walls of magnificent buildings tottering to the earth below; above a great number of rude hillocks, under which were deposited the remains, in clusters, of those deathless heroes who fell in the field of battle. The scene was inexpressibly solemn, when I considered that perhaps, whilst I was musing on the objects around me, I might be standing over the remains of a dear brother, whose blood had stained these hallowed walks."[2]

Several days passed before the body of Warren was found. "The rosemary and cassia," Governor Gore says, "adorned and discovered his hallowed grave."[3] It was identified on the 4th of April, covered with about three feet of ground, much disfigured; "yet it was sufficiently known by two artificial teeth, which were set for him a short time before his glorious exit."[4] On the same day, Hon. James Sullivan, by order of a committee of the Massachusetts House of Representatives, who had been appointed to erect a monument to his memory, reported that the

---

[1] Arthur Lee's Letter, Oct. 30, 1777. This quotation from Virgil is thus rendered by Dryden: —

>Let me with funeral flowers his body strow:
>This gift which parents to their children owe,
>This unavailing gift, at least, I may bestow.

[2] Warren's Journal.   [3] Oration, 1783.
[4] New-England Chronicle, April, 1776.

THE CLOSING SCENE. 523

Lodge of Freemasons of which he was late Grand Master were desirous of taking up his remains, and burying them with the customary solemnities of the craft, and that Warren's friends consented to the proposition. The committee recommended that the lodge have leave to carry out their intention "in such manner as that the government of the colony might hereafter have an opportunity to erect a monument to the memory of that worthy, valiant, and patriotic American."[1]

The remains, placed in an elegant coffin, were removed from the hill to the State or Town House, at the head of State Street. On Monday, the 8th of April, they were "re-interred with as great respect, honor, and solemnity as the state of the town would permit," the "New-England Chronicle" says. "The procession began from the State House, and consisted of a detachment of the continental forces; a numerous body of the Honorable Society of Free and Accepted Masons (of which fraternity the general was Grand Master throughout North America);[2] the mourners; a number of the members of the two houses of the Honorable General Assembly; the selectmen and inhabitants of the town. The pall was

---

[1] Journals of Massachusetts House of Representatives.

[2] The following appeared in the "Boston Gazette" of April 8, 1776: —

BOSTON, April 8, 1776.

Notice is hereby given to all the brethren of the Ancient and Honorable Society of Free and Accepted Masons, that this day will be re-interred the remains of the late Most Worshipful Joseph Warren, Esq., Grand Master of Ancient Masonry for North America, who was slain in the Battle of Bunker Hill, June 17, 1775. The procession will be from the State House in Boston, at four o'clock, P.M., at which time the brethren are requested to attend with their clothing and jewels.

By order of the Right Worshipful Joseph Webb, Esq., Deputy Grand Master.

WILLIAM HOSKINS.

supported by the Hon. General Ward, Brigadier-General Frye, Dr. Morgan, Colonel Gridley, the Hon. Mr. Gill, and J. Scollay, Esq. The corpse was carried into King's Chapel, where the Rev. Dr. Cooper made a very pertinent prayer on the occasion; after which Perez Morton, Esq., pronounced an ingenious and spirited oration." This production contains a warm panegyric on Warren's private and public life. At its conclusion, the orator advocated independence. "Shall we," his words are, "still contend for a connection with those who have forfeited not only every kindred claim, but even their title to humanity! forbid it the spirit of the brave Montgomery! forbid it the spirit of the immortal Warren! forbid it the spirits of all our valiant countrymen! who fought, bled, and died for far different purposes. . . . They contended for the establishment of peace, liberty, and safety to their country; and we are unworthy to be called their countrymen, if we stop at any acquisition short of this."

The remains were deposited in the tomb of George Richards Minot, a friend of the family. Nearly half a century afterwards, in 1825, when those who took part in these ceremonies had died, and the place of deposit had become unknown, the relics were discovered in the Minot Tomb, in the Granary Burying-ground. They were identified by the nephew of the general, Dr. John C. Warren, by the eye tooth, and the mark of the fatal bullet behind the left ear. They were placed in a box of hard wood, and removed to the Warren Tomb, in St. Paul's Church, Boston. The box bears a silver plate with the following inscription: "In this tomb are deposited the earthly

THE CLOSING SCENE. 525

remains of Major-General Joseph Warren, who was killed in the Battle of Bunker Hill, on June 17, 1775."[1] They are now in the Forest Hills Cemetery.[2] I have aimed to trace faithfully the career of Joseph Warren.[3] It is characterized by rare singleness of aim. He grasped as by intuition ideas that are fundamental and vital; and he sought by applying them to promote the good of his country. He

---

[1] Warren Genealogy, 47.   [2] They were removed Aug. 3, 1855.

[3] Most of the circle of patriots in which Warren moved, lived to see the independence of their country. Otis, though but the wreck of himself, died in May, and Samuel Cooper in December, 1783. Cushing died in 1788, Bowdoin in 1790, Hancock in 1793, Phillips in 1804, Gerry in 1814, James Warren and Revere in 1818, and John Adams in 1826.

The "Chronicle" of July 17, 1777, has a notice of the death of Dr. Thomas Young, one of the senior surgeons of the military hospital at Philadelphia; and this, I suppose, was the intrepid patriot who took so bold a part in the action of Boston. He removed to Newport before the beginning of hostilities.

Joshua Henshaw, of the Board of Selectmen, died in Dedham, on the 5th of August, 1777. The "Chronicle" of the 21st has a fine tribute to his services and character, in which it is said: "He was a gentleman of an engaging aspect and deportment, of solid, unaffected piety, of sober and amiable manners, of untainted integrity and honor, of sincere and steady friendship, of great compassion to the distressed, and benevolent to all." As selectman, councillor, and in other public trusts, he evinced ability and patriotism; and, so long as he was capable of attending to any thing on earth, he preserved an unabated attachment to the great cause of America, and died in the pleasing hope of its success."

John Scollay died on the 15th of December, 1790, aged seventy-nine. In an obituary, it is said, that from early life he was distinguished as a firm supporter of the civil and religious rights of this country, and as such was respected and honored by his fellow-townsmen. He was chosen a fire-ward in 1747; and he discharged its duties until within a few years of his death. In 1754, he was chosen a selectman, and rendered the town service in this office nearly to the end of his life. "In his domestic relations, he was all that could make a husband, a parent, or a friend desirable." He took a deep interest in ecclesiastical affairs, was a devout worshipper, and "met his death not only with the calmness and fortitude of the man, but with the humble submission and animated hopes of the Christian."

Samuel Adams died in 1803. What Forster says (in his "Arrest of the Five Members") of Hampden and Pym may be said of Adams and Warren: "These great men went in perfect harmony together. They shared the same beliefs and purposes, the same hopes and resolves, the same enemies and friends in common, to the end."

was a type of American nationality, as it rose to grasp " Liberty and Union." He loved this cause more than he loved his life; and was ever ready to peril his all in its behalf. He evinced a sound judgment, had clear conceptions of political questions, and was animated by patriotic motives. His integrity, capacity for public service, talent for writing, fervid eloquence, cool courage, promptitude of action, large love for his countrymen, and commanding genius, endowed him with the magic spell of influence, and the power there is in a noble character. His utterances and his work constitute an enduring memorial of his fame. He was not permitted, like many co-patriots, to live long, and, after the enjoyment of tokens of public confidence, to witness in coming days the greatness of the structure of which he did so much to lay the foundation: but he was destined to fall " ere he saw the star of his country rise; " and even in his death to benefit the cause which it was his ruling passion to promote. He dwells in memory as the young, brave, blooming, generous, self-devoted martyr, awakening the purifying emotions of admiration, tenderness, and love of the country. The influence of such a character is not confined to contemporaries. As the friends of liberty from all countries and throughout all time contemplate it, they may feel their better feelings strengthened, and gather from it a kindred virtue.[1]

---

[1] The friends of liberty, from all countries and throughout all time, as they kneel upon the spot that was moistened with the blood of Warren, will find their better feelings strengthened by the influence of the place, and will gather from it a virtue in some degree allied to his own. — *Everett's Warren*, 183.

APPENDIX.

APPENDIX.

I.

THE SUFFOLK RESOLVES.

THE following document is copied from " The Essex Gazette," of the 20th of September, 1774 : —

At a meeting of the delegates of every town and district in the county of Suffolk, on Tuesday, the 6th of September, at the house of Mr. Richard Woodward, of Dedham, and, by adjournment, at the house of Mr. Daniel Vose, of Milton, on Friday, the 9th instant, — Joseph Palmer, Esq., being chosen moderator, and William Thompson, Esq., clerk, — a committee was chosen to bring in a report to the convention; and the following, being several times read, and put paragraph by paragraph, was unanimously voted, viz : —

Whereas the power but not the justice, the vengeance but not the wisdom, of Great Britain, which of old persecuted, scourged and exiled our fugitive parents from their native shores, now pursues us, their guiltless children, with unrelenting severity; and whereas, this then savage and uncultivated desert was purchased by the toil and treasure, or acquired by the valor and blood, of those our venerable progenitors, who bequeathed to us the dear-bought inheritance, who consigned it to our care and protection, — the most sacred obligations are upon us to transmit the glorious purchase, unfettered by power, unclogged with shackles, to our innocent and beloved offspring. On the fortitude, on the wisdom, and on the exertions of this important day is suspended the fate of this New World, and of unborn millions. If a boundless extent of continent, swarming with millions, will tamely submit to live, move, and have their being at the arbitrary will of a licentious minister, they basely yield to voluntary slavery; and future generations shall load their memories with incessant execrations. On the other hand, if we arrest the hand which would ransack our pockets; if we disarm the parricide who points the dagger to our bosoms; if we nobly defeat that fatal edict which proclaims a power to frame laws for us in all cases whatsoever, thereby entailing the endless and numberless curses of slavery upon us, our heirs and their heirs for ever; if we successfully resist that unparelleled usurpation of unconstitutional power, whereby our capital is robbed of the means of life; whereby the streets of Boston are thronged with military executioners; whereby our coasts are lined, and harbors crowded with ships of war; whereby the charter of the colony, that sacred barrier against the encroachments of tyranny, is mutilated, and in effect annihilated; whereby a murderous law is framed to shelter villains from the hands of justice; whereby that unalienable and inestimable inheritance, which we derived from nature, the constitution of Britain, which was covenanted to us in the charter of the province, is totally wrecked, annulled and vacated, — posterity will acknowledge that virtue which preserved them free and happy; and, while we enjoy the rewards and blessings of the faithful, the torrent of panegyric will roll down our reputations to that latest period, when the streams of time shall be absorbed in the abyss of eternity.

Therefore we have resolved and do resolve, —

1. That, whereas His Majesty George the Third is the rightful successor to the throne of Great Britain, and justly entitled to the allegiance of the British realm, and, agreeable to compact, of the English colonies in America, — therefore we, the heirs and successors of the first planters of this colony, do cheerfully acknowledge the said George the Third to be our rightful sovereign, and that said covenant is the tenure and claim on which are founded our allegiance and submission.

2. That it is an indispensable duty which we owe to God, our country, ourselves, and posterity, by all lawful ways and means in our power, to maintain, defend, and preserve those civil and religious rights and liberties for which many of our fathers fought, bled, and died, and to hand them down entire to future generations.

3. That the late Acts of the British Parliament for blocking up the harbor of Boston, and for altering the established form of government in this colony, and for screening the most flagitious violators of the laws of the province from a legal trial, are gross infractions of those rights to which we are justly entitled by the laws of nature, the British Constitution, and the charter of the province.

4. That no obedience is due from this province to either or any part of the Acts above mentioned; but that they be rejected as the attempts of a wicked Administration to enslave America.

5. That so long as the justices of our superior courts of judicature, court of assize, and general goal delivery, and inferior courts of common pleas in this county, are appointed, or hold their places by any other tenure than that which the charter and the laws of the province direct, they must be considered as under undue influence, and are therefore unconstitutional officers, and as such no regard ought to be paid to them by the people of this county.

6. That if the justices of the superior court of judicature, court of assize, &c., justices of the court of common pleas, or of the general sessions of the peace, shall set and act during their present unqualified state, this county will support and bear harmless all sheriffs and their deputies, constables, jurors, and other officers, who shall refuse to carry into execution the orders of said courts. And, as far as is possible to prevent the inconveniencies that must attend the suspension of the courts of justice, we do earnestly recommend it to all creditors to exercise all reasonable and generous forbearance to their debtors, and to all debtors to discharge their just debts with all possible speed; and if any disputes concerning debts or trespasses should arise, which cannot be settled by the parties, we recommend it to them to submit all such causes to arbitration; and if the parties, or either of them, shall refuse so to do, they ought to be considered as co-operating with the enemies of this country.

7. That it be recommended to the collectors of taxes, constables and all other officers who have public moneys in their hands, to retain the same, and not to make any payment thereof to the province or county treasurers, until the civil government of the province is placed upon a constitutional foundation, or until it shall otherwise be ordered by the proposed Provincial Congress.

8. That the persons who have accepted seats at the Council Board by virtue of a mandamus from the King, in conformity to the late Act of the British Parliament, entitled, An Act for regulating the Government of the Massachusetts Bay, have acted in direct violation of the duty they owe to their country, and have thereby given great and just offence to this people. Therefore,—

Resolved, That this county do recommend it to all persons who have so highly offended by accepting said department, and have not already publicly resigned their seats at the Council Board, to make public resignations of their places at said Board, on or before the twentieth day of this instant September; and that all persons neglecting so to do shall, from and after that day, be considered by this county as obstinate and incorrigible enemies to this colony.

9. That the fortifications begun and now carrying on upon Boston Neck are justly alarming to this county, and give us reason to apprehend some hostile intention against that town, more especially as the commander-in-chief has in a very extraordinary manner removed the powder from the magazine at Charlestown, and has also forbidden the keeper of the magazine at Boston to deliver out to the owners the powder which they lodged in said magazine.

10. That the late Act of Parliament for establishing the Roman-Catholic religion and the French laws, in that extensive country now called Canada, is dangerous in an extreme degree to the Protestant religion, and to the civil rights and liberties of all America; and therefore, as men and Protestant Christians, we are indispensably obliged to take all proper measures for our security.

11. That whereas our enemies have flattered themselves that they shall make an easy prey of this numerous, brave, and hardy people, from an apprehension that they are unacquainted with military discipline, we therefore, for the honor, defence, and security of this county and province, advise, as it has been recommended to take away all commissions from the officers of the militia, that those who now hold commissions, or such other persons, be elected in each town as officers in the militia as shall be judged of sufficient capacity for that purpose, and who have evidenced themselves the inflexible friends to the rights of the people; and that the inhabitants of those towns and districts who are qualified, do use their utmost diligence to acquaint themselves with the art of war as soon as possible, and do for that purpose appear under arms at least once every week.

12. That during the present hostile appearances on the part of Great Britain, notwithstanding the many insults and oppressions which we must sensibly resent, yet, nevertheless, from our affection to His Majesty, which we have at all times evidenced, we are determined to act merely upon the defensive, so long as such conduct may be vindicated by reason and the principles of self-preservation, but no longer.

13. That, as we understand it has been in contemplation to apprehend sundry persons of this county who have rendered themselves conspicuous in contending for the violated rights and liberties of their

countrymen, we do recommend, that, should such an audacious measure be put in practice, to seize and keep in safe custody every servant of the present tyrannical and unconstitutional government throughout the county and province, until the persons so apprehended be liberated from the hands of our adversaries, and restored safe and uninjured to their respective friends and families.

14. That, until our rights are fully restored to us, we will to the utmost of our power (and recommend the same to the other counties) withhold all commercial intercourse with Great Britain, Ireland, and the West Indies, and abstain from the consumption of British merchandise and manufactures, and especially of East-India teas and piece goods, with such additions, alterations, and exceptions only as the Grand Congress of the colonies may agree to.

15. That, under our present circumstances, it is incumbent on us to encourage arts and manufactures amongst us by all means in our power: and that Joseph Palmer, Esq., of Braintree; Mr. Ebenezer Dorr, of Roxbury; Mr. James Boyes, and Mr. Edward Preston, of Milton; and Mr. Nathaniel Guild, of Walpole, — be and hereby are appointed a committee to consider of the best ways and means to promote and establish the same, and report to this convention as soon as may be.

16. That the exigencies of our public affairs demand that a Provincial Congress be called, to concert such measures as may be adopted and vigorously executed by the whole people; and we do recommend it to the several towns in this county to choose members for such a Provincial Congress, to be holden at Concord, on the second Tuesday of October next ensuing.[1]

17. That this county, confiding in the wisdom and integrity of the Continental Congress now sitting at Philadelphia, will pay all due respect and submission to such measures as may be recommended by them to the colonies, for the restoration and establishment of our just rights, civil and religious, and for renewing that harmony and union between Great Britain and the colonies, so earnestly wished for by all good men.

[1] This resolve does not in the least militate with the seventh resolve of the County of Essex, then unknown to this convention, for choosing representatives to meet agreeable to the Governor's precept at Salem, the fifth day of October, as the gentlemen chosen representatives may also be empowered to act in the Provincial Congress, after having despatched their business as members of the General Court; and it is hoped that the towns in this county will choose their Representatives, and empower them to act in a Provincial Congress in the same manner as is proposed by the County of Essex.

18. Whereas the universal uneasiness which prevails among all orders of men, arising from the wicked and oppressive measures of the present Administration, may influence some unthinking persons to commit outrage upon private property, we would heartily recommend to all persons of this community, not to engage in any routs, riots, or licentious attacks upon the properties of any person whatsoever, as being subversive of all order and government, but, by a steady, manly, uniform and persevering opposition, to convince our enemies, that, in a contest so important, in a cause so solemn, our conduct shall be such as to merit the approbation of the wise, and the admiration of the brave and free of every age and of every country.

19. That should our enemies, by any sudden manœuvres, render it necessary for us to ask the aid and assistance of our brethren in the country, some one of the committee of correspondence, or a selectman of such town, or the town adjoining, where such hostilities shall commence, or shall be expected to commence, shall despatch couriers with written messages to the selectmen or committees of correspondence of the several towns in the vicinity, with a written account of such matter, who shall despatch others to committees or selectmen more remote, till proper and sufficient assistance be obtained; and that the expense of said couriers be defrayed by the county, until it shall be otherwise ordered by the Provincial Congress.

Voted, That Joseph Warren, Esq., and Dr. Benjamin Church, of Boston; Deacon Joseph Palmer, and Colonel Ebenezer Thayer, of Braintree; Captain Lemuel Robinson, William Holden, Esq., and Captain John Homans, of Dorchester; Captain William Heath, of Roxbury; Colonel William Taylor, and Dr. Samuel Gardner, of Milton; Isaac Gardner, Esq., Captain Benjamin White, and Captain Thomas Aspinwall, of Brookline; Nathaniel Sumner, Esq., and Mr. Richard Woodward, of Dedham, — be a committee to wait on His Excellency the governor, to inform him that this county are alarmed at the fortifications making on Boston Neck, and to remonstrate against the same, and the repeated insults offered by the soldiery to persons passing and repassing into that town; and to confer with him upon those subjects.

Attest:

WILLIAM THOMPSON, *Clerk.*

II.

EULOGIES ON WARREN.

The "New-England Chronicle" of the 22d of June, 1775, contained a brief account of the Battle of Bunker Hill, but did not mention the death of Warren. The next issue, on the 29th, contained the following: —

> On Saturday, the 17th of June, 1775,
> fell in battle,
> In the American Army,
> Major-General JOSEPH WARREN,
> A Gentleman worthy that office, to which, the Day before,
> by the free votes of his Countrymen,
> He was honorably elected.
> As a Friend to Britain, he wished the mutual happiness
> of her and America;
> And, conscious their Interests were inseparable,
> He strenuously opposed the unjust Claims
> of a venal Parliament,
> *Who attempted to ruin the latter, by depriving them of their Rights
> sacred by* CHARTER.
> Twice to crowded Audiences,
> He wail'd the fate of those massacred March 5, 1770;
> and twice
> Received the Thanks of his Fellow-Citizens therefor.
> To enumerate his Virtues
> would be a Subject worthy of an abler Pen.
> Sufficient for us, we add,
> He by them has laid the Foundation of a Fame
> that shall not be impaired
> by the Tooth of Time.
> *Over his Grave his mourning Countrymen may justly say,*
> Here lies the Body of a worthy Man,
> Whose Name shall live, and fill the World with Wonder.
> Although his Ashes scarcely fill an Urn,
> His Virtues shall remain when we have left the Stage:
> His praises shall be spoke for many an Age to come.

The "Pennsylvania Magazine" for June, 1775, printed in Philadelphia, has "an Eulogium" on Warren, which is said to have been supplied by a gentleman of that city. It was copied into the "Boston Gazette." The following is an extract: —

"It is impossible to do justice to his full-orbed character. He filled each of the numerous departments of life that were assigned to him so well, that he seemed born for no other. He had displayed, in the course of three and thirty years, all the talents and virtues of the man, the patriot, the senator, and the hero. He was unlike the Spartan general only in not expiring in the arms of victory. But even in this unfortunate event he has served his country; for he has taught the sons of freedom in America, that the laurel may be engrafted upon the cypress, and that true glory may be acquired not only in the arms of victory, but in the arms of death."

The "Pennsylvania Packet" of July 3, 1775, had the following eulogium, which I copy from the "Massachusetts Spy, or American Oracle of Liberty" of the 26th of July, 1775: —

AN ELEGY TO THE MEMORY OF DOCTOR WARREN. — Warren the learned, brave, and good, — amiable and esteemed in his private character, admired and applauded in his more public sphere. He was an eminent physician. a sincere and affectionate friend, and a faithful, undaunted asserter of his country's rights; in defence of which he nobly fell with a true magnanimity and heroism of soul becoming the great cause in which he struggled, and which did honor to the dignity of the station in which his country had a few days before placed him.

> He's gone, — great Warren's soul from earth is fled;
> Great Warren's name is numbered with the dead.
> That breast where every patriot virtue glowed;
> That form where nature every grace bestowed;
> That tongue which bade in freedom's cause combine
> Truth, learning, sense, and eloquence divine;
> That healing hand which raised the drooping head,
> Which led pale sickness from her languid bed,
> Are now no more: all, wrapt in sacred fire,
> On Liberty's exalted shrine expire:
> While the great spirit which the whole informed,
> Glowed in the breast, and every feature warmed,
> Mounts midst the flame to its own native heaven,
> Where angels' plaudits to his deeds are given.
> Methinks I see the solemn pomp ascend, —
> See every patriot shade his soul attend:
> Immortal Hampden leads the awful band,
> And near him Raleigh, Russell, Sidney, stand;
> With them each Roman, every Greek, whose name
> Glows high recorded in the roll of fame,

Round Warren press, and hail with glad applause
This early victim in fair freedom's cause;
With generous hearts the laurel crown they twine,
And round his brows they bind the wreath divine.
Oh glorious fate, which bids the gloomy grave
Throw wide the gates of triumph to the brave!
Sure, godlike Warren, on thy natal hour,
Some star propitious shed its brightest power;
By nature's hand with taste, with genius formed,
Thy generous breast with every virtue warmed;
Thy mind, endowed with sense, thy form with grace,
And all thy virtues printed in thy face;
Grave Wisdom marked thee as his favorite child,
And on thy youth indulgent Science smiled;
Well pleased, she led thee to her sacred bower,
And to thy hands consigned her healing power.
Still more to bless thee, soothing Friendship strove,
And bade thee share in Adams', Hancock's love;
With them united in great freedom's cause,
Thou stoodst the brave asserter of her laws;
While, ever watchful for thy country's weal,
No arts could warp, no dangers damp thy zeal.
Thy grateful country, to thy virtues just,
To thee committed each important trust;
Called thee o'er all her councils to preside,
And midst this storm the helm of State to guide.
Equal to all : alike in all thou shined,
The patriot, friend, and counsellor combined.
Heaven saw thy virtues to perfection soar,
Till nature failed, and earth could bear no more!
Approving saw, and burst the bonds of clay,
Which staged thy passage to the realms of day;
And that e'en death might to thy fame conspire,
Bade thee on freedom's glorious field expire;
Allowed thee once to mingle in the strife,
That thou mightst give thy country e'en thy life;
Bade liberty and honor guard thy grave,
And countless thousands for thy mourners gave.
And dare we, then, thy sacred triumphs mourn,
Or with the fear of grief profane thy urn?
Illustrious shade! forgive our mingled woes,
Which not for thee, but for our country flows:
We mourn her loss, we mourn her hero — gone!
We mourn thy patriot soul, thy godlike virtue flown.
But, oh! from yon bright realms vouchsafe to bend
On us thy looks, and to our fate attend;
Thy country's guardian angel deign to prove,
And watch around us with thy wonted love;

Still o'er our councils may thy soul preside,
Thy light direct us, and thy genius guide;
Let thy great spirit glow in every breast,
And be thy virtue on each heart impressed:
So shalt thou not alone in glory stand,
And other Warrens shall adorn our land.

The following lines were printed on a broadside, and are copied from the "Historical Magazine" for April, 1861:—

LINES
Sacred to the Memory of Joseph Warren, who fell in the Battle at Charlestown, fighting gallantly for his Country.

Such their Care for all the Great,
Whensoe'er they meet their fate;
Shades heroic throng around,
Pleas'd to tend th' expiring Ground;
Pleas'd to mark the favour'd Place
Where they end their glorious Race,
Round the Turf, or grassy Sod,
Palms with Yews they learn to nod;
There, by silent Luna's Rays,
Oft a fun'ral dirge they raise.
So, on some appointed Hill,
Heav'n's last Mandate to fulfill,
When with Blood they seal their Cause,
Die to save their Country's Laws,
Joy'd at such a nameless Sight,
Countless Worthies quick alight;
Rapt in soft, celestial Flames,
Stepping to sublimest strains,
Thus in solemn Pomp they rove,
There admire a Brother's Love:
As the mystic March goes round,
All the neighb'ring Vales resound.
Thus, when WARREN late was slain,
Passing Mourners heard them plain.
    "CATOS, HAMPDENS, SYDNEYS, come,
Ye of BRITAIN, GREECE, or ROME,
YE for JUSTICE who did plead,
Ye for FREEDOM who did bleed,
Quit a While th' elysian Land,
Join in one harmonic Band,
Come, instal a HERO NEW,
Who deserves to rank with you;
Bring the laurel leaf along,
Swell the chorus with Conq'ror's Song,

Slav'ry clanks her Chains in vain,
Despots there shall never reign :
Yet fair *Liberty* shall stand,
Yet shall sway that happy Land ;
Yet her godlike sons shall rest,
Of their Birthrights still possest.
They the World throughout shall save,
They shall make the Timid brave.
Tho' their present peace is marr'd,
Tho' their future Struggle hard,
Britain's Sons, degen'rate grown,
For their Folly yet shall mourn.
Griev'd their ancient Sires look down,
Curse their Measures, give a Frown,
Swear the Glory is transferr'd,
YOUNG AMERICA's preferr'd ;
Heav'n is fixt her ardent Friend,
She shall see a glorious End ;
Long in Bliss her Sons shall reign,
Till their native Skies they gain ;
Join Orchestras, chant AMEN!"

  Quite o'erwhelm'd with swooning Joy
(So extatic such Employ)
Passing Mourners, waking found
Neither Shades nor faintest Sound.
Hear, ye Sons of Freedom, hear,
Banish hence your ev'ry Fear ;
Trust, for once, a Prophecy,
Know, the *Period* draweth nigh.   B. B.

PROVIDENCE, July 27, 1775.

Dr. Solomon Drowne sent the following lines, in a letter addressed to his brother, William Drowne, and dated Providence, R.I., Aug. 12, 1775, which are copied from the "Historical Magazine" for March, 1861 : —

And is it so ?
Is WARREN, then, no more ? Alas! too true.
"He's gone! my Patriot Warrior's gone!"
New Albion's Genius cried ; and " He is gone!"
Remurmured all around. Heart-rending thought!
How sunk my spirits, when the baleful sound
First shocked mine ear. But why bewail a death
So glorious, which might rather in our breasts
Excite becoming envy ? Yes, he fell
A willing sacrifice, in the great cause
Of human kind, his COUNTRY's cause, which he

> Had plead so well. Heroic fortitude,
> An honest zeal, a Scipio's martial flame,
> A Cato's firmness, Tully's eloquence,
> Were all his own. Thus great in public life;
> Nor less the *milder* virtues of his soul.
> Philanthropy his gen'rous bosom swayed, —
> Beneficence marked well the steps he trod.
> View him in the sphere of his profession;
> See, at the sick bedside his anxious care.
> With countenance benign, see him stretch forth
> His healing hand to yield the kind relief:
> If medicines failed, his gentle accents and
> His soothing words revived the fainting heart.
> But silent now that tongue, and cold that hand
> So oft employed in heavenly deeds like these, —
> *That* tongue, that moved at will the attentive throng,
> *That* hand, to dire distress a cheerful aid.
> WARREN[1] the great, the good, is now no more:
> He's left this earth, to hail those blesesd abodes
> Where NORTHS shall vex not, and the virtuous rest.
>
> PHILATROS.

The following ode has been ascribed to Arthur Lee. I copy from the "American Museum," vol. v. 1790: —

ODE

To the memory of Dr. Joseph Warren, the celebrated Orator, who was slain upon the Heights of Charlestown, fighting for the Liberties of America, on the seventeenth day of June, 1775.

> O great reverse of Tully's coward heart,
>   Immortal Warren! you suffice to teach,
> The orator may fill the warrior's part,
>   And active souls be joined with fluent speech.
>
> Shall not the speaker, who alone could give
>   Immortal reviviscence to the dead,
> Changed to a hero now, for ever live,
>   In fame's eternal roll, with those he led?
>
> Let North and Sandwich take the meaner shame
>   Of blustering words, unknown to hardy deeds!
> And callous G—— superior merit claim,
>   In grinning laughter, while his country bleeds.

---

[1] In him, great LIBERTY has lost a most noble and worthy son, the community where he resided a useful member, and free-born AMERICANS a brother, — a strenuous friend   S D.

Boston's first sons in prostrate numbers lay,
  And freedom tottered on destruction's brink;
Warren stept forth to solemnize the day,
  And dared to speak what some scarce dared to think.

Yet, glorious honor! more than one man's share,
  He in his latest, as his earliest breath,
In camp or forum, equally could dare,
  And seal his bold philippic with his death.   LUCIUS.

III.

CHILDREN OF WARREN.

The four children of Warren, on the death of their mother (Everett's Warren, 179), were committed to the care of their maternal grandmother. Their names were Elizabeth, Joseph, Mary, and Richard. A name made illustrious was their only inheritance (Sparks's Life of Arnold, 126). Immediately after their father's death, the masonic fraternity contributed liberally to their necessities (Moore's Masonic Memoir of Warren, 118). On the 31st of January, 1777, on the motion of Samuel Adams, Congress resolved that the eldest son "should be educated at the expense of the United States." He says (Febuary 1, 1777), in a letter to James Warren, "I moved in Congress, that the eldest son of our deceased friend, General Warren, might be adopted by the continent, and educated at the public expense. The motion was pleasing to all; and a committee was appointed to prepare a resolve. . . These things I would not have yet made public."

About the month of April, 1778, General Arnold — who made the acquaintance of Warren in Cambridge — was informed that the children "had been entirely neglected by the State;" when, in a letter dated July 15, 1778, addressed to Miss Mercy Scollay, — the greater portion of which is printed (Sparks's Arnold, 127), — he contributed five hundred dollars for their support, and expressed generous sentiments for their welfare. Warren was betrothed to this lady for a second wife (Loring's Orators, 49). In another letter, addressed to Dr. Townsend, dated August 6, 1778 (printed in the Life of John C. Warren, ii. 56), Arnold expresses similar sentiments. In the next year, there was additional correspondence on the care of the children. A letter addressed to Samuel Adams and John Hancock, on the 19th of November, 1779, by Elbridge Gerry and James Lovell, elicited the following: —

BOSTON, Dec. 20, 1779.

GENTLEMEN, — Since my last letter to you, I have had an opportunity of conversing with Dr. John Warren, brother of our deceased friend, concerning the situation of his children. He tells me, that the eldest son was, as early as it could be done, put under the care and tuition of the Rev. Mr. Payson, of Chelsea; a gentleman whose qualifications for the instructing of youth, I need not mention *to you.* The lad still remains with him. The eldest daughter, a miss of about thirteen, is with the doctor; and he assures me, that no gentleman's daughter in this town has more of the advantage of schools than she has at his expense. She learns music, dancing, writing and arithmetic, and the best needle-work that is taught here. The doctor, I dare say, takes good care of her morals. The two younger children, a boy of about seven years, and a girl somewhat older, are in the family of John Scollay, Esq., under the particular care of his daughter, at her most earnest request; otherwise, I suppose, they would have been taken care of by their relations at Roxbury, and educated as farmers' children usually are. Miss Scollay deserves the greatest praise for her attention to them.' She is exceedingly well qualified for her charge; and her affection for their deceased father prompts her to exert her utmost to inculcate in the minds of these children those principles which may conduce " to render them worthy of the relation they stood in " to him.

General Arnold has assisted, by generously ordering five hundred dollars towards their support. This I was informed of when I was last in Philadelphia. I called on him, and thanked him for his kindness to them. Whether he has done more for them since, I cannot say. Probably he originated the subscription you have mentioned to me. I have omitted to tell you, that, two years ago, I was in this town, and made a visit to the present General Warren, at Plymouth. His lady was very solicitous that the eldest daughter should spend the winter with her, and desired me to propose it to miss. I did so; but I could not prevail upon her. She said that Mrs. Miller (Mr. Charles Miller's lady), at whose house she then was, did not incline to part with her; and that it would be a breach of good manners, and ungrateful for her, to leave Mrs. Miller against her inclination. She very prettily expressed her obligations to both those ladies, and thus prevented my saying any more. I am very certain it was Mrs. Warren's intention to give her board and education. You know the distinguished accomplishments of that lady. I think it does not appear that *Betsey* has been altogether friendless and "deserted," or that the others are in danger of "suffering irreparably on account of their education." Yet, as I am very desirous that they should have the greatest advantage in their growth into life, I shall, among other friends, think myself much obliged to any gentleman who, from pure and *unmixed* motives, shall add to those which they now enjoy.

I have not yet had the honor of an interview with Mr. ―――― since I sent him the letter which you wrote to us jointly, and requested his sentiments thereon. Adieu, my dear friends, and believe me to be,

Respectfully yours,

Hon. ELBRIDGE GERRY and   SAMUEL ADAMS.
JAMES LOVELL, Esqrs.

General Arnold applied to Congress for a provision to support the children. On the 1st of July, 1780, is the following record:—

On motion of Mr. Livingston, seconded by Mr. Adams, Congress came to the following resolutions:—

Whereas Congress have thought proper to erect a monument to the memory of Major-General Warren, in consideration of his distinguished merit and bravery, and to make provision for the education of his eldest son; and whereas it appears no adequate provision can be made out of his private fortune for the education and maintenance of his three younger children; therefore—

Resolved, That it be recommended to the executive of Massachusetts Bay to make provision for the maintenance and education of the said three children of the late Major-General Warren.

Resolved, That Congress will defray the expense thereof, to the amount of the half-pay of a major-general, to commence at the time of his death, and continue until the youngest of the said children shall be of age.

"General Warren," Sparks says (Life of Arnold, 128), "had been dead five years, and the annual amount of half-pay was somewhat more than thirteen hundred dollars, making the sum due nearly seven thousand dollars, besides the future stipend. In the congratulatory letter which Arnold wrote to Miss Scollay on this event, only six weeks before the consummation of his treachery, he reiterated his ardent concern for the welfare of the children."

Dr. John Warren, the general's youngest brother, on his marriage took the children to his home (Everett's Warren, 179). Both the daughters were distinguished by amiable qualities and personal beauty, and were highly accomplished.

Elizabeth, born in 1765, became in 1785 the wife of General Arnold Welles; died without issue in Boston, July 26, 1804, at thirty-nine years of age, and was buried from her residence in School Street.

Joseph was born in 1768; graduated at Harvard College in 1786; was an officer at the Castle; and died while on a visit to Foxboro', at the house of his uncle Ebenezer. The following is the inscription on his tombstone: "Sacred to the memory of Joseph Warren, son of the late Major-General Joseph Warren, who died suddenly, April 2, 1790, Æ. 22. Be ye also ready."

Mary was twice married. Her first husband was Mr. Lyman, of Northampton. She lost all her children by this marriage (Mrs. Paine's Letter). Her second husband was Judge Richard E. Newcomb, of Greenfield, Mass., who, in a letter dated April 14, 1843, says, "My late wife, Mary, was the youngest and only surviving child of the late Gen. J. Warren. She died on February 7, 1826; leaving an only child, a son, who bears the name of his grandfather, Joseph Warren. He is an attorney-at-law, and now lives at Springfield, in this State. He, with the exception of his two children, is the only descendant, in a direct line, of him who fell on Bunker Hill." Both of these children are (1865) living. One is the wife of Dr. Buckminster Brown, and resides in Boston.

Richard, according to the letter of S. Adams, born about 1772, was engaged in mercantile business in Alexandria (Mrs. Paine's Letter in Life of J. C. Warren, ii. 24); returned to Boston; and died in the family of his uncle, Dr. John Warren, at the age of twenty-one.

IV.

RELICS OF WARREN.

I have seen several interesting relics of Warren, which were procured and preserved by the late Dr. John C. Warren. One is the manuscript of the oration which he delivered on the 6th of March, 1775. It is in a black cover, and is in a large, round handwriting. It has few interlineations. Another relic is a small Psalm Book, which a British soldier said that he took out of Warren's pocket, and as such sold it to Dr. Samuel Wilton of London, who sent it to Dr. William Gordon with the request that it should be delivered to Warren's relatives. It was printed at Geneva, in 1559. On the inside cover is written, "North America. Taken at ye Battle of Bunker Hill, June 17, 1775, out of Dr. Warren's pocket." The name, "Thomas Knight," is written at the end of the volume. These relics, with a sword, which was owned by Warren, are in the possession of Dr. J. Mason Warren, who has also Warren's day-book, containing entries by him from May 4, 1774, to April 17, 1775. I have mentioned on page 167, that there are fragments of a prior day-book. These books show Warren's professional connection with the families of the popular leaders. At the celebration of June 17, 1836, in Charlestown, Hon. A. H. Everett exhibited the bullet which he regarded as the one that killed Warren. (See Loring's "Hundred Boston Orators," p. 67.) The "Historical Magazine" of December, 1857, has an interesting paper by Mr. Loring, on the relics of Warren.

V.

MONUMENTS TO WARREN.

The Massachusetts House of Representatives on the 4th of April, 1776, in giving the Lodge of Freemasons leave to bury the remains of Warren, reserved a right to erect a monument to his memory; and, on the 12th of February, 1818, it ordered a committee to consider the expediency of building a monument of American marble: but the right remains unexercised.

The Continental Congress, on the 31st of January, 1777, on the motion of Samuel Adams, appointed Messrs. Rush, Heyward, Page, and S. Adams a committee to consider what honors are due to the memory of General Warren; who submitted their report on the 8th of April, 1777, when Congress voted: —

That a monument be erected to the memory of General Warren, in the town of Boston, with the following inscription: —

> In honor of
> Joseph Warren,
> Major-General of Massachusetts Bay.
> He devoted his life to the liberties
> Of his country;
> And, in bravely defending them, fell
> An early victim,
> In the Battle of Bunker Hill,
> June 17, 1775.
> The Congress of the United States,
> As an acknowledgement of his services
> And distinguished merit,
> Have erected this monument
> To his memory.

Though it stands in the journals of Congress that "a monument was erected" (see the vote on page 544), and in 1850 a memorial was presented in the Senate for an appropriation for a statue, the vote remains, like a similar one in relation to Washington, without effect.

The honor of raising a memorial to Warren, on the spot where he fell, belongs to King Solomon's Lodge of Masons, of

Charlestown. It was chartered by the "Massachusetts Grand Lodge," which was established by Warren. The charter was not granted until the 6th of September, 1783 (Moore's Memoir, 122). This Lodge (Nov. 11, 1794) appointed a committee "to erect such a monument in Mr. Russell's pasture" (which was on what is now called Breed's Hill), as would do honor to the Lodge, in memory of their late brother, M.W. Joseph Warren, and draw upon the treasury for the expense. Hon. James Russell gave the land for this purpose. This committee caused to be erected a Tuscan pillar eighteen feet in height, built of wood, placed on a brick pedestal eight feet square and ten feet high. On the top was a gilt urn, on which, with masonic emblems, were the words J. W. The south side of the pedestal contained this inscription:—

Erected A.D. MDCCXCIV,
By King Solomon's Lodge of Freeemasons,
constituted in Charlestown, 1783,

IN MEMORY OF

MAJOR-GENERAL JOSEPH WARREN,

AND HIS ASSOCIATES,

who were slain on this memorable spot, June 17, 1775.

"None but they who set a just value upon the blessings of Liberty, are worthy to enjoy her. In vain we toiled; in vain we fought; we bled in vain, if you our offspring want valor to repel the assaults of her invaders."

Charlestown Settled 1628.
Burnt 1775. Rebuilt 1776.
The enclosed land was given by Hon. James Russell.

This monument cost about one thousand dollars. It was dedicated on the 2d of December, 1794, when a procession consisting of the masonic fraternity, the municipal authorities, revolutionary officers, children of the schools, and citizens, was formed at "Warren Hall," and "walked in solemn silence to the hill;" when a circle was formed round the pillar, and John Soley delivered an address, in which he termed the hill "Mount Warren." The procession returned to Warren Hall, where a eulogy was pronounced by Dr. Josiah Bartlett. The memorial reflected great credit on King Solomon's Lodge.

APPENDIX. 549

This monument stood on the ground which is now Concord Street, a few rods from the present structure, and was kept in repair by King Solomon's Lodge until 1825, when it was presented with the land to the Bunker-Hill Monument Association. King Solomon's Lodge, in 1845, procured an exact model of the pillar, of the finest Italian marble, which was executed by one of the best American artists, and was placed within the obelisk. This was dedicated with imposing masonic ceremonial. On this occasion one of the speakers was the venerable John Soley, who presented the working-tools to the Grand Master. The model bears the following inscription: —

"This is an exact model of the first Monument erected on Bunker Hill. Which, with the land on which it stood, was given, A.D. 1825, by King Solomon's Lodge, of this town, to the Bunker-Hill Monument Association, that they might erect upon its site a more imposing structure. The association, in fulfilment of a pledge at that time given, have allowed, within their imperishable obelisk, this Model to be inserted, with appropriate ceremonies, by King Solomon's Lodge, June 24th, A.D. 1845."

At a meeting of the Bunker-Hill Monument Association on 1st of July, 1850, Colonel Thomas Handasyd Perkins tendered one thousand dollars towards a monument in honor of Warren, when a committee decided upon a statue, which it was first designed to place in Faneuil Hall. Other subscriptions having been made, a statue was executed by Henry Dexter, a native artist; and, on its completion, it was determined to place it on the battle-field. The heirs of John C. Warren now contributed the splendid pedestal of verd antique, on which the statue stands; and a building was built for its reception. "The statue is seven feet high, of the best Italian marble, and weighed in the block about seven tons. It is draped in the costume of the revolutionary period. The right hand rests upon a sword, the left being raised as in the act of giving emphasis to his utterance. The chest is thrown out; the head, which is uncovered, is elevated; and, upon the broad brow, and the firm, manly features of the face, thought and soul are unmistakably stamped" (Cambridge Chronicle, June 6, 1857). This statue was dedicated on the 17th of June, 1857, with magnificent ceremonies; an account of which is contained in a volume entitled "Inauguration of the Statue of Warren, by the Bunker-Hill Monument Association." One of the speakers, Henry J. Gardner, Governor of Massachusetts, said, on the battle-ground, "This mighty multitude has assembled, women and men, the statesman, the soldier, the orator, the citizen, those placed in authority, these various benevolent and fraternal associations, all, the old, the young, of every calling and every station, to aid, by their presence and their sympathy, in doing honor to the patriot and the martyr, by dedicating the statue of General Joseph Warren."

This occasion was emphatically national in its character. Warren was also eulogized on the great day (1825) of laying the corner-stone of the Bunker-Hill monument, when Lafayette was present, and sat among two hundred veterans of the Revolution, of whom forty were survivors of the battle. Daniel Webster then uttered before them the following apostrophe: —

"But ah! Him! the first great martyr in this great cause. Him! the premature victim of his own self-devoting heart! Him! the head of our civil councils, and the destined leader of our military bands, whom nothing brought hither but the unquenchable fire of his own spirit! Him! cut off by Providence in the hour of overwhelming anxiety and thick gloom; falling ere he saw the star of his country rise; pouring out his generous blood, like water, before he knew whether it would fertilize a land of freedom or of bondage! — how shall I struggle with the emotions that stifle the utterance of thy name! Our poor work may perish; but thine shall endure! This monument may moulder away! the solid ground it rests upon may sink down to a level with the sea; but thy memory shall not fail! Wheresoever among men a heart shall be found that beats to the transports of patriotism and liberty, its aspirations shall be to claim kindred with thy spirit!"

INDEX.

A.

Abbot, Samuel, 244.
Adams, Abigail, 268, 521.
Adams, John, 10, 15, 19, 24, 51. Frames instructions, 67. Cited, 107, 143, 151, 164, 169. On the massacre, 150. Removes to Braintree, 165, 187, 212. On S. Adams, 212. On the answers to Hutchinson, 223, 224. On the tea, 279, 281, 284, 295. On parties, 301. Member of Society for the Bill of Rights, 229, 313. In town-meeting, 320. Delegate, 324, 338. On Suffolk resolves, 366. On forming government, 386. Cited, 200, 425, 491. Death of, 525.
Adams, John Quincy, 268.
dams, Samuel, thesis of, 9. Character of, 25. On Warren, 26, 202, 229, 427, 526, 542, 544. On Board of Customs, 53. On the Liberty, 58. Cited, 80, 94. Author of Boston "Appeal," 114. On troops, 117. Speech of, 137, 144. Description of, 143. An incendiary, 159, 233. On Hutchinson, 159, 160, 204. On local government, 160, 377. The Father of America, 162. On opposition to, 181, 182. On parties, 183. On Hillsborough, 185. On union, 188, 190, 194, 196, 292. Moves a committee of correspondence, 200. Letters of, cited, 196, 205. On the Boston report, 206, 207. Faith of, 212. Mode of life of, 212. On Virginia resolves, 221. Author of reply to Hutchinson, 224. On the tea issue, 247, 258, 261, 263, 265, 271, 276, 279. Joy of, 281. On a post-office, 297. On political prospects, 298. Fame of, at fifty-two, 302. On the Port Act, 303 Action of, 305, 307, 310. On a premature conflict, 312. On delegates to congress, 316, 322, 324, 325. The King on, 330. Attachment of to Great Britain, 332. On the Regulating Act, 333, 334. Goes to congress, 338. Testimonials to, 338. On the people, 388. On hostilities, 411. On the Tories, 426. On British officers, 438. On the Nineteenth of April, 454, 455, 458, 459. Death of, 526.
Adm, John R., 457.

Albemarle: "Life of Rockingham," 49.
Allen, James, cited, 146.
Ames, Ellis, 167, 546.
Amory, John, 310.
Andrews, John, cited, 310, 311, 338, 359, 446.
Appleton, Nathaniel, 229, 244, 290, 379.
Army, British, 291, 300, 315, 410, 450. — See "Troops" and "Removal of the Troops."
Army, standing, 74, 84, 86, 101.
Arnold, Benedict, 474, 500, 542, 543, 544, 545.
Association, American, 407.
"Atlantic Monthly," 99.
Attucks, Crispus, 127.
Austin, Benjamin, 137.
Austin, John Williams, 516.
Austin, Samuel, 137, 257, 438 439, 465, 476.

B.

Baldwin, Loammi, 227.
Baltimore, Letter from, 317.
Bancroft, George, 2, 26, 86, 93, 146, 202, 302, 307, 311, 317, 327, 338, 340, 342, 352, 358, 382, 409, 410, 415, 422, 442, 446.
Barber, Nathaniel, 201, 240.
Barré, Colonel, 58, 115, 151.
Barrett, James, 384.
Barrington, Lord, 96.
Bartlett, Josiah, 549.
Beacon Hill, 80, 82, 83.
Belknap, Jeremy, 287, 469.
Bernard, Francis, character of, 29. Cited on parties, 30. On the press, 36. On insurrections, 37, 39, 56, 62, 76, 80, 81. On "A True Patriot," 41, 42, 44, 46, 48. On introducing troops, 53, 73, 75, 76, 79, 83. On a riot, 59, 60. On town-meeting, 64, 65, 69. On Circular Letter, 72. On "Reader, Attend," 77. On the convention, 89, 91. On the charter, 95. On quarters for troops, 100. Superseded, 105. Cited, 106, 151, 165, 264. Death of, 526.
Bigelow, Timothy, 385.
Bill of Rights, 313.

[551]

Bill of Rights Society, 229, 313.
Blodgett, Samuel, 227.
Boston, character of, 15. Small pox in, 15. Parties m, 17, 29. Clubs of, 49. Vote of, m Faneuil Hall, 54. Riot in, 57. Petition of, 63. Vote of, on troops, 68. Call of a convention by, 84 Memorial of, 88. Denunciation of, 95. Troops landed in, 99. "Appeal to the world" by, 114. Removal of troops from, 149. Eulogy on, 152, 224, 225. Committee of correspondence chosen by, 201. Report adopted by, 206, 213, 217, 236 Commendations of, 266. Tea destroyed at, 280. Suffering of, 310. Relief of, 324. Fortification of, 359. Instructions of, 379. People of characterized, 473, 478, 479.
"Boston Gazette," foundation of, 34.
Bourgate, Charlotte, 127.
Bourne, Melatiah, 64.
Bowdoin, James, 10, 23, 24, 76, 156, 259, 320, 324, 334, 338, 360.
Boyle, John, cited, 461, 518.
Boylston, Thomas, 83, 321.
Boynton, Richard, 201.
Bradford, John, 83, 201.
Brewer, Jonathan, 469.
British officers, behavior of, 428, 437, 446.
Brookline, letter from, 336.
Brown, Buckminster, 546.
Brown, Peter, 515, 517, 578.
Bruce, Captain, 267, 271.
Buckingham, Joseph T., 218.
Bunker Hill, on the occupancy of, 504. Occupied, 507. Battle of, 513-519.
Burch, William, 52.
Burke, Edmund, 19, 183.
Burns, Robert, cited, 282.

C.

Cadet company, 51, 53, 308. Order to, 249, 250.
Caldwell, James, 128.
Caldwell, Captain, 140.
Cambridge, action of, 214, 256. Gathering at, 353, 356.
Camden, Lord, 96.
Cannon, report on, 472.
Cape Fear, letter from, 336.
Carmarthen, Lord, remark of, 402.
Carnes, Joshua, 167.
Carr, Dabney, 226.
Carr, Colonel, 121, 128, 134, 141.
Carr, Patrick, 128.
Cartwright, John, 299.
Caucus, or Corcas, 50. — See "Clubs."
Chalmers, George, 452.
Chandler, John, 164.
Charleston, letter from, 237.
Charlestown, burning of, 516.
Chatham, Lord. 211.
Cheever, David, 389.
Cheever, Ezekiel, 240.

Chester, Captain, 501, 512.
Choiseul, cited, 97.
"Chronicle of the Times," cited, 324.
Church, Benjamin, 64, 66, 137, 171, 194, 195, 201, 202, 206, 225, 240, 534.
Circular Letter, Mass., 39, 71, 72, 90.
Clarke, Jonas, 451, 457.
Clarke, Richard, 238, 240, 250, 254, 262.
Clubs, 49, 50, 169, 170, 238, 441.
Coffin, Colonel, 308.
Coffin, Captain, 267.
Cohasset, militia of, 404.
Committees of correspondence, design of, 181, 189. Origin of, 200 Conferences of, on the tea issue, 252, 253, 265, 270. On the Port Bill, 300. On the Regulating Act, 348. On the troops, 383, 446.
Committee of correspondence, Boston, 200, 202, 203, 205. Report framed by, 206, 217. Faith of, 221. Circular of, 236. On the tea issue, 218, 252, 255. On the post-office, 297. On the Port Act, 300, 305, 313. On the Regulating Act, 333; its action, 343, 380, 383, 446.
Committee of correspondence, inter-colonial, 226, 227.
Committee of correspondence, Mass., letter of, 237.
Committee of safety, Boston, 149, 334.
Committee of safety, Mass., 389, 390, 406, 412, 419, 458, 466, 468, 470, 472, 473, 482, 490, 491, 502, 504, 513.
Congress, general, germ of, 94. Suggested, 182, 224, 225, 231, 292, 296, 314. Action for, 322 Time of, fixed, 323. Delegates to, chosen, 324, 338. Reliance on, 361, 375, 386, 397. Reception by, of Suffolk resolves, 366, 373, 378. On views of, on local government, 386. Pledge of, to Massachusetts, 388 Obedience to, 400, 403, 407. Advice of, asked by Massachusetts, 476, 487, 501. Requested to adopt the army, 485. Its advice on forming a local government, 511.
Congress, Provincial, proposed, 349. Time of, fixed, 361. Delegates to, chosen, 378. Meeting of, 376, 384. Action of, on forming government, 385, 444, 445. Chooses a committee of safety, 389, 412. Chooses general officers, 390. Proceedings of, 394, 397, 444, 445, 449, 509.
Convention of 1768. Proposed, 78. Adopted, 86. Call of, 89. Meeting of, 90. Parties in, 93. Address of, 93. Effect of, 95.
Consignees, tea. — See "Tea, consignees"
Connecticut, action of, 415, 416, 475.
Cooper, Samuel, 10, 15, 72, 82, 118, 135, 166, 169, 225, 305, 448, 452, 526.
Cooper, William, 24, 68, 135, 138, 155, 178, 202, 229, 333. Character of, 480.
Cooper, William, jun., 480.
Copley, John S., 136, 238, 263, 264.
Coronation Day, 90.

INDEX. 553

Corner, Captain, 57, 58.
Council, on the press, 42. On the troops, 75, 260 On the tea issue, 252, 259.
Council Chamber, 143.
Counsellors, mandamus, 334, 340.
Courts, powers of, 235.
Cowardice, 418, 451, 452.
Cowley, Abraham, prophecy of, 425.
Crafts, Thomas, 115.
Cushing, Thomas, 24, 64, 76, 82, 83, 87, 91, 103. 114, 135, 136, 139, 165, 166, 171, 187, 196, 229, 290, 324, 330, 333, 338, 382, 526.

D.

Dalrymple, Lieutenant Colonel, 100, 116, 131, 134, 138, 139, 141, 142, 145, 150, 156.
Dalhousie, Earl of, 115.
Dana, Edmund, 19, 20.
Dana, Francis, 448.
Dana, Richard, 64, 66, 83, 103, 114, 171, 172, 178, 195.
Danforth, 259, 353.
Dartmouth, Lord, appointment of, 185. On judges' salaries, 186. On the tea issue, 254, 255. On penal acts, 334, 471.
Davis, Caleb, 201.
Dawes, William, 455.
De Berdt, Dennis, 64, 66, 88.
Dennie, William, 201, 240.
De Tocqueville, 23, 98.
Devens, Richard, 384, 387, 412.
Dexter, Henry, 549.
Dexter, Samuel, 259, 397, 491.
Dickinson, John, 33, 52.
Dillaway, C. K., 12.
Donation committee, appointed, 306, 344. Letters of, to Stonington, 345. Preston, 346. East Haddam, 354. Norwich, 350. Middletown, 391. Montreal, 442. Falmouth, 423.
Donations, for Boston, 324, 325, 443.
Dorchester, vote of, 270.
Dorr Harbottle, 40.
Douglas, Robert, 227.
Downer, Eliphalet, 461
Drayton, William Henry, 424.
Drowne, Solomon, 540.
Drowne, William, 540.
Durand, cited, 97.
"Duyckinck's Cyclopedia," cited, 405.

E.

East Haddam, letter to, 353
East-India Company, 234, 289.
Edes, Benjamin, 35, 40, 44, 48, 493.
Eliot, Andrew, 46, 56, 75.
Eliot, John, 10, 36, 51, 56, 90, 93, 135, 162, 163, 166, 169, 170, 456, 462, 468.
Episcopal clergy, card on, 381.
Eustis, William, 168, 342, 456, 513.

Everett, Alexander H., cited, 1, 2, 3, 5, 6, 28, 526, 546.
Everett, Edward, 330, 429.

F.

Falmouth, letter of, 422.
Faneuil, Benjamin, jun., 238.
Faneuil Hall, fame of, 23, 24. Refusal of, 54 — See " Town meetings " and " Public meetings."
" Farmer's Letters," 51, 52.
Fayerweather, Thomas, 167.
Fifth of March, massacre on, 127. Commemoration of, 158, 171, 225, 295, 427.
Fisher, Jabez, 389, 412.
Flag, red, 61. Union, 105, 232, 240. Motto on, 403, 426.
Flucker, Thomas, 186, 324, 364.
Forrest, James, 184.
Foster, Amos, 519.
"Fourteenth of August," celebration of, 19, 76, 231.
Frankland, Lady, 491.
Franklin, Benjamin, 115, 119, 299. Letter of, 315, 409, 411, 448.
Franklin, William, 216.
Freedom and Equality, 21, 23.

G.

Gadsden, Christopher, 336.
Gage, Thomas, 73 Offer of troops by, 75, 77. Visits Boston, 100. Orders troops away, 104. Appointed governor, 307. Dissolves the General Court, 324. Receives the penal acts, 334. Action on, 339, 348, 351, 418, 503. Fortifies Boston Neck, 359. Reply of, 362. On the Suffolk resolves, 367. On supplies, 383. On the Provincial Congress. 396, 417. Military operations of, 422, 453, 455, 513. Views of, 467, 471, 479, 483. Death of, 518.
Gardner, Henry, 384.
Gardner, Henry J., 550.
Gardner, Isaac, 524, 550.
Gardner, Thomas, 304, 337, 384.
Gardner, William, 534
General Court, powers of, 31. On the press, 41. Petition for the meeting of, 83, 187. Divisions in, 162. Session of, at Salem, 315. Dissolution of, 324.
George III., 119, 157, 233, 327, 331, 400, 408, 442.
Germaine, Lord George, 399.
Germany. popular power in, 98.
Gerry, Elbridge, 194, 384, 397, 413, 510, 525.
Gibbon, Edward. cited, 154.
Gill, John, 10, 35, 40, 44, 48, 493.
Gill, Moses. 385, 389.
Goddard. William, 296, 297.
Goldthwait, Ezekiel, 137.

Gordon, William, 34, 123, 124, 331, 517, 546.
Gore, Christopher, 520, 522.
Gorham, Nathaniel, 384.
Graves, Admiral, 333.
Gray's ropewalks, 121, 122.
Gray, Samuel, 128.
Green-Dragon Tavern, 115, 170, 187, 225, 441.
Green, Samuel A., 437.
Greene, Joshua, 166.
Greenleaf, Jonathan, 384.
Greenleaf, Joseph, 201, 229, 290, 313.
Greenleaf, Sheriff, 81, 263.
Greenleaf, William, 83, 135, 201.
Grenville, George, 41, 77.
Gridley, Benjamin and John, 167.
Griffin's Wharf, 267.

H.

Hall, Benjamin, 389.
Hall, Captain, 254.
Hallowell, Benjamin, 57, 58, 59, 60, 272.
Hancock, John, 10, 23, 24. Negatived as councillor, 56. Owner of the sloop "Liberty," 57. On quelling a riot, 58, 59, 60. On committees, 63, 64, 68, 82, 87, 137, 142, 171, 178, 334, 438. Hutchinson on, 162. Popularity of, 163. At variance with S. Adams, 163, 165, 187. Declines to act in the council, 193, 251. Moderator, 193, 243. Thanked by Marblehead, 213. On the tea issue, 240, 243, 249, 257, 258. One of the guard, 280, 286. Commander of the Cadets, 249, 253, 421. Oration of, 296. An arrest of, ordered, 307. The king on, 330. Delegate to the Provincial Congress, 378. Chosen president, 383, 384, 390, 445. Member of the committee of safety, 389, 412. Chairman, 390. On the nineteenth of April, 451, 459. Selectman, 465. Death, 525
Hand-bills, 37, 61, 67, 123, 239, 255, 271, 413.
Hastings House, 510.
Hawley, Joseph, 224, 372, 420, 494.
Heath, William, 384, 389, 397, 412, 450, 458, 460, 461, 462, 503, 506, 515, 534.
Henry VIII., statute of, 98.
Henshaw, Joshua, 64, 114, 137, 142, 465, 525.
Hill, Alexander, 201.
Hillsborough, Lord, 46, 48, 72, 73, 75, 103, 114, 117, 160, 185.
Holden, William, 534.
Hollis, Thomas, 211.
"Hollister's History of Connecticut," cited, 346.
Holyoke, Edward, 9.
Homans, John, 534.
Hood, Commodore, 55, 73, 74, 101, 116.
Hooton, Elizabeth, 14.
Hooton, Richard, 14.

Hostilities, views of, on beginning, by Dartmouth, 411. S. Adams, 411. J. Adams, 386. Hawley, 420. J. Quincy, jun., 421. Warren on, 434. Provincial Congress on, 449.
Hulton, Henry, 52.
Hutchinson, Elisha, 238.
Hutchinson, Thomas, remark of, on independence, 23. On the theories of the patriots, 31. On the libel case, 43, 44. On the clubs, 50. On sending for troops, 53. Sent for by Bernard, 62, 64, 65. Cited, 68. On town-meetings, 71, 199. On the people, 72, 74, 75. On the call of a convention, 87. On the troops, 100, 121, 122. Acting governor, 106. His character, 107. On suppressing public meetings, 112, 119. On their influence, 114. On the public peace, 117. On firing on the people, 118. His bearing on the night of the massacre, 129. On the Sixth of March, 141-147. His reasons for the removal of the troops, 148. Cited, 155. On J. Quincy, jun., 156. On the faction, 158. On S. Adams, 159. On the patriots, 159-162. On Otis, 164. On Cushing, 166. On political prospects, 170. On Warren's oration, 178. On Hillsborough, 185. Appointed governor, 186. Hopes the Union is broken, 188. His views on local government, 189, 221. On the judges' salaries, 190. On the source of political evils, 192. On committees of correspondence, 202, 233. Speech of, to the general court, 222, 224, 227. On the tea issue, 246, 247, 249, 252, 258, 259, 260, 261, 262, 263, 265, 268, 269, 272, 277, 281. On the effect of the destruction of the tea, 292. His departure for England, 308. Interview with the king, 327. Letters of, 486, 493. His view of the army, 502. His death, 502.

I.

Inches, Henderson, 137, 178, 465.
Independence suggested, 198, 428, 435 Disclaimed, 408, 409, 364. Tendency to, 220. Charged, 51, 303.
"Independence the object of Congress," cited, 303.
Ingersoll, Colonel, 55.
Inspection committees, 406, 407.
Insurrection, charge of, 37. — See "Bernard, Francis."
Irving, 58, 147.
Irving, George, 310.
Irving, John, 259.

J.

Jackson, Joseph, 64, 114, 137, 178, **465**.
Jeffries, Dr. John, 519.

INDEX. 555

Jefferson, Thomas, cited, 302.
Jeffries, Daniel, 178.
Johonnot, Gabriel, 240.
Jones, Joseph, 178.
Journalism in Boston, 34.
Judges' salaries, 181, 186, 188.
Junius, 55, 120.

K.

Keith, Sir John Murray, 408.
Kent, Benjamin, 64, 82, 114, 271.
King Solomon's Lodge, 547, 549.
Knapp, Samuel L , 11, 429, 439, 462.
Knight, Thomas, 546.
Knowlton, Colonel, 514.
Knox, Henry, 126.
Knox, William, 77.

L.

Lamb, John, 297.
Langdon, Samuel, 498.
Lawrence, Samuel, 519.
League and Covenant, 313, 314, 325.
Lee, Arthur, 204, 224, 247, 288, 289, 418, 447, 488. On Boston, 224, 422, 522, 541.
Lee, Jeremiah, 389–397.
Lee, William, 472.
Leland, John, 516.
Leonard, Judge, 259.
Leslie, expedition of, 422.
Liberty, on, 176, 232, 317, 345, 395.
Liberty Hall, 61, 240.
Liberty Pole, 120.
Liberty Song, 405.
Liberty Tree, 37, 54, 55, 59, 61, 90, 105, 239, 240.
"Liberty and Union" motto, 403.
Lincoln, Benjamin, 383, 384, 389.
Lisle, David, 57, 61.
Livingston, Edward, 47.
Lloyd. James, 13–17.
Loring, James S , 546.
Local government, views of, 29, 31. Claim of, 68. Re-organization of, urged, 95. Hutchinson on, 110, 159, 160, 189, 192, 221. Violation of, 160. On *quo warranto* against, 166. Practical, grasp of, 171, 172. May on, 172. Warren on, 175, 178, 208, 340, 354, 357, 375, 385. Maintenance of, 185. Aggression on, 186, 188, 334, 361, 391. Right of, 208, 221, 340, 348. On the formation of, 355, 375, 376, 377, 386, 390, 397, 408, 444. On the necessity of, 357. Charters of, 372. Dissolution of, 373. The people on, 376, 377. Congress on, 378, 386, 388. Middletown on, 391. Franklin on, 400, 409. The issue on, 409, 422, 477, 481, 483, 485, 487, 488, 495. Advice of Congress on, 512.
Lovell, James, 157, 544.
Lucas, Dr., 158.

M.

Mackay, Alexander, 104, 116.
Mackay, William, 201.
Magoon, E. L., 429.
Magna Charta, 90, 208.
Mahon, Lord, 97, 183, 278.
Maine's "Ancient Law," cited, 28.
Malcom, Daniel, 64, 83.
Marblehead, 213, 270.
Marshall, Thomas, 195, 476.
Marshfield, 422.
Mason, Jonathan, 137, 465.
Masonic fraternity, 13, 115, 289.
Massachusetts, action by, urged, 32. Description of, 370. Charter of, 372 People of, 372. Views of, 378. Pledge to, 388. Object of, 408. Follows the general congress, 390. Preparation in, 404. Advice to, 511.
"Massachusetts," cited, 200.
Maverick, Samuel, 128.
Mayhew, Jonathan, 24.
Maynard, Horace, 510.
"May's Constitutional History," cited, 49, 472.
McDougal, Alexander, 120, 474.
Medford, eulogy on Boston, 152.
Mifflin, Thomas, 248.
Millar, Charles, 422, 544.
Minot, George Richard, 524.
Mohawks, 279, 280.
Molesworth, Sir William, 172.
Molineux, William, 23, 24, 83, 137, 142, 178, 187, 201, 240, 258, 265, 403.
Moncrief, Major, 501.
Monk, Christopher, 439.
Montague, Admiral, 269, 278.
Moore, Frank, "Diary of the Revolution," cited, 285, 452
Moore, Charles W., 13, 115.
Morton, Perez, 14, 27, 34, 35, 462, 524.
Municipal Reform Bill, 98.
Murray's Barracks, 101, 120, 124, 125, 127.

N.

"Nancy Dawson," tune of, 118.
Newbury Bridge, 59.
Newcomb, Richard E., 545.
Newell, Timothy, 187, 195, 465, 476.
"New-England Courant," 50.
Newport, letter to, 290, 398.
New York, on the tea, 283.
Noddle's Island, 482.
Non-importation agreement, 158, 343.
North, Lord, 95
North Carolina, on the tea, 283.
North-end Caucus, 50, 169, 238.
Norwich, letter to, 350.
"Novanglus," cited, 200.

O.

Observations on the Port Bill, cited, 393.
Old Brick Meeting-house, 124.
Old Charter, 89, 371, 376, 386.
Old South Meeting-house, 39, 62, 65, 139, 146, 173, 257, 258, 259, 278, 477.
Oliver, Andrew, 186, 356.
Orne, Azor, 384, 412.
Otis, James, 10, 35. Speech of, 38, 39, 64, 65. Moderator, 62, 82, 83. Cited, 86, 87, 92, 93, 96. Negatived as councillor, 56. Aids in quelling a riot, 58. Reference to, 68, 81, 157, 162, 163, 165, 169, 187, 195, 196, 201, 202. Cited, on the power of courts, 235. Death, 526.

P.

Paddock, Adino, 83, 420.
Paine, Mrs , 545, 546.
Paine, Robert Treat, 324, 338, 385, 396.
Palmer, Joseph, 389, 412, 521, 529, 534.
Palmer, Richard, 360.
Parsons, Samuel H., 225.
Patronymica Britannica, cited, 4.
Paxton, Charles, 52, 54, 67.
Payne, Edward, 64, 66.
Payson, Rev. Mr., 543.
Pemberton, Samuel, 156, 171, 465.
Percy, Lord, 455, 457, 460, 462.
Perkins, Dr., 16.
Perkins, Thomas Handasyd, 549.
Philadelphia, letter from, 56. On the tea, 230.
Phillips, William, 24, 56, 76, 137, 142, 177, 195, 229, 316, 334, 339, 376, 465, 526.
Pickering, John, 283, 284.
Pierpont, Robert, 201.
Pietas et Gratulatio, 11.
Pigeon, John, 389, 412, 482.
Pitts, John, 244, 339, 340, 465, 476.
Pitts, James, 145, 259.
Pomeroy, General, 141
Pomeroy, Seth, 384, 390, 412.
Popular leaders, names of, 24. Theory of, 32. Use of the press by, 35, 183. Aims of, 57, 97, 113, 116, 181, 191, 307. Care of their cause, 129, 132 Fidelity to social order by, 32, 38, 117. On the tea issue, 267, 274. On arrests of, 307, 524. The King on, 330.
Port Act, 299, 300, 310, 311, 312, 313, 316, 319, 320, 435.
Powell, William, 244.
Preble, Jedediah, 390, 412.
Prescott, James, 384.
Prescott, Judge William, 515.
Prescott, Col. William, 337, 511, 517.
Press, on the service of, 35, 39, 41. On the liberty of, 43, 45, 46, 47, 48. Tone of, 92. On politics, 170, 183, 198, 214, 230. On the tea issue, 234, 245, 255, 269, 270. On Union, 369.

Preston, Captain, 126, 127, 128, 130, 131, 151.
Preston, letter to, 346.
Proctor, Edward, 261.
Provincial Congress. — See " Congress, Provincial."
Providence, faith in, 219, 220, 231, 245, 298.
Public meeting, on the seizure of the " Liberty," 61. On the massacre, 134. On the tea question, 240, 257, 271, 274, 313.
Public meetings, right of, 49. Effect of, 94, 95. Legality of, 97. Hutchinson on, 114. Speakers at local, 213.
Public opinion, reliance on, 32. Influence of, 70. Progress of, 94. Formation of, 114. Demand of, 133, 140. Expression of, 214, 217, 235, 273, 424, 429.
Putnam, Daniel, 505, 515.
Putnam, Israel, 341, 505, 513, 514, 515.

Q.

Quincy, Josiah, 64, 334.
Quincy, Josiah, jun., 10, 24, 26, 35, 39, 55, 64, 74, 92, 156, 157, 169, 187, 188, 201. Speech of, 276. Life of, cited, 169. Vindication of the destruction of the tea, 284. On union, 156, 157. On hostilities, 421. Death of, 470. Letter to, 394.
Quincy, Norton, 389.
Quincy, Samuel, 64, 83, 103, 290.

R.

Ramsay, David, 332.
Rand Dr. Isaac, 18.
Reed, Joseph, Letter to, 486.
" Reed's Life of Joseph Reed," cited, 295.
Regulating Act, signed, 327. Character of, 331, 340. Reception of, 332, 335. Resistance to, 348, 349, 361, 366, 400.
Removal of the troops, question of, 101, 133. Petition to the king for, 102, 105. Instructions on, 114. Demand for, 134, 137, 141. S. Adams on, 144. Counsel on, 147. Effected, 150. Views of, 151.
Report, Boston, of 1772, authors of, 206. Abstract of, 207–211. Circulation of, 213. Effect of, 214–217. Criticism on, 216. Hutchinson on, 211, 221. — See " Boston."
Revere, Paul, 24, 51, 115, 225, 279, 307, 323, 366. 382, 388, 441, 454, 455.
Rives, William C., 218.
Robinson, John, 52.
Robinson, Lemuel, 534.
Rogers, Jacob, 457.
Rogers, Nathaniel, 136.
Romney, 55, 57, 61, 63, 88.
Rotch, Francis, 254, 269–277.
Rowe, John, 63, 64, 68, 83, 321, 465.

INDEX.

Roxbury, character of, 5.
Royall, Isaac, 259, 294.
Ruddock, John, 64, 83, 137, 465.
Russell, James, 259, 548.
Russell, Earl, 259.

S.

"Sagittarius's Letters," cited, 157.
Sargeant, Colonel, 470.
Savage, Samuel Phillips, 271.
Sayre, Stephen, 160.
Scollay, John, 187, 253, 259, 262, 281, 465, 476, 525.
Scollay, Mercy, 542, 543.
Selectmen, boards of, 464.
Sewall, Samuel, 465.
Shelburne, Lord, 37, 38, 40, 41, 42, 151.
Sheriff, Captain, 77.
Sibley, John L., 419.
Slave, purchase paper of, 166.
Slavery, Hutchinson on, 167. S. Adams on, 207.
Slaves, agreement for, 167.
Small, Major, 341, 518.
Smith, Col., expedition to Concord, 456.
Smith, Adam, cited, 210.
Snider, funeral of, 120.
Social order, the patriots on, 33, 499.
Solemn League and Covenant, 333, 357.
Soley, John, 548, 549.
Somerby, Horatio G., 4, 53, 61, 62.
Sons of Liberty, 17, 37, 79, 104, 107, 111, 188, 248.
South Carolina, word from, 336, 401.
Spear, Pool, 136.
Stamp Act, 17, 20, 23. Anniversary of the repeal of, 54, 55
Standing army, 74, 101.
St. Andrew's Lodge, 13, 115.
Stevens, Samuel, 5.
Stedman, Ebenezer, 215.
Stonington, letter to, 345, 346.
'Stories of General Warren," 6, 8.
Story, Ebenezer, 171, 465.
Stoughton, convention at, 339, 341.
Suffolk county Convention, 360.
Suffolk resolves, occasion of, 327. Reported, 361. Boldness of, 365. Reception of, in Congress, 366. Endorsement of, 366. Effect of, 367. Copy of, 549.
Sullivan, James, 385, 522.
Sumner, Nathaniel, 534.
Supplies, refusal of, 383.
Sweetser, John, 201.
Sweetser, Seth, 237.

T.

Tarring and Feathering, 329.
Taylor, William, 534.
Tea Act passed, 233.
Tea duty, Hutchinson on, 157.
Tea, consignments of, 233, 234.
Tea, compensation for, 304, 310, 316, 320. Franklin on, 315.
Tea, consignees of, 238. Warned to resign, 239. Refusal of, 240. Letter of, 251. Application of, to the council, 243. Action of, 244. Fears of, 258. Retire to the castle, 259. Ask time, 261.
Tea, destruction of, 281. Vindicated, 284. Denounced, 285. Effect of, 288, 292, 293, 299, 308, 311, 424.
Tea ships, 250, 258. Arrival of, 254, 267. Legal status of, 268. Guard of, 267, 280.
Tea issue, character of, 249, 273, 283.
Temple, John, 52, 61.
Thacher, Oxenbridge, 24, 35.
Thayer, Colonel, 342.
Thomas, Isaiah, 35.
Thomas, John, 413.
Thompson, William, 360.
Tories, views of, 17, 51, 94, 122, 399, 529, 534. Threats of, 92. Object of, 180. On the Suffolk resolves, 368.
Town meetings, 49, 69, 114, 200, 204.
Town meeting on the Revenue Act, 37. On the sloop "Liberty," 62. On the troops, 82. On the massacre, 139. On commemoration, 171. On judges' salaries, 193, 198. On the tea question, 243, 251. On the Port Act, 305, 320. On the Regulating Act, 379.
Townsend, Dr., 513.
Tradesmen, meeting of, 306, 317.
Trial by jury, 209.
Troops asked, 53, 73. Ordered to Boston, 72, 73. Landing of, 99. Insults of, 118. Removal of, 150.
Trowbridge, Judge, 165.
"True Patriot, A," 40, 44, 45, 47.
Tudor, William, 33, 38.
Tyler, Royal, 61.

U.

Union, idea of, 10, 156, 335. A plan of Providence, 191, 219, 231, 291, 345. Warren on, 22, 53, 345, 354, 361, 376, 392, 435, 443. Pledge of, 52, 361, 369, 388. Spirit of, 72, 266, 387, 417. Hutchinson on, 111, 159, 188, 222, 224. Importance of, 111, 161, 183, 188, 354, 377, 443, 444, 449. The first object, 161. The desire for, 161, 221, 355. Virginia on, 226. Toast on, 232. Alarm of the Tories at, 236, 409, 413. Extent of, 283. "A new Union," 292. Hancock on, 296. S. Adams on, 188, 299, 332, 377. The press on, 198, 306. Effect of the Port Act on, 301, 314. Effect of the Regulating Act on, 333, 336. Gage on, 367, 396. Hawley on, 375, 421. Demand of, 400. Result of reached, 401. Exultation at, 401. Meaning of, 402. Flag of, 105, 232, 403. Manifestation of, 324, 411. Firmness of, 448.

Made in the USA
Lexington, KY
19 July 2018